Heritage Matters

SPORT, HISTORY, AND HERITAGE

STUDIES IN PUBLIC REPRESENTATION

HERITAGE MATTERS

ISSN 1756–4832

Series Editors
Peter G. Stone
Peter Davis
Chris Whitehead

Heritage Matters is a series of edited and single-authored volumes which addresses the whole range of issues that confront the cultural heritage sector as we face the global challenges of the twenty-first century. The series follows the ethos of the International Centre for Cultural and Heritage Studies (ICCHS) at Newcastle University, where these issues are seen as part of an integrated whole, including both cultural and natural agendas, and thus encompasses challenges faced by all types of museums, art galleries, heritage sites and the organisations and individuals that work with, and are affected by them.

Previously published titles are listed at the back of this book

Sport, History, and Heritage

Studies in Public Representation

Edited by

JEFFREY HILL, KEVIN MOORE
AND JASON WOOD

THE BOYDELL PRESS

First published 2012
The Boydell Press, Woodbridge

ISBN 978–1-84383–788–6

The Boydell Press is an imprint of Boydell & Brewer Ltd
PO Box 9, Woodbridge, Suffolk IP12 3DF, UK
and of Boydell & Brewer Inc.
668 Mt Hope Avenue, Rochester, NY 14620–2731, USA
website: www.boydellandbrewer.com

The publisher has no responsibility for the continued existence or accuracy
of URLs for external or third-party internet websites referred to in this book,
and does not guarantee that any content on such websites is,
or will remain, accurate or appropriate.

A CIP record for this book is available
from the British Library

Papers used by Boydell & Brewer Ltd are natural, recyclable products
made from wood grown in sustainable forests

MIX
Paper from
responsible sources
FSC® C013604

Printed and bound in Great Britain by
CPI Group (UK) Ltd, Croydon, CR0 4YY

Contents

Illustrations

COVER IMAGES
(Top) 'The Splash'. The statue of the footballer Tom Finney is sited over a fountain and is based on a famous photograph of Finney sliding through a waterlogged pitch during a match between Chelsea and Preston North End at Stamford Bridge in 1956. *Jason Wood*

(Middle) The Webb Ellis Cup.   *Courtesy of World Rugby Museum*

(Bottom) Race-day ticket of 1996. This piece of ephemera makes the point that the Indy consciously represents the races' past, present and future as a continuum.   *IMS*

Acknowledgments

Much of the work for this book has resulted from a series of workshops that took place between 2006 and 2008, funded by an award from the Arts and Humanities Research Council's Research Networks and Workshops Scheme. Jeffrey Hill (Principal Investigator), Kevin Moore and Jason Wood (co-Investigators) wish to thank the AHRC for the award, which made the present book and various other outcomes of the workshops possible.

Thanks are also due to Professors John Bale, Dave Russell and John K Walton, who served as external assessors for the research project. The editors are grateful for their help and guidance. In addition to those who have contributed a chapter to this book, many colleagues from higher education and professional practice helped form the network and attended the workshops. The editors gratefully acknowledge their interest, participation and ideas. Professor Richard Holt agreed to undertake the task of writing the Afterword, and to him we also extend our thanks.

Thanks are also due to the following institutions, which kindly provided accommodation and support for the workshops: De Montfort University, Leicester; the Wimbledon Lawn Tennis Museum and the All England Lawn Tennis Club, Wimbledon; the University of Central Lancashire, Preston; the National Football Museum, Manchester; Liverpool Football Club, Anfield, Liverpool; the MCC Museum and Lord's Cricket Ground, St John's Wood, London. The editors, authors and publisher wish to thank all the individuals and institutions who granted permissions to reproduce copyright material.

Finally, the editors wish to acknowledge the support of the Series Editors at the International Centre for Cultural and Heritage Studies at Newcastle University, and in particular the invaluable work of Catherine Dauncey; Rohais Haughton and the production team at Boydell and Brewer; and James Panter of the International Centre for Sport History and Culture at De Montfort University for his work in assisting with the arrangements for meetings, circulating minutes and notices, and maintaining the project website.

Sport, History and Heritage:
An Investigation into the Public Representation
of Sport – Editors' General Introduction

Jeffrey Hill, Kevin Moore and Jason Wood

This book has its origins in a series of seminars funded by the Arts and Humanities Research Council between 2006 and 2008.[1] The fundamental aim of the project was to bring together groups of academics and practitioners from history, museum and heritage studies, and related fields. Previous contact across these disciplines had been minimal, though there was common ground awaiting exploration and development. Essentially, all participants had an interest in sport and in the public representation of it in particular. In the absence of an existing joint forum for the sharing of experiences, the AHRC project – 'Sport, History, and Heritage: an investigation into the public representation of sport' – was designed to create just such a multidisciplinary meeting place: a crossroads for knowledge exchange that would point ways forward for this field of study and at the same time influence museum and heritage practice.

From the outset of the project it was generally agreed among participants that sport had become an integral part of British culture and an important aspect of life in a globalised world. Ideologically, sport was seen to convey powerful messages, contributing to the shaping of an understanding of society and the identities by which people defined themselves. A significant part of this process had to do with history and a sense of the past: what we might describe as the phenomenon of 'sports heritage' (Wood 2005). While the importance of sporting activity had been recognised in academic circles through the growth since the 1980s of 'sport history', and in popular writing and discourse for far longer than that, in the growing and related fields of heritage and museum studies scholars had yet to be fully persuaded of its importance. Moreover, interaction in any systematic form with historical studies was negligible. The synergies and inter-relationships between history, heritage and museology still needed to be explored and their multidisciplinary potential released.

Although the various disciplinary approaches to sport had operated for the most part as separate spheres, one point of convergence was gradually emerging, stimulated perhaps as much by popular interest and initiatives as by any academic prescience. This was the growing popularity of sports museums, the collecting of sporting memorabilia of various kinds, and the frequent sense of alarm felt at the disappearance of historic sports venues as a result of urban redevelop-

1 The editors would like to express their thanks to the AHRC for financial support from the Research Network and Workshops scheme to convene eight seminars over a period from the autumn of 2006 to the summer of 2008. It enabled in all some 40 specialists from a range of fields – including history, sociology, museum studies, heritage studies, art history, tourism studies, town planning, business studies, geography, architecture, museum and heritage professionals and sports businesses – to be brought together for discussions on several aspects of the theme of the public representation of sport.

ment. As in continental Europe and North America, the public sphere seemed more animated by these matters than academic circles. By the end of the 20th century a 'public sport history' had become a buoyant if inchoate movement constituted by a variety of people who brought to sports heritage the passion of the sports fan. In some cases it spoke for individuals, in others for highly professionalised corporate bodies seeking to bring heritage ideas into their businesses. When, therefore, academic practitioners perceived the need for a forum of debate on this whole issue, the consideration of philosophical and methodological strategies could not be the sole objective; these concerns had to be brought into contact with popular conceptions of the sporting past and the action that accompanied them. The AHRC project, therefore, needed to have a broad approach to the important questions: what is sports heritage, who creates it, and where is it going?

The uncertainties implied in these questions betray a sense that sports heritage was 'betwixt and between': lacking an academic 'home', pulled between the scholarly and the popular, the commercial and the voluntary, and without a clear centre or trajectory. From this a number of further research questions followed. Where does sports heritage differ, if at all, from the history of sport? What understandings of history underpin sports heritage? How far do practical considerations (eg finance, acquisitions, preservation, public taste) affect current philosophies and policies? To what extent can the intangible (eg a sense of place and identity) be incorporated alongside the material culture of sport? What are the choices in protecting and celebrating historic places, as against virtual representations; and what might be the implications of this for historians? How do museum and heritage site visitors react to representations of sport, and how is feedback responded to?

When conceived in this way the project's objectives were innovative. The one national body dedicated to the study of sport history (the British Society of Sports History) had shown little interest in facing up to such questions. This is perhaps unsurprising. The Society's main purpose had been to establish a rigorous set of questions and methods that would ensure a serious study of sport. In spite of having a proportion of members who were not professional academics, attention to popular history had been slight. Similar priorities had affected professional bodies in the museum and heritage sectors. In heritage studies, for example, research had been yet more limited, both in concept and extent. While there had been several course initiatives in higher education, usually at the postgraduate level, their emphasis tended to fall on traditional topics: the country house, for example, figured far more prominently in the syllabus than sports grounds. Thus the formation in the autumn of 2004 of the Sports Heritage Network (SHN), representing all the major sport museums in the UK, was a crucial initiative and a formative influence in shaping what became the project from which this book springs. The SHN, now progressing strongly, aims to strengthen the network of institutions working within the field of sports heritage and to inspire public involvement in sport and its history. For example, in 2005 it applied successfully to the Museums, Libraries and Archives Council (MLA) for a grant to support the appointment of a research officer to map and define for the first time the nature of sports heritage resources held within UK museums, libraries and archives (Hood 2006; Sports Heritage Network 2011).

The intervention of the SHN raises a major question, which recurs in much of what follows in this volume. In an area such as sports heritage, where commercial and institutional developments have often run ahead of academic debate, and where there is strong centrifugal potential, can a public history of sport ever hope to accommodate all interests? It is worth reminding ourselves of two layers of popular historical consciousness identified in Jerome de Groot's recent work (de Groot 2009). We might call them the *commercial* and the *amateur*. They have long been evident in writing about sport. Each presents quite different problems. Commercial public history in sport is found, among other places, in club programmes and museums, radio and television broadcasting, sportspeople's autobiographies, magazines and newspapers, even radio phone-ins – all of which serve to stimulate a popular historical consciousness, though essentially as a commodity: something bought and sold in the market place. Influenced by commercial considerations, the historical can come across in a marginalised or distorted way. This is seen most clearly in broadcasting, where the audience's perceived preferences, together with technical limitations in the material available, shape the orientation of programming. The BBC's flagship football show *Match of the Day* may be taken as an example; not only is its content wholly confined to the Premier League but the programme displays virtually no sense of a pre-Premier League history of the game. Its presenters and pundits rarely reflect on historical precedents, in spite of the fact that viewers' knowledge of past matches and players might be acute. ITV's recent televising of the FA Cup has, to be sure, used title sequences with images of past games, at least recognising a long history of the Cup competition – albeit a history constituted for the most part by filmed and televised matches. Another television programme, *Empire of Cricket*, was more self-consciously historical in its content though again, because confined in its sources to visual representations, it was inevitably weighted to the more recent past, for which there was ample video-recorded material (BBC 2009). Historical bias is most often seen in sport museums, especially those run by leading clubs and organisations, where what Vamplew has called the 'glory side' of sport predominates (Vamplew 2004). It is assumed, presumably, that visitors do not like to be associated with losers.

When we look at the amateur layer of the public history of sport we find a strong tradition of localism, usually in the form of club-based histories written by amateur enthusiasts. Much of it is recorded in Richard Cox's monumental bibliographies (Cox 2007). This layer also contains a more informal stratum of historical consciousness, a sporting example of Michael Billig's 'banal nationalism' (Billig 1995): in other words, an almost unnoticed reproducing of collective memory through the constant flagging of history in a variety of forms; perhaps its most important aspect is the *oral* discourse of sport found in the workplace, home and pub. It is recreational and not, in the main, profit-driven, though of course it provides the readership and viewing audience who consume commercial sport products. Getting into this 'subterranean' sense of the past is difficult. When it surfaces from the banal and everyday depths into a conscious formal endeavour to represent sport in the public domain – memorialising local heroes such as footballer Jackie Milburn in Newcastle, preserving famous sporting sites, collecting and maintaining written and visual archives, even seeking to capture the 'feel' of a sport space, something attempted by Nick Hornby in his best-selling novel *Fever Pitch* (Wood 2005, 143) – it can bring us quickly back up to the commercial.

A further crucial strand of amateur sports history is the preservation of archives and artefacts by individuals, reflecting in part the lack of interest in sport by museums and archives. While sports museums, as this volume explores, are an increasingly important part of the museum sector, the preservation of material by private collectors is often the only way unique material is preserved. This now has a commercial aspect, with the development over the past 20 years of a substantial and growing market for sports memorabilia. The private preservation and commer-cialisation of sports heritage needs significant further study.

Recognising these layers of activity is important. In the final analysis, however, they present two overriding concerns about sports heritage. The first is about the precise nature of the connection between 'history' and 'heritage': where does the one end and the other begin? It is not always obvious what the essential differences are. Now that heritage has established itself as a force with both commercial and academic compartments it is important to determine what its relationship to the discipline of history is. Both clearly exhibit a fascination with, and notion of, 'the past' and what it has bequeathed to the present. But when the idea of inheritance is treated as unproblematic we run into difficulties. It is not *obvious* what the legacy of the past is; it results from a process of *negotiation* between what people from the past have wished to pass on as their legacy to future generations, and the wish of those future generations, for their part, to accept or reject the bequest. In both history and heritage there is, therefore, a tension between what has been *bequeathed* and what it is felt should be *retrieved/preserved*. Some groups have a strong sense of their own importance in society, and therefore a keen historical consciousness, shown in a desire (indeed, a duty) to keep records and maintain archives; others don't, which is why we know more about the history of the Cabinet than of cabinet-makers, and in sport more about the MCC than we do about local cricket clubs.

A second concern is about *content*. The transforming of the past into a story about the past (in other words, into 'history') takes place in a context of power, between those who think they are important and those who do not – or, to put it more precisely, those who have been encouraged by that very process of history-making to consider themselves as unimportant. This is why people need to have a critical perspective on the past, to *question* and *contest* the legacies of dominant historical narratives, to *reclaim* and *re-interpret* the past; and in relation to heritage to ask, as the writer Iain Sinclair did in a recent critique of the Olympic Development Agency's claim to be protecting the heritage of east London, 'whose heritage?' (Sinclair 2008).[2]

We offer the following chapters as a contribution to the formulating of answers to questions raised by the uneasy tensions that make up the field of sports heritage.

BIBLIOGRAPHY AND REFERENCES

Billig, M, 1995 *Banal Nationalism*, Sage Publications, London

Cox, R, 2007 International Bibliography of Publications on the History of Sport …, *Sport in History* 27 (4), 505–621

de Groot, J, 2009 *Consuming History: Historians and Heritage in Contemporary Popular Culture*, Routledge, London

Empire of Cricket, 2009 (television film), BBC, London

Harrison, R (ed), 2010 *Understanding the Politics of Heritage*, Manchester University Press, Manchester

Hood, A, 2006 *Sports Heritage Network Mapping Survey: An Overview of Sports Heritage Collections*, Sports Heritage Network/MLA

Sinclair, I, 2008 The Scam of Scams, *London Review of Books* 30 (12), 17–23

[2] These, and similar important issues, are further dealt with in *Understanding the Politics of Heritage* (Harrison 2010).

Sports Heritage Network, 2011 *Our Sporting Life*, available from: http://www.oursportinglife.co.uk [21 June 2011]

Vamplew, W, 2004 Taking a Gamble or a Racing Certainty?: Sports Museums and Public Sports History, *Journal of Sport History* 31 (2), 177–91

Wood, J, 2005 Talking Sport or Talking Balls? Realising the Value of Sports Heritage, *Industrial Archeology Review* XXVII (1), 137–44

History, Heritage and Sport

1

Sport, History and Imagined Pasts

Jeffrey Hill

Commenting on recent political pronouncements about the need to teach British school-children a more factual, narrative and national form of history, the historian Richard J Evans makes a fundamental point: 'History is a critical academic discipline whose aims include precisely the interrogation of memory and the myths it generates' (Evans 2011, 12). Contrary to what many people seem to believe, there is no fixed content to 'the past'. What we remember and study from the past – in other words, what we construe as 'history' – is infinitely variable and, what is more, contestable. The very content and interpretation of history is dynamic, subject to continuing debate and disagreement. Those who like cut-and-dried solutions to problems will find only frustration in a discipline that constantly throws up new challenges to existing 'truths'.

Paradoxically, what makes the subject yet more problematical is its very accessibility. Unlike some other subjects, history demands relatively few technical skills from those wishing to practise it and enjoy the rewards their labours bring. History's democratic nature is evident in the vast range of public history now available, whether in the form of commercially produced versions (eg television programmes, magazines, historical novels) or in the 'do-it-yourself' amateur histories composed by all those who make use of local archives of one kind or another (de Groot 2009). The subject has become in itself almost a modern leisure industry, the public (or 'popular') output of which far outstrips in volume the history taught and produced in the academy.

Sport is a clear case in point. The history of sport has taken hold over the past 30 to 40 years in universities, where in research output and teaching it has acquired a particular form. In essence, historians and sociologists have attempted to 'academic-ise' sport history: to make of it a 'discipline' that converges with other disciplines (such as politics, literature and film studies, geography, business studies and anthropology) in the serious study of sport, while at the same time aligning sport history with methods and debates arising from congruent branches of main-stream history. The process has usually resulted in the play element of sport being sidetracked in favour of bringing to the fore the economic, social and political circumstances that have shaped the development of sport and games. The purpose is also to show the functions and influences that sport exercises in modern society. It is an understanding of sport that was summed up in the title of C L R James' classic book on cricket, *Beyond a Boundary* (James 1963). In its relatively short life-span, academic sport history has tended to focus upon elite, commercialised sport from the perspective of the developed world, though in the recent past important shifts of emphasis have been initiated to encompass issues of gender, ethnicity and race within a broader canvas that comprises non-elite sport and the developing world (Hill 2010).

As against these developments, however, there is a more demotic form of sport history that the academy has been drawing away from. It has a lineage that goes back at least to the 18th century. This particular strand of historical consciousness has dealt in the things that have traditionally constituted a popular (and usually male) understanding of sport: the famous matches, the heroic individuals, the evolving tactics, the group loyalties and quite simply the pleasures, whether of participation or merely watching, to be derived from sporting contest. There is little formal or critical sensibility in this public discourse comparable to that assumed in academic sport history, but it has nonetheless to be taken seriously. It might, indeed, be a more *authentic* expression of the sport experience than that found in academic publications. While to an extent it can be understood as a spontaneous expression of popular interests – such as might be found in, for example, pub talk or football terrace exchanges – it is nonetheless stimulated and guided by specific agents of knowledge. They have traditionally been found in print culture, to which in the more recent past has been added various electronic forms of mediation. To be a sport enthusiast involves being informed by this vast but somewhat inchoate cultural baggage accumulated from the past and the present (Hill 2010). It is a powerful engine of memory.

When we leave aside the specialised (and rather narrow) field of the experts and move into this realm of the popular – what nowadays is increasingly (and somewhat misleadingly) termed 'public history' – there is a need to disentangle some threads: in brief, to distinguish between what is 'history' and what are stories about the past that might better be described as 'myth'. Myth is not necessarily untruth or fiction. It might contain elements of verifiable truth. Its real purpose, however, is not to represent past events with complete accuracy so much as to tell a story that conveys important ideas about the present and its relationship to the past. Rather than seeing myth as untruth, therefore, we might better render it as 'ideology': something that represents a particular vision of an individual or group and their place in an evolving historical process. Setting aside sport for a moment and turning to another field of popular entertainment, the point is well illustrated by the award-winning film *The King's Speech* (Hooper 2010). The narrative time of this film covers some 15 years in Britain before World War II, with its central story the struggle of the Duke of York (later King George VI) to overcome, with the help of a speech therapist, a stammer that seriously affected his public appearances and, in a more general sense, the standing of the monarchy. The personal drama, climaxing in an efficiently stage-managed radio broadcast made by the king from a recording studio on the outbreak of war, is framed by two major political episodes in British history – the Abdication Crisis of 1936 and the coming of war in 1939. While the film strives for historical accuracy in representing the built and material environment, and attempts to cast actors who bear some resemblance to the historical figures portrayed, its treatment of the political process is far less constrained by a sense of veracity. The story is told with a large serving of hindsight, the script inscribed with a sense of foreboding about the coming war. However, it makes no mention of the British government's attempts to avert conflict through the foreign policy of appeasement and the domestic implications this had for the Conservative Party. The story gives only marginal attention to the leading politicians of the 1930s (Baldwin and Chamberlain), while at the same time emphasising the figure of Winston Churchill. Churchill appears in situations that his political position at the time would simply not have warranted, even doing things contrary to the stance Churchill actually took.[1] It seems more than likely that the film-makers' intention was to employ the Churchill character because the resonances in the name and persona, which the actor playing the part developed almost to

---

[1]　Churchill was out of government for ten years until recalled in Chamberlain's war cabinet (September 1939); he himself described the period as his 'wilderness years'. In the film we see the Churchill character counselling the Duke of York during the Abdication Crisis when in reality Churchill supported Edward VIII.

caricature proportions, would be readily seized upon by a modern international audience.[2] In doing so they were also able to invoke a layer of historical understanding embedded in popular memory. The 'idea' of Churchill has survived, when that of other politicians has been largely forgotten, because it has long been incorporated into a familiar strand of national heritage. Because of his role as wartime leader, Churchill has emerged as the embodiment of all that is British. He denotes a time of national heroism – 'our finest hour' – when the country was united behind its king and prime minister, standing alone against a powerful foe. By thus building its story upon such myths, *The King's Speech*, which had the potential to cast a subtly subversive eye over the British monarchy's problematical relationship with its subjects, became instead yet another comforting version of 'our island story'.

Does any of this matter? Not, presumably, for film producers, whose main concern is doubt-less box office takings. More importantly, for many members of the audience, the film would seem 'true': it looks right, and has known political events and real figures as reference points to complement its (largely fictionalised) interpretation of the daily life of the monarchy. Here 'myth' takes the place of history. It is myth not in the sense of 'untruth' but as a story that makes free with evidential accuracy to provide a statement about a nation's development. It produces a text that suits particular tastes, markets and political ideologies, while hardly measuring up to what academic historians would accept as 'history'.

Such manipulation of fact and interpretation is common across all areas of popular culture, and sport is no exception. The point is well illustrated by one of the outstanding English sporting myths of the 20th century – that relating to the opening of Wembley Stadium in 1923. The football ground known to several generations of supporters as the home of the FA Cup Final was completed as part of a larger campus in north London that accommodated the British Empire Exhibition, held in 1924 and 1925. The stadium, which long outlasted the Exhibition, was none-theless known for many years after as the 'Empire Stadium'. The first event staged there was the 1923 Cup Final between Bolton Wanderers and West Ham United, an occasion which almost immediately acquired legendary status in football folklore, largely as a consequence of inad-equate event management. In short, the stadium was overcrowded; many more people than could reasonably be accommodated gained admission to the match. It was a potentially dangerous situation and the pitch had to be cleared of spectators by mounted policemen before play could begin. Press photographs featured what appeared to be a lone policeman on a white horse (in reality a rather drab grey) successfully doing his job (in fact there were other mounted officers). The story of the 'White Horse Final' thus began, and was retold for many years. Wembley started its life as a sporting venue, therefore, endowed with instantaneous myth. More important than the facts of the situation were the connotations of the story, the moral implications. The white horse and the crowd was a story about English people behaving in a calm, orderly manner when directed by the forces of law which implicitly made comparisons with the supposed irrational behaviour of hot-headed foreigners (Hill 2005).

Wembley's development thereafter contrasts with that of previous sites of the FA Cup, notably the Crystal Palace in south London, which staged the Final between 1894 and 1914 and which was remembered with some fondness in later years for the good-natured holiday atmosphere

---

2   This point was acknowledged by the film's 'royal adviser', Hugo Vickers: http://www.guardian.co.uk/film/2011/jan/09/how-historically-accurate-is-the-kings-speech [20 January 2011].

that had prevailed there. A Wembley Final, on the other hand, had become, by the mid-1920s, much more of a state occasion. Military bands and community singing were complemented by the presence of the monarch (or high-profile members of the royal family), the singing of the national anthem and the broadcasting of the proceedings from 1927 onwards by the BBC. Most significant of all, perhaps, was the singing before the start of play of the hymn 'Abide With Me'. This might seem strange to 21st-century readers. 'Abide With Me' was a popular hymn at funerals. It dealt with the subject of death. Why sing it at a football match? The answer is that it was popular, it was felt that it fitted well into the community singing, and it was an easy tune to follow for an untrained and vast (100,000) audience; above all, it seemed to catch the mood of the times. It related strongly to the feelings of loss among members of the crowd and the listening public, many of whose loved ones would have perished in the Great War that had come to an end only a few years before. It is hardly surprising that the singing of 'Abide With Me' was experienced as a deeply moving event, a moment of remembrance that expressed the shared grief of a nation (Hill 2009).

The continuing vitality of the White Horse myth is explained by its repetition in football histories, memoirs, boys' magazines and annuals, and newspaper accounts of Cup Finals across at least the first half of the 20th century. Popular sport memory is replete with such stories, some of which are examined in this section of the volume. They serve to link the present with the past while perpetuating ideologies about the place of sport in the fabric of the nation. Often the stories are more compelling and influential than that of football and Wembley, and have come both to fulfil an important commercial imperative and to form a symbol of a sport's identity. Jed Smith's chapter deals with one of the most important of these myths – the William Webb Ellis myth, a famous and remarkably durable story about the origins of the modern game of rugby which describes how, in the 1820s, a boy at Rugby School picked up a football and ran with it. Smith shows how the legend has survived, notwithstanding a complete absence of historical evidence to sustain it, and indeed ample evidence to support a far more rational explanation of rugby's origins and dissemination. Smith's analysis points up the appeal of simple stories and takes us beyond the myth into issues relating to the game's power structures and the value to them of a myth of origin. In the late 19th and much of the 20th century the Webb Ellis story turned on tropes of social class, masculinity, amateurism and Britishness, all of which endowed rugby with an appearance that distinguished it alongside its competitor sports, in particular the rival Northern Union game, which in time became known as Rugby League. At the very end of the 20th century, at the point when the relationship between these two codes was mellowing and, it might have been imagined, the old-fashioned values residing in rugby's traditional themes were becoming anachronistic, the Webb Ellis myth actually tightened its hold on the popular imagination. When rugby embraced commercialism and professionalism in the mid-1990s, jettisoning the amateur code that had been its defining characteristic for a century, the game's leaders paradoxically launched the new era by deploying afresh the Webb Ellis story. For example, the new Rugby Union World Cup competition was played for the 'Webb Ellis Cup' and pubs bearing the name of the game's 'founder' appeared in sites as hallowed as Rugby and Twickenham. Such 'banal' identification was important; as Smith observes, it connoted 'heritage, longevity of interest and (ironically) knowledge of the game's origins and history' (Smith, Chapter 2, 39).

Thus, from such peculiar versions of history springs something called 'heritage', a concept intimately connected to public history and one central to this volume (Lumley 2005). But in the form we encounter it, in this section 'heritage' means something rather different from the professionalised and technical approach to preserving the built environment of the past that falls within the remit of bodies such as English Heritage. Rugby's heritage, for example, involves the perpetuation of an imagined past, or an imagined past event at least. The point may be developed further, as Anthony Bateman does in his chapter, in relation to the history and in particular the *literature* of cricket. Few team games have generated a literature to match that of cricket. Since the appearance in the early 1830s of John Nyren's reminiscences of the champions of his Hambledon youth (Nyren 1833), cricket and its players have been celebrated in writing. The output has been immense and wide-ranging: historical accounts (as in Nyren's classic text); stories of the game and its play in extensive press reports; technical analyses in numerous coaching manuals; autobiographies of players and administrators; a rich tradition, both factual and fictional, of self-consciously *belle-lettrist* representations of the game in verse, short stories and serialisations; and, perhaps most famously, Wisden, the annual almanack that from its inception in 1864 has been almost the defining text of cricket – the 'cricketer's Bible', as many have described it. As Bateman shows, a good deal of this literature has been not only Anglo-centric but *southern* English centred, with an insistence on the essence of cricket as being in a rural environment where the game stands as a symbol of a natural social hierarchy. It has been through such pastoral themes that the notion of cricket as a game untainted by political considerations has been constructed, reinforcing in turn images of an idealised past. This ideology reached its apogee in the interwar years and in particular in the writings of Neville Cardus, music and cricket correspondent (a fitting juxtaposition) of the *Manchester Guardian* from the early 1920s until his death more than half a century later. Cardus' affectionate, nostalgic and highly romanticised descriptions of the cricketers of the game's 'Golden Age' (c. 1890–1914) contributed strongly to a notion of England's inheritance: he was, says Bateman, 'the supreme celebrant of cricket … and was from there constructed as a central figure in the discourse of the national culture' (Chapter 3, 38). Cricket took its place as one of the signifiers of a conservative and backward-looking 'Englishness', and thus a game presented as being apolitical was subtly imbued with a decidedly political quality. In much the same way, in politics itself, Stanley Baldwin (three times Conservative prime minister in interwar Britain) presented himself and his party to the electorate as 'non-political', speaking for the nation when their opponents represented only sectional interests (McKibbin 2010, chapter 3).

The history of sports such as cricket, with a long past, is always likely to become intertwined with 'heritage'. Longevity in itself generates a sense of tradition. In fact, the powerful heritage of cricket has bequeathed images of its past that have necessitated a serious re-appraisal from members of the newer academic history in recent years. In the wake of the Trinidadian radical writer C L R James, cricket's past and the influences it has spread have prompted a scrutiny from which a revision of the very idea of cricket has emerged. Class, gender and race assumptions that have been inscribed in the game's history are being overturned in some of the newer academic and journalistic writings on cricket (Bateman and Hill 2011).

What of boxing, another sport with a long history? It had a leading part, as pugilism, in the commercialisation of sport in and around London during the 18th century. Legends emerged with it. Most, as may be imagined for an individualised sport, have to do with famous fighters, especially those who showed great courage. Many stories also give a special emphasis to the place of 'community' in the sport – the community, for example, of the gym; of the neighbourhood in which the fighter grew up; of the nation itself when honour is at stake in international contests; or (an image writers and film-makers have often been attracted by) of the criminal community that both supported and profited from professional boxers. Neil Skinner and Matthew Taylor's chapter examines the difficult concept of community in relation to representations of boxing, looking in particular at a project initiated by the London Ex-Boxers' Association (LEBA). This organisation, which in itself forms a community, has sought through both an exhibition at Hackney Museum and its own website to keep alive memories of boxing in London. The venture, from which varied notions of 'community' have emerged, was deemed worthy of financial support from the Heritage Lottery Fund, no doubt because of LEBA's attempt to make its project into a people's history. Skinner and Taylor's analysis of the ways in which boxing is represented here leads, as we must expect from academic history, to critical (though not negative) conclusions about public history of this kind. Boxing was in some measure responsible for giving credence to the idea of the 'East End', around which so many of the memories of London have been constructed. Sport has undoubtedly provided a major prompt in stimulating an interest among members of the public in the history of their own lives and districts, but, as with other projects, some of the assumptions that govern LEBA's choice of subject matter are open to question. There is, for example, a nostalgic conception of a socially and ethnically harmonious East End community, with emphasis falling on the recent past and, for the most part, on well-known boxing heroes rather than less celebrated figures. There is also a vision of boxing as a specific *occupational* community – that of the boxers themselves, their internal relations and group dynamic – a sub-cultural 'community within a community' (Skinner and Taylor, Chapter 5, 73). The LEBA project provokes interesting thoughts about the elusive issue of community and how this is articulated in the inter-relationship between memory, heritage and history, as well as concerns for all who trespass into these areas about how *interpretation* is implanted, and often obscured, in the very process of making history.

The formal exhibiting of visual representations of sport is also the subject of Ray Physick's chapter on the *Football and the Fine Arts* exhibition, an initiative of the Arts Council and the Football Association (FA) in 1953. The exhibition was held in London towards the end of that year and toured the country for several months thereafter, visiting a number of provincial galleries and museums. Responses to it were varied. Interest from the public was in some towns very keen (as in Birkenhead), in others (Blackpool) disappointing. The official art world was generally condescending towards the idea of football art: 'Many of the pictures', said the art correspondent of *The Times*, 'have the look of works done to order on a not very congenial theme' (Physick, Chapter 4, 51). Some, however, gave a much warmer reception to the attempt to bring a subject that had mass popular appeal into the world of serious art. Physick shows that the exhibition in general succeeded in establishing that sport could inspire good art (one of the prize-winners was L S Lowry) and that this was not a new thing – there had in Britain been a tradition of sport painting, of which well-known artists such as C R W Nevinson and Cyril Power were a part. Physick also highlights the characteristics displayed in much of this art. It was essentially conservative, realist in form, with ample references to the social context of the game: football locations (from professional club grounds to street-corner pitches), crowd dress and behaviour, on-field action and portraits of famous players. Lowry's prize-winning *Going to the Match*, for example, has a hurrying mass of his distinctive figures being drawn into the professional football ground, as workers might be similarly sucked into the factory gates. The 1953 exhibition came at a time long before football was accepted as part of 'mainstream' culture, and seems in retrospect a forlorn effort at bringing art to the masses, an early and not very successful attempt to fuse elite and popular culture. It was an age when, similarly, the academic world showed little or no inclination to bring sport under its purview as a serious object of study. But Physick argues that, if its immediate impact was slight, the exhibition helped to energise new artistic attitudes, from which sprang later and more readily appreciated fine art initiatives such as *Offside* (Manchester, 1996) and *One Love: The Football Art Prize* (The Lowry Galleries, Salford, 2006).

All the visual and written forms we have considered so far have had an important part to play in people's perceptions of sport. From them an *ideology* of sport is crystallised. Yet their influence, even that of literature, has become minor compared to the medium with which sport, in the early 21st century, is virtually synonymous: television. It is well-nigh impossible to gauge the precise extent of television's relationship with sport, though few would deny that in volume its reach is global and that its ubiquity has wrought profound changes upon sport – though whether for good or ill is a subject of endless debate. Considering the massive presence of television in our lives, and the varied means through which it is now available to us, it is difficult to imagine a world in which television occupied only a minor role. Tim O'Sullivan's account of the televising in Britain of the 1948 summer Olympic Games reminds us of such a time. O'Sullivan deals with a period when television broadcasting had only recently emerged from a suspension of the service in wartime, and possessed (by later standards) a miniscule *regional* audience. In the late 1940s television was available only to viewers in the Home Counties. As a newcomer in the media it had to vie for attention with other, more influential means of communication, notably radio and the daily press. What is more, there was resistance from some potential viewers; many regarded the television set as a distraction from more fulfilling activities. The BBC itself, to an extent, reinforced this notion, advising its audience to be 'selective' in its viewing habits and providing a very limited schedule of programmes. Nonetheless, the opportunity to transmit Olympic athletics and swimming and boxing events from Wembley stadium and the adjacent Empire Pool was not missed, and by thus seizing the moment important precedents were set for future sport broadcasting by the Corporation itself and, after 1955, Independent Television. The Olympic Games, held in London at a time when other countries were, for a variety of reasons, not in a position to act as host,[3] brought a certain amount of prestige to Great Britain which was augmented by the BBC's attempting of what was the first large-scale international televised sporting event. As O'Sullivan shows, presentation was constrained by time (the restricted television schedule) and technical limitations (the difficulties of installing outside broadcast equipment in all the various athletics locations). Thus swimming, boxing and track and field events tended to predominate, with the all-important commentary provided by voices of the 'right' type. Received pronunciation was essential for an organisation still influenced by the Reithian principle that public broadcasting should be serious and educational. Even commentary on association football – the 'people's game' – was given to the plummy-voiced Raymond Glendenning. Nonetheless the broadcasting of the 1948 Games represented a moment of modernity in a context of post-war austerity. There was a very strong sense that the BBC, in its endeavours of 1948, was representing at one and the same time both Britain and sport itself, and that the image conveyed from the Olympic Games should be complimentary to both. Britain's willingness to host the Games was an indication of forward thinking, with television a symbol of the technology of the future. The

---

3 London had in fact been nominated by the International Olympic Committee to host the 1944 Games (not held because of the war). For an excellent discussion of the economic and political context of the 1948 Games see Holt and Mason 2000.

eminent Olympian Lord Burghley spoke in the *Radio Times* of making a contribution 'however humble, to the real progress of mankind' (O'Sullivan, Chapter 6, 86).

The chapters in this section of the book examine a small selection of forms through which an idea of sport is created. Each chapter in its way deals with an aspect of what is often loosely described as 'the media', a term nowadays associated largely with electronic means of communication. But books, museums, exhibitions and even more informally generated stories – such as the William Webb Ellis legend – have their part to play in shaping the meanings that people attach to sport. In an age when sport has a massive worldwide impact in both an economic and a cultural sense these mediations of sport make an important ideological input to the construction of the identities by which we understand ourselves. Senses of nationhood, locality, social class, gender, age and ethnicity can each become bound up with an understanding of sport communicated through the media forms we have discussed. As a further ingredient in this complex process, a sense of history is often invoked. It is not always (perhaps even only rarely) the kind of historical understanding that professional historians would recognise. Nonetheless it is there, an important dimension among many others of the appeal that sport radiates. Whether there for entertainment or for a more serious educational purpose, it should not be ignored as merely trivial. To return to the point with which we began this chapter: the constant accompaniment of all historical understandings and interpretations should be a degree of scepticism on the part of the reader, viewer and listener. The history of sport generates a plenitude of myths and memories, which in turn demand careful and critical interrogation.

BIBLIOGRAPHY AND REFERENCES

Bateman, A, and Hill, J, 2011 *The Cambridge Companion to Cricket*, Cambridge University Press, Cambridge

De Groot, J, 2009 *Consuming History: Historians and Heritage in Contemporary Popular Culture*, Routledge, London

Evans, R J, 2011 The Wonderfulness of Us (the Tory Interpretation of History), *London Review of Books*, 17 March, 9–12

The Guardian, 2011 *How historically accurate is The King's Speech? Hugo Vickers, royal adviser on the film The King's Speech*, interview by Jon Henley, 9 January [online], available from: http://www.guardian.co.uk/film/2011/jan/09/how-historically-accurate-is-the-kings-speech [20 January 2011]

Hill, J, 2005 The Day Was an Ugly One: Wembley, 28th April 1923, in *Soccer and Disaster: International Perspectives* (eds P Darby, M Johnes and G Mellor), Routledge, London, 28–44

—— 2009 War, Remembrance and Sport: Abide with Me and the FA Cup Final in the 1920s, in *Sporting Sounds: Relationships Between Sport and Music* (eds J Bale and A Bateman), Routledge, London, 164–78

—— 2010 *Sport in History: An Introduction*, Palgrave Macmillan, Basingstoke

Holt, R, and Mason, T, 2000 *Sport in Britain 1945–2000*, Blackwell, Oxford

Hooper, T (dir), 2010 *The King's Speech*, See-Saw Films, UK

James, C L R, 1963 *Beyond a Boundary*, Hutchinson, London

Lumley, R, 2005 The Debate on Heritage Reviewed, in *Heritage, Museums and Galleries: An Introductory Reader* (ed G Corsane), Routledge, Abingdon, 15–25

McKibbin, R, 2010 *Parties and People: England 1914–1951*, Oxford University Press, Oxford

Nyren, J, 1833 *The Young Cricketer's Tutor, Comprising Full Directions for Playing … Cricket (including 'The Cricketers of My Time, or recollections of the most famous old players)*, C C Clarke, London

2

Discredited Class-war Fable or Priceless Promotional Asset? The Duality of Rugby Union's William Webb Ellis Foundation Myth

Jed Smith

Introduction

The very first words in Tony Collins' definitive *A Social History of English Rugby Union* offer no ambiguity: 'Of the little that is known about William Webb Ellis, we can be certain of one thing, he did not invent the game of rugby football' (Collins 2009, vii). Collins' statement is a direct strike against the traditional story that sits as the foundation stone of rugby football history: that Ellis, in 1823, took the ball in his arms during a game at Rugby School and ran forwards with it, thus creating the defining feature of the sport of rugby football. Collins' claim that Ellis played no role in either the creation or evolution of the game would not have raised a single eyebrow among those who have actually taken the time to examine the origins of rugby football. The view that the William Webb Ellis foundation story is a myth, with no more truth behind it than a fanciful piece of fiction, is one shared by the majority of those that have assessed the primary evidence with impartial eyes.

As a perspective on the game's origins, the view articulated by Collins has had currency for many decades and a completely unchallenged consensus within academic circles in recent years. However, shortly after Collins' book was published, England's Rugby Football Union (RFU) – the largest national governing body among the many rugby-playing nations – decided that one of its major administrative buildings was to be renamed 'Webb Ellis House' in honour of rugby football's 'founding father'. One can picture Collins shaking his head in silent resignation as yet another brick was added to the ever-expanding edifice of the William Webb Ellis myth. The Ellis story may have been carefully unravelled and shown to be a myth by a host of researchers, but instead of quietly dying away it has not only survived but actually flourished. A dichotomy is now present where two intransigent and entirely opposed factions co-exist as, not for the first time, sports historians sit in one corner while a sport's marketers, its governing bodies and the broader population sit in the other. How the Ellis myth has evolved and mutated and how we find ourselves at this impasse is as remarkable as the creation of the myth itself.

Sporting Mythology

Sports history as an academic, rather than amateur, concern is still relatively youthful. Much of the sporting historiography published prior to the 1970s came from the pens of well-meaning amateurs who typically had a vested interest in the sport, often as administrators, and no incli-

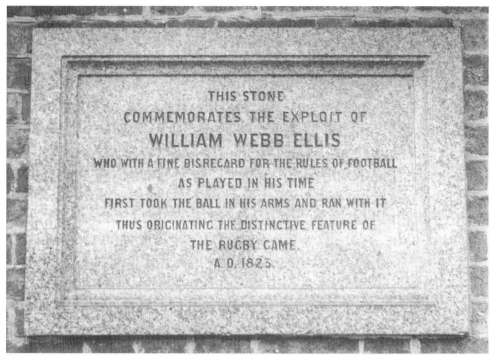

FIG 2.1. THE WILLIAM WEBB ELLIS PLAQUE AT RUGBY SCHOOL.

nation to provide anything other than a promotion of their beloved game or club through the retelling of accumulated tales of daring. Their sports history is usually defined by an absence of deep or wide-ranging research (or at least any direct references to source material), a lack of objective analysis, and sweeping conclusions.[1] The same approach can be seen in the sports museums of the era, which aspired to be little more than glorified trophy cabinets dedicated to on-field success.

Sport, with its inherent inter-sport and intra-sport rivalries and adrenalin-induced passions, is an ideal environment within which mythology can take root and flourish. This is especially true for eras that were almost entirely free from critical and impartial analysis, and the William Webb Ellis foundation story contains all of the fertile ambiguity that such a myth might require. The claim for Ellis' solo action in running with the ball for the first time, and the importance attached to that action, was made in the late 19th century. In 1900 it was edited down to its very essence and carved into stone at Rugby School.

The Rugby School plaque (Fig 2.1) is intriguingly worded, providing a very loose framework that allows for flexibility of interpretation depending upon one's view of the world. It is a

---

[1]   The work of certain sport writers prior to the 1970s, such as Percy M Young on Association Football and cricket writers, including John Arlott and Rowland Bowen, may have been informed by the use of primary sources and extensive research, but their writings seldom made links with wider economic, social or political factors, in comparison with the approach from the 1970s onwards.

freedom of interpretation that has certainly contributed to the story's popularity and aided its growth: Ellis the rebel, bucking the rules and thumbing his nose at authority; Ellis the educated young gentleman, using the in-bred initiative of his social class; or Ellis the innovator, reflecting a nation's inventive and entrepreneurial spirit. The idea of a single individual altering the course of events in the sporting world, or in any other sphere of activity, is immensely attractive, implying that any of us has the same capacity to make a fundamental impact. The story has had potent currency for well over a century, and can be interpreted to 'prove' any number of assumptions: the pre-eminence of England as rugby football's founder and (therefore) moral or legal guardian; the position of the male at the centre of sporting evolution and progress; the dominance of a certain educated class within the game; and (in this particular context) the importance and pre-eminence of a particular school. Since 1995, when the game of rugby union was formally opened up to professional players and significant financial investment, the Ellis story has also gained a new lease of life as a supreme marketing tool. Few other major sports can lean on such a concise and attractive foundation story to capture the imagination and inspire the public to participate (play, officiate, administer, volunteer or purchase product) or spectate (in person or through the media). Elsewhere, baseball's Abner Doubleday creationist myth has been successfully challenged and a step by step evolution, rather than a 'big bang' event, is typically recognised as the developmental model for most major sports.

The Myth's Origins

The first major history of rugby football, written by Reverend Frank Marshall, did not mention William Webb Ellis at all, despite being written in close proximity to Ellis' life and times. Many pages of Marshall's book were instead dedicated to tracing the slow development of the game from as far back as a Roman ball-carrying game named *Harpastum*. Writing in the last decades of the 19th century, Marshall claimed that rugby football was the 'legitimate refinement of the rough and crude games which in their main features are undoubtedly the source from which the Rugby game and the Rugby game alone are the true issue' (Marshall 1892, 2). His work was republished twice, but this insightful element of his work was entirely overshadowed by events to come.

It is extraordinarily beneficial (but also entirely frustrating, given the myth's widespread acceptance and endurance) that we know how the flawed Ellis story came into existence. We can trace the myth almost back to its very source because it was first propagated in the public domain. Having come to light in the letters pages of *The Meteor* (journal of The Old Rugbeian Society), it was then investigated by the Old Rugbeian Society, who published their conclusions and, more importantly, their assembled evidence (Old Rugbeian Society 1897). One can see quite clearly the glaring omissions and the numerous contradictions in the evidence that have allowed so many researchers to be critical of the Old Rugbeians and which make the myth so easy to deconstruct and refute. The Ellis myth is not centred on the creation of a fictitious person – William Webb Ellis certainly existed and football games were definitely being played at Rugby School in the early 1820s. However, the fascinating gradual evolution (and formal acceptance in 1841) of running with ball in hand in the Rugby School football game was discarded by the Old Rugbeian Society who, instead, added the considerable weight of their support to a far simpler and more attractive tale.

Matthew Holbeche Bloxam is the oft-quoted source of the story, the first to name Ellis in this context. A pupil at Rugby School from 1813, Bloxam had departed before 1823, the date of the alleged event with which he will be forever associated. In 1876 a debate raged in *The Standard*. Was the (by now) international game of rugby football a continuation of the ball-handling traditions of ancient folk football games, or a more recent innovation? Bloxam claimed that running with the ball in hand had been invented at Rugby School, but he had no idea when or how. Later in the same year, however, he claimed in a letter to *The Meteor* that he had since ascertained that William Webb Ellis was the originator of handling in Rugby School football games. In 1880 Bloxam again wrote to *The Meteor* following a related editorial in *The Times*. Ellis was named again and the story fleshed out, but Bloxam's original 1876 source remained unnamed. In 1887 Montague Shearman published *Athletics and Football*, in which he claimed that Rugby School had always played a 'primitive' handling game (Shearman 1887). It was this publication that allegedly inspired the Old Rugbeian Society to appoint a sub-committee in July 1895 to examine the origins of their School's game with particular reference to Bloxam's claims.

Thomas Hughes, author of *Tom Brown's Schooldays* (1857), and 14 other old boys of Rugby School responded to the sub-committee and they all inferred a slow evolution in the laws surrounding handling. Not one of the old boys who contributed to the sub-committee's research could attest to ever having heard about the Ellis story, let alone corroborate the details. They confirmed that during the late 1830s (and certainly not as early as 1823), running with the ball in hand was gradually accepted and only formally legalised for the first time in the early 1840s – just in time for the first written laws in 1845. Thomas Hughes had entered Rugby School in 1834 and he declared that 'The "Webb Ellis tradition" had not survived to my day' (Old Rugbeian Society 1897, 13). Prior to the first written laws, every aspect of the game – its laws, traditions and memories of great feats of bravery – were all passed on as oral history and yet no mention of Ellis' seemingly monumental act had survived even a decade. As Collins points out, 'There can be no doubt that if the Webb Ellis story had contained a shred of truth, Hughes would have woven it into *Tom Brown's Schooldays*, a veritable compendium of folklore about Rugby School' (Collins 2009, 3). Even if Ellis *had* performed the feat attributed to him by Bloxam, the fact that it had not been remembered means that it had no impact at all on the development of the game. Bloxam had died prior to the sub-committee's work, so could not be cross-examined, and Ellis himself had died in 1872 – prior to Bloxam 'naming' him for the first time in 1876. Despite living long enough to see the schoolboy pastime become an international sport, Ellis (Fig 2.2) never spoke a reported word on the subject.

Despite the damning evidence provided by the interviewees, Bloxam's story was not buried. In fact the sub committee were remarkably keen to name Ellis and the following conclusion was issued in their 1897 report: 'though we have been unable to procure any first hand evidence of the occurrence, we are inclined to give it our support' (Old Rugbeian Society 1897, 11). The fine detail of the correspondence contained within their published report provided all of the evidence that could ever have been required to paint a picture of gradual evolution and acceptance of ball handling – not of a single action generating a new sport. The sub-committee's conclusions were therefore misguided and wide of the mark. However, the real tragedy came when the infamous plaque was subsequently placed in Rugby School's grounds in 1900. The sub-committee's conclusions, when distilled down to their bare bones and with all context and caution removed, advocated a 'Big Bang' theory. It is the plaque, rather than the more cautious claims of the 1897 report, that would be seen by millions and its message would be disseminated far and wide. The plaque appeared to confer absolute authority on the story despite the fact that (to paraphrase

Fig 2.2. William Webb Ellis.

David Smith, Gareth Williams, Huw Richards and others) the finest disregard on display was actually for the rules of evidence (Smith and Williams 1980; Richards 2006).

The importance and impact of the 1900 plaque cannot be overestimated, not only in legitimising and disseminating the story but in the confusion that arose due to the use of the word 'football'. Over subsequent decades the word was appropriated within Britain and elsewhere for almost exclusive use by followers of the Association Football (soccer) code and the plaque is therefore often misinterpreted as being a claim that Ellis picked up a soccer ball. The intention of the plaque's wording was to express that Ellis had taken the ball in his arms (ie caught a rugby ball) but it seems to imply that rugby football is a bastard offspring of the round ball game. The widespread confusion thus created provides a tangible and significant reason for wanting to disseminate a more accurate and considered version of events, rather than bursting the Ellis 'bubble' simply as an exercise in academic point scoring.

DISSEMINATION

In 1905 the first New Zealand ('All Blacks') team toured Britain and made what was to become a standard touring team pilgrimage to Rugby School. In a subsequent book the team's captain and vice-captain claimed, having seen the 1900 plaque, that there was 'very clear evidence' of Ellis' deed (Gallagher and Stead 1906, 12). Ellis may have been conspicuous by his absence in most other books up to the early 1920s (Marriott 1922), but a 1923 'centenary' game at the School (England and Wales v Scotland and Ireland) sealed the story's ascendancy and henceforth the tale seems to have become an accepted standard. England captain 'Dave' Davies claimed that 'one William Webb Ellis picked up the ball and ran with it' (Davies 1923, 20), and in 1930 the *Football Records of Rugby School* used 1823 as its 'year zero'. The official history of the Football Association states that the Ellis story is 'the accepted origin of the Rugby game' (Green 1953, 12) and the following year Morris Marples asked his readers not to 'grudge [Ellis] his monument, and the celebrity which, somewhat belatedly, was bestowed on him by the Old Rugbeians in 1895' (Marples 1954, 118). After 1958 a second Ellis 'monument' made its way into the public domain following Ross McWhirter's discovery of Ellis' grave in Menton, France. By the time that the RFU's centenary season came around in 1970/71, the Ellis story was being used explicitly to promote the sport. The RFU commissioned a quasi-documentary film which featured Arthur Lowe as a Rugby School master who bellows out the film's title – *William Webb Ellis, Are You Mad?* – at the appropriate moment. The film was created specifically as an educational and promotional tool, with rugby clubs able to borrow canisters of the film from the RFU to play on projectors in their club houses. When the author worked for the RFU from the mid-1990s requests for information about the film were still being received by the organisation on a regular basis, suggesting that it had generated a great deal of interest while in circulation.[2] However, at the same time that the myth was taking root in rugby football's collective psyche, some writers were, no doubt to Morris Marples' displeasure, starting to begrudge Ellis.

CREEPING DOUBT

In the RFU's first official history, published in the mid-1950s, O L Owen reminded his readers that 'Mr Bloxam was not an actual eye-witness, for he had left Rugby a few years earlier' and that 'anyone with an open mind must take into account the fact that the evidence about the man is entirely hearsay and long delayed' (Owen 1955, 25). Further doubt was articulated by others over the following decades, as expressed in Hope Simpson's subtle questioning of the tradition (Simpson 1967) and Malcolm Lee's detailed synopsis, while master in charge of football at Rugby School:

> There is little evidence to support the popular belief that William Webb Ellis created a new form of football.... If you look at the notes of the Bigside Levees – notes made by the boys

---

[2] The film *William Webb Ellis, Are You Mad?* was eventually removed from circulation and distribution by the RFU during the 1980s. This was not because of historical inaccuracies but because the organisation was aware that the scenes involving a clubhouse full of 'typical' rugby players and their lecherous behaviour and commentary were attracting a negative reaction.

themselves – you will see that the rules were discussed almost every time the boys went out to play and that adjustments were frequently made. (Reason and James 1979, 9)

These carefully worded warnings came from figures held in high regard within the sport who had obviously reviewed at least some of the source material, but they were isolated voices and were never likely to inspire an 'about turn' in thinking.

Academia Steps In

During the 1970s a number of social historians, such as Stedman-Jones, Joyce, E and S Yeo and Hobsbawm, recognised the value of sport history as a previously untapped resource and started to exploit the possibilities that a serious analysis of the subject offered their discipline. They perceived that sport responded to social (as well as political and economic) developments and so, by examining sport, they could gain a greater insight into society's relations and views in areas such as nationalism, gender, class and race. These historians paved the way for a new examination of sports history, shorn of its bluff and mythology. Research was given a previously absent academic vigour and sports such as rugby football were examined for the first time in the wider context of Victorian and 20th-century social history. A key text was *Gentlemen, Barbarians and Players* (1979), within which Dunning and Sheard assigned many pages to the early development of the game and, by necessity, to understanding and analysing Ellis' alleged role. Objective and dispassionate, they confirmed the concerns of Owen, Simpson, Lee *et al* when they concluded that the Ellis story was an invented tradition, suggesting that 'it is just not sociologically plausible that a deeply entrenched traditional game could have been changed fundamentally by a single act, particularly that of a low-status individual such as Webb Ellis is reputed to have been' (Dunning and Sheard 1979, 61).

Dunning and Sheard were also able to place the myth into a wider context and to speculate about how and why it came into being. They highlighted the remarkable coincidence that the Old Rugbeian Society's investigation commenced in mid-1895, almost to the month that growing divisions within the game exploded in a painful split into the rival sports of broadly working-class rugby league and broadly middle-class rugby union. They surmised that the endorsement of an origin myth by the Old Rugbeians was a last-ditch attempt to assert Rugby School's position of authority over a sport within which they were losing any last vestiges of control. They were also interested in the reductionist element of the Ellis myth, highlighting instead the complex developments in other facets of the game, such as H-shaped goals and try scoring, which were equally distinctive features, but which the overly simplistic myth of sport creation ignored entirely.

The work of Tony Mason, Wray Vamplew, Gareth Williams and others placed the history of sport into the context of national identity and professionalism and also allowed sports to be systematically compared and contrasted (Mason 1980; Vamplew 1988; Smith and Williams 1980). This new breed of sports historiography legitimised serious analysis of the subject and also raised the bar for those writing from a sports background rather than coming through academia. Throughout this period the Ellis story took an increasing number of body blows, including Don Atyeo's claim that 'Unfortunately, the Ellis saga is a blatant fiction, perpetuated by an overly loyal gathering of Rugby Old Boys more than half a century later' (Atyeo 1979, 196). It was suggested that 'whether the evolution of the rugby game owes anything at all to William Webb Ellis must be doubtful' (Smith and Williams 1980, 21), while Richard Holt concluded that Rugby School's 'claim to ownership of the game was based upon the most flimsy evidence and designed primarily to counter the later pretensions of rival northern clubs' (Holt 1989, 85). The *Encyclopaedia Britannica* carries no reference to William Webb Ellis or to his alleged action.

Interpretations of the reasons behind the myth's creation and its enduring popularity are many and varied. First, there is a view that Ellis is an example of Victorian Britons' widely held Carlylean view that great deeds could only be assigned to great individuals.[3] The Old Rugbeian Society had been provided with a name by Bloxam and it is possible to imagine that the only thing that would have prevented Ellis' elevation by the Society in 1897 would have been the naming of an alternative, chronologically earlier, 'hero' figure.

Second, Rugby School was certainly keen to reassert itself off the field in the early 1890s, having been defeated on the field during inter-school matches in the mid-1870s, which led to a long-term suspension of such fixtures. Rugby clubs and other rugby-playing schools were starting to utilise the RFU's 1871 'universal' laws of the game, but Rugby School, naturally, still considered itself to be the authentic guardian of the sport and jealously retained its own version of the laws, refusing to join the RFU until 1892. The Ellis story provided an unequivocal statement about ownership of the game, taking all emphasis away from the centuries-long development of ball-handling football games (and the influence that they must have had on the boys of Rugby School) and, instead, placing Rugby School squarely at the centre of the sport's evolution.

Finally, Dunning and Sheard's view in relation to rugby league warrants closer attention. Nineteenth-century workplace reforms had provided a half-day holiday on Saturday which had facilitated the creation of mass working-class participation in sporting culture, including rugby.[4] A typical middle-class reaction to this incursion was to create exclusive sporting environments where they retained sole 'ownership' and were able to maintain their middle-class values. According to this interpretation, the Ellis foundation myth legitimised the hardline policy of the RFU towards a faction of their own northern clubs and, ultimately, the split with the Northern Union. The Ellis story allowed the rugby game to be seen in a distinctly middle-class context, through its primary association with Rugby School, and certainly not as the continuation of the older lineage of folk football as had been played by individuals from the lower social orders. Tony Collins' recent work in the field outlines how the dissemination of the Ellis myth was an integral part of the creation of an amateur ideology for the game of rugby union (in direct opposition to, and as a result of, moves towards professionalism in the game in the north of England) and stresses that 'Matthew Bloxam's assertions would have remained an antiquarian's eccentric belief … had it not been for the battle for rugby's soul that raged from the mid-1880s' (Collins 2009, 35).

---

3   This is the same worldview that saw Queen Boudica's celebration in verse and her casting in bronze for a prime London location on a Thames-side plinth, despite having actually sacked London and razed it to the ground. Irony or evidence were seldom allowed to encroach.

4   During the second half of the 19th century a series of Factory Acts and associated legislation in the United Kingdom introduced reforms which included the provision of compulsory workplace closure for many industries at 2pm on Saturdays. In the absence of opportunities to play sport on Sunday, the newly acquired free time during daylight hours provided a chance for large swathes of the population, all living in close proximity within the industrial heartlands, to participate and spectate. The designated workplace closure time inspired the still-widespread tradition of football matches (of all codes) starting at 3pm on a Saturday afternoon.

An Uneasy Co-existence

The published research of the late 1970s and early 1980s might have managed to successfully uproot the deeply embedded Ellis myth had there not been significant resistance. Challenges came (and continued to come) from those who held dear the romanticism and value of the story but were never able to hold up a shred of supporting evidence because no such material exists. The story continued to flourish, even if renditions of the tale were henceforth often tempered with the subtle addition of an 'alleged' or a 'claimed'. When authors, such as former Rugby School librarian Jennifer Macrory, attempted to defend the story they were inevitably forced to make claims ('All the evidence supports [the sub-committee's] finding') which were quite blatantly false (Macrory 1991, 35). Even Macrory was unable to ignore the flaws in her own theory and the errors that have contributed to the confused historiography: 'The big mistake made by the Old Rugbeian Society was in the wording of the plaque.... They intended to celebrate the game, but instead created a myth' (Macrory 1991, 35).

Following the creation of the plaque (1900), the playing of the 'centenary' match (1923) and the production of the RFU film (1971), the next key building block in the Ellis myth followed the acquisition made in 1986 by the International Rugby Football Board (now International Rugby Board – IRB) of a small silver cup and cover trophy. The cup was purchased to be utilised as a winner's trophy for the nascent Rugby World Cup tournament, due to be held in Australia and New Zealand the following year. The purchase was made by one of the RFU's representatives on the IRB Committee, John Kendal-Carpenter, and, with so much else to manage and prepare, the organising committee were happy to accept his suggestion that the trophy be gilded and named the 'Webb Ellis Cup' (Fig 2.3). This decision, and the enormous success of the associated four-yearly tournament, sent the Ellis story global.

In 1996 the author commenced employment as Curator at the Museum of Rugby, Twickenham (now World Rugby Museum), and spent over a decade dealing with the duality of the story. During his first year in post the author received correspondence from the historian Wray Vamplew, asking how the museum dealt with the Ellis myth. The answer was that the museum used the word 'alleged' extensively and was cautious about giving succour to myth promoters; for example, it had to counter significant RFU pressure in order to decline the potential donation of a replica statue of Ellis that had been offered for display. The original Graham Ibbson statue (modelled on the figure of the sculptor's own son, since no likeness is known to exist of William Ellis as a schoolboy) was unveiled immediately outside Rugby School in 1997. Text on the sculpture's plinth nods to the revisionist academics by avoiding the words 'invention' or 'creation', instead suggesting that Ellis was a local boy who 'inspired' the game of rugby football. However, the very existence of the statue, rather than the subtle phraseology, is what will be remembered by those who have seen it.

By the mid-1990s rugby union history texts and the newly emerging rugby history websites carried a consensus among those who had examined the Ellis evidence. 'The only thing that is for certain', says Bath, 'is that Rugby School's William Webb Ellis did not spontaneously invent the game' (Bath 1997, 8); Zavos refers to 'the continuation of the hoax' (Zavos 1998, 158); and Collins suggests that it is 'possibly the most famous example of myth-making in British sport' (Collins 1998, 5). For the first time, the myth was deconstructed in the greatest communication medium – television. The BBC's 1999 television series and associated, identically named publication *The Union Game* was groundbreaking in offering up many contemporary theories

FIG 2.3. THE WEBB ELLIS CUP.

and conclusions about the game's international evolution and role in a populist way. That a public school elite created and supported the Ellis story because they were 'anxious to confirm possession of a game ... split in two' (Smith 1999, 14) may not have been what rugby followers were expecting to hear when they tuned in – probably hoping, instead, to be treated to the usual highlights reel of renowned players scoring acclaimed tries.

However, paying absolutely no heed, the Ellis juggernaut rolled on relentlessly. The IRB's decision in 1995 to open up the previously amateur rugby union game to professionalism was a decisive turning point in the game's evolution. In this new age of commercialised rugby union, with its marketing departments and brand strategies, the Ellis myth took on a powerful new significance. In 2003 Rod and Lawrence Ellis sold their world-famous Gilbert rugby ball (and netball) brand but retained control of the Gilbert Museum (of rugby football) located directly opposite Rugby School. Utilising their surname in a manner that, it can be safely assumed, they perceived as allowing them to continue to successfully tap into the heritage of the game, the town and the School, they started the Webb Ellis brand of rugby union balls. This development has seen the Webb Ellis name take the field for the first time, courtesy of high-profile licence agreements with the Welsh Rugby Union and the European Cup competition. Concurrently, the Gilbert Museum became the Webb Ellis Rugby Football Museum. A stone's throw away in Rugby town centre is the William Webb Ellis public house and an identically named establish-

FIG 2.4. THE WILLIAM WEBB ELLIS PUBLIC HOUSE, LONDON ROAD, TWICKENHAM.

ment was opened in the centre of Twickenham, not a mile from the famous stadium, in 2003 (Fig 2.4). The name is a perfect, semi-coded marketing tool for a public house in proximity to a large rugby ground. It provides an obvious link with the game for anyone with even a passing interest, but is not overtly specific to a particular nation, region or club. It suggests heritage, longevity of interest and (ironically) knowledge of the game's origins and history, yet it is simultaneously not so blatant that it might dissuade anyone antipathetic towards the sport from passing over the threshold. The thoughts and findings of rugby historians were of absolutely no interest.

ELLIS COMES HOME

England's victory in the 2003 Rugby World Cup competition – the first victory by a northern hemisphere nation – inspired enormously enhanced interest in the game within the winning nation. In addition the RFU gained, as a physical manifestation of England's victory, possession of the Webb Ellis Cup for two years, prior to transferring it to the French Rugby Federation in advance of their 2007 tournament. The presence of the trophy only served to magnify the intransigent views of the Ellis story. On the one hand, the period offered an extraordinary opportunity to utilise the heightened interest in the sport (and its senior trophy) to present a balanced and historically sound reading of the game's origins. Alternatively, various marketing and promotional departments had a once-in-a-lifetime opportunity to utilise their two years with the trophy to provide a lasting legacy of participation in the game once the initial post-tournament surge of interest had waned. They had no interest in anything other than using a swift and simple exploitation of the Ellis myth to grab headlines and increase traffic and footfall wherever the trophy went. The author experienced a number of RFU planning meetings in late 2003 which became animated when the two philosophies clashed. The end result was a compromise whereby the 2004–5 *Sweet Chariot* trophy tour vehicle that transported the Cup across England, to be seen by over a million people, contained a considered interpretation of the origin myth on an associated graphic panel. This interpretive approach – still naming Ellis, but stressing the involvement of countless others in the game's development and downplaying the 'Big Bang' theory – was rolled out wherever possible. However, in most cases publicity and press releases took every opportunity to latch onto links (real and imagined) with Ellis at the expense of detail as the vehicle traversed the country.

ELLIS FOR THE GREATER GOOD

Twenty-first century academic and research-led publications continue to attack the Ellis myth, as exemplified by Huw Richards' declaration that: 'Codification, not some mythic act of invention … is the key moment in a game's history' (Richards 2006, 27). There are even encouraging signs that those who write rugby history from a non-academic perspective – such as the keen amateur historians who have continued to produce club history books for many decades – are no longer rolling out the myth unchallenged in their introductions and opening chapters. The availability of numerous well-researched rugby histories by Tony Collins, Huw Richards and others is having the effect of filtering down a more accurate version of the story. A case in point is Alan Turley's book tracing the early decades of rugby in New Zealand, which contains the traditional retelling of the Ellis story, followed by a disclaimer that, 'whether deserved or not, Webb Ellis has been given an exalted place in rugby tradition. No other sports code today can boast such an iconic figure' (Turley 2008, 36). This view is one that continues to be held by many who perceive enormous value in rugby having what Turley calls 'a unique heritage'. Even the IRB, owners of the Webb Ellis Cup and the body ultimately responsible for the game's health and promotion, is forced to acknowledge that question marks hang over Ellis' action. They declare that 'The legend of William Webb Ellis, who is credited with first picking up the football and running with it, has doggedly survived the countless revisionist theories' in their key publication, the official *Laws Of The Game* (IRB 2010).

In very few countries does rugby union have sporting predominance and the game is typically engaged in a constant battle for column inches, attention or even survival against stronger footballing foes. In this media-driven contemporary sporting world, the Ellis myth continues to serve a role as an easily digestible and accessible introduction and point of difference. Sean Fagan is a historian of both rugby codes working within the Australian media, where rugby union can hope for little more than to secure the third rung on the nation's football ladder at the expense of soccer (after Australian Rules Football and rugby league). Fagan is a respected researcher and writer who is fully aware of the fundamental flaws in the legend but who references the Ellis myth uncritically to get a point across in a crowded marketplace (Fagan 2010). He is unapologetic about utilising the Ellis foundation story because:

just mentioning WWE is an easy metaphor for referring to the start of the game, when speaking on rugby features in a cross-code context. People are so familiar with the WWE myth (and accept it), that it is much simpler/quicker/briefer to just go with the flow … there's little space to divert for a few paragraphs to explain why it is a myth. (Fagan 2010)

He goes on to suggest that if he does not mention Ellis in the popular media his readers struggle for context. He admits that 'I'd rather not perpetuate the myth, but on the other hand I want to draw people into rugby history – "for the greater good!"' (S Fagan *pers comm*).

The William Webb Ellis myth is, as with other myths, not simply an untruth or a lie. It is a story that has grown because it has served, and continues to serve, a multitude of purposes. For many people over many decades it has served to offer a simple explanation to questions that actually require complex answers and, in some cases, cannot and may never be fully answered: Where does the game come from? Whose game is it? How did it develop in the way that it did? Why do some people play it, while others look elsewhere? The role of the historian is not only to show where the myth is at variance with the evidence but also to explain why a myth persists, despite the finest disregard for the rules of evidence.

Bibliography and References

Atyeo, D, 1979 *Blood and Guts: Violence In Sport*, Grosset and Dunlap, New York

Bath, R (ed), 1997 *The Ultimate Encyclopedia of Rugby*, Carlton, London

Collins, T, 1998 *Rugby's Great Split: Class, Culture and the Origins of Rugby League Football*, Frank Cass, London

— 2009 *A Social History of English Rugby Union*, Routledge, London

Davies, W J A, 1923 *Rugby Football*, Websters, London

Dunning, E, and Sheard, K, 1979 *Barbarians, Gentlemen and Players*, Martin Robertson, London

Fagan, S, 2010 *No place for Folau in game of mum-friendly soccer* [online], 13 June, available from: http://www.smh.com.au/afl/afl-news/no-place-for-folau-in-game-of-mumfriendly soccer-20100612-y4r1.html [14 June 2010]

Gallagher, D, and Stead, W J, 1906 *The Complete Rugby Footballer*, Methuen and Co Ltd, London

Green, G, 1953 *The History of the Football Association*, Naldrett Press, London

Holt, R, 1989 *Sport And The British: A Modern History*, Clarendon Press, Oxford

International Rugby Board, 2010 *Laws Of The Game: Rugby Union 2010*, International Rugby Board, Dublin

Macrory, J, 1991 *Running With The Ball: The Birth of Rugby Football*, Collins Willow, London

Marriott, C J B (ed), 1922 *The Rugby Game and How To Play It*, Athletic Publications Ltd, London

Marples, M, 1954 *A History of Football*, Secker and Warburg, London

Marshall, Rev F (ed), 1892 *Football: The Rugby Union Game*, Cassell, London

Mason, T, 1980 *Association Football and English Society 1863–1915*, Harvester, Sussex

Old Rugbeian Society, 1897 *The Origin of Rugby Football: Report (with appendices) of the Sub-Committee of the Old Rugbeian Society*, A J Lawrence, Rugby

— 1930 *Football Records Of Rugby School 1823–1929*, George Over, Rugby

Owen, O L, 1955 *The History of The Rugby Football Union*, Playfair, London

Reason, J, and James, C, 1979 *The World Of Rugby: A History of Rugby Union Football*, BBC, London

Richards, H, 2006 *A Game for Hooligans: The History of Rugby Football*, Mainstream, London

Shearman, M, 1887 *Athletics and Football*, Longmans, Green and Co, London

Simpson, J B H, 1967 Rugby *Since Arnold: A History of Rugby School from 1842*, Macmillan, London

Smith, D, and Williams, G, 1980 *Fields Of Praise: The Official History of the Welsh Rugby Union 1881–1981*, University of Wales Press, Cardiff

Smith, S, 1999 *The Union Game: A Rugby History*, BBC Books, London

Turley, A, 2008 *Rugby: The Pioneer Years*, Harper Collins, Auckland

Vamplew, W, 1988 *Pay Up and Play The Game: Professional Sport in Britain, 1875–1914*, Cambridge University Press, Cambridge

Zavos, S, 1998 *Ka Mate! Ka Mate! New Zealand's Conquest of British Rugby*, Viking, Auckland

3

Cricket Writing, Heritage and Ideology

Anthony Bateman

> Have you not ever felt the urge to write
> Of all the cricket that has blessed your sight? (Blunden 1945, 5)

There is little doubt that of all sports to have originated in the British Isles, cricket is the most literary. In 1991 the updated edition of Padwick's *Bibliography of Cricket* listed over 10,000 items, a figure that is now likely to have increased exponentially given the global growth in cricket's popularity, particularly in South Asia (Eley and Griffiths 1991). As well as the sheer quantity of cricket books, the sport has attracted the attention of a great many literary figures and this has lent the game a distinctly bookish aura, something that has tended to privilege it socially and culturally over other sports. In addition to portrayals of cricket by such resoundingly canonical literary figures as Charles Dickens and E M Forster, cricket developed a tradition of cultured belletrism, a body of reflexive prose and poetry that to a great extent defined cricket's meaning and set out the parameters of how the sport could be commemorated and remembered. Ever since Mary Russell Mitford included a description of a country cricket match in *Our Village* (1824–32), a heritage of literary representations of cricket tended to privilege the past over the present, the rural over the urban and the amateur over the professional while, at the same time, setting out conservative ideals of social and gender relations. In short, it created an ideology of cricket that continued to hold sway well into the 20th century. This chapter seeks to trace the emergence and development of this discourse and to examine both its subsequent canonisation and the ensuing valorisation of cricket within English national culture.

Although a number of cricket poems appeared in the 18th century, such as William Goldwin's 'In Certamen Pilae; Anglice, A Cricket Match' and James Love's 'Cricket, an heroic poem', the first full-length prose description of cricket appears in Mary Russell Mitford's classic account of rural life, *Our Village*. Written at a time of significant social change – a second wave of land enclosure and sizeable migrations from the country to the expanding urban centres – Mitford's work shares with William Cobbett's *Rural Rides* (1830) a preoccupation with chronicling a fast-disappearing way of life. In this sense Mitford's village cricket field is already a heritage site, something at odds with modernity and its emerging commercial culture:

> I doubt if there be any scene in the world more animating or delightful than a cricket-match:- I do not mean a set match at Lord's Ground for money, hard money, between a certain number of gentlemen and players, as they are called – people who make a trade of that noble sport, and degrade it into an affair of bettings, and hedgings, and cheatings … nor do I mean a pretty *fete* in a gentlemen's park, where they show off in graceful costumes to a gay marquee of admiring

belles.… No! the cricket that I mean is a real solid old-fashioned match between neighbouring parishes, where each attacks the other for honour and a supper, glory and half-a-crown a man.

(Mitford 1992, 131–2)

The same is true of John Nyren's *The Cricketers of my Time*, a work written with the assistance of John Keats' close friend Charles Cowden-Clarke and first published in serial form in *The Town* in 1832. Nyren had been a leading player at the famous Hambledon club in Hampshire during the late 18th century and the book is a nostalgic reconstruction of a lost golden age of cricket. Here the rambunctious energies and virility of late 18th-century rural cricket provide a point of contrast to the apparently temperate, effete and Europeanised present:

There was high feasting held on Broadhalfpenny during the solemnity of one of our grand matches. Oh! it was a heart-stirring sight to witness the multitude forming a complete and dense circle around that noble green. Half the county would be present, and all their hearts with us – Little Hambledon pitted against all England was a proud thought for the Hampshire men … How those fine brawn-faced fellows of farmers would drink to our success! And then, what stuff they had to drink! – Punch! – not your new *Ponche à Romaine*; or *Ponche à la Groseille*; or your modern cat-lap milk-punch – punch be-devilled; but good, unsophisticated, John Bull stuff – stark! – that would stand on end – punch that would make a cat speak!

(Nyren 1998, 71–2)

Despite its resolutely unpuritanical attitude to strong liquor, cricket's Victorian literary gate-keepers loved Nyren's book and, during the second half of the 19th century, it became the urtext of the sport's literary canon. The Reverend John Mitford's review of the book (1833) has become a canonical text in itself and, in the latter decades of the 19th century, numerous editions of Nyren appeared. Even before cricket became properly established as a genuinely national game the sport was besotted with its literary past.

The 1860s witnessed a significant growth in the publication of cricket books, including the first edition in 1864 of *Wisden Cricketers' Almanack*, a yearbook that has since been afforded a quasi-Biblical status in the cricket canon. As cricket became a genuinely national and increasingly imperial pastime, a number of the sport's literary figures began to organise its discourses retrospectively so that a canon of authorised texts emerged that were deemed suitable models for cricket's literary representations. At the same time the growth of cricket literature neatly dovetailed with the contemporary 'discovery of rural England' (Howkins 1986, 63–88). In the context of fears about racial degeneration and the survival of England's pre-industrial structures, the popularity of cricket literature in the 1890s echoed the broader revival of folk-custom and culture typified by Cecil Sharpe's folk-dance movement (Boyes 1993; Matless 1998; Hughes and Stradling 2001). Although pastoralism had been a consistent feature of the English literary tradition, there was a marked proliferation of such discourse in the late Victorian and Edwardian period (Williams 1975, 1). For the urban middle class, literary visions of the countryside seemed to offer escape from the tyranny of industrialism and the ideological tensions of modernity (Wiener 1992, 51). Cricket literature formed part of this broader cultural context because it was a now well-established literary medium through which reassuring images of the rural could be disseminated. Indeed, influential and popular ruralist publishing houses, such as Country Life, published cricket books (Hutchinson 1905). In his poem 'Ecstasy' (1898), the prolific cricket litterateur E V Lucas elevated the rural and ancient associations of the game to the level of apotheosis by figuring village cricket as a ritualised act of pagan nature worship. Muscular Christianity has here given way to the hedonistic literary cult of the 'Gospel of Joy', with nature becoming the source of an English masculine cultural identity, 'Stout of heart, clean of limb, steady of eye':

> Twenty-Two Englishmen, blithesome and vigorous,
> On with your flannels, and haste to the game;
> Greet the Earth-Mother, and meet the sun face to face,
> Offer your brows for the kiss of his flame!
> Children of Midsummer, Sons of the Open Air,
> Here in this meadow, this fair summer day,
> Here 'mid the song o' birds, here 'mid the hum o'noon,
> Here will we play! (Frewin 1964, 179–80)

A less pantheistic variant of this contemporary literary ruralism located the essence of Englishness in the country house. In the 1890s – a period of economic downturn and a degree of social unrest – the cult of the country house provided reassuring romantic images of the countryside for a middle-class urban readership. In this literature the country squire was invariably portrayed as the embodiment of Englishness and as the benevolent head of a harmonious quasi-feudal social order with his elegant house the architectural focus of this national imaginary (Wiener 1992, 50). A contemporary fashion for country-house cricket among the socially privileged neatly dovetailed with this prevailing literary conceit. Whole weeks could be dedicated to this leisurely form of cricket, and, although it was primarily a social occasion for the elite, estate workers and local villagers often took part in the matches. When L P Hartley nostalgically portrayed an Edwardian country-house game in his novel *The Go-Between* (1953), both Lord Hugh Trimingham ('a pretty bat') and his rival in love, the local farmer Ted Burgess, participate, albeit on opposing sides (Hartley 1977, 177–89). For the cricketer Albert Knight (or, at least, his likely co-writer E V Lucas), the ease and luxuriance provided by country-house cricket not only contrasted with the sordid commercial realities of top level cricket but also pointed to nothing less than a Morrisian rural utopia:

> Country House cricket reminds one of days spent in eating apples under an old tree, reading the 'Earthly Paradise' of William Morris. It is the cricket of an Eden future when we shall saunter through the fields, 'without tomorrow, without yesterday', nor scent laziness in ease, nor distrust good-humoured chaff as incompatible with seriousness. (Knight 1906, 284–5)

In contrast to the Muscular Christian version of the sport, Knight here projects cricket both forward and backwards into a future that magically recaptures a pre-industrial society, free from the earnest religious pieties and work ethic that underpinned the creation of modern industrial Britain.

The elegiac had been an element of cricket writing as far back as Nyren, and during the later 19th century it continued to form part of a broader discourse of English remembrance. One of the most famous cricket poems, Francis Thompson's 'At Lord's' (1897), begins:

> It is little I repair to the matches of the Southron folk,
> Though my own red roses there may blow;

> It is little I repair to the matches of the Southron folk,
> Though the red roses crest the caps, I know.
> For the field is full of shades as I near the shadowy coast,
> And a ghostly batsman plays to the bowling of a ghost,
> And I look through my tears on a soundless-clapping host
>   As the run-stealers flicker to and fro,
>   To and fro:
> O my Hornby and my Barlow long ago! (Thompson 1913, 305)

Thompson had spent six years in Manchester as a failed medical student before moving to London, where he became closely associated with the aesthetic movement and incurably addicted to opium. He composed several cricket poems, which, according to his biographer Everard Meynell, 'are all lamentations for the dead' (Meynell 1926, 34). As well as the profoundly elegiac quality of 'At Lord's', it is significant that the match Thompson reconstructs was not actually played at Lord's, but at Manchester's Old Trafford ground between Lancashire and Gloucestershire in 1878. Meynell recounts that the young Thompson 'was much at the Old Trafford ground, and there he stored memories that would topple out over one another in his talk at the end of his life' (Meynell 1926, 31). With its deliberately archaic diction, the text is an act of wistful recollection that plays upon the image of the 'shadowy coast' ('coast' being an obsolete term for a borderland or frontier) as a temporal, and not merely a spatial, concept. 'Coast' is a long-established literary metaphor of death, yet its shadowy quality implies only a vague or illusory boundary between the dead and the living, between past and present. Equally, although the conflation of Lord's with Old Trafford could be attributed to the unreliability of an opium-addled memory, the confusion is in keeping with a poetic schema in which temporal and spatial boundaries are deliberately ambiguous. This schema enables both the nation's past and present and the geographical disparity of nation and empire figured by the names of its individual (yet interchangeable) cricket grounds to merge into a single, ordered place of Englishness. But the image of the spectral did not simply create and invoke the national sport's traditions and hagiology; in conjunction with the metonymically interchangeable cricket field, the generic figure of the spectral cricketer was an integral feature of cricket writing's ability to reproduce Englishness in the past, present and future. The itinerant ghosts haunting the generic English cricket field represent a national community that can constantly imitate itself across time and geographical space (Baucom 1999, 150).

This theme is also evident in a speech written by the author of *Peter Pan*, J M Barrie. The speech was given at a dinner to mark the arrival in England of the Australian Test team in 1926, was subsequently reprinted in *The Times* and now forms part of the sport's literary canon. It was conventional for major literary figures to speak at such events (as part of the elaborate ritualism of empire which surrounded colonial cricket tours) in order to validate cricket culturally and sanctify the bonds of empire it represented. As well as producing the most famous narrative of perpetually arrested adolescence, *Peter Pan* (a fiction that had profound resonances after the truncation of so many young lives in the war), Barrie frequently wrote on cricket and sought to enshrine the links between the sport and the literary field by organising a writers' cricket team known as the Allahakbarries which, before the war, had regularly included authors such as Arthur Conan Doyle and P G Wodehouse (Barrie 1927; Allen 1988). The Australian players may have been surprised to learn from Barrie that 'the great glory of cricket does not lie in Test Matches, nor county championships, nor Sheffield Shields, but rather on village greens, the cradle of cricket'. Like many interwar cricket writers, Barrie's speech positions the contemporary practice of Test cricket within a broader discourse of cultural crisis by defining it as little more than a part of ephemeral modernity: 'As the years roll on they become of small account; something else soon takes its place, the very word may be forgotten'. Against this fallen image of impermanence, village cricket signifies sameness, not only through history but across geographical space, a quality that endows this auratic English locale with an imperial dimension: 'but long, long afterwards, I think, your far-off progeny will still of summer afternoons hear the crack of the bat and the local champion calling for his ale on the same old bumpy wickets'. This generic location possesses not only an ability to transcend imperial space, but can enforce a diachronic conformity in which past and present merge into one. The aesthetic space of the rural cricket field can thus imaginatively obviate the violent separations of war: 'It has been said of the unseen army of the dead, on their everlasting march, that when they are passing a rural cricket ground the Englishman falls out of the ranks for a moment to look over the gate and smile. The Englishman, yes, and the Australian' (Barrie 1926). Such synoptic imperial imagery had specific resonances at this time. In Australia a series of economic and political factors, in conjunction with perceptions of the serious shortcomings of British leadership in the war (particularly at Gallipoli), were hastening and intensifying calls for the devolution of imperial power (McDevitt 2004, 83–8). In its very denial, Barrie's speech articulates with this context, for, although it eschews the blatant empire-binding rhetoric of much late 19th-century and early 20th-century cricket discourse, the village green is nevertheless a symbol of an imperial culture whose past, present and future would be fundamentally the same.

NEVILLE CARDUS AND THE HERITAGE OF CRICKET

> Cardus! Thou shouldest be living at this hour
> The game hath need of thee … (De Silva 2004)

Like many of his fellow writers, Barrie admired the cricket journalism of the game's most celebrated chronicler, Neville Cardus (1888–1975). Cardus was born in Rusholme, Manchester, and in 1919 began writing on cricket for the *Manchester Guardian* under the *nom de plume* of 'Cricketer'. His deeply nostalgic and stylistically florid representations of cricket have subsequently afforded him a revered status in the sport's literary canon. More than any other cricket writer, Cardus has become a construct who transcends the fields of 'cricket literature' and 'literature' to become a component of the national culture. The canonisation of Cardus started soon after the beginning of his career when, in 1921, the influential organicist literary figure H J Massingham invited him to contribute an article to the *Nation*. Subsequently Cardus' 'William Gilbert Grace' appeared in Massingham's *The Great Victorians*, 'Cricket Fields and Cricketers' in *A Hundred Best English Essays* and 'Cricket and Cricketers' and 'A Sentimental Journey' in two English prose textbooks for schools, one of which was published by the English Association (Ratcliffe 1931, 68–78; The English Association 1936, 30–34). In his autobiography, Cardus acknowledged the support he had received in the 1920s from a number of influential conservative literary figures, such as J C Squire and Hugh Walpole (Cardus 1947, 183–4). His first three cricket books were published by Housman's friend and publisher, Grant Richards, and his fourth, *Cricket* (1930), appeared as part of Squire and Viscount Lee of Fareham's Longmans' *English Heritage Series* with an introduction written by Squire himself. Other titles in the series included *The English*

Constitution, *Shakespeare*, *Fox-hunting*, *English Music* and *English Folk Song and Dance*. Equally implicated in the contemporary literary construction of Englishness, *English Cricket* (1945) was published in *Writers' Britain* alongside titles such as Edmund Blunden's *English Villages* and Vita Sackville-West's *English Country Houses*. Cardus later contributed a chapter on cricket to a book on British heritage published to mark the 1951 Festival of Britain (Cardus 1951). Clearly Cardus' representations of cricket provided a number of influential cultural figures and publishing houses with images of how they believed England and Englishness should be reproduced. Cardus' cricket writings have frequently been reprinted, anthologised and edited, and all recent English anthologies of cricket prose include at least one essay by him. Conversely, forms of literary criticism were a major constitutive discourse in the making of Neville Cardus. The first cricket writer to be knighted, he became the supreme celebrant of cricket (and particularly the cricket of the interwar period), and was from there constructed as a central figure in the discourse of the national culture. His death in 1975 prompted a flurry of tributes from journalists and literary figures. For John Arlott (himself an important figure in the making and remaking of the cricket canon as both critic and writer), Cardus created modern cricket writing and was:

> The first writer to evoke cricket; to create a mythology out of the folk hero players; essentially to put the feelings of ordinary cricket watchers into words. [...] There can never be a greater cricket writer that Neville Cardus. He created it. Others performed what he showed them. There is not one of his juniors who has not been affected by him, and few who have not, shamelessly, copied him. (Brookes 1978, 6)

Cardus' response to modernity was also manifest in the major contribution he made to the literary construction of a late Victorian and Edwardian 'Golden Age' of cricket. The Golden Age was a temporal utopia situated between about 1890 and 1914, a pristine point of contrast to the interwar practice of cricket, and, by implication, to the politics, industrial processes and aesthetics of the contemporary national culture. Cardus' Golden Age presented a naturally hierarchical social order in which the aristocracy display their inherent superiority through elegant and effortless bodily performance:

> During the golden age of English cricket, the public school flavour could be felt as strongly as in any West End club. When Spooner or K L Hutching batted on a lovely summer day you could witness the fine flowerings of all the elegant cultural processes that had gone to the making of these cricketers; you could see their innings as though against a backdrop of distant playing fields, far away from the reach of industry, pleasant lawns stretching to the chaste countryside, lawns well trimmed and conscious of the things that are not done. (Cardus 1930, 106)

Golden Ages recur in literary and cultural history as retrospective critiques of the loss of feudal or aristocratic social orders (Williams 1975, 35). Cardus was not only celebrating the bodily performance of pre-war batsmen such as Spooner and Hutching, but the economic conditions and social relations that seemingly enabled such displays of aristocratic and upper-middle-class style to arise. Cardus elegised the loss of a social hierarchy that was supposedly uncomplicated by the economic transformations and social mobility of the interwar years. The construction of cricket's Golden Age formed part of a broader literary rewriting of the late Victorian and Edwardian eras as an image of a less complex, 'depoliticised' national community.

Cardus' R H Spooner was one of the most important figures in the discourse of cricket's Golden Age. Spooner was a public-school-educated Lancashire amateur whom Cardus had watched at Old Trafford as a boy. Although he played the majority of his cricket before the war, Spooner made a few appearances for Lancashire at the beginning of Cardus' career as a cricket writer. His subsequent account of a Spooner innings – one hugely influenced by the Victorian aesthete Walter Pater – is a paean to the past that inscribes upon Spooner's body the aura of the reified art work:

> In and through the art of batsmanship we have come to know Spooner as intimately as if he had written Sonnets to a Dark Lady. Walk at random on a cricket field and see Spooner make his off-drive. You have no need to be informed that Spooner is batting. The stroke can be 'attributed' with as much certainty as any canvas by Paul Veronese. That graceful forward poise, the supple play of the wrists! (Cardus 1922, 110)

In contrast to what Cardus often described as the dull mechanical reproduction of cricket at the time, Spooner's bodily performance is valorised as the product of individual creative genius and evinces a Leavisite 'vitality' of expression.

By the early 1930s Spooner had become a major text in Cardus' construction of the Golden Age, as his essay 'The Batsmanship of Manners' shows. Here Cardus did not merely eulogise his boyhood batting idol, but symbolically outlined a simplified vision of English society, a hierarchical and essentially rural society in which deference and ties of service bound the social ranks together. As the embodiment of an old aristocratic order, Cardus' Spooner is a golden boy of this Golden Age, an effortless and refined stylist whose play is utterly dignified and devoid of violence. Cardus' studied attention to language foregrounds the need for modes of representation that are themselves apposite stylistic vehicles for the construction of a particular aesthetic of Englishness: 'Straight from the playing field of Marlborough he came and conquered – nay, the word conquered is too hard and aggressive for Spooner: he charmed and won our heart and the hearts of his opponents' (Cardus 1934, 83). Cardus often unfavourably characterised northern cricket of the 1920s and 1930s as expressing the region's historical associations with industrialism, utilitarianism and, even more concerning, trade unionism and socialism: 'Too many Lancashire, Nottinghamshire, and Yorkshire elevens have overdone the collectivist philosophy, turning out just "utility" teams, mechanically efficient' (Cardus 1922, 32). However, Spooner's *habitus* produces a mode of embodiment that associates him with the gentility of the southern shires rather than the industrial heartland of his native county:

> Spooner told us in every one of his drives past cover that he did not come from the hinterland of Lancashire, where cobbled streets sound with the noise of clogs and industry; he played always as though on the elegant lawns of Aigburth; his cricket was 'county' in the social sense of the term [...]. I'll swear that on that day long ago there were tents and bunting in the breeze of Manchester while Spooner's bat flicked and flashed. (Cardus 1934, 83)

Spooner's body is here endowed with the ability to represent the country house and the public school in the most alien and industrial of environments:

> He was the most lyrical of cricketers, and for that reason he had no need to play a long innings to tell us his secret. The only difference between 30 by Spooner and 150 by Spooner

was a matter of external and unessential form or duration; the spirit moved him from the very beginning. A rondo by Mozart is just as complete as a symphony by him [...] and a single stroke by Spooner was likewise a quality absolute, beyond the need of mensuration or any mathematical means of valuation whatever. [...] as well count the words in a poem or the notes in an allegro. (Cardus 1934, 83)

Cultured and elegant batting is not only an index of Spooner's heredity (as Cardus later wrote, 'What's bred in the bones comes out in an innings' (Cardus 1930, 77)) but represents a form of art-for-art's-sake in which the scoring of runs is of secondary importance to the display of style. Accordingly, Cardus' florid prose, replete with allusions to literature and classical music, is carefully constructed so as to create a sense of the aesthetic quality of Spooner's batting and to divorce it from any taint of utility value. Here, as in so many Cardus essays, there are echoes of the aesthetic movement's doctrine that great art aspires to the condition of music. Indeed, the 'Mozartian' grace and charm of Spooner's play leads Cardus at the conclusion of the essay to make claims in more general terms for cricket's status as art, and to rail against those who would think otherwise. At the same time, with its emphasis on the aesthetic – rather than athletic – qualities of Spooner's batting, a softer, more feminised rhetoric of cricketing heroism emerges that is distinct from the dominant Muscular Christian constructions of the field:

And Spooner's cricket in spirit was kin with sweet music, and the wind that makes long grasses wave, and the singing of Elisabeth Schumann in Johann Strauss, and the poetry of Herrick. Why do we deny the art of a cricketer, and rank it lower than a vocalist's or a fiddler's? If anybody tells me that R H Spooner did not compel a pleasure as any compelled by the most celebrated Italian tenor I will write him down a purist and an ass. (Cardus 1934, 87)

Cardus' nostalgic feudal social vision was rendered by an aetheticisation of the amateur/ professional divide that structured cricket's social relations until 1963. In creating a cast of pre-war professional cricketers, Cardus used the literary stereotype of the simple countryman to endow them with a bucolic charm that highlights by antithesis the pedigree of the Gentlemen. As well as providing humorous, homespun comments, they are presented as good honest artisans in the manner of the contemporary organicist writings of H J Massingham. In his deeply nostalgic essay 'Good Days' (1931), Cardus reveals himself as a shameless purveyor of a feudal vision of rural England. In this piece Cardus introduced the figure of 'Old William' (Bill Attewell), an ex-Nottinghamshire professional who was subsequently a cricket coach at Shrewsbury school, where, for a time, Cardus acted as his assistant. Like Massingham's Samuel Rockall, Cardus' Old William is organically embedded in a rural environment and thus beyond temporal change. Unlike Cardus' interwar professionals, Old William's body does not disrupt the aesthetic ideals of cricket discourse and can thus be seamlessly merged into the English rural landscape: 'he seemed as permanent at Shastbury as the ancient oak tree' (Cardus 1934, 101). With this organic image connoting organic social order, his respectful comments, patronisingly rendered by Cardus, exemplify social deference and serve to underline the pedigree of Spooner and its relationship to the gentlemanly batting aesthetic: '"It were a pleasure to bowl to Maister Spooner [...] his batting were as nice as he were hisself"' (Cardus 1934, 83). Within the narrative's logic of distinction, a sense of Cardus' own cultural capital is produced through a condescending description of Old William's theory of literature: 'And something about the oak and the ash and a summer of "wet

and splash". He was fond of that one, because the rhymes brought it within his view of poetry'
(Cardus 1934, 103). Compounded of the innocent swain with a home-spun, folkloric wisdom
and the salutary Wordsworthian archetype, Old William is resolutely pre-modern rather than
upwardly mobile or acquisitive: 'He was one of the old school of professional cricketers; I cannot
see him in a Morris-Cowley, as any day I can see many contemporary Test match players. And
I cannot see him in suede shoes, or any sort of shoes. William wore enormous boots which
has some sort of metal protection built into the edge of the heel. You could hear him coming
up the street miles away' (Cardus 1934, 102–3). Here Cardus shares with Leavis a Kenneth-
Grahame-like hostility to the motor car as a symbol of modernity and conspicuous consumption,
while Old William's footwear loudly announces his unambiguous class status and unimpeach-
able masculinity at a safe distance. Old William represents an ideal of a mythical economically
and socially immobile social formation that in its political deference merely consented to, and
complemented, the cultural authority of the public-school-educated elite: 'I am glad that he
loved Shastbury and knew it was a beautiful place' (Cardus 1934, 103). In these nostalgic evoca-
tions of Spooner and Old William, Cardus was presenting a more desirable picture of an Englishness based upon both social cohesiveness and clearly demarcated inequality under aristocratic
benevolence.

CONCLUSION

Although Cardus was guilty of producing a fictional construction of the past, it is an historical
perspective of significance and one that, as Arlott noted, was highly influential and widely reproduced in the literature of cricket. The 1997 reprinting of Cardus' *English Cricket*, along with other
titles in the original *Writers' Britain* series, such as Edmund Blunden's *English Villages* and Vita
Sackville-West's *English Country Houses*, suggests that cricket, and particularly Cardus' romantic
version of it, is still packaged as a 'heritage item'. For a period in the 1980s and 1990s this indeed
did seem to be the case. The sale of school playing fields for the purposes of building development led to less youth participation in the sport, while an inconsistent England Test side hardly
inspired the nation. Much mainstream cricket writing wallowed in nostalgia to the extent that
in 2000 the editor of *Wisden*, Stephen Moss, complained:

> The rosy-eyed romantics should declare and let the revisionists into bat. Subvert the stereotypes
> of cricketing parsons and public schools, hymn the joys of global cricket, let writing play its
> part in re-energising the game for a new age, a generation less devoted to a dreamy past … we
> want our prose in black and white, not purple. Its anglocentricity is absurd for a game where the
> balance of power now lies on the Indian subcontinent and in Australia. The commemoration of
> the past is dangerous for a sport which must quickly find a role for the future. Cricket writing,
> like cricket as a whole, must remake itself … Wit, vision, a close reading of the game, a sense
> of its languor and lunacies, rather than unremitting reverence, should henceforth dictate the
> play, dominate the field. (Moss 2000, 30)

Much of what Moss says is indisputable, yet he suggests that at the beginning of the new
millennium cricket writing remained a heterogeneous body of work. This is to overlook the
publication of a number of major texts that had already challenged this Anglo-centric and
nostalgic tradition. First among these books was the appropriately titled *Beyond a Boundary*,

by the Trinidadian Marxist C L R James. In this groundbreaking work James placed cricket, both English and West Indian, within its historical and social context to show how the game was inextricably bound up both with British imperial ideals *and with resistance to them* (James 1963). The politics of James' cricket writings still remain an embarrassment to many of the sport's traditionalists, but since its publication in 1963, other writers – most notably Derek Birley and Mike Marqusee – have adopted a less than reverential stance on many of cricket's most cherished myths and obfuscations, particularly the long-held misconception that cricket is somehow above and beyond politics (Birley 1979; Marqusee 1994).

Since 2000 both cricket and cricket writing have experienced huge changes. The shift of power, noted by Moss, from England to the Indian subcontinent has been further consolidated, particularly with the emergence of the Indian Premier League Twenty/20 competition in 2007, a glitzy, unashamedly populist packaging of the shortest form of the game that has produced vast television revenues in South Asia and beyond. The irrationality of any lingering Anglo-centricity was highlighted in 2000 when the International Cricket Council moved its headquarters from London to Dubai. The opening match of the 2010 English season took place not at Lord's but in Dubai when, complete with an experimental pink ball, the action unfolded under floodlights.

Side by side with these developments, cricket writing itself is changing, not least as a result of the emergence of new forms of media. The internet is now a major agent in the dissemination of cricket discourse and a plurality of voices now surround the game, less reverential to the game's traditions and more international in complexion. Nevertheless, a rich heritage of cricket literature remains for us to cherish, question and analyse. Another important recent development is the work of a number of scholars from disparate fields – social history, sociology and literary and cultural studies – who have brought to bear in their analyses of cricket and its literature academic rigour and scholarly objectivity. In so doing they have revealed much about cricket's ideological role within Britain and its former empire as well as the politics underlying the sport's social, race and gender relations (Bateman 2009; Bateman and Hill 2011; Beckles and Stoddart 1995; Williams 1999; Williams 2001). Cricket's literary heritage is no longer merely a means of nostalgic escape but a body of texts crucial to the reconstruction and interpretation of a nation and its empire's past.

BIBLIOGRAPHY AND REFERENCES

Allen, D R, 1988 *Peter Pan and Cricket*, Constable, London

Barrie, J M, 1926 *Cricket*, The Author, London

— 1927 *The Greenwood Hat*, P Davies, London

Bateman, A, 2009 *Cricket, Literature and Culture: Symbolising the Nation, Destabilising Empire*, Ashgate, Farnham

Bateman, A, and Hill, J (eds), 2011 *The Cambridge Companion to Cricket*, Cambridge University Press, Cambridge

Baucom, I, 1999 *Out of Place: Englishness, Empire and the Locations of Identity*, Princeton University Press, Princeton

Beckles, H, and Stoddart, B (eds), 1995 *Liberation Cricket: West Indies Cricket Culture*, Manchester University Press, Manchester

Birley, D, 1979 *The Willow Wand: Some Cricket Myths Explored*, Queen Anne Press, London

Blunden, E, 1945 (1944) *Cricket Country*, The Reprint Society, London

Boyes, G, 1993 *The Imagined Village: Culture, Ideology and the English Folk Revival*, Manchester University Press, Manchester

Brookes, C, 1978 *English Cricket: The Game and its Players Through the Ages*, Reader's Union, Newton Abbot

Cardus, N, 1922 *A Cricketer's Book*, Grant Richards, London

— 1930 *Cricket*, Longmans, London

— 1934 *Good Days*, Jonathan Cape, London

— 1947 *Autobiography*, Collins, London

— 1951 Cricket, in *Our Way of Life: Twelve Aspects of the British Heritage*, Country Life, London, 141–52

De Silva, A, 2004 'Cardus', in *'A Breathless Hush…': The MCC Anthology of Cricket Verse* (eds D R Allen and H Doggart), Methuen, London, 311

Eley, S, and Griffiths, P, 1991 *Padwick's Bibliography of Cricket: Volume 2*, McKenzie, London

The English Association, 1936 *English Essays of Today*, Oxford University Press, Oxford

Frewin, L (ed), 1964 *The Poetry of Cricket: An Anthology*, Macdonald, London

Hartley, L P, 1977 (1953) *The Go-Between*, Penguin, London

Howkins, A, 1986 The Discovery of Rural England, in *Englishness: Politics and Culture 1880–1920* (eds R Colls and P Dodds), Croom Helm, London, 63–88

Hughes, M, and Stradling, R, 2001 *The English Musical Renaissance 1840–1940: Constructing a National Music*, Manchester University Press, Manchester

Hutchinson, T, 1905 *Cricket*, Country Life, London

James, C L R, 1963 *Beyond a Boundary*, Hutchinson, London

Knight, A E, 1906 *The Complete Cricketer*, Methuen, London

Marqusee, M, 1994 *Anyone But England: Cricket and the National Malaise*, Verso, London

Matless, D, 1998 *Landscape and Englishness*, Reaktion Books, London

McDevitt, P F, 2004 *'May the Best Man Win': Sport, Masculinity and Nationalism in Great Britain and the Empire, 1880–2004*, Palgrave Macmillan, Basingstoke

Meynell, E, 1926 *The Life of Francis Thompson*, Burns, Oates and Washbourne, London

Mitford, M R, 1992 (1824–32) *Our Village*, Bracken Books, London

Moss, S (ed), 2000 *Wisden Cricketers' Almanack*, John Wisden, London

Nyren, J, 1998 (1832–33) *The Cricketers of My Time*, Robson Books, London

Ratcliffe, A (ed), 1931 *Prose of Our Time*, Nelson, London

Thompson, F, 1913 *The Collected Poetry of Francis Thompson*, Hodder & Stoughton, London

Wiener, M, 1992 *English Culture and the Decline of the Industrial Spirit 1850–1980*, Penguin, London

Williams, J, 1999 *Cricket and England: A Cultural and Social History of the Inter-War Years*, Frank Cass, London

— 2001 *Cricket and Race*, Berg, Oxford

Williams, R, 1975 (1973) *The Country and the City*, Oxford University Press, Oxford

4

Football and the Fine Arts:
The Football Association Art Competition and Exhibition, 1953

RAY PHYSICK

In 1953, as part of its 90th anniversary celebrations, the Football Association (FA), in conjunction with the Arts Council of Great Britain, organised a *Football and the Fine Arts* competition in London, followed by a national tour. Artists were invited to submit entries 'dealing with a game of association football in England, or any scene directly connected' with the sport. According to Sir Stanley Rous, the aim of the exhibition was to break down the 'barrier between football and art' (*Birkenhead News* 1954). J St John, the key organiser of the exhibition and subsequent tour, suggested that: 'The worlds of art and football were not so far apart. The excitement of admiring paint skilfully applied to the canvas was not so far removed from the artistry of men like Mercer, Puskas and Matthews' (*Liverpool Daily Post* 1954).

St John developed his point by congratulating the FA on the idea of the exhibition, saying: 'art today needed a new form of patronage' and he hoped 'that other bodies would follow the example of the FA' (*Liverpool Daily Post* 1954). As well as the 90th anniversary of the FA, the other context of the exhibition was the establishment, immediately after World War II, of the Arts Council, the remit of which was to encourage wider participation in the arts.

From the outset the Arts Council oversaw and selected the work to be exhibited, a situation with which the FA was happy to concur. The guidelines for submissions to the competition stated that there 'would be no limitations on the artist's style; symbolic treatment would receive the same consideration as more naturalistic treatment' (*Football and the Fine Arts* 1953, 1). The response to the FA's invitation was overwhelming, with a total of 1710 pieces of art submitted for the consideration of the judges.[1] Entries were divided into four categories: paintings; drawing and watercolours; engravings and lithographs; and sculptures. Prizes for the competition totalled £3000: £1000 each for paintings and sculptures and £250 each for drawings and watercolours and engravings and lithographs, together with 20 Honourable Mentions worth £25 each. The judges finally chose 152 artworks for the three-week-long exhibition, which was held at the International Faculty of Arts, Park Lane House, between 21 October and 7 November 1953.[2] Although

---

[1] The four judges were Professor William Coldstream from the Slade; Sir John Rothenstein, director of the Tate; Sir Philip Hendy, director of the National Gallery; Philip James, director of the Arts Council.

[2] Most sources give the figure of 152 artworks (an overall figure also given in the Exhibition Catalogue), broken down into: 78 paintings; 28 drawings and watercolours; 24 engravings and lithographs; and 22 sculptures. However, the final programme listed in the Arts Council archive lists 156 artworks: 81 paintings; 29 in the

the exhibition was given a royal opening by HRH Princess Alice, Countess of Athlone, who also bought Lilla Fox's painting *Boys Playing Football*, the idea for the exhibition was conceived before the schedule for the Coronation of Queen Elizabeth II was announced. The majority of the work was also shown on the subsequent year-long national tour that took the exhibition to 12 English towns and cities, as well as Aberdeen. Each gallery showed the exhibition for a three-week period.[3]

This chapter will assess the significance of the 1953 exhibition. Owing to limitations of space I will confine my analysis to the two-dimensional work that was chosen by the judges. The work will be assessed in the context of the traditions of British art and the extent to which the artwork informs us about football. The art critic Herbert Read has commented that: 'In its plainest manifestations art always embodies some interpretation of life' (Read 1974, 171). The chapter will show that the *Football and the Fine Arts* exhibition successfully revealed the cultural context of football in the immediate post-war period. To fully appreciate the significance of the 1953 exhibition it will be necessary to briefly consider what type of football art preceded the exhibition.[4] The chapter will conclude by looking at the ways the exhibition influenced subsequent generations of artists whose work is either totally focused on football or has been influenced by it.

FOOTBALL ART PRIOR TO 1953

The first line of the *Football and the Fine Arts* souvenir booklet confidently states that: 'Compared with cricket, there is no tradition in Britain of football painting' (*Football and the Fine Arts* 1953, 1). However, this statement is only partially accurate, as football, in one form or another, had been represented in the visual arts for hundreds of years prior to the exhibition. There are several important paintings showing football in a social setting prior to codification of the game in 1863. Perhaps the most important one is Thomas Webster's oil painting *Foot-Ball*, which was exhibited at the Royal Academy in 1839, the year after it was painted. There are also numerous examples that show football being played in a rural or public-school setting.[5]

---

drawing and watercolours class; 24 engravings/lithographs; and 22 sculptures. Prizewinners were as follows: Paintings: four shared £1000: Brian Robb, *Football*; L S Lowry, *Going to the Match*; L L Toynbee, *Midweek Practice at Stamford Bridge*; Alfred Daniels, *Fulham FC*. Watercolours: one winner received £250: Susan Benson, *Stamford Bridge Stadium*. Engravings and Lithographs: five winners received £50 each: Arthur Goodwin, *Saturday Afternoon*; Susan Benson, *Saving a Goal*; Geoffrey Clarke, *Study of the Ball Striking the Net*; Michael Rothenstein, *Moment of Victory*; Robert Taverner, *The Changing Room*. Sculpture: only £600 of the £1000 was awarded: two winners received £150: F B McWilliam, *Football*; Jack Daniel, *Footballers*; three received £100: Willi Soukop, *Goalkeeper*; Roger Young, *Spectators*; Peter L Peri, *The Players*. The 20 Honourable Mentions broke down as follows: paintings 14; watercolours 3; engravings and lithographs 2; sculpture 1.

3   Many other galleries and museums expressed interest in hosting the exhibition. Some had to refuse owing to lack of space, others because their programme was already fully booked for the year ahead.

4   When referring to visual images of football I will use the term football art. In my PhD thesis I have argued that football artwork should be regarded as a distinct genre (genre meant as artworks depicting scenes of everyday life, rather than genre meant as a categorisation of form). *The Guardian*, in reviewing the 1966 exhibition 'Football' at the Manchester Art Gallery, stated that football painting is a genre and should not be judged simply on painterly qualities or an artist's technique (*The Guardian* 1966). In this context genre in art is determined by the subject matter. For definitions of genre visit the Tate gallery website at: http://www.tate.org.uk/collections/glossary/definition.jsp?entryId=333.

5   See the Priory and FIFA art collections at the National Football Museum for such examples. A print of the Webster painting was on show at the NFM prior to its closure in 2010.

In the period following the codification of football in 1863, up to the outbreak of war in 1914, football grew exponentially from a game largely played at and between public schools to a sport that attracted millions of spectators in large conurbations. Moreover, following the establishment of the Football League in 1888 the game emerged as a genuine mass spectator sport; by 1900 several clubs were drawing regular crowds in excess of 20,000 (Russell 1997). In the same period football became increasingly covered in local and national newspapers and in illustrated periodicals such as the *Illustrated London News* and *The Graphic*, as well as in dedicated sports papers such as the *Athletic News*. All of these publications were established in the 19th century. Sports coverage was seen as essential by newspaper proprietors to attract and increase circulation, with visual depictions of sport seen as an important part of this strategy. Until the launch of the *Daily Mirror* – the first newspaper to use photographs exclusively for illustration – in 1903, newspapers would employ artists to draw cartoons and engravers to produce images using woodblock and lithographic processes. Many of these visual images provide an essential reference point for football historians when looking at the early development of the game. Football was also given wide visual circulation in popular art through postcards, posters and in magazines (Chazaud 1998, 7). It is estimated that in the early years of the 20th century companies producing popular art employed 20,000 artists to paint and design popular images of everyday life. Many of the postcards produced depicted various aspects of the game, reflecting its mass appeal. These illustrations included leading players of the day, club squads, players in action and instructional postcards that showed potential players how to shoot or take a corner or a throw-in, among other skills. Among the key artists were S T Dadd, Amos Ramsbottom and Fred S Howard, who between them painted thousands of football images (Krieger 1983).

Visual representations of football in the media coincided with the emergence of Realism in art. Realism introduced revolutionary change in the way artists presented their subject matter: it enabled them to depict scenes from the real world. The 19th-century context of Realism was that mimesis was an 'active reflectionism', a method for transmitting knowledge through art, a 'knowledge that was external to art itself', but art that informed the viewer about society (Mosquera 1994, 76–80). Realism emerged in France but in Britain its counterparts can be found in the pre-Raphaelites and later in the Camden Town and Euston Road Groups. Popular artistic representations of football were clearly influenced by Realism. Likewise, the style of paintings exhibited in 1953, with few exceptions, was overwhelmingly presented in the genre of Realism with an emphasis on reflecting the cultural impact of football inside and outside football stadiums.

Although the majority of early football images stem from popular art, there are several examples of fine art; among the best are a watercolour by William Hodgson and two oils paintings by Duncan Grant and Clarence Bretherik. The Hodgson and Grant images need not delay us, as these paintings both represent football prior to the dominance of the sport professionally. Bretherik's painting, dated 1897, is of an actual match in Lancashire in front of a large crowd, possibly marking a special occasion such as a cup tie.[6] Unfortunately, the actual location of the football ground has not been identified but, compared with the Hodgson and Grant paintings, this is a modern scene, one recognisable to any present-day football fan. The painting is in the

---

6   The painting is in the Priory Collection but has not been loaned to the National Football Museum. Much of the information relating to the painting has been extracted from the Priory Collection notes associated with the painting.

tradition of Realism, art that informs the viewer about an emerging cultural activity. Bretherik's painting shows steep terrace embankments packed with supporters, indicating that football at this stage was attracting large crowds: it is almost certainly a match between two professional teams. This is hardly surprising given that Lancashire was the birthplace of the professional game in the 1880s. The painting has significance, as such scenes would only become fully popularised through photography in the first decade of the 20th century.

Although in the interwar years cricket was still regarded as Britain's national sport, it was football that had the genuine mass spectator base and was, particularly in working-class areas, the *de facto* national sport. This situation is reflected in the growing importance of the FA Cup Final following the opening of Wembley in 1923, an event that impressed football upon the consciousness of the mass of the population. Radio coverage of the finals from 1927 took the sport into people's homes and served to intensify the cultural significance of the game. This is the background to the growing interest in football shown by a number of artists during this period. L S Lowry's football paintings from the interwar years show football being played in parks and on local playing fields, themes that were recreated by other artists for the 1953 exhibition. Other significant artists in this period include Paul Nash, C R W Nevinson and Carel Weight, who all produced influential pieces of art that had football to the fore. Moreover, London's transport companies, prior to 1914, had engaged artists to paint posters that advertised the best way to get to a football ground by bus or tube. This continued in the interwar years, with particularly striking posters being designed each year for the FA Cup Final. Among the most significant poster-producing artists were Sybil Andrews and Cyril Power, both of whom produced woodcuts that conveyed the fast pace of football and other sports.[7]

The above survey shows that prior to 1939 there was a small but growing number of artists who were attracted to football as a subject for their work. In the post-1945 period this trend continued and was given further impetus by the decision to hold a football art exhibition in 1953.

The Exhibition and Tour: Role and Responses of the Arts Council

In the immediate post-war period the Arts Council of Great Britain was established, replacing the wartime Council for the Encouragement of Music and of the Arts (CEMA). The primary objective of the new body was to 'encourage knowledge, understanding and practice of the arts' with an emphasis on broadening the base and the audience for the arts.[8] According to *The Manchester Guardian*, paraphrasing J M Keynes, the first chairman of the Arts Council, the new body was to: 'be concerned with nourishing a living interest in the arts all over Great Britain and with raising the standard of presentation in the metropolitan centres … [and] to foster a high standard in the arts of the nation and to make them as widely accessible as possible' (*Manchester Guardian* 1945,

---

[7]   Some London Transport football posters are in the National Football Museum. They can also be viewed online at: http://www.ltmcollection.org/posters/themes/theme_sub.html?IXtoptheme=Sport&IXthemeid=1. KU.U. Prints of Paul Nash and Sybil Andrews' work can also be found in the British Museum. Nevinson's painting *Any Wintry Afternoon* is on permanent display at the Manchester Art Gallery.

[8]   The quotation is from Sir John Anderson, Chancellor of the Exchequer, speaking in the House of Commons, 12 June 1945, cited in Steyn 2008, 155, and *The Manchester Guardian* 1945, 3.

3). Clearly, the newly formed Arts Council was a body that was committed to taking the arts to a wider public and the sponsoring of the FA exhibition was an obvious indication of this aim.

Although the costs for the original exhibition were met by the Arts Council, escalating overheads for the nationwide tour forced Philip James, Director of the Arts Council, to write to Sir Stanley Rous asking for a contribution of £500 from the FA towards the tour. James explained to Rous that hiring fees for artists for the year-long tour would amount to £1000, with transport costing an additional £700. Upon Rous' recommendation the FA eventually acceded to James' request (James to Rous, Archive of Art and Design).

Initially regional galleries were offered the tour free of charge but because of higher than expected costs, and despite the donation from the FA, the Arts Council was forced to levy a hire charge of £1 per day for the exhibition. This fee proved too much for some galleries, who had been initially informed that only insurance and transport costs would fall upon them. Galleries that declined after initial interest included the Walker Art Gallery in Liverpool, Burnley, Stafford and Rochdale. Other galleries, such as Birmingham, had rejected 'the football exhibition' from the outset (Correspondence, Archive of Art and Design).

Birmingham's response reflects the view held by the majority of art critics and curators and some academics – and which has only recently begun to change – that most football-related art produces pictures 'that might appeal more to the public than the art critic' (Lanfranchi *et al* 2004, 147). Indeed, reports from regional art galleries to the Arts Council about the exhibition reinforce Lanfranchi's comment: the extant regional reports do reveal that the exhibition was popular with the viewing public, especially when the artworks were shown alongside football artefacts. During the course of the year December 1953–December 1954, more than 85,000 visitors attended the exhibition. However, attendance was variable; some areas saw record crowds and others a poor response. The Williamson Art Gallery in Birkenhead, for example, attracted over 21,000 people, almost a quarter of the aggregate total. In comparison, Sheffield and Blackpool had disappointing attendances, totalling 7000 and 2000 respectively for the two three-week periods. Reporting to J St John, Joanna Drew of the Arts Council observed that: 'The exhibition had its greatest success at Birkenhead as you can see from the numbers, it created an unprecedented stir in a town which doesn't take to art exhibitions' (Drew to St John, Archive of Art and Design).

However, to what extent art was the attraction is open to question. Birkenhead adopted the strategy of showing the four Football League Championship trophies, the FA Cup, Stanley Matthews' cup winners' medal and personal souvenirs from the collection of Ralph (Dixie) Dean, the former Everton centre-forward, as well as several souvenirs from the Everton and Liverpool trophy rooms. This seems to have been a decisive factor in attracting visitors, the majority of whom would never have seen trophies such as the FA Cup close up. The first day's attendance at the gallery totalled 1500, compared to the weekday average of 30. The next best attendance on the tour was at Manchester, with nearly 12,000 visitors, while Bootle attracted 5000 visitors. Some galleries were clearly disappointed with the attendance. At Bradford, for example, attendance totalled 5773 for the duration of the exhibition. Expressing his disappointment, the art director of Cartwright Hall partly blamed the poor weather but overall 'it [the exhibition] did not appeal to anything like the extent we had anticipated, despite the fact there are two Football League Clubs in the city'. The gallery had expected to draw a minimum of 3000 persons for each week of the exhibition (Cartwright Hall to Arts Council, Archive of Art and Design). Overall, however, the Arts Council was pleased with the tour. Writing to Rous, Phillip Green, the director of the Arts Council, informed him that:

On the whole it has been extremely successful and particularly well received at Sheffield and Birkenhead and at Wolverhampton, where it was pronounced the most popular exhibition of the year. At Salford and Bradford the success was not so great but at Luton … seven hundred people attended in 1½ hours and it … attracted an entirely new public to the gallery. (Green to Rous, Archive of Art and Design)

Wolverhampton had adopted a similar strategy to Birkenhead by displaying the Division One League Championship and the FA Cup, both of which were held by two local teams at the time of the exhibition: Wolverhampton Wanderers and West Bromwich Albion respectively.

Those who saw the exhibition were generally excited by the content on show. In contrast, the response of some regional curators towards the content was somewhat condescending. At Leeds the curator reported that the exhibition 'irritated those who knew about football and failed to satisfy those who knew about painting'. An unnamed regional association wrote to the Arts Council stating that 'the show was an excellent scheme by the Football Association but I doubt whether it did much good for the cause of art'.

Scott Campbell from the North East Arts Council reported that the region had three show-ings, at Sheffield, Leeds and Bradford. He agreed with the sentiments expressed by Leeds and went on to say:

People with whom I discussed the show – painters and others – disliked it more often than not for the reasons Musgrave [of Leeds Art Gallery] suggests. My personal impression was one of size and garishness … Three huge rooms full of footballers is too much for anyone, especially in view of some of the horrors included. (Regional Reports Archive of Art and Design)

Getting away from curatorial impressions, a report from another unnamed region stated that 'visitors to the exhibition were pleased to see contemporary painters facing up to the expression of such a popular theme in so many varied ways'. The Kettering curator noticed that:

some visitors came to see the exhibition primarily for its subject. Visitors of this type preferred the more straightforward pictures such as No2 (Allinson: At The Goalmouth) and the various dressing room scenes. They were plainly bewildered by such pictures as No1 (Adams: The Two Captains) and No26 (Feiler: Mousehole v Paul). These visitors often had technical comments to make about the inaccuracies in the pictures (eg goalkeepers do not have numbers as other players). Such pictures as No8 (Bone: Arromanches, 1944), No47 (Lamb: Village Football), No49 (Lowry: Going to the Match), No69 (Tucker: A promising Lad) and No76 (Williams: Highgate Schoolboy) were popular and there was a good deal of interest in the sculpture, particularly in No150 (Wood: Player in Wire). (Regional Reports Archive of Art and Design)

Although the FA and the Arts Council placed no restriction on the style of work it would seem that the more popular works were those that were presented in the Realist tradition.[9]

---

9   Although most of the work in the exhibition was presented in Realist form, there were several Modernist artists who had work selected by the judges. These included: Michael Rothenstein, Walter Hoyle, Daphne

The Artwork in Context

According to the artist Mark Wallinger, artistic practice should get under the skin of the viewer and challenge people's received opinions of the way artists cover a particular subject (Wallinger and Warnock 2000, 133). The themed nature of *Football and the Fine Arts* produced a challenging exhibition: for the first time in the history of football an exhibition of fine art gave the public the opportunity to view the game through the imaginative eye of the artist. Moreover, as regional reports above show, the exhibition got under the skin of and irritated the art establishment, a situation that *The Times* arts correspondent also confirms: 'Many of the pictures and sculptures have the look of works done to order on a not very congenial theme' (*The Times* 1953).

In contrast, *The Manchester Guardian*, commenting upon the Manchester leg of tour, argued that:

> football provides the artist with a great variety of excellent pictorial materials which he [sic] had hitherto neglected – panoramic crowd scenes, figures in vigorous action and in strikingly dramatic attitudes, formal patterns of goalposts and nets, striped jerseys, and great corrugated iron stands, geometrically marked out fields, spectators underneath giant advertisements hoardings, and small dirty boys in back streets and empty plot. (*Manchester Guardian* 1954)

In general, however, the art establishment recoiled from the subject matter of the exhibition. One is reminded of the conservative attitude of the Royal Academy in the late 19th century towards the artists who sought to combine social conscience and documentary in their work. Such work, like the artwork contained in the 1953 exhibition, was also looked upon condescendingly by the art establishment (Treuherz 1987).

The main source for images of football is journalistic photography. Unlike the photo-journalist, however, the artist does not seek to give an exact representation of cultural practice but rather to present personal impressions of life or an aspect of life. This explains the response of the public, as outlined in the report from the Kettering gallery, to some of the more abstract works in the exhibition, most notably the Feiler painting. Several regional reports indicated that the exhibition did bring new audiences into the galleries; the majority of these new visitors were probably working-class football supporters, many of whom would not have been exposed to abstract art before. However, the varied nature of the exhibition reinforces my earlier comment that there was something in it to accommodate all tastes, especially the paintings that were documentary in nature.

Not all of the paintings from the exhibition have survived, but, using the 75 reproductions and the full list of exhibitors presented in the exhibition catalogue, it is possible to break down the paintings into various subject categories. Excluding action scenes, such as goalmouth tussles, there were some 40 images that showed football stadiums, most of which have football fans either approaching the stadium or packing the terraces. London grounds dominate, particularly Stamford Bridge and The Valley, but there are also interesting paintings of the Goldstone Ground (Brighton), Fratton Park (Portsmouth), Brunton Park (Carlisle) and three of Burnden Park (Bolton). Lowry's painting of Burnden Park, *Going to the Match*, has, since the exhibi-

Chart, Clifford Fishwick and Paul Feiler. It is impossible to provide a definitive list as many paintings have not survived or are not readily accessible.

tion, emerged as the most important painting that was on display in 1953. The Professional Footballers' Association bought the painting in 1999 for £1.9m. Gordon Taylor, the PFA Chief Executive, regards it as the most important football painting since for him it represents 'the heart and soul of the game and the anticipation of fans on their way to a match' (BBC News 1999).

Compared with modern British grounds, which are generally poor architecturally, some older grounds do have some excellent architectural features. Gerald Cains' painting *Saturday Taxpayers* shows a section of Fratton Park which reveals a 'classic [Archibald] Leitch balcony, with his trademark criss-cross steelwork in blue on a white background' (Inglis 1996, 294). But in general the paintings reveal the poor conditions under which fans had to watch football in the 1950s. Cundall's painting, and others of Stamford Bridge, shows a vast stadium that had limited cover for the majority of fans.

Other interesting contrasts captured by the artists are the differences between fans attending a league match and those attending a FA Cup tie. Very few fans at league games are portrayed displaying their team's colours through the wearing of a scarf, rosette or hat, whereas for cup ties the opposite is the case. R A Bailey's line and wash image *The Cup Tie* depicts raucous fans wearing such regalia as well as swirling football rattles above their heads. K Lek's wood engraving *Off To The Match* shows this even more graphically, while the celebrity nature of a cup tie is brilliantly captured by Michael Rothenstein's abstract engraving *Moment of Victory* which, among other things, shows football rosettes swirling like Catherine wheels.

Somewhat surprisingly, perhaps, the next most popular scene represented in the exhibition is football being played in a community setting. There are approximately 27 such paintings showing football being played on council-owned playing fields or on the common, in the street or on wasteland near to or in close proximity to houses. The football action illustrated in these paintings is far more satisfying than the stylised images that show football being played between top-level league teams. These non-professionals are shown playing football with more freedom; the situational goalmouth scenes present in the league games, in general, show a somewhat static view of the game, with perhaps the notable exception of Michael Ayrton's painting *Arsenal v Aston Villa*. The communal football images in the exhibition show football being played on makeshift areas, a situation that was not uncommon in the 1950s. This was a period when streets in working-class areas were largely free of motor cars and waste ground near houses was used for all sorts of pastimes: scenes brilliantly shown in *Tomorrow's Professionals* by W H Newton Taylor, which shows boys playing in the back entry as mothers look on. Another painting, *On the Heath* by Paul Bullard, shows how important playing fields were, and are, for the myriad of football teams that play in local leagues at weekends.

Approximately 15 artists covered action on the pitch. Many of these paintings were long shots that showed a full stadium with players on the pitch and place the stadium in its wider environment, showing, among other things, the close proximity of residential housing and industrial complexes such as power stations and mills to places of leisure. However, the most satisfying paintings in this section are those that focus on the fans on the terrace talking passionately about the game. One such image, *Offside Dispute* by Victor John Kuell, shows an angry young man pointing his finger towards the penalty area while talking to two elderly fans, presumably about the injustice of the goal awarded by the referee.

Football, of course, is about scoring goals, and there are several paintings showing just this. Perhaps the best painting in this section is a surrealist-influenced oil painting by Walter Hoyle simply titled *Goal!* The goal net, which seems to wrap around the players, acts as a metaphor for the entangled goalmouth area which shows opposing players tangled up in each other's challenges. The goalkeeper has missed the ball, which has been headed towards the goal and is about to cross the line. The whole scene gets across the physicality of the game, the efforts players make both to score and to stop goals being scored. In a single image the artist has captured the great intensity of the game and successfully communicated the reason why we play and watch football.

Surprisingly, the portrait section of the exhibition was small; only nine were chosen by the judges. The approach of the artists towards portraiture was traditionalist. It is important to note that portraits are more than just a record of the great and the good; they often reflect social realities (Brilliant 1991, 7–21). Three of the most prominent portraits in the exhibition were of Raich Carter, Wally Barnes and Frank Swift, all very fine players in their day. There were, however, no paintings of Stanley Matthews, the most famous British footballer of the era, or of Billy Wright, the England captain at the time of the exhibition. Each player's national identity is given prominence; in the case of Barnes and Swift, for example, they are seen wearing the kit of their national team, while the painting of Carter, who is wearing the colours of Hull City, has a badge in the top left corner which is inscribed with the word 'England'. The paintings present the footballer as a role model, as men of substance who have strong allegiance to their country.

Superficially, the paintings in the exhibition demonstrate that the artists approached their subject matter in a conservative manner. Their approach to the subject, as indicated above, with a few exceptions, was overwhelmingly Realist. However, the artists did not focus merely on pitch action; they presented the viewer with a wider view of football that included the players in contemplative mood in the dressing room before and after the match, the empty stadium, the stadium full of fans watching the action, fans approaching the stadium and the celebratory nature of being at and going to a match. In other words, taken as a whole, the exhibition encompassed many aspects of the game, including how ordinary people in the community played and watched football.

The artist Frank Auerbach has commented that when painters arrange things on a surface they need to have 'a permanent sense of the tangible world'. Such awareness enables artists to not merely reflect the world, but to make a permanent statement about it (The Hard-Won Image 1984, 26). Overall, the 1953 exhibition shows how a significant portion of the population accessed and received their leisure: the football ground paintings in particular show them in locations very close to the place of work and close to where people lived. In this respect the exhibition brought together a body of work that was not only socially relevant at the time but that has also provided sports historians with lasting images of how football was embedded into the mores of society. The exhibition also prefaced the modern era of football, a period that has seen the high art of painting seeking out football rather than the other way round.

Conclusion

The 1953 exhibition focused upon in this chapter marks an important milestone in the visual representation of football. The exhibition was pioneering in the sense that it attempted to attract a sceptical art world to football; it was also the first art exhibition dedicated to football that was presented through a network of publicly owned galleries (Wingfield 1998). The response of the artists, the Arts Council and art galleries from around the country demonstrates that football was, even in 1953, the only national sport that was capable of attracting such broad support for a nationwide art exhibition about a particular sport. While critical acclaim was generally lacking for the exhibition, and subsequent tour, it did demonstrate that art could be taken into areas of the population that had hitherto been ignored by the art establishment. It also demonstrated that working-class people could be attracted to art given the right subject matter or approach by artists and art galleries, and that art can be popular in style and subject without compromising its quality. As with all exhibitions, the work exhibited in 1953 was of mixed quality. Works by Lowry, Rothenstein, Fishwick and Colquhoun stood out against the lesser works, but given the broad sweep of the exhibition it was a remarkable achievement that the exhibition was seen as both a success and of a good standard by the organisers (Green to Rous, Archive of Art and Design).

The FA had hoped that the exhibition would act as a catalyst to promote further interest in football by artists. The FA's interest in football art was long in gestation. Examples of football art can be found in the FA yearbooks, where for six years, between 1949 and 1955, articles looked at how football had been depicted in art since the Middle Ages up to the modern day. Particularly poignant is the 1951–2 yearbook, which reproduced seven football images drawn by school-children for the *Daily Express*. This edition of the yearbook also carried information about the *Football and the Fine Arts* competition. Despite this huge effort by the FA to promote football-related art, however, the art world reverted to type following the exhibition and once again, with some notable exceptions, largely ignored football. However, as football became an increasingly dominant leisure pastime and as its exposure on television became more extensive artists, as well as academics, have taken a growing interest in the game. These two groups have sought to assess the significance of football in the context of wider cultural processes taking place in society. Indeed, one of the major factors in the increasing interest in football by artists is their increasing desire to reinterpret popular culture, of which football is a significant part. The establishment of the Premier League in 1992 seems to have provided the catalyst for a new generation of artists, who not only feature football in their work but have began to take up major societal issues such as identity, racism, commodification and globalisation – issues that are of increasing importance in football. Two exhibitions of note held during Euro '96 were, firstly, *Offside*, held between 17 June and 26 September 1996 at the Manchester Art Gallery, and subsequently at three other galleries, which explored a diverse range of societal issues through football art. This exhibition was in many ways the reverse of the 1953 exhibition. It received wide critical acclaim from the art world but little response from football fans (*Offside* 1996). The second was *England's Glory*, hosted in a private gallery in Cork Street, London; this was a more commercial exhibition that included artwork from the 1953 exhibition, prints as well as work by contemporary artists. The gallery has subsequently hosted several other football art exhibitions.

Ten years after *Offside* and *England's Glory*, the sporting goods manufacturer Umbro sponsored *One Love: The Football Art Prize* at the Lowry galleries in Salford. Like *Football and the Fine Arts* of 1953, the aim was to attract work from as wide a range of artists as possible. In the event more than 800 entries from professional and amateur artists were received. The choice of the Lowry Galleries to host the exhibition was poignant. Lowry, whose painting *Going to the Match* was one of the winners of the FA competition in 1953, is now on permanent display at the Gallery thanks to the Professional Footballers' Association. The exhibition was in many ways a hybrid of the 1953 and 1996 exhibitions: Realist-style paintings were juxtaposed alongside more Modernist styles. The winner of the competition was Manchester artist Ben Kelly, whose work is, fittingly, influenced by Lowry (Fig 4.1). The exhibition was very popular and in many ways showed that the aims of 1953 – to have artists consider football as a worthy subject for art – had finally been fulfilled. Lynn Barber, in a humorous but complimentary review, endorses this view:

Fig 4.1. Ben Kelly: *The Final Whistle*, winner of the One Love: Football Art Prize held at the Lowry Galleries in 2006.

Why have artists wasted so many centuries painting nudes, landscapes, Madonnas, flowers, still lifes, when they could have been painting football all this time? When you think about it, it's the ideal subject. It has everything – colour, movement, passion, triumph and disaster, men with big thighs. Think what Michelangelo could have done with a football team – he really missed out. Anyway, football's proper place as an inspirer of art has finally been recognised in a competition called 'One Love: The Football Art Prize'. (Barber 2006)

It may have taken more than 50 years to materialise but the hopes that Rous and the FA had in 1953 were finally realised. The *One Love* exhibition was not only a celebration of football but recognition that football was among those activities that sat at the pinnacle of national culture. *Art Monthly* summed up the nature and role of art in society when reviewing the *Offside* exhibition and indicated why football had become a legitimate area for artists to explore:

All kinds of people, including artists, take an interest in football yet it is perhaps only in recent years that it has been possible for artists confidently to include the game in the subjects of their work. There would have been a time when this exhibition, if it happened at all, would likely have taken an oppositional stance to the game and the (male) myopia for which it is meant to stand. Current art discourse is less antagonistic towards aspects of a more general culture and the game itself has come a long way in shrugging off the dark atmosphere of violence which surrounded it during the 1970s and the early '80s. (*Art Monthly* 1996)

Football provides some of the most powerful metaphors around and artists are going to use its social and cultural significance in their work. Moreover, the landmark FA exhibition is the reference point for most artists who seek to reference football in their work.

Bibliography and References

The Archive of Art and Design (at the Victoria and Albert Museum, London), n.d. Letters, circulars and reports relating to the *Football and the Fine Arts* exhibition

Art Monthly, 1996, London, July–August

Barber, L, 2006 The art of football [online], *The Observer*, 12 November, available from: http://www.guardian.co.uk/football/2006/nov/12/1 [3 February 2011]

BBC News, 1999 *Footballers' union nets Lowry* [online], 1 December, available from: http://news.bbc.co.uk/1/hi/uk/545023.stm [18 October 2011]

Birkenhead News, 1954 Art Gallery is treasure-house of famous trophies, 3 February (newspaper cuttings file in the Williamson Art Gallery, Birkenhead)

Brilliant, R, 1991 *Portraiture*, Reaktion Books, London

Chazaud, P, 1998 *Art et Football 1860–1960*, Mandala Editions, Toulaud

England's Glory: An Exhibition of Football, 1996 Gallery 27, London

FA Year Books, 1949–1955 Football Association, London

Football and the Fine Arts exhibition catalogue, 1953 Naldrett Press, London

The Hard-Won Image exhibition catalogue, 1984 Tate Gallery, London

Inglis, S, 1996 *Football Grounds of Britain*, Collins Willow, London

Krieger, E, 1983 *Good Old Soccer: the Golden Age of Football Picture Postcards*, Longman, London

Lanfranchi, P, Eisenberg, C, Mason, T, and Wahl, A, 2004 *100 Years of Football: The FIFA Centennial Book*, Weidenfeld & Nicolson, London

Liverpool Daily Post, 1954 Art and Sport From New Alliance, 3 February (newspaper cuttings file in the Williamson Art Gallery, Birkenhead)

McNay, M G, 1966 Football in the Frame, *The Guardian*, 12 July and 26 July, 7

Manchester Art Gallery archives (Manchester Art Gallery): letters, circulars and reports relating to the *Offside* exhibition

Manchester Guardian, 1945 C.E.M.A. Will Continue Its Work Under a New Title: The Arts Council of Great Britain, 13 June, 3

— 1954 Art and Football: Novel Exhibition Come to Manchester, 30 March, 5

Mason, T, 1996 Game of the North? in *Sport and Identity in the North of England* (eds J Hill and J Williams), Keele University Press, Keele

Mosquera, G, 1994 Marxist Aesthetics, and Abstract Art, *Oxford Art Journal* 17 (1), 76–80

Offside exhibition catalogue, 1996 Institute of International Visual Arts and Manchester City Art Gallery, Manchester

One Love: The Football Art Prize exhibition catalogue 2006, The Lowry, The Lowry Press, Salford Quays

Panofsky, E, 1972 *Studies in Iconology*, Harper Row, New York

Read, H, 1974 *The Meaning of Art*, Faber and Faber, London

Russell, D, 1997 *Football and The English*, Carnegie Publishing, Preston

— 2008 Associating with Football: Social Identity in England, 1863–1998, in *Football Cultures and Identities* (eds G Armstrong and R Giulianotti), Macmillan, London

Steyn, J, 2008 Realism versus Realism, British Art of the 1950s, *Third Text* 22, March, 145–56

The Times, 1953 Football in Art: Competition Works go on Show, 21 October, 10

Treuherz, J, 1987 *Hard Times: Social Realism in Victorian Art*, Manchester City Art Galleries, Manchester

Wallinger, M, and Warnock, M, 2000 *Art for All? Their Policies and Our Culture*, Peer, London

Wilson, S, and Lack, J, 2008 *Tate Guide to Modern Art Terms*, Tate Publishing, London

Wingfield, M, 1998 *Sport and the Artist – Volume 1: Ball Games*, Antique Collectors' Club, Woodbridge

5

'It's Nice to Belong':[1] Boxing, Heritage and Community in London

Neil Skinner and Matthew Taylor

The development of pugilism and modern boxing in Britain has always been closely associated with London and its people. From Jack Broughton, a former waterman from Wapping who formulated the first written rules in 1743, through to Aldgate's Daniel Mendoza, arguably the first great 'star' of the ring in the late 18th and early 19th centuries, and post-war champions such as Henry Cooper and Frank Bruno, Londoners have played a central role in the history and culture of the sport. So too have famous London venues such as Broughton's boxing academy off Tottenham Court Road, the National Sporting Club in Covent Garden and, more recently, York Hall in Bethnal Green. Few would doubt Stan Shipley's assessment that London was Britain's boxing 'capital' for most of its modern history; nor, as Kasia Boddy's cultural history of the sport shows us, that many of the popular representations of British boxing in television, film, literature and art relate to its metropolitan subculture (Shipley 1989, 94; Boddy 2008).

For much of its history boxing has been portrayed as a sport in crisis and decline. Such concerns prompted nostalgic reflections and a search for the essence of the sport in its past. In the interwar years the perceived dangers of Americanisation, corruption and commercialisation led boxing columnists to fondly recall encounters from the prize-ring and the earliest gloved fights. By the 1960s and 1970s changing leisure patterns, alternative forms of entertainment, suburbanisation and television coverage had led to a decline in participation and attendances. The 1930s and 1940s were now perceived as boxing's 'golden years', when thousands of registered fighters fought in nightly promotions in the big cities. By contrast, small hall boxing had 'almost died' and there were only a few hundred professional fighters by the early 1970s – a figure which, despite an increase to around 600 during the unemployment of the 1980s, had dropped to just 40 by 1996 (Shipley 1989, 96; Cooper 1972, 29; Odd 1978, 239; Holt and Mason 2000, 64).

Some commentators connected boxing's apparent post-war decline to the disappearance of traditional working-class communities. Poverty and hunger may have been one of the motivations to take up the sport but fighters were also thought to have flourished in Britain's tough, close-knit urban neighbourhoods (Holt 1989, 301–2; Sugden 1996, 92–3). Despite significant changes, Shipley argued in 1989, boxing had remained 'a working-class sport' and one that 'has tenaciously claimed a sense of place'. 'Boxers have always been seen as coming from a working-class community', he went on, although 'whether the community remains is another matter' (Shipley 1989, 110–11).

---

[1] The phrase is the motto of the London Ex-Boxers' Association and is used in much of its publicity, on its website and in the 'East End Boxing Lives' exhibition.

The link between boxing and 'community', though often asserted, has rarely been adequately explored by writers, sociologists and historians. This chapter aims to do this by focusing on public representations of boxing's history and heritage in London. It looks, firstly and briefly, at how London's boxing past has been represented in popular literature. The main part of the article then focuses on the 'East End Boxing Lives' project organised by the London Ex-Boxers' Association (LEBA). In particular, it explores how representations of boxing's past have been developed, arranged and, where possible, engaged with through the project's website and a related exhibition at Hackney Museum. In so doing it draws on academic debates around history, memory and 'historical distance' to consider how LEBA's portrayal of London boxing positioned its audience in relation to the 'lives' it narrated and depicted.

Boxing and Community

'Community' has always been a difficult concept for scholars to pin down. It has, as Richard Dennis and Stephen Daniels have pointed out, been 'used to perform many different functions in the description and analysis of society', with a resulting lack of consensus over definitions and meanings. Some of its appeal might be explained by an assumed positive connotation of social belonging. For Raymond Williams it was a concept that, unlike related terms such as 'state', 'society' and 'nation', seemed 'never to be used unfavourably' (Dennis and Daniels 1994, 202). Its connection to the concept of 'class' has been a topic of particular debate. While 19th-century social investigators and some historians saw 'community' in terms of social mixing and cross-class loyalties, the historical orthodoxy now is to relate it more to social segregation and class solidarity. As Trevor Griffiths has suggested, rather than being presented as 'the converse of class', 'community' might reasonably be seen 'as complementary, enhancing our appreciation of the complexity and richness of class identities' (Griffiths 2001, 11).

Historians of the British working class have dealt with the concept in a number of ways. For John Benson, in his study of the pre-World War II era, a sense of community was built upon and derived from kinship and neighbourhood ties. It thus needed to be understood 'both spatially and socially: as a geographical area and as a group of people to which its members feel that they belong'. Clearly defined communities emerged, in this view, in circumstances where the social and economic structure was relatively homogenous, where residential patterns were stable, where the community was geographically isolated and where a 'communality of interest' was consequently pronounced. The era of the 'traditional' working-class community may have begun to unravel with wider industrial changes and the building of new out-of-town estates in the interwar years, but, for those on lower wages at least, ties of community 'survived remarkably unscathed' into the 1940s and 1950s (Benson 1989, 118, 124–5, 133).

Although not all historians have been as sensitive as Benson to the definitional complications of 'community' and its relationship to categories such as 'kinship' and 'neighbourhood', many have concurred with his view of its far-reaching significance in working-class social life (Savage and Miles 1994). Some have given considerable credence to the idealised celebrations of community solidarity portrayed in certain working-class autobiographies. For Andrew August, for example, the working-class community of the late 19th and early 20th centuries should be understood as a close-knit group of families, friends and neighbours bonded by common experiences and practical support networks. Its essence was its spatial and cultural insularity, and the 'dense web of interdependence and intimacy' that developed out of poverty and crowded living conditions (August 2007, 105).

In a recent study of local identity in east London between the wars, Benjamin J Lammers distinguished between two specific meanings of the term 'community'. The first related to a local-ised conception of street and neighbourhood support and assistance, encapsulated in the notion of 'the working-class street in which doors were unlocked and neighbours helped one another out in times of need'. The second referred to a larger East End community which bound together the localised communities of the first. This was not, in Lammers' words, 'the intimate face-to-face community of the working-class street' but 'a largely imagined community that gave birth to the quintessential working-class figure, the East Ender' (Lammers 2005, 332–3). Changes in work, leisure and politics led, in this view, to a broadening of horizons and an increasing tendency to identify with those beyond the narrow confines of family, friends and acquaintances. It was also, crucially in Lammers' view, a multi-ethnic community in which Jews and non-Jews could both belong.

The notion of different layers (or levels) of community belonging is particularly relevant in relation to boxing in general and London boxing in particular. Lammers suggests professional football as an important facet of the emergence of 'a common commercial culture' knitting localised communities and the Jewish and non-Jewish populations together during the 1920s and 1930s (Lammers 2005, 338–9). For all that supporting a football club was undeniably a significant expression of local community identity, boxing was arguably a more subtle and powerful marker of community affiliation and pride. As one of us has argued elsewhere, identi-ties of place were a fundamental part of boxing's popular appeal. Not only were boxers billed as coming from a particular locality (fighting 'out of' Greenwich or Stepney, according to the popular parlance) but they were also often attached to a particular hall in a specific geographic area (Taylor 2009, 147–8; Shipley 1989, 111). Ties and attachment to people and places operated at a variety of levels, and as a boxer progressed through the ranks he could come to be seen as representing wider communities, the population of a town or city, a region and perhaps even an entire nation (Taylor 2008, 33).

A final conception of 'community' relevant for our purposes is the notion of boxing itself as an occupational community. We are not referring here to the idea of a traditional, stable and homogenous community dominated by a particular occupational group – typically coal miners, dockers or shipbuilders – though this does have some overlap with the notions of 'community' discussed above. Rather, taking a cue from Graeme Salaman, the concept of an 'occupational community' as understood here relates to any type of occupation involving 'a close relationship between work and non-work activities, values, relationships, interests and identities'. Members of such occupational communities shared common value-belief systems, derived much of their self-image from their occupations and preferred friendships and associations with work colleagues than with those outside their occupational group. The result was a common ideology that stressed 'their distinctiveness and isolation from the rest of society' (Salaman 1975, 234, 231). Sociological writing on boxing has argued that it represents a distinct subculture with its own value system based on discipline and self-sacrifice. Moreover, the boxing club and gymnasium could be consid-ered a world of its own, an occupational refuge isolated and enclosed from the neighbourhood outside (Sugden 1996, 182–4; Wacquant 2004, 17–27). Boxing, in this sense, might be consid-ered a distinct occupational community, part of and yet separated from the wider communities from which it drew its membership and its strength.

Representing London's Boxing Past

Representations of boxing in London have been many and varied. It is not the intention here to analyse comprehensively the range of depictions of the sport and its social and cultural milieu. Rather, we want to focus briefly on a tendency in some literary representations to locate boxing within a particular segment of London working-class life. In his comparative sociology of boxing in Northern Ireland, the United States and Cuba, John Sugden emphasised the historical and cultural connections linking boxing with inner-city life, and its associations with poverty, violence and crime (Sugden 1996, 181). Boxing was in some respects regarded as a natural product of the 'ghetto', reflecting the harsh realities of life on the streets. But, as we have observed, the boxing club or gym also represented a sanctuary from it, 'an island of order and virtue' in Loïc Wacquant's phrase, where aggression and violent tendencies could be channelled to good effect (Wacquant 2004, 17). From the 1880s, amateur boxing clubs in London and elsewhere were set up by social and religious reformers in poor areas with the hope of improving the physical and moral well-being of the masses. Boxing was seen as a form of rational recreation and the notion that it helped keep young boys and working men off the streets and away from trouble was, as Sugden has suggested, axiomatic both inside and outside the sport's subculture (Boddy 2008, 95; Dawes 1975, 57; Sugden 1996, 182).

Literary representations of boxing in late Victorian and Edwardian Britain can be usefully read in connection with the sensationalist inquiries of Andrew Mearns and William Booth and the sociological investigations of Charles Booth and others into the living conditions of the urban poor. The East End of London was a particular focus of attention for writers, journalists and middle-class 'explorers' (Fishman 1988). Arthur Morrison's *Tales of Mean Streets*, published in 1894, was important in this context as a powerful fictional portrayal that aroused 'further concern for the deprived working-classes of East London' (Krzak 1983, 12). It is telling that boxing, a sport Morrison was apparently familiar with as participant and observer, was the centrepiece of one of the stories. 'Three Rounds' is the tale of Neddy Milton, a casual labourer and boxer who turns up at the Prince Regent pub in Bethnal Green tired and hungry but with no choice but to fight in the nine-stone competition. The fight is 'hard labour' for Neddy and, though he wins, he receives no interest from the potential backers who might have helped 'mend his fortunes'. Boxing here is depicted as a core element of working-class leisure in the East End and a significant form of casual labour. But the odds are ultimately stacked against the poor and downtrodden fighter, whose chances of being 'taken up' are limited (Morrison 1983, 83–94; Boddy 2008, 125).

Boxing also played a central role in Robert Machray's *The Night Side of London*, first published in 1902. Machray, a novelist and journalist for the *Daily Mail*, included three vivid boxing scenes in his travelogue of the 'haunts and havens' of the night-time capital. He and illustrator Tom Browne moved from the doctor's room, bar and 'theatre' of the prestigious National Sporting Club to witness a 'fine exhibition of scientific boxing' at Bob Habbijam's School for Neophytes in Newman Road, Oxford Street, and then, most interestingly, on to a Saturday programme at the notorious Wonderland in Whitechapel. Machray had no interest in documenting 'the worst and most devilish features' of the city and, indeed, his descriptions of boxing were for the most part positive and affectionate (Machray 2002, 251, v). Wonderland, for example, with its boisterous clientele and garrulous refreshment vendors, offered 'illuminating glimpses into East End life'. Particularly notable for Machray was the good behaviour of the crowd, even when the referee judged one of the bouts to be a draw, which pleased nobody. Indeed, 'the orderliness of the crowd is remarkable, considering its extent and composition. And in all this building there is not a single policeman to be seen!' (Machray 2002, 259, 261). Other writers were less convinced. James Butler, for one, recalled violent incidents at Wonderland and other London venues in the early decades of the 20th century involving rival race gangs and other criminal groups (Butler and Butler 1956, 15–22).

What representations such as these had in common was the tendency to place boxing at the margins of respectable middle-class metropolitan culture. Often the sport was positioned geographically on the periphery, in the poorer areas of the East End in particular. At other times, boxing was associated with the city at night, and with accompanying perceptions of fear, danger and crime (Morton 1941, 383–5). Boxing halls and clubs were not always depicted as dens of vice and immorality; in some cases quite the opposite was true, and they were seen as places where discipline, orderliness and honesty prevailed in spite of the chaos outside. Yet, significantly, this was an activity that existed below the surface of mainstream everyday life: a culture that 'the outside world may not know much about', in Machray's words (Machray 2002, 251). Fighting may have been learned on the street, an emerging arena of working-class recreation and sociability, but organised boxing took place away from it and was therefore easily visible only to those who chose to seek it out (Beaven 2005, 89). Journalists and social investigators portrayed it as the sport of the back alleys, basements and backrooms of London's densely packed working-class neighbourhoods: an activity that flourished in the dark corners of the capital.

THE LONDON EX-BOXERS' ASSOCIATION AND 'EAST END BOXING LIVES'

The London Ex-Boxers' Association (LEBA) was founded in 1971 by Alf Paolozzi, with the assistance of former British champion Len Harvey and Jack Powell, the organisation's first secretary. The idea to create a forum where ex-boxers could 'meet friends and former opponents in a social environment' was not entirely new. Paolozzi had been inspired by attending a meeting of former boxers in Kent, while similar developments were soon underway in Merseyside and elsewhere. LEBA was one of a number of prominent associations that developed an important charitable role alongside its primary functions of providing sociability and welfare for its members. By 2010 it had over 600 members and was one of 43 former boxers' associations in Britain (LEBA 2010; Physick 2009). Regular meetings, monthly newsletters and annual awards ceremonies have helped to facilitate communications between members, while on a national level the 'Old Timers' column in *Boxing News* has for some time publicised the activities of EBAs across Britain. Existing at least partly for the opportunities they provide for 'mutual reminiscence' and commemoration, organisations such as LEBA have a particularly significant mnemonic function. It is useful in this sense to regard them, in Geoffrey Cubitt's words, both as 'forums for the production and reproduction of shared knowledge pertaining to the past of the collectivity' and as 'environments that condition the way in which individuals remember' (Cubitt 2007, 133).

The connection between memory and social belonging is particularly evident if we look more closely at LEBA and its 'East End Boxing Lives' project. The origins of the project can be traced back to similar initiatives in Merseyside and Scotland. Both the Merseyside EBA and the Scots Boxing Hall of Fame secured Heritage Lottery Fund (HLF) grants to develop popular heritage projects during the mid-2000s. The Mersey Boxing Archive involved the collection of 60 video biographies of former boxers and the digitisation of hundreds of boxing-related images and

Fig 5.1. The Ring pub on Blackfriars Road commemorates one of the capital's most important venues. Long defunct, The Ring retains a central place in the memory of the London boxing community.

boxing memorabilia. The '8, 9, 10 and Out' project had similar aims: to document aspects of Scottish boxing history through collecting archives and memorabilia and conducting new oral history interviews. These would then be made publicly available by means of a touring exhibition and a project website (Merseyside & Wirral Ex-Boxers' Associations 2007; HLF 2006; 2005).

The success of the Merseyside project led directly to the LEBA initiative: indeed, Ray Physick, a freelance researcher and project director on the former, took a central role from the very beginning of the LEBA project. LEBA's initial objectives were to gain sufficient funding for a permanent Hall of Fame, or museum, for London boxing. An initial HLF application proved unsuccessful but £50,000 was secured in June 2009 to fund the more modest 'East End Boxing Lives' project. It aimed to 'trace' the history of the sport from 1891 to 1990 (though the starting-point was subsequently moved back to the 18th century) and to explore and celebrate the heritage of boxing in London through an archive of interviews, digitised images and memorabilia. The centrepiece of the project was to be 15 case studies of East End boxers spanning the centuries. The intention was then to make the archive public through a project website and a related exhibition. In a press statement, Sue Bowers of HLF London underlined the community agenda at the heart of the project: 'Boxing clubs have long been part of the East End's social fabric and this project will bring to life their achievements in both helping community cohesion and creating champions' (HLF 2009).

The LEBA project fits closely in certain respects with the burgeoning in recent years of community-based web archives. As Jerome de Groot has suggested, such projects have proved important in allowing groups with little involvement or interest in conventional historical narratives to actively participate in creating and controlling their own archives (de Groot 2009, 100). Democratisation, access and empowerment have been central objectives: in the LEBA case, members were trained to conduct interviews while local boxing clubs and school pupils were marked out as playing a key role in the gathering of material for the website. In de Groot's view, community archives have 'the potential to enable the community to engage with its history directly, develop skills related to information management and reach a wider audience'. The online format of such collections also allows users the opportunity to contribute to and shape the development of the archive. This, it is argued, 'strengthens existing communities as well as creating the possibility for new ones' (de Groot 2009, 100–101).

The choice of 'boxing lives' case studies reflected the project's stated aim of viewing boxing as 'a force for racial and social integration' and celebrating the diverse cultural heritage of the East End (LEBA 2010). Jewish fighters from the 18th century (Daniel Mendoza) to the 20th century (Ted 'Kid' Lewis and Jack 'Kid' Berg) were especially prominent, while those from Italian (Teddy Lewis and Dominic Bergonzi), Irish (Billy Graydon), North African (Charlie Magri) and Afro-Caribbean (James Cook) backgrounds are also included. Chronologically, the focus was, perhaps not surprisingly, on the relatively recent past. Only three of the boxing lives covered the pre-1900 era. Four careers were centred on one of British boxing's perceived 'golden ages', between the wars, but, significantly, over half of the case studies were of boxers who fought mainly in the post-war period, all of whom are still alive. To some extent this may reflect the personal networks and connections of the LEBA membership, as well as the importance to the project of conducting as many video interviews as possible with the boxers themselves. Moreover, while the majority of the chosen boxers were well-known names, and some were former champions, a handful were less celebrated, representing the rank-and-file of the sport and potentially offering a more balanced view of the lives and lifestyles of boxing 'men' than can be gleaned from conventional boxing literature.

A closer look at the online archive itself indicates another salient element of the LEBA project: the link between 'place' and 'memory'. LEBA proposed from the beginning to look at 'defunct and existing boxing venues', elevating the boxing hall to a central position in the 'lives' it intended to record (LEBA 2010). The boxing hall is, as Physick has written in relation to Liverpool boxing, 'a place where the intimacy of the boxing fan merges with the boxer.... The fight fan is at one with the boxer while boxers feed off the atmosphere generated in the boxing stadium' (Physick

2008, 9). For participants and spectators both, it can be seen as a crucible of memory (see Fig 5.1). In the context of the LEBA project, venues therefore played an important role in linking the individual lives of those who fought to the collective memories of the wider community. The website makes this connection in a number of ways. First of all, it has a 'London Boxing Map', with the location and details of over 60 East London venues. All of these locations are cross-referenced with the image archive, and many, particularly the better-known venues such as Premierland, Shoreditch Town Hall and York Hall, have a page of related photographs and scans of boxing bills that electronically 'link' the 'lives' of boxers with the places they boxed. In addition, a number of the video interviews of the chosen boxers (Billy Graydon's is an example) specifically focus on 'favourite venues' and recollections of boxing in the halls and arenas of the East End.

In common with other forms of 'digital history', the most important element of the LEBA website was not the content so much as the opportunity it offered for users to engage and connect with, and to contribute to, the 'East End Boxing Lives' project. Neither the information provided nor the perspectives advanced were presented as being definitive or complete. Although it claimed to tell 'the story of London boxing from its beginnings in the eighteenth century to the present day', by definition the architecture of the website meant that information was not presented in linear, narrative form but was multi-layered and inter-linked (LEBA 2010; Cohen and Rosenzweig 2005). Users could access specific pages on particular boxers and venues without the need to assimilate a wider sense of chronology and context. As Mark Moss has argued, history presented in digital form is 'not bound to traditional orderly presentations but rather … is … "fragmentary" and "multiple". History gets conflated and can be both present and past, not necessarily closed and final.' It also encourages users to become 'active agents in the discovery of the history process' (Moss 2008, 205, 204). Moreover, in this case, while the backbone of the 'story' was LEBA's, the website was open and interactive in the sense of offering users the opportunity to comment upon and add their memories and experiences of East End boxing.

The 'East End Boxing Lives' Exhibition

Between 25 January and 30 April 2011 Hackney Museum hosted LEBA's 'East End Boxing Lives' exhibition. It was not the first exhibition of its kind in a London museum. Between May and September 2007 the Jewish Museum in London held an exhibition entitled 'Ghetto Warriors: Minority Boxers in Britain'. Curated by Ruti Ungar, an academic based in Berlin and an expert on boxing in Georgian Britain, the exhibition also produced an impressive accompanying book of essays by academics on the history and representation of Jewish and Black British boxers (Berkowitz and Ungar 2007). But it was also linked to a broader initiative, based around the work of Clive Bettington and the London Jewish Cultural Centre, to establish a Jewish boxers' Hall of Fame; an initiative that, like LEBA's original plans for a London boxing Hall of Fame, aimed to secure wider community and academic support.

'East End Boxing Lives' was a small exhibition of 99 square metres housed in one of Hackney Museum's temporary exhibition spaces on the ground floor of the Technology and Learning Centre in Reading Lane. Like the website, the exhibition consisted of a selection of photographs, boxing bills and posters, video interviews and pen portraits of boxers. The main difference from the website in terms of content was the inclusion of boxing artefacts and memorabilia, which play, of course, a crucial role in the physical space of a museum gallery. Indeed, four glass-cased displays of artefacts relating to the careers of particular boxers occupied the centre of the exhibition space. Around the walls the narrative of the exhibition was communicated through a series of textual, photographic, physical and audio-visual displays.

One of the striking features of the exhibition was the importance attached not just to the memories of boxers and their families but to the process of remembering. Academic historians have long found the relationship between history and memory a problematic one. While some have connected the two as related concepts, for others they are fundamentally opposed: 'memory, so to speak, is history's defining "other" – a contrasting and radically different form of knowledge' (Cubitt 2007, 31; Lowenthal 1985, 212–14). For producers of public history such as museum curators, the relationship is no less complex. Gaynor Kavanagh has argued that museums and exhibitions should be seen as 'places where memories and histories meet, even collide'. The museum's role is thus not just to identify and record memories through artefacts and oral testimony but also to connect individual memories to broader, formal interpretations of the past; to 'bridge the gap', in other words, between history and memory (Kavanagh 1996, 13, 9). Susan A Crane likewise sees museums as a particularly evocative site where the subjective and the objective can interact 'in an ongoing reciprocal mediation' (Crane 2000, 7). Critiques of sports museums have tended not to fully acknowledge the complexities of this interplay (Lindberg 1990; Vamplew 1998; Reiss 2003, 105), but the best sports museums and exhibitions have certainly responded to it. The National Football Museum, for example, was adjudged to have bridged the gap between history and memory by focusing first on the experiences of fans and then relating this in other displays to a broader narrative of developments in the social history of football. In this way, visitors were 'encouraged to relate their personal identities, experiences and memories to the wider mesh of the game's history' (Johnes and Mason 2003, 130).

'East End Boxing Lives' foregrounded boxers' memories in a number of ways. To the left of the entrance was a reconstruction of a 'traditional' working-class sitting room, complete with a sofa, armchair, standard lamp, coffee table, sideboard and boxing trophies, memorabilia and photographs displayed in a cabinet and on the walls (see Fig 5.2). On the coffee table were seven folders collecting the 'Boxing Memories' (newspaper clippings, articles, published and unpublished 'life stories' and so on) of seven East End fighters. On the sideboard were bound archive copies of boxing magazines and a couple of boxing books, as well as the exhibition visitors' comments book. A video screen on the wall above the sideboard showed a series of edited interviews (many selected from those on the website) of boxers talking about their careers on a constant loop. This was a space for memory, where visitors were encouraged to sit down, listen and read about the boxing experiences of others, but also, crucially, to talk about these with fellow visitors and relate them to their own individual or family memories. The video recollections of the boxers and their families, the folders of written memories and the space itself: all of these worked to stir and evoke individual and collective memories in visitors. What is more, though the boxers' memories were particular and individual (and 'placed', significantly, in a domestic setting), through the process of communication to multiple visitors they could be regarded as important public records and a central strand of one of the exhibition's key themes: the linking of boxing 'lives' with the broader memory of the East End community (Thomas 2008).

Memory was also evoked in imaginative ways through the display and arrangement of artefacts. Despite the growth of audio, film and interactive exhibits, objects remain at the heart of most museums, and exploring 'people's relationship with material culture' is still among their chief objectives (Moore 1997, 48). There is, as we know, a particularly diverse and rich material

FIG 5.2. THE SITTING ROOM AREA OF THE 'EAST END BOXING LIVES' EXHIBITION.

culture associated with sport, especially in relation to fans, who might objectify their attachment to a team or individual sportsperson by collecting shirts, tickets, autographs, cigarette cards or other memorabilia. As in other sports, objects mattered to those who practised and followed boxing. The equipment of the sport – shorts, boots, robes and even gum-shields – was meaningful to the boxers and, by association, to their fans (Moore 1997, 126–30). Posters and boxing bills both recalled a moment in time and place and helped to chart a career in progress, as did medals, trophies and, at the highest level, championship belts. Successful boxers, like other athletes, were often photographed surrounded by shields and trophies, the material record of their achievements. Later, after the career had ended, such objects (often displayed prominently in the home) continued to carry meaning as a powerful reminder of the past, but also a symbol of identity, for the boxers themselves, or perhaps their relatives, friends or supporters. For museum curators, the dilemma is how to interpret objects of this kind and communicate to visitors a sense of what they meant (and mean) to those who owned them (Johnes and Mason 2003, 127–8).

'East End Boxing Lives' achieved this, at least in part, by grouping related objects together and connecting these to the 'lives' of boxers, and to particular themes, sketched out elsewhere in the exhibition. One case of artefacts was themed around the Olympic and Commonwealth Games and included, among other objects, Ron Cooper's travel pass and identity card from the 1948 London Olympics, the vest and tracksuit Mickey Pye wore at the 1962 Commonwealth Games and the dressing gown worn by Sylvester Mitte at the Montreal Olympics of 1976. A photograph and a small amount of text were sufficient to explain what the items were and to whom they belonged but comparisons between the Games and the different eras in which they took place were encouraged simply from the clustering and positioning of this range of objects. Elsewhere, some interesting ideas about the casual nature of professional boxing in the immediate post-war years, its relationship to full-time work and the significance of both in terms of shaping self-identity could be drawn from the positioning of Teddy Lewis' fish porter's hat alongside his skipping robe and boxing boots.

Another display featured a diverse collection of souvenirs related to the broader culture of boxing: books, programmes, magazines, photographs, as well as an ashtray from Jack Solomons' Devonshire Club and a Repton Boxing Club pennant. The significance of artefacts to the process of remembering was conveyed here through the various objects relating to Teddy Baldock, World Bantamweight Champion in 1927 and one of the most prominent figures in the history of East London boxing. The group of connected Baldock objects included his gloves, a photograph of him with the world title belt, a programme of the 1927 title contest against Archie Moore at the Royal Albert Hall, copies of contemporary sporting newspapers with Baldock pictured on the front page and, finally, a copy of a recent biography of Baldock written by local historian Brian Belton with the help of Baldock's archivist and grandson Martin Sax (Belton 2008). Interviews with Sax and his mother (Baldock's daughter) Pam were also among those shown. Moreover, though not a formal part of the exhibition, leaflets promoting a fund to support the erection of a statue of Baldock in Poplar as 'a lasting memorial' to the boxer were also displayed prominently.

While the artefacts had a central role, the exhibition also included a significant narrative element. To the right of the entrance, and following the wall round to the back of the exhibition space, were a series of panels introducing the project and providing a thematic anchoring to the rest of the displays. The first panel on the history of LEBA and the origins of the project identified the boxers themselves as the main focus of the exhibition. Separate panels of text and photographs on the infrastructure of professional boxing – venues, promoters and unions and

FIG 5.3. A DISPLAY OF CHAMPIONSHIP BELTS, BOXING SHORTS AND OTHER MEMORABILIA BELONGING TO JAMES COOK, IAN NAPA AND JASON MATTHEWS AT THE 'EAST END BOXING LIVES' EXHIBITION.

associations – bookended two chronological panels on bare knuckle boxing and the introduction of the Queensberry Rules that provided a brief but important historical background for the 20th-century focus of the bulk of the exhibition. Also significant was the inclusion of two further contextualising panels on boxing's 'Fight against Racism' and, more surprisingly perhaps, women's boxing. Both of these rooted recent advancements and achievements (the successes of ethnic minority boxers, the licensing of female fighters and the inclusion of women's boxing in the 2012 Olympics) in the 18th century, thus connecting past and present but drawing clear distinctions between the social and cultural contexts of the prize-fighting era and modern boxing. Unlike some sports exhibitions, 'East End Boxing Lives' did address issues of racial and sexual discrimination with some success in the limited space available; indeed, the 'immigration history' of boxing, in particular, was woven throughout the exhibition, from the biographical panels on Ted Lewis and Jack Berg to James Cook's championship belt (see Fig 5.3) and Dave Starkey's 'Star of David'-emblazoned boxing shorts (Panayi 2010, 9).

'Every form of historical representation', Mark Phillips has written, 'must position its audience in some relationship of closeness to or distance from the events and experiences it describes'. Museum displays demonstrate more clearly than most, for Phillips, how to engage the emotions of the audience through advances in technology and design as well as by widening the social lens. They can become a space that 'includes and surrounds' the visitor, inviting him or her 'to imagine the past as a field of experience rather than an object of study' (Phillips 2004, 95, 93). By focusing on the memories of boxers, the objects they kept and the lives they led, 'East End Boxing Lives' did not deny the temporal distance between the past and the present but managed to provide a sense of affective and ideological proximity to the experiences portrayed. Those looking for an objective and scholarly analysis of the social history of boxing in East London were likely to be disappointed, of course, but then, as with many exhibitions, its aim seems to have been not so much to inform as to connect, engage and involve the visitor with the displays and to encourage them to reflect upon their own memories of, and relationship with, boxing in the East End.

A small but successful way in which the exhibition negotiated the distance between the lives of its boxers and its visitors was in simply listing the name and locality of scores of East End boxers – non-champions as well as champions – on spaces on the walls of the gallery. The authors witnessed a number of visitors spending considerable time perusing the lists, picking out individual names and discussing these with fellow visitors. Some may have known the boxers mentioned, or have had an older relative who did, or perhaps had just heard or read about them. But the place-names were equally important, reminding the visitor of the East End's rich boxing heritage and, for locals perhaps, encouraging an immediate and emotional engagement with men who 'belonged' and possibly still 'belong' to 'their' community.

A sense of closeness and connection to the theme of the exhibition could also be detected in some of the responses conveyed in the visitors' book. A number of the visitors articulated their 'place identity' alongside their comments and signatures in the same ways as boxers were billed (from 'Bethnal Green', 'Hackney', 'Hoxton' etc). Those who had boxed included the era in which they fought, their weight, championships won, and so on; others did the same for fathers, uncles and grandfathers. The small number of comments that were critical tended to highlight the omission of certain boxers or boxing clubs, or the assumed under-representation of boxers from 'their' part of the East End. More generally, some visitors drew links between personal experiences and the broader 'memories' encapsulated in the exhibition. It was good, one commented, to celebrate working-class culture and heritage 'for a change', especially the history of Jewish and Black boxers. Another recalled watching boxing at the Devonshire Sporting Club as a teenager and meeting 'Harry Mizler, Kid Berg and other Jewish boxers'. 'The fight game was rather different in the 30s, 40s and 50s', the same visitor reflected rather nostalgically: 'The exhibition brought back memories of Hackney/East End as I remembered it as a child' (Hackney Museum 2011).

Concluding Thoughts

Community is a powerful theme in the popular and academic history of British boxing. The fortunes of both are often assumed to have been inseparable, with boxers, clubs and venues emerging as the embodiment of late Victorian working-class community solidarity and then declining in the post-war era as 'traditional' communities were torn apart. Popular histories have invariably featured boxing as part of the story of the East End's past and as an important element of the cultural identity of the area. One writer has claimed the East End to have been the 'birth-place' of boxing, while another suggested that Daniel Mendoza was 'the earliest folk hero of the East End … the first lad from the densely crowded streets around Aldgate to … become … a national figure' (Tames 2004, 9; Palmer 2000, 35). Boxing played a small but not insignificant part in these narratives of the 'making' of a place called 'the East End'. Along with, and connected to, the legendary deprivation, poverty and crime of the area, boxing helped to position 'the East End' as a place apart, distinct and separate from other parts of the city and the country.

For many, no doubt, the 'East End Boxing Lives' project evoked memories of place and identity that they felt had long disappeared. There is more than a hint in some responses to the exhibition of what Doreen Massey has termed an 'essentialist' view in which '"the past" is seen … to embody the real character of the place' (Massey 1995, 183). Boxing, like the strong sense of community attachment that it was felt both to reflect and reinforce, was, in this view, not what it used to be. It was simply not central to people's lives any more. So while the exhibition may have successfully engaged the emotions of many of those who visited, and connected their lives to those of the boxers, it might also have reminded them of what had changed and what had been lost.

The LEBA project also demonstrated the multi-faceted character of 'community' in relation to boxing. At one level it foregrounded the highly localised communities characterised by the street, neighbourhood and borough. The constituent parts of the East End – from particular buildings and streets outwards – were named and 'represented' on the website and in the exhibition. The 'London Boxing Map' allowed visitors to locate themselves spatially and temporally in relation to famous East End venues and sites past and present. It encouraged them to think about their sense of place and the alignment between individual and community identity (Field 2008, 119). At another level, the project was about the 'imagined community' of a wider East End. This was the place that had intrigued writers in the past and continued to fascinate journalists in the present. The mythology of the East End still had a powerful romantic appeal. Boxing's 'spiritual home', wrote *The Sun*'s Colin Hart in his review of the exhibition, 'lies deep in the heart of East London's meanest and most poverty-stricken streets' where 'empty bellies rather than burning ambition … fuelled the great fighters who emerged from that tough, uncompromising environment' (Hart 2011).

That the East End and its boxing had been shaped by influences and individuals from the 'outside' was also acknowledged and integrated into the project. Nobody visiting the website or the exhibition could have been left in any doubt that the 'community' being documented and celebrated was multicultural and multi-ethnic, and had been for centuries. Jewish, Irish, Italian and Afro-Caribbean boxers were chosen as case studies and the complex relationships between local, national and ethnic identities were offered for reflection in a number of the interviews, photographs and artefacts.

At the core of the LEBA project, however, was another understanding of 'community': the occupational community of the boxers themselves. While there is no doubt that the connections between individual 'lives', wider histories and community memories were for the most part imaginatively constructed, we should not forget that at the heart of the project was an activity and a subculture that relatively few visitors would ever have experienced at first hand. At this level, the project might be seen as a public extension of the mutual reminiscence and commemoration of LEBA meetings and social events. It is not a criticism to observe that one facet of 'East End Boxing Lives' was a celebration of the shared experiences and values of a relatively insular community of boxers and ex-boxers. This was an element of the project with which 'outsiders' could empathise but to which they could never truly belong: a community within a community.

BIBLIOGRAPHY AND REFERENCES

August, A, 2007 *The British Working Class, 1832–1940*, Longman, Harlow

Beaven, B, 2005 *Leisure, Citizenship and Working-Class Men in Britain, 1850–1945*, Manchester University Press, Manchester

Belton, B, 2008 *Teddy Baldock: The Pride of Poplar*, Pennant Books, London

Benson, J, 1989 *The Working Class in Britain, 1850–1939*, Longman, London

Berkowitz, M, and Ungar, R (eds), 2007 *Fighting Back? Jewish and Black Boxers in Britain*, Department of Hebrew and Jewish Studies, University College London, London

Boddy, K, 2008 *Boxing: A Cultural History*, Reaktion, London

Butler, J, and Butler, F, 1956 (1954) *The Fight Game*, The Sportsmans Book Club, London

Cohen, D J, and Rosenzweig, R, 2005 *Digital History: A Guide to Gathering, Preserving and Presenting the Past on the Web* [online], available from: http://chnm.gmu.edu/digitalhistory/ [12 February 2011]

Cooper, H, 1972 *An Autobiography*, Cassell, London

Crane, S A, 2000 Introduction: Of Museums and Memory, in *Museums and Memory* (ed S A Crane), Stanford University Press, Stanford, CA, 1–13

Cubitt, G, 2007 *History and Memory*, Manchester University Press, Manchester

Dawes, F, 1975 *A Cry from the Streets: The Boys' Club Movement in Britain from the 1850s to the Present Day*, Wayland Publishers, Hove

de Groot, J, 2009 *Consuming History: Historians and Heritage in Contemporary Popular Culture*, Routledge, Abingdon

Dennis, R, and Daniels, S, 1994 'Community' and the Social Geography of Victorian Cities, in *Time, Family and Community: Perspectives on Family and Community History* (ed M Drake), Blackwell, Oxford, 201–24

Field, S, 2008 Imagining Communities: Memory, Loss and Resilience in Post-Apartheid Cape Town, in *Oral History and Public Memories* (eds P Hamilton and L Shopes), Temple University Press, Philadelphia, 107–24

Fishman, W J, 1988 *East End 1888: A Year in a London Borough among the Labouring Poor*, Duckworth, London

Griffiths, T, 2001 *The Lancashire Working Classes, c.1880–1930*, Clarendon Press, Oxford

Hackney Museum, 2011 East End Boxing Lives Exhibition Visitors Book

Hart, C, 2011 Boxing's history in East End, *The Sun* [online], available from: http://www.thesun.co.uk/sol/homepage/sport/boxing/3432238/Boxings-history-in-East-End.html [10 April 2011]

Heritage Lottery Fund (HLF), 2005 *Case Study: '8, 9, 10 and out' Boxing Project* [online], available from: http://www.hlf.org.uk/ourproject/Pages/`8,9,10andout'BoxingProject.aspx [12 April 2011]

— 2006 *Project: Merseyside Former Boxers' Association* [online], available from: http://hlf.org.uk/ourproject/Pages/Mar2006/a6548730–3091–465b-a141–4d4f190 [12 April 2011]

— 2009 East End's boxing lives revealed with Heritage Lottery help [online], available from: http://www.hlf.org.uk/news/Pages/LivesofEastEndboxersrevealed.aspx [12 April 2011]

Holt, R, 1989 *Sport and the British: A Modern History*, Clarendon Press, Oxford

Holt, R, and Mason, T, 2000 *Sport in Britain, 1945–2000*, Blackwell, Oxford

Johnes, M, and Mason, R, 2003 Soccer, Public History and the National Football Museum, *Sport in History* 23 (1), 115–31

Kavanagh, G, 1996 'Making Histories, Making Memories', in *Making Histories in Museums* (ed G Kavanagh), Leicester University Press, London, 1–14

Krzak, M, 1983 Preface, in *Tales of Mean Streets* (A Morrison), The Boydell Press, Woodbridge, 7–17

Lammers, B J, 2005 The Birth of the East Ender: Neighborhood and Local Identity in Interwar East London, *Journal of Social History* 39 (2), 331–44

Lindberg, R, 1990 Review of '"Say It Ain't So Joe": The 1919 Black Sox Scandal' exhibition, *Journal of Sport History* 17 (1), 118–21

London Ex-Boxers' Association (LEBA), 2010 *East End Boxing Lives* [online], available from: http://www.londonexboxers.org.uk/ [18 December 2010]

Lowenthal, D, 1985 *The Past is a Foreign Country*, Cambridge University Press, Cambridge

Machray, R, 2002 (1902) *The Night Side of London*, Bibliophile Books, London

Massey, D, 1995 Places and their Pasts, *History Workshop Journal* 39, 182–92

Merseyside & Wirral Ex-Boxers' Associations, 2007 *Mugs Alley Souvenir Issue*, Self-published, Liverpool

Moore, K, 1997 *Museums and Popular Culture*, Leicester University Press, London

Morrison, A, 1983 (1894) *Tales of Mean Streets*, The Boydell Press, Woodbridge

Morton, H V, 1941 *London*, Methuen & Co, London

Moss, M, 2008 *Toward the Visualisation of History: The Past as Image*, Lexington Books, Lanham, MD

Odd, G, 1978 *Len Harvey: Prince of Boxers*, Pelham, London

Palmer, A, 2000 (1989) *The East End: Four Centuries of London Life*, 2 edn, John Murray, London

Panayi, P, 2010 *An Immigration History of Britain: Multicultural Racism since 1800*, Longman, Harlow

Phillips, M S, 2004 History, Memory and Historical Distance, in *Theorizing Historical Consciousness* (ed P Seixas), University of Toronto Press, Toronto, 86–102

Physick, R, 2008 *Liverpool's Boxing Venues*, Sport Media, Liverpool

— 2009 Boxing on Merseyside, paper presented at the conference *Sport and Oral History*, April, University of Huddersfield

Reiss, S, 2003 History, Memory and Baseball's Original Sin: The Telling and Retelling of the Black Sox Scandal, *Journal of Sport History* 30 (1), 101–7

Salaman, G, 1975 Occupations, Community and Consciousness, in *Working-Class Images of Society* (ed M Bulmer), Routledge & Kegan Paul, London, 219–36

Savage, M, and Miles, A, 1994 *The Remaking of the British Working Class, 1840–1940*, Routledge, London

Shipley, S, 1989 Boxing, in *Sport in Britain: A Social History* (ed T Mason), Cambridge University Press, Cambridge, 78–115

Sugden, J, 1996 *Boxing and Society: An International Analysis*, Manchester University Press, Manchester

Tames, R, 2004 *East End Past*, Historical Publications, London

Taylor, M, 2008 Class and Sport in Britain, 1850–1939, *Leidschrift* 23 (3), 25–37

— 2009 Round the London Ring: Boxing, Class and Community in Interwar London, *The London Journal* 34 (2), 139–62

Thomas, S, 2008 Private Memory in a Public Space: Oral History and Museums, in *Oral History and Public Memories* (eds P Hamilton and L Shopes), Temple University Press, Philadelphia, 87–100

Vamplew, W, 1998 Facts and Artefacts: Sports Historians and Sports Museums, *Journal of Sport History* 25 (2), 268–82

Wacquant, L, 2004 *Body and Soul: Notebooks of an Apprentice Boxer*, Oxford University Press, New York

6

Television and the 'Austerity Games': London 1948

Tim O'Sullivan

Introduction

The Olympic flame has been extinguished; Fanny Blankers-Koen, that extraordinary Dutch athlete, and the other heroines and heroes have returned to the bosoms of their families; and Wembley Stadium reverts to dog racing and similar local pursuits. It must be for other nations to record what they think of Britain's achievement as a host, but the general impression appears to be that, granted the restrictions in our pinched Europe, we did not do too badly. […] the broadcasting arrangements went pretty smoothly. One hundred and fifty BBC commentators and reporters and one hundred and twenty representatives of overseas broadcasting organisations functioned from the old Palace of Arts; eighty-five lines connected Wembley with Broadcasting House; and the number of recordings made each day was prodigious. Those happy enough to enjoy the pleasures of television also appear to have been well satisfied, the more enthusiastic viewers remarking that it was as good as going to the Games. (*The Listener* 1948a)

The BBC has paid around £40–50 million for the broadcast rights to the London 2012 Olympic Games. For that amount of money taxpayers will be able to enjoy 5,800 hours of content. Do the sums. That is 242 days and nights bleary-eyed straight on the couch. […] That means that every hour of every sport will be aired. The 5,800 hours of host content will all be in high definition. (Magnay 2010)[1]

In a recent public lecture, Barbara Slater, BBC Director of Sport, presented an insightful account of the sports broadcasting 'journey' to London 2012 (Slater 2011). In particular, she noted the ways in which one could 'track' the development of many key broadcast innovations through the developing 20th-century coverage of the Olympic Games and that this persists beyond the millennium, into the present, digital, 21st century times. The 'modern' in the 'Modern Olympic Games' cannot be easily separated from their mass, ultimately global *mediation* and availability; initially by press coverage, then via film, newsreel and radio, and finally by television and its subsequent online mutations. A cursory list of the 'great leaps forward' would note that the first London Olympics in 1908 received excited and exciting press and still photographic coverage plus early experimental silent film record. In 1928, Amsterdam provided the first truly sound broadcast, 'radio games'. In 1936, Berlin hosted and projected the first 'film and television games',

---

[1] The coverage will deliver 24 simultaneous live streams (four times more than Beijing), bringing live sport from every venue where it is happening. 'The choice will be yours not ours'; see: http://www.bbc.co.uk/blogs/ rogermosey/. My thanks to Mike Penson, BBC TV Sport for this and other data.

edgy and heavily propagandised, with television coverage and reception based on a non-domestic model of cinematic, 'closed-circuit', public viewing.[2] After this, for the first time, London in 1948 transmitted the Games to domestic TV sets; Tokyo in 1964 was the first satellite, globalised games; Mexico in 1968 became the first Games (for some) in colour. Later, in the developing post-analogue era, Sydney in 2000 saw the rise of the website as an alternative access point, and Athens in 2004 became the first 'red button' Games, allowing limited viewer choice and interactivity. Beijing in 2008 achieved a massive, record global TV reach, with extensive interactive replay activity on demand. The weight of this history sets the scene for London 2012. As Slater suggested in her talk, for the BBC, the challenge for this next 'step change' is for another 'Coronation moment' – nothing less; the most comprehensive coverage of The Olympic Games to date. A crucible for attention on the world stage, which is charged with 'bringing the Nation together' while also asserting outwardly a 'different face of Britain – modern not heritage' to the world, and achieving new, technically unimagined possibilities; fully comprehensive coverage of all events for the first time and furthermore, fully in tune with all digital broadcast and mobile, interactive platforms. These will be the red button, selective and interactive Olympic Games, empowering choice which matches the total menu of events as they take place, with the dynamics of individual selection. These Games will run to a complex set schedule over 17 days, in locations in London and around the UK; but you, the viewer, will be able to navigate your very own 'virtual Olympics'.

Many commentators have noted the historical parallels between London 1948 and London 2012, in particular developing the analogy of the 'Austerity Games'. Needless to say, 'Austerity' Britain in 1948, as Kynaston (2007, 19) and others[3] have noted, however, was a very different state and condition to that of the present economic and social conditions; the result of a prolonged and terminally exhausting period of total war, rather than spiralling levels of national and consumer debt and associated complex fiscal and financial crisis. In spite of this however, it might be argued that in both cases 'The Games' and what they symbolised were, and are, intimately linked to their particular depressed political and economic circumstances; a 'way out', or at least a diversion, projecting their respective aspirant and rejuvenating images of a 'new' Britain; forward, rather than backward-looking.

In the light of this, the following brief account sets out to assess the significance of the BBC television coverage of the 1948 London Olympic Games. No recordings of the television coverage of these Games survive although some radio coverage and a range of newsreel films do exist in various archives.[4] In looking through the contemporary commentaries of the day however, one significant issue recurs; televising the Games in 1948 was seen overwhelmingly as a scientific and technical challenge and achievement; the forms of programming that emerged and their cultural consequences were largely ignored.[5] Initially, some attention is given to the broad context of

---

[2]   Akin to the relatively recent use of mega-digital screens in public squares and spaces; large screen relay coverage of football finals, rock concerts or other civic ceremonies, for instance; the widely relayed and networked marriage of Prince William to Kate Middleton in April 2011.

[3]   See also Hampton 2008 for a related discussion and Simon Jenkins: http://www.guardian.co.uk/commentisfree/2008/oct/24/olympics-london-sport [24 October 2011]

[4]   See, for example, *A Very British Olympics* (2005), narrated by Alan Coren, a popular, tongue-in-cheek account of the Games and their humorous 'austerity moments' (transmitted 23 October 2005, BBC4).

[5]   See, for example, the discussion by Hotine (1949), 'Broadcasting the Olympic Games', and de Lotbiniere (1948), 'The Biggest Outside Broadcasting Operation in History'.

television in Britain at the time. The discussion then analyses the scheduling of the Games in July 1948 and develops themes concerning the commentators and the critical reception of the first television Games.

Post-War TV

> Whilst sound broadcasting settled down to consolidate its war-time gains, television began again from nowhere and suddenly revealed itself as a power to be reckoned with. Between 1945 and 1950 it passed from being a scientific achievement, a futuristic novelty, into being a successful rival to the older medium as a source of entertainment for the modern home. [...] The future had changed hands. The fact was that people wanted to look as well as listen.
>
> (Gorham 1952, 234)

Transmission of the nascent, BBC 'high definition' Television Service was abruptly halted days before the outbreak of war in September 1939. When the service recommenced in June 1946, Maurice Gorham had already been in post as Head of the Television Service for six months. The official decision to re-continue British television transmissions after the war had resulted from a rather shadowy Committee of Inquiry, led by Lord Hankey. This had been established in secret in September 1943 and two years later the Committee's conclusion that 'television is here to stay' was officially given the green light by the Labour government. The resultant 405 line BBC Service from Alexandra Palace began again on 7 June 1946 and the following week's broadcast schedule included regular but sound-only news bulletins, as well as *The Silence of the Sea*, starring Kenneth More – the first full-length post-war television drama. The following day, with Freddie Grisewood and Richard Dimbleby as commentators, the Television Service covered the Victory Parade with great success. This was the first in a long line of post-war BBC Television outside broadcasts which aimed to televise and hence relay significant events for domestic reception and to mediate national civic rituals with due television pomp and ceremony.[6]

However, by March 1947 there were fewer than 20,000 licensed TV sets capable of operating in the UK – the great majority of them in the London area – and progress was slow in developing transmission to 'the regions' and to a genuinely national audience.[7] In part this was due to delays in developing a national television transmission system. Hankey had recommended a network of six transmitters to service major centres of population but these were yet to be completed in the conditions of post-war austerity. As Gorham was to note however, there were other crucial factors that inhibited the growth of the television-viewing public in Britain at this time:

[6] See Chaney (1983). Televising VE Day was followed by subsequent BBC TV milestones: the first televised Royal Wedding of Princess Elizabeth to Prince Philip in November 1947; the London Olympics in July 1948; the Festival of Britain in May 1951; and most famously, The Coronation in June 1953. This history of major outside broadcast (OB) events have understandably entered into BBC mythology and in the particular context of sporting occasions, the name, and larger-than-life presence and achievements of S J de Lotbiniere ('Lobby') – first in radio and then in television in the period under discussion – cannot easily be missed. See for instance Haynes (2010) for an engaging and informed account.

[7] For relevant discussion see Silvey (1974) and Briggs (1995).

This was not because people did not want television after the war but because they could not get it. There were no sets. There was no such thing as 'sales resistance' in those early years; every dealer had waiting-lists and every set that left the manufacturers found its way into a home, but supply fell far short of demand. (Gorham 1952, 237)

Supply eventually began to catch up with demand by the late 1940s when TV set production reached 1000 per day and the new combined TV/radio licences were selling at the same pace.[8] However, British television in the late 1940s and early 1950s faced considerable problems and expansion was slow; by the time of the 1948 Games, for instance, a mere 4.3 per cent of the adult population of Britain had a television set in their homes: some 70,000 receivers. Without hire purchase, credit or rental arrangements at this time, the cheapest television, for instance a Phillips model with a 9½ inch monochrome screen (measured diagonally), cost as new between 50–60 guineas, equivalent to at least two full months' wages for a skilled, industrial worker. On the one hand, this was due to technical, investment and related-market factors, but there were also other complications.

In particular, within the BBC at this stage, television remained very much the 'upstart and unanticipated offspring' of radio, perhaps understandably, as more than 11 million British households had radio licences at the time and the wireless had significantly proved its worth as *the* domestic medium during the war and in its immediate aftermath. Significantly, in 1947–8 for instance, only £716,666 was allocated to TV, with £6.5 million going to the senior, sound-only services (Hotine 1949, 146–9). Furthermore, the frustratingly slow and protracted technical expansion of television, its expense for consumers, national (non)availability and disappointing related domestic take-up were a focus for some cautionary, if not outright regressive voices within the BBC itself (including the influence of the then Director General, Sir William Haley) who identified television as *the* threat to radio sound broadcasting. Even Robert Silvey, the Head of Listener Research at the BBC (Listening *and Viewing* Research from 1948 onwards) confessed himself at this stage no convert, and he had decided views about the value of television viewing at the time. In the first place he argued that television paled when placed alongside the extremely high standards of radio broadcasting. By comparison, he admitted, the picture was 'very primitive' and caused him headaches, the programmes themselves he found to 'contain much which is of very little appeal'; and finally he argued the 'sheer palaver' involved in watching the set – extinguishing the lights, moving the furniture and consequent domestic upheaval – was unwarranted and disruptive (Kynaston 2007, 212–3).

In these views he echoed many of the widespread, contemporary assessments of the new sound *and* vision medium. One especially rich example in particular was the research carried out to document everyday life in Britain by the Mass-Observation movement from 1937 onwards. In their project to produce an 'anthropology (or science) of our selves' (brought about by their chance meeting via *The New Statesman*), the work of Charles Madge, Humphrey Jennings and Tom Harrisson and their extensive network of intellectuals, artists, volunteer diarists, panellists and observers provides a fertile and diverse account of British cultural life of the time and the

---

[8]   Geddes (1991) provides a valuable if lonely analysis of the industrial production of radio and television sets relevant to this period.

attempts to adjust to social change.[9] Their studies of 'Worktown' (Bolton, Lancashire, UK) and more particularly of cinema-going (Richards and Sheridan 1987) are acknowledged, and distinctive historical sources, relating principally to the immediate pre-war, wartime and immediate post-war experience. However, in April 1949 they published a fascinating and groundbreaking survey of public attitudes towards the new medium of television,[10] some five months after the televised Games, and two key questions were put to the M-O National Panel ('a predominantly middle class group, generally above average in intelligence and education'). First: How do you feel about having television in your own home? Second: if you had a television set, how do you think it would affect your home leisure pursuits? (Mass-Observation (hereafter M-O) 1949, 1)

Significantly, of the 684 people who replied to the survey, only 2 per cent actually owned a television set and about 10 per cent lived in areas where television was 'not yet visible'. Almost 40 per cent of the M-O Panel respondents had *never seen* television and a further 20 per cent reported having seen TV only once, 'before the war'. In spite of this, the report offers rich insights – 'thick descriptions' – of how television was 'imagined' at the time by *potential* viewers/buyers. In fact, about half of the Panel were strongly committed to having a set in their own home, typically on grounds of enhanced domestic entertainment and educational facilities, but status pretensions and aspirations were also clearly evident in many of the responses: 'If I could afford it I should certainly like to have a set in the same way as I should certainly like to have a car, a private swimming pool and other good things of life!' (27 year-old Housewife) (M-O 1949, 3).

Others played harder to get, and were more resistant to the lure of the 'goggle-box': 'I do not particularly wish for a set in my home, as I think it rather a temptation to waste time. However, if the system comes to my town, I may purchase a unit' (M-O 1949, 4).

Against such positive, if wishful dreams of luxury, about one-third of the respondents were definitely hostile to the idea of having a television in their own home, citing the cost of investment in an as yet unproven apparatus as the principal reason. Related 'drawbacks' to television in the home were perceived in its ability to displace and draw attention and concentration away from other more 'worthwhile' pursuits or activities ('a colossal waste of money and time'), and in its perceived, destabilising impact on the existing 'hub' of household arrangements, with what for many was identified as 'synthetic entertainment':

I have no desire whatsoever to have a set myself. I think it encourages the growing tendency for passive pastimes, and that this tendency should be prevented if possible. Since television involves a semi-darkened room and concentration of eyes and ears, it is particularly crippling for any other activity; and it is unnecessary as pleasure for our ears and eyes are already well catered for, with wireless, concerts, cinemas, theatres, etc. I myself would far rather do something more actively creative with my spare time than sit and look at what is given out to us on a television set (24 year-old Research Chemist). (M-O 1949, 6)

---

[9] The Mass-Observation Archive is housed in the Special Collections section of the Library at the University of Sussex, Brighton, UK; see: www.massobs.org.uk. For useful references, see Mass-Observation (1939), Calder and Sheridan (1984) and Jeffrey (1978).

[10] See Mass-Observation (1949); it is also interesting to note Tom Harrisson's reflections on the changing status of television some ten years later in *The Telly: How Important?* Chapter 12 in Harrisson (1961).

Perhaps this is why responses to questions about the future development of television were overwhelmingly in favour of more outside broadcasts, for more television of respectable and spectacular record, a seemingly unmediated mirror, the 'window on the world', where TV simply seemed to replace the eye at the live event. Having a television in the home was also identified as an obvious reason for decreased wireless listening and cinema-going was also expected to suffer. Other home pursuits predicted to be most affected were reading and knitting. Home life – as it was known – would be in chaos:

> I view the possibilities of having a set in the house with mixed feelings. There are so many things I can do in my leisure time while listening to and enjoying the wireless, for example, reading, carving and modelling, gardening. I am so afraid that television would prove so attractive that my spare time would be spent straining my eyes looking into a fixed distance screen (32 year-old School Teacher). (M-O 1949, 5)

> Apart from the wasted evening's prospect, what housewife (middle or any other class) would have the time to sit down and watch television in the morning and afternoon? With the radio women can work and hum with 'Housewives Choice'. With television they would not be able to watch the screen and make the pastry. What mysteries would be brought forth from the oven at dinner time, due to the irresistible distractions of the cathode tube? (24 year-old Clerk).
> (M-O 1949, 7)

> I believe that television makes family home life almost impossible. For 2–3 hours every evening the family must sit in darkness gazing at the screen – mother cannot knit, father cannot read, the children skimp through their homework and stay up late. No one can have a conversation, no letters get written, and friends calling are not welcomed since they break the sequence (35 year-old Laboratory Technician). (M-O 1949, 28)

For others however, the promise of television transcended its perceived, problematic presence in the home:

> I should like to have a television set in my home, whilst admitting it has some drawbacks: eg it demands an undivided attention and a darkened room for perfect viewing. It nevertheless possesses the power of providing me with the *otherwise unattainable* (My emphasis: 32 year-old Commercial Traveller). (M-O 1949, 6)

Only eleven of the people questioned mentioned sports and television, one commenting that: 'Whether or not sports meetings (boxing and football in particular) will be televised will depend on the stadium owners, but I think it is doubtful whether television can ever take away completely the thrill of actually seeing the game' (24 year-old student) (M-O 1949, 23). On the other hand, one respondent remarked: 'The Olympic Games and Test Matches of last summer were almost too good to be true' (41 year-old Schoolmaster) (M-O 1949, 15).

From outside the BBC in this period, the disturbing novelty of television had also encountered a similar period of doubt, contradictorily mixed with enthusiasm and commercial unease, if not direct hostility, from bodies like The Newspaper Society, and from British film producers, exhibitors and distributors and music hall and theatre managers. In sport, The Epsom Grandstand Association refused to have The Derby horse race televised and the Football League and the British Boxing Board of Control also boycotted television coverage in this period. The use of any popular music was also an issue at this time due to uncertainty over the acquisition of television rights.

Schedules

Nowadays, TV schedules cannot be contained. A digital television, on-screen electronic menu is necessary to view the full range of options and specialist, 'generic' channels devoted to cookery, lifestyle, sport, comedy, history, films and so on. Furthermore, the notion of 'live' TV has also been by-passed by record and replay systems. TV screens are also no longer 'one-way', as they have converged with computerised interactive systems from games to home shopping and Google. Increasingly, television is accessed by laptop, mobile phone, and iPad. Analogue newspapers and magazines struggle to contain the uncontainable, the full range of what is available and what you can choose. By comparison, just over 60 years ago, on the single BBC channel of the time, television transmission times remained very limited. In the *Radio Times*, radio schedules for the Home, the Light and Third programmes dominated, with a small, two page section at the end of each issue devoted to television programmes. The schedule architecture of the time was primitive and, to the modern eye, laughably thin. Looking at the TV schedule for the week of Sunday 18 July, the week before the Games commenced for instance, most days began with an hour-long programme between 11am and midday, a 'demonstration film' for retailers' purposes. This was followed by an hour of afternoon programmes between 3–4pm. This slot often targeted female viewers with programmes like *For the Housewife* ('W P Matthew shows how to prepare a wall for distempering, Philip Harben makes a basic salad dressing'), *Designing Women* ('which deals with good design in the home in an amusing way') or *In Our Garden* (where Members of the League of Health and Beauty gave a display of physical fitness exercises and Fred Streeter demonstrated how to take cuttings for next year). From this time on, there was a break in transmission until 8.30pm – an extended version of what became known as the 'toddlers' truce' – a period when it was assumed that all households would be too busy with domestic routines, preparing and eating meals, returning from work, putting children to bed and so on, to view television. The evening schedule which started at 8.30pm usually consisted of a play, in this instance *Dandy Dick* or *Virtuoso*, or a variety, cabaret musical sequence, *Hulbert Follies* or *Café Continental*. The evening ended with 15 minutes of *Newsreel* followed by the sound-only *News* at 10pm. This pattern of scheduling epitomised BBC television provision through the late 1940s and into the 1950s when the forces of demand and competition began to introduce significant changes in time and content. Outside broadcasts were, however, permitted to extend beyond these times and the BBC coverage of the 1948 London Olympics was an important, early example of the power of televised media sporting events to colonise and extend the schedule framework. On Thursday 29 July 1948, between 2.30pm and 5pm, viewers were treated to an extended sequence of coverage which included the Opening Ceremony in the Stadium at Wembley with the King, H M George VI (after his therapy recently dramatised in the film *The King's Speech*), the march past of the competitors from the 62 countries involved, the release of 7000 pigeons, the arrival of the Olympic Torch and the taking of the Olympic Oath by the athletes. At 8 o'clock in the evening, half an hour of coverage came from the Empire Pool with swimming, pushing *The Long Mirror* by J B Priestley further back into the evening.

From then on, and for the next two weeks, at the end of each day's TV transmission, the following day's coverage was announced and outlined in sound only. The Games captured substantial segments of the schedule as they unfolded, on average 3.5 hours per day were covered, with some days more than five hours of broadcasting devoted to the various competitions (viewers were advised that 'selective viewing is essential'). Swimming, athletics and boxing predominated because the key locations for television OB cameras – themselves technically imperfect and in very short supply – were Wembley Stadium (Athletics and field events) and the Empire Pool (Swimming and Boxing). A hint of some of the difficulties encountered is given in the *Radio Times* for Friday 30 July '8.45 app. Olympic Games: If light permits a further visit will be made to the Empire Pool during the evening'.[11] Coverage of events was supplemented with interviews and BBC records indicate that it was felt a great achievement that athletes were interviewed to camera, out of breath and in the case of the swimmers, 'while still wet'. While by comparison BBC radio coverage of the Games was more extensive, detailed and comprehensive and attracted vastly superior numbers of listeners than the viewers of TV, many involved in the television operation saw this as a key opportunity to provide a salutary challenge to radio. Ian Orr-Ewing, BBC Outside Broadcasts Manager for instance noted that 'Britain's Television Service is going to be "on show" to thousands of overseas commentators and visitors […] it is hoped the programming will be to the credit of British Television throughout the world' (Orr-Ewing 1948, 25). In the absence of any archival recordings of the television coverage of The London Games in 1948, it is difficult to assess the extent to which such credit was achieved. Some anachronistic evidence indicates that the TV coverage was claimed to be almost as good as 'being there', although at that time there was also a widespread view that there could be no televised substitute for the 'real thing', real spectatorship, actually 'being there'. However, it can be safely assumed that the coverage was partly mesmerised by the technical miracle of its own image, the simple relay of the picture of the event, happening 'as you watched it', in your home. Beyond this, it is undoubtedly the case that the modern TV viewer would identify the coverage as dated, technically crude, restricted and jingoistic but with a familiar focus on dramatic moments and performers; including those of Gailly, Wint, Anderson, Gardner, Gibson and above all, Fanny Blankers-Koen, the 'Flying-Housewife'.

Questions of Commentary

While the production of live, moving pictures of the events and competitions were central to the BBC television mission and its coverage of the Games in 1948, also on the frontline were a new breed of specialised professional mediators: television commentators. The OB TV coverage of the time may have been understood primarily as a technical set of challenges for the BBC, but the transition from radio commentary to television commentary also required important, demanding and interesting adjustments. For the senior, sound-only service, commentary was everything, whether for sporting spectaculars or for civic ceremonies. On the wireless, without the appropriately measured and informed (largely BBC Received Pronunciation, 'institutional voice') commentary to act as the eyes of the listener, there was little that could be intelligible. For television however, commentary had to proceed according to a different set of ground rules,

---

[11] For an insight into the technical aspects of the operation see Haynes (2010), Orr-Ewing (1948) and de Lotbiniere (1948).

informed by an acknowledgment that both parties to the broadcast could actually see the action, thus rendering certain aspects of radio commentary superfluous and redundant. The 'asymmetric relationship' between broadcaster and *listener* and broadcaster and *viewer* required a paradigm shift and an adjustment of the terms of engagement and the 1948 Games were a key moment of transition in this respect.[12]

Richard Haynes has provided an insightful and detailed account of the development of BBC sports commentary from the pre-war to post-war era. Inevitably, this is part and parcel of the mythic story of the larger-than-life character and influence of Seymour Joly de Lotbiniere, better known as 'Lobby', BBC Director of Outside Broadcasts 1935–52. One of Lobby's key and recurrent challenges in the period was negotiating and managing the institutional politics and practices of commentators and commentary, through the period which encompassed the establishment and take-off of television. In this interesting history, as Haynes notes:

> During the war new commentators had come to prominence including Richard Dimbleby and Wynford Vaughan-Thomas, both cutting their teeth on sports OBs before venturing wider to cover life from 'The Front' and state occasions. Others like Raymond Glendenning and Rex Alston became the BBC's most prominent voices on sport, first during the reduced hours of coverage from sport in the war years, then subsequently on the wide array of sports broadcasting that grew from 1946. Between them Glendenning and Alston covered football, rugby union, golf, greyhound racing, motor racing, cricket, boxing, horse racing, tennis and athletics. In October 1945 there was already a feeling that Glendenning was being overstretched and overused across his main sports of football, boxing and horse racing. With the prospect of covering the 1948 Olympic Games in London new commentators were at a premium.
>
> (Haynes 2009, 8–9)

In the light of this situation, a whole new generation of recruits for television commentary for the Games and beyond were procured and enlisted,[13] some on the basis of their journalistic credentials but in the *Radio Times* at the time for instance, one might be forgiven for reading an emphasis not only on sporting knowledge or experience, but also an over-riding masculine (commentators were men) validation derived from their respective records of wartime service. In a sign of the times for instance, the profiles published introducing Roy Moor, Pat Landsberg, Ian Orr-Ewing, Jack Crump, John Webb and Freddie Milton all fore-grounded their war-time records; 'served in North Africa', 'was at El Alamein with 10th Armoured Division', 'was in Italy with the 8th Indian Division', 'Captain in Royal Artillery in Burma', 'Wing Commander and served in North Africa, Italy, France and Germany' (*Radio Times* 1948), as much as their sporting expertise.

The pedigrees, if not the dilemmas of the commentator for BBC television as opposed to radio, particularly in the sphere of sports coverage, had already surfaced in records of viewer opinion. Some weeks before the commencement of the Games for example, the *Radio Times*

---

[12] See Tolson (2006, 109) and Crisell (1986, 119) for relevant and interesting discussions of radio and television commentary.

[13] This was the period when the voices of Kenneth Wolstenholme, Peter West, Max Robertson, Brian Johnston, Peter Dimmock, Harry Carpenter, Murray Walker and Raymond Baxter were introduced and 'tuned' to broadcasting, especially television commentary.

had featured an article, 'Problems of the Commentator', by P H Dorté, BBC Head of Television Outside Broadcasts and Films, where he responded to viewers' letters, 'typical of those which pour into Alexandra Palace'. In particular, he responded to the following three edited and sharply contrasting opinions, which he labelled 'annoying', 'pleasing' and 'worrying':

> But it was ruined for us by the incessant talk of the commentator. Doesn't he realise that we viewers can see the competitors just as well as he can?

> My sincere congratulations to your Outside Broadcast commentators; they give me just the information that I want to have to supplement the picture.

> But all the viewers around here (incidentally we are some seventy miles from Alexandra Palace) agree that the commentators should talk more. We can't always follow the ball, and if a game that is being televised is also being broadcast we invariably switch off the Television sound and listen to the Home or Light Programme commentary; it's so much fuller. (Dorté 1948, 25)

Dorté's response indicated that the television commentator's job was to supply the viewer with those facts which the camera cannot establish. Whereas the sound broadcasting commentator's role was to paint a word picture of the general scene, the TV commentator could to some extent ignore these generalities, as the picture makes these largely self-evident. However, the television commentator had to be aware – 'keep at the forefront of his mind' – the point that information which will be 'welcomed by one viewer may be resented by another, who may consider that the commentator is talking down to him'. As he went on to argue:

> What are we doing about it all? Quite frankly we are trying to compromise while at the same time remembering that our first duty lies in looking after the average viewer who lives within the official range of Alexandra Palace, and who has bought a medium-priced television set of average performance. Putting it another way, we are assuming that our commentators are talking mostly to those who have an average appreciation of the game which we are televising, and who are seeing it very nearly as clearly as the commentators themselves can see it.
>
> (Dorté 1948, 25)

The extent to which viewers could be relied upon to enjoy this simultaneous clarity of vision was an assumption which, like the sets themselves, was not always reliable during the 1948 Olympics.

REFLECTION: SOME THINGS CHANGE, SOME THINGS STAY THE SAME?

> We are the hosts at these Games; we have a reputation for hospitality, good sportsmanship, tolerance and kindliness, so let us each and every one do our uttermost to show our visitors that this reputation is well founded. It is very certain that by doing so we can be satisfied that we are making a contribution, however humble, to the real progress of mankind. (Burghley 1948, 3)

For all the prodigious and ground-breaking political, technical and institutional efforts and achievements involved in bringing the 1948 London Olympics to a successful conclusion in 'austerity' Britain, and to relay them 'world-wide' on radio and in more domestic and limited terms on broadcast television to small, almost 'experimental' domestic TV audiences, as Haynes has noted: 'the information on radio and television audiences for the 1948 Olympics is pretty thin' (2010, 1042). The televised events seem to have vied with the partly overlapping radio coverage of the England v Australia Test Match of that year (Bradman's last series in England). The conditions of film and newsreel coverage of the Games, by comparison with that of TV, are briefly but usefully outlined in Hampton's account (2008, 111–26). Asa Briggs notes that for television viewers, the new, improved Emitron cameras which were employed required much less lighting, and produced a 'velvety quality' for some viewers, akin to 'high-grade photographs' (Briggs 1995, 248), but this was by no means uniformly reported.

The 'Critic on the Hearth', for *The Listener*, in 'A view from the Games', reviewed the television coverage, beginning by extolling the exciting climax of the 'small television screen' images of the last moments of the Zatopek – Reiff 5000 metres event, which Zatopek narrowly lost; 'in the flash of an eyelid […] bruised and defeated, but an inspiration, an illumination'. While admitting generally that 'from watching the television screen I should say that these cameras gave a very good account of themselves all through the Games', the reviewer however went on to compare this British effort against the grain of the 'screen version of the Games held in Berlin in the middle nineteen-thirties, with Goering, genial in a floppy straw hat, and Hitler febrile with excitement over every German victory', as a 'vast and gleaming […] demonstration in architecture and organisation of military panoply and splendour'. By comparison,

> … Supposing that the organisers of the 1948 Games wanted to create an effect of shabby, shoddy muddle, then, judging from the television screen, they too succeeded in their aim. Seen from an armchair, the Games seemed to have neither comprehensive plan nor individual impressive-ness of presentation. On the television screen they looked like some haphazard athletic events run together at the last moment by an incompetent spiritual instructor who had counted on the annual Sunday School treat being washed out by rain. (*The Listener* 1948b)

The television clarity, the coverage, the debates and the historical context of the London Olympic Games have been transformed almost beyond the bounds of generational memory and imagination in the intervening years between 1948 and 2012. In the light of this, what can be gained from any critical attention given to the cultural history and heritage of the 1948 moment? In brief, the significance of the 1948 BBC Television coverage of the Games, as Haynes (2010, 1030) has argued, is three-fold; it signalled the possibilities of new, mutual relationships between the BBC and sporting bodies; it provided the BBC with a challenge which severely tested their 'blueprint' technical and production capabilities in the new era of the emergent television service; and for television sales and viewers it was an early but significant post-war moment of important, added stimulus. More generally however, the 1948 BBC TV Olympics operation marked the first 'recognition' of the real possibilities of *television* coverage of sport and provided a template of very basic expectations; that we should be able to 'witness',[14] live, OB-mediated coverage of events and, hence, that there could be a televisual alternative to the 'being there' experience and that raw television pictures of events should be accompanied by informed commentary and interviews. From this point on, any Games worth their salt provided the TV-mediated, and if possible enhanced, the '*otherwise unattainable*' (see MO respondent quoted earlier in this chapter).

---

[14] See Ellis (2000) for a relevant discussion of this period and its televisual formations.

Once again however, televising the Games provides the ultimate challenge to British broadcasters, eager to respond and to emphasise the moment of pure technical progress and, as a result, to distance themselves and us from the primitive but nevertheless nostalgically charged past. As BBC 1 announces that it will screen a one-off, 90-minute TV drama about the story of 'Bert and Dickie' (Bushnell and Burnell), unanticipated Gold Medal Olympic Double Sculls winners in 1948 (Conlan 2011), in the 2012 run-up to the Games, Ralph Rivera, BBC Director of Future Media argues: 'The Olympics will do for digital media what the Coronation did for television' (quoted in Solon 2011). In 1948, with the assistance of very early TV coverage, Britain won 3 Gold, 14 Silver and 6 Bronze medals.

BIBLIOGRAPHY AND REFERENCES

Briggs, A, 1995 (1979) *The History of Broadcasting in the United Kingdom, volume IV: Sound and Vision 1945–55*, Oxford University Press, Oxford and New York

Burghley, Lord, 1948 The Spirit of the Games, *Radio Times*, 23 July, 3

Calder, A, and Sheridan, D (eds), 1984 *Speak for Yourself: A Mass Observation Anthology, 1937–49*, Jonathan Cape, London

Chaney, D, 1983 A Symbolic Mirror of Ourselves: Civic Ritual in Mass Society, *Media, Culture and Society* 5, Academic Press, London, 119–35

Conlan, T, 2011 BBC to air 1948 Olympics drama, *The Guardian*, 26 May, available from: http://www.guardian.co.uk/media/2011/may/26/bbc1-olympic-games [24 October 2011]

Crisell, A, 1986 *Understanding Radio*, Methuen, London and New York

Dorté, P H, 1948 Problems of the Commentator, *Radio Times*, 13 June, 25

Ellis, J, 2000 *Seeing Things: Television in the Age of Uncertainty*, IB Tauris, London and New York

Geddes, K, 1991 *The Setmakers: A History of the Radio and Television Industry*, BREMA, London

Gorham, M, 1952 *Broadcasting & Television Since 1900*, Andrew Dakers, London

Hampton, J, 2008 *The Austerity Olympics*, Aurum Press, London

Harrisson, T (ed), 1961 *Britain Revisited*, Victor Gollancz, London

Haynes, R, 2009 'Lobby' and the Formative Years of Radio Sports Commentary, 1935–52, *Sport in History* 29 (1), 25–48

— 2010 The BBC, Austerity and Broadcasting the 1948 Olympic Games, *The International Journal of the History of Sport* 27 (6), April, 1029–46

Hotine, L, 1949 Broadcasting the Olympic Games, in *BBC Year Book, 1949*, BBC, London

Jeffrey, T, 1978 *Mass Observation – A Short History*, CCCS Stencilled Paper No 55, University of Birmingham

Kynaston, D, 2007 *Austerity Britain 1945–48: A World to Build*, Bloomsbury, London

The Listener, 1948a Editorial, 19 August, Issue 1021, 262

— 1948b 'Critic on the Hearth': Television, A View of the Games, 2 September, Issue 1023, 354

Lotbiniere, S J de, 1948 The Biggest Outside Broadcasting Operation in History, *Radio Times*, 9 July, 3

Magnay, J, 2010 Two Years to Go: Full Coverage, *The Daily Telegraph*, 27 July, 18

Mass-Observation, 1939 *Britain*, Penguin, London

— 1949 *Mass-Observation's Panel on Television* (M-O Archive File 3106), Mass-Observation, London

Orr-Ewing, I, 1948 Televising the Olympic Games, *Radio Times*, 23 July, 25

Radio Times, 1948 Television's Commentators This Week at the Olympic Games, *Radio Times*, 30 July, 26, and 6 August, 26

Richards, J, and Sheridan, D (eds), 1987 *Mass-Observation at The Movies*, Routledge and Kegan Paul, London and New York

Silvey, R, 1974 *Who's Listening? The Story of BBC Audience Research*, Allen & Unwin, London

Slater, B, 2011 'Sports Broadcasting – a Journey to London 2012', public lecture at University of Leicester, Leicester, UK, Thursday 10 March

Solon, O, 2011 BBC talks up 2012 Olympics' value for digital media, *wired.co.uk*, 18 April, available from: http://www.wired.co.uk/news/archive/2011–04/18/ralph-rivera-bbc-olympics [24 October 2011]

Tolson, A, 2006 *Media Talk: Spoken Discourse on TV and Radio*, Edinburgh University Press, Edinburgh

Museums and the Representation of Sport

7

Sport in Museums and Museums of Sport:
An Overview

Kevin Moore

Sport is an increasingly important part of global culture. Museums are an increasingly significant way in which culture, through displays of material culture, is reflected and interpreted worldwide. How, then, is sport reflected in museums? This chapter will consider the development of sport in museums, and dedicated sports museums, but with a particular emphasis on these developments in the context of the UK.

There is growing academic interest in sport in museums and sports museums, but the literature is as yet relatively limited and many questions remain unexplored (see, for example: Adair 2004; Alegi 2006; Brabazon 2006a; Brabazon 2006b; Brabazon and Mallinder 2006; Danilov 2005; Forslund 2006; Frost 2005; Johnes and Mason 2003; Kellett and Hede 2008; Kohe 2010; Moore 2003a; Moore 2003b; Moore 2004; Moore 2008; Moore 2009; Moore 2012; Osmond and Phillips 2011; Phillips 2010; Phillips 2012b; Phillips and Tinning 2011; Ramshaw 2010; Redmond 1971; Smith 1999; Snyder 1991; Vamplew 1998; Vamplew 2004; Wood 2005). Fundamentally, we still have little understanding of how and why sport has been reflected in museums and how and why sport museums have developed. This chapter addresses these questions, but much further research and analysis is required. Much of the academic analysis of sport in museums to date has focused on the kind of histories portrayed, arguing that much on offer reflects a nostalgic and corporate view of sport. I will also consider how valid such academic critiques of sport in museums are. Woven into this analysis will be a brief consideration of the contributions made by the four further chapters in this section of this volume.

What do we mean by a museum? As I have explored elsewhere, there is no single universally accepted definition, with variation but overlap between those of the International Council of Museums (ICOM), the American Association of Museums (AAM) and the UK's Museums Association (MA) (Moore 1997, 13–14). A problem in the UK (and internationally) is that 'museum' is not in any way a protected term – unlike, for example, 'university'. In the UK anyone can establish a 'museum' – even in their own home – and promote it as such, and there are many examples of this. To protect the sector, there is in the UK an accreditation scheme for museums formerly operated by the Museums, Libraries and Archives Council (MLA), a government-funded body which sets standards in museums. MLA was abolished by the government in 2011 and its responsibilities taken over by Arts Council England (ACE). This is unlike the situation in the USA, where the comparable scheme is run by the AAM rather than by a government quango. In the analysis below, it will be considered whether such formal schemes are too constrictive in terms of the defining and understanding of sports museums and sport in museums.

Before we consider the dedicated sports museums, we must ask how and why sport has been reflected in museums more generally. The way in which non-sport museums have engaged with sport is an important topic which has been even less addressed by academics than that of sports museums, and it deserves much further attention. I have argued that sport, as part of popular culture, was (and to a significant extent is still) regarded as 'other' in terms of the dominant ideological position of museums, which, despite some democratisation in recent years, remain 'temples of high culture' in the UK. Traditionally, the purpose of museums was to identify and validate high culture, defined in binary opposition to popular or 'low' culture (Moore 1997; 2008).

This has begun to change over the past two decades. Increasingly museums have created temporary exhibitions exploring aspects of sport in relation to their subject matter. Those relating to sports science, such as the Science of Sport, by the UK's Science Museum, have been particularly popular. There have been an increasing number of displays exploring the fine and decorative arts of sport, such as the 'Courage Exhibition of National Trophies' at the Victoria and Albert Museum (V&A) in 1992 (Victoria and Albert Museum 1992), 'British Sporting Heroes' at the National Portrait Gallery in 1999 (Huntington-Whiteley 1999), 'Champions' at the National Portrait Gallery in 2008, and 'Fashion V Sport' at the V&A in 2008 (Salazar 2008). Social history museums have increasingly reflected the history of sport, partly because of the populist appeal of such displays, which attract audiences generally under-represented in museums (ie working-class people). This has most notably been achieved through the large number of temporary exhibitions in UK museums in recent years on the history of individual football clubs or football more generally in a town or city.

It is an assumption, rather than fully established fact, that museums have previously ignored sport in displays. Indeed, the 1953 *Football and the Fine Arts* touring exhibition, explored in Chapter 4 of this volume, indicates that this assumption needs to be further explored. Historians need to turn their attention, to, for example, the International Sporting Trophies Exhibition held in London in 1933 and the National Sporting Trophies exhibition in London in 1951. Atherton has examined in detail the theft of the Jules Rimet Trophy (the FIFA World Cup Trophy up to 1970) from an exhibition in London in 1966 during the build-up to the FIFA World Cup Finals (Atherton 2008). We have some knowledge of the collections relating to sport held in non-sport museums in the UK as a result of a major survey. In 2004, the major UK sports museums came together to establish the Sports Heritage Network (SHN) with the mission: 'To strengthen the network of institutions working within the field of sports heritage, and to inspire public involvement in sport and its history'. The SHN secured funding from the MLA to undertake a mapping survey to identify sporting collections held in museums, libraries and archives in the UK. The survey also identified governing bodies, clubs and other institutions that hold collections which may be made available to the public or to those undertaking research (Hood 2006).

The survey, undertaken by museum consultant Annie Hood, found that the museums of sport in the SHN have extensive knowledge about the heritage of their respective sports, but that they were not fully aware of what was held in more general museums and archives. Outside of the major sports even less was known about where sports heritage artefacts and archives were held. The report concentrated on collections in the public domain. The survey was limited to competitive and active sports and did not include games and pastimes. It identified that the distinction is not always clear cut and that there are many sports where recreation and competition are hard to divide, such as in motor sports and cycling. A questionnaire was circulated to 440 museums, starting with all museums with sporting collections identified in searches, to which were added the major regional museums and a selection of local and military museums. A healthy 206 questionnaires, or 47 per cent of the total, were returned. The information was supplemented by an earlier survey carried out by the Council of Museums in Wales (CMW) in 2002, *A Survey of Sporting Collections held by CMW Member Museums*.

In 1998 Vamplew commented that 'curiously most non-sport museums appear to have very few sporting artefacts on their accessions register, and even those are rarely documented in detail' (Vamplew 1998, 269). The survey found that, contrary to this, in addition to the dedicated sports museums, Britain's museums, libraries and archives held a wealth of material relating to sporting heritage, with 12 museums holding large sporting collections and the vast majority of museums holding at least some sporting material. There were 36 museums devoted entirely to sport and over 2000 further sporting collections within the country's institutions. This material had been 'hidden' through the classification systems in museums, which tend to focus on the type of materials (fine art, decorative art, silver, textile, ceramic, paper etc), rather than the subject matter. Even within social history collections, sporting material could be classified as 'leisure', 'recreation' or 'pastime'.

However, the report made it clear that sporting history was under-represented in Britain's local and regional museums, with much of the material collected in an *ad hoc* fashion: 'Locally unusual sports are given prominence in many cases which is an obvious part of the remit of a museum but often mainstream sports with local importance have been neglected. Much material relates to historical sports and little thought is given to contemporary collecting' (Hood 2006, 11). The survey revealed that, of the 206 social history museums that completed the questionnaire, only 32 had collecting policies that referred specifically to sporting artefacts. Yet

> There would seem to be a heartening change in that an increasing number of archives and museums are reviewing their contemporary collecting policies and in those realising that sport is important to their communities. The number of museums showing interest in staging sports related exhibitions and the high level of positive responses to the survey are perhaps a reflection of this change. This interest will only increase in the run up to the 2012 Olympics.
>
> (Hood 2006, 4)

This latter comment has proved highly prescient. For the London 2012 Olympics and Paralympics the Sports Heritage Network has developed a project called 'Our Sporting Life', to encourage and assist exhibitions of sports history in towns and cities across England. The take-up has exceeded all expectations, with 115 local sports history exhibitions taking place. This will be the largest exhibition festival ever held across England on any subject, and will reach an audience of at least 500,000 people. There is clearly huge latent public interest in sports history. It is also taking sports history to new audiences, with the exhibitions taking place not just in museums but also in other locations, such as sports and leisure centres, places where people are actively participating in sport (see www.OurSportingLife.co.uk).

Although Hood found that some of the key sports are well represented in museum collections, she also established that much sports heritage material is held in private hands and that museums that have put on sporting exhibitions have relied heavily on loans from both sports clubs and private individuals. The major governing bodies of sport were contacted to see if they had an overview of collections in their sport. A total of 200 questionnaires was sent out, and 73 were returned (37 per cent). While this gave an idea of the material held by the governing bodies, it revealed little about collections at sports club level. Subsequently the SHN has made contact with the governing bodies of more than 100 sports. What this has revealed is that many governing bodies do hold some historical material without defining this as a 'museum'; and, secondly, that for almost every sport there are a number of private collectors who have safeguarded major collections on the history of the sport, which are in some cases termed by the private collectors as 'museums'. These private collectors are generally of two kinds: those people connected with a sport who often had an administrative role within a club or governing body, who have preserved the heritage of the sport in the form of archives and artefacts in an individual capacity where there was a lack of interest from the relevant organisations; and wealthy individuals who have built up collections through purchases at auction and other means as part of the growing market for sports memorabilia, particularly in the UK, in the last 20 years. This phenomenon and its impact on sport in museums is worthy of further study in its own right. Both these kinds of private collection are of significance to the heritage of sport. The collections of the former may be stored (sometimes literally) in garages and back bedrooms, but are still an important part of Britain's sporting heritage.

There are an increasing number of dedicated sports museums around the world. Of course, the parameters of this depend on the definition of sport used. Danilov has undertaken two pioneering mapping studies of global sports museums and halls of fame, the second of which is 'the first comprehensive reference to sports museums and halls of fame worldwide' (Danilov 2005, 1; see also Danilov 1997). This work is already out of date, however, with significant developments in the sports museums sector since 2005, but it is still a starting point of value. Danilov gives a figure of 580 sports halls of fame and museums in 46 countries. However, it is unclear how many of these are 'museums' in terms of the AAM, MA or ICOM definitions. Danilov includes both 'halls of fame' and 'museums' – 'Approximately half are "halls of fame", with the others being split almost equally between those called "museums" and combination "museums and halls of fame"' (Danilov 2005, 11) – and loosely defines these by their interpretative approach rather than by their governance or purpose: 'Sports museums are similar to traditional historically oriented museums, with the emphasis generally on collections and exhibits of artefacts, memorabilia, photographs, films, and other materials relating to the history, highlights and principal figures of the field' (Danilov 2005, 11), whereas 'halls of fame often consist merely of wall plaques with brief biographies and photographs or etchings of the enshrined'. However, in the third category – 'hall of fame and museum' – 'most of the more popular museums and halls of fame combine these elements in imaginative ways and add interactive computerized exhibits, videos, multimedia shows, and other high-tech ingredients' (Danilov 2005, 18). These divisions between and definitions of 'museum', 'hall of fame' and 'hall of fame and museum' need to be considered further – and one could add 'museum and hall of fame'. Nor does Danilov define 'sport', while he includes museums and halls of fame of 'games like checkers, chess, and marbles, and such fields with sporting elements as automobiles, aviation and firearms' (Danilov 2005, 3). North America dominates, with more than 400 of the total in the USA and the second greatest number, 39, in Canada. The cultural meaning and significance of this North American preponderance remains to be explored. Within the threefold typology of 'museum', 'hall of fame' and 'hall of fame and museum' Danilov offers a further level of classification: sports museums can be multi-sport and international, national, regional or even for an individual college or university; single sport and international, national and regional; dedicated to a single sports man or woman; or dedicated to a single event, such as an Olympic Games (Danilov 2005, 12–13). Again, this approach is useful but needs much further exploration.

Moving beyond the limitations of Danilov's work, Phillips has developed a very helpful typology of sports museums, drawing on and adapting Gordon's classification for museums more generally (Phillips 2012a). Phillips considers the limitations of this fourfold typology – all such approaches inevitably over-simplify – but it remains very helpful to our understanding. Phillips' typology of sports museums is fundamentally as follows:

- Academic: the formal, usually publicly funded museums (conforming to the ICOM definition of a museum)
- Corporate: those run by sporting clubs and governing bodies, with some better termed Halls of Fame
- Community: the local, largely volunteer-run
- Vernacular: sporting artefacts in other settings, such as shops, bars and restaurants – including equivalents to the 'Hard Rock Café'

Phillips' classification embraces not just what we might term the 'formal' museum – academic and corporate – to also include and consider the 'informal' – community and vernacular.

Historically there has been a relative absence of, in Phillips' terms, 'academic' sports museums. There were clearly issues of social class and cultural value at work here. Museums were traditionally temples of high culture; sport, as part of popular culture, was 'other', though there are of course differences between sports. Today we have a growing but still relatively small number of museums that can be described as 'academic'. In the UK, for example, the Urbis building in Manchester city centre will become in 2012 the new public face of the National Football Museum in an £8.5 million development. This is a highly symbolic and major step forward in the recognition of the value of sports museums in the UK (Figs 7.1 and 7.2). Yet this is one of only four sports museums in the UK with museum accreditation status with MLA (now ACE).

'Corporate' museums, including Halls of Fame, established by sports governing bodies or clubs, have a much longer history, particularly in the USA, and are also increasingly popular globally. They are criticised by academics, as we shall see, for tending to pander to the nostalgic desires of their audience, for being largely public-relations vehicles for sport governing bodies or clubs and for being prone to bias in favour of sponsors. While such claims, as we shall explore below, do have some merit, it is far too simplistic to dismiss all as offering a partial, commercialised history. Many employ professionally qualified curatorial staff and operate in a manner very close to that of the 'academic' sports museums. Only their lack of independence in governance from their sport's governing body or club prevents many of them from securing museum accreditation status. The difference between many 'corporate' and 'academic' sports museums is paper thin. 'Community' and 'vernacular' sport museums have been even less considered, though an edited volume by Phillips explores these (Phillips 2012b). Community is a particularly interesting category in sports museums, potentially embracing every sports club in the world, as all tend to display in some form the club's history and achievements. Phillips' typology is a useful starting point for much-needed further study of sports museums.

The history of the development of sports museums has only been sketched to date by Danilov, who, as we have seen, is as concerned with halls of fame as museums (Danilov 2005, 5–10). While the National Mountaineering Museum, Turin, has a claim to be the world's oldest sports

FIG 7.1. THE NEW NATIONAL FOOTBALL MUSEUM, URBIS BUILDING, MANCHESTER.

Fig 7.2. The new National Football Museum from Cathedral Gardens, Manchester.

museum (1874), we need to be careful regarding the definition of a museum. There is a difference between a collection owned by a private individual or club for the benefit of its members and a publicly accessible museum. Depending on the definition of a museum, the MCC Museum at Lord's opened in 1953 – or 1864. A number of sports museums began to develop in Europe from the 1910s onwards, such as the Olympic Museum in Lausanne (1915), though not in its current form. The first sports halls of fame and museums in the USA developed in the 1930s, most notably the Baseball Hall of Fame and Museum in Cooperstown, which was founded in 1936, opening to the public in 1939. Again, however, we need to be careful regarding definitions. While the Baseball Hall of Fame and Museum today fits with the ICOM and AAM definitions of a museum, this has not necessarily been the case throughout its history, as a 'hall of fame' rather than a 'hall of fame and museum'. From the 1950s sports museums began to develop in Eastern Europe as a glorification of Communist sporting triumph. But we know as yet very little as to how and why sports museums have developed in different contexts and cultures, revealing contrasts between, for example, North America and Eastern and Central Europe in the Communist era. The history of the development of sports museums awaits the serious attention of historians.

As sport has globalised, so sports museums are rapidly becoming a global phenomenon. But do sports museums matter? If museums have a value, if sport is an important part of culture, then sports museums potentially have value. But how is this value defined and by whom? This relates to wider debates about how we measure the value and effectiveness of all types of museums. Do we need dedicated sports museums? Does this marginalise sport from the mainstream museum agenda? How far should all history museums (or science museums or art galleries for that matter) reflect sport? The danger of dedicated sports museums is that it enables other museums to continue to largely ignore sport. And what is the relationship between museums of individual sports and regional, national or international museums of all sports? These are all questions which await consideration. Further, the position of sports museums within the wider museums sector has been relatively unexplored. A PhD research project on this subject with regard to the UK is now underway, funded by the Arts and Humanities Research Council (AHRC) and led by Professor John Hughson, University of Central Lancashire, and myself.

Though the UK was the birthplace of modern sport, the history of the development of sports museums in the UK is as, if not even more, unstudied as the development of sports museums globally. The foundation dates of the UK's major sports museums are notably recent compared with those in the USA, so that while the MCC Museum opened to the public in 1953, the other major museums are of more recent origin, as follows:

- Wimbledon Lawn Tennis Museum – 1977
- National Horseracing Museum – 1983
- British Golf Museum – 1990
- World Rugby Museum – 1996
- River and Rowing Museum – 1998
- Scottish Football Museum – 2000
- National Football Museum – 2001

As I have argued elsewhere, this comparative lateness in the development of the UK's sports museums relates to the perceived lack of value and relevance placed on sport by the wider museums sector, reflecting in turn issues of high and popular culture in museums, and ultimately issues of class (Moore 1997; 2008). Why, for example, was it that the National Soccer Hall of Fame and Museum opened in the USA in 1979 but that the National Football Museum for England, the birthplace of Association Football, opened in 2001?

Hood identified 36 sport-specific museums in the UK, ranging from the national to museums for more minor sports and individual sports clubs. In Phillips' typology they are academic, corporate and community. Hood states that while there is no national sports museum for Britain,

> National museums for sport have been established for most of the key sports; the MCC Museum for cricket; the National Football Museum, Scottish Football Museum and Welsh Football Museum Project for football; the British Golf Museum for golf; the National Horseracing Museum for horseracing; the River & Rowing Museum for rowing; the Museum of Rugby for rugby and Wimbledon Lawn Tennis Museum for tennis. (Hood 2006, 4)

This is questionable on a number of counts. The Wimbledon Lawn Tennis Museum and the MCC Museum at Lord's may be *de facto* national museums for their sports but institutionally are not and do not claim to be, but are rather museums of sporting clubs. The River and Rowing Museum may also *de facto* be the national museum of its sport, but it is also a museum of the River Thames and the history of Henley; and the rugby museum at Twickenham is now rebranded as the World Rugby Museum!

The Hood report identified the major sports without a dedicated museum as athletics and boxing, but there is also no dedicated museum in Britain for the Olympics, despite London being the only city to host the games three times, nor of the Paralympics, despite this originating in the UK. For Rugby League there is, in Phillips' terms, a 'vernacular' rather than an academic or corporate museum, in the basement of the George Hotel in Huddersfield, where the sport was founded. How might we explain these gaps and the narrative of the development of sports museums in the UK? It might be argued that historically sport featured only in museums where it could either be considered as art or reflected the sporting pastimes of the higher social classes, such as hunting and shooting. The works held by the British Sporting Art Trust, established in 1977, reflect both these points to an extent. While cricket is not *per se* an upper-class game, the MCC at Lord's epitomised the upper-class control of the game up to the 1950s, so it is indicative that the first major dedicated sports museum in the UK was the MCC Museum. While there are also other factors at play, the timing of the foundation of the museums of major sports in the UK reflects the social position of the sports, with the museums of the sports controlled and dominated by the higher social classes being formed first, while that for football – the most working-class of these sports, but by far Britain's leading sport – is the most recent.

This point relating to social class is reinforced when we consider those major sports which still do not have museums. Athletics is not a major spectator or participant sport in the UK so its absence is perhaps not a surprise and does not directly relate to this class issue. However, the absence of a museum for rugby league (setting aside the 'vernacular' museum, the Gillette Rugby League Heritage Centre at the George Hotel, Huddersfield) links to this class analysis. Rugby league is a double 'other': it is both working class *and* northern (Russell 2004, 257–62). The Rugby Football League (RFL) has for more than 15 years been exploring the possibility of establishing a museum more akin to that of the other major sports, rather than a collection on show in a hotel. Boxing is also a working-class sport in the UK.

All this demonstrates that museums of sport are a relatively recent phenomenon in the UK, and that sports with a higher social class involvement developed museums first, while those with stronger working-class (and northern) associations developed museums later, or not at all as yet. While popular culture has made significant strides in UK museums since the publication of my book *Museums and Popular Culture* in 1997, sports museums have faced an additional barrier to popular culture, as sport is perceived by many as not a part of culture, but separate and, indeed, perhaps in opposition to it. This perception of sport as *not* culture, though largely unspoken, is a feature of the museum and wider cultural sector in the UK. It is institutionalised at the highest levels in government, where we have the Department for Culture, Media *and* Sport (my italics). As Germaine Greer has argued,

> Football counts as culture just as much as opera does … a Martian social anthropologist would be excused for wondering if the British, or at any rate their elected representatives, have any idea what culture is. If they did, DCMS would have been called Culture (Media and Sport). To list media and sport as co-equal with culture is like referring to food, eggs and chips as separate categories. The government's category mistake leads us all into conceptual quagmires out of which dangerous speculations and asinine pretensions arise like poisonous mists. (Greer 2008)

The current annual budget of the Department for Culture, Media and Sport (DCMS) for museums is over £300 million, but none of this funding is contributed to sports museums.

Given the lack of support from government for even the national sports museums in the UK, the issue of sustainability is vital. As Danilov comments, 'not all sports museums and halls of fame succeed' and, indeed, he lists a significant number of failures. Frost has explored the failure of the Australian Football League Hall of Fame, which has wider resonance (Frost 2005). Dunbar's chapter in this volume is therefore very timely and instructive, in that it demonstrates how a major English football club with a distinguished history and presence in the current Premier League decided not to set up a museum but instead an online archive and community learning and outreach programme. This is a model of sustainability which other football and sporting clubs could follow, as some have opened museums which have subsequently closed and others are currently considering opening museums. Yet, at the time of writing, while the Everton Collection has a secure long-term home in Liverpool Record Office, the sustainability of the project itself, the ongoing interpretation of the collection for the public benefit, is not secured.

Academic analysis of sports museums to date has tended to focus on the issue that they reflect an uncritical, celebratory history: 'sports museums cater to the nostalgia market and have, almost without exception, institutionalised the concept of a "golden age" in virtually every sport. Errors of fact and interpretation persist and myths are perpetuated despite historical research to the contrary ... Jingoism at national and club triumphs abounds' (Vamplew 1998, 270, 272). Further, 'few make connections between sport and the social setting in which it operated' (Johnes and Mason 2003, 120). The concern is that many are delivering an ersatz sports history to their substantial audiences.

There is no doubt that this critique has some justification, at least in terms of some 'corporate' museums. For example, museums at Association Football clubs tend to be income-generating and public-relations vehicles for the club, focusing on success and marginalising difficult and controversial issues. This reflects the funding and governance of these museums. They are part of the football clubs, usually part of the commercial arm, and staff creating the museums may experience censorship or practise self-censorship: 'A major difficulty is the formal and informal pressure that sponsoring bodies can exert on nominally independent institutions' (Vamplew 2004, 187).

However, this point regarding censorship or self-censorship in the 'corporate' sports museums has been assumed rather than studied and proven, with the exception of Vamplew's work on the National Horse Racing Museum. Given that this Museum has now moved to charitable trust status and achieved national registration status with MLA, it is highly unlikely that this accusation can now be made. In addition, many corporate museums employ professionally trained staff who are experts in their sport and in museum practice, and it would not be their intention as far as possible to engage with censorship or self-censorship. This is not to say that this prevents such practices, but that the case for them happening is largely unproven.

Danilov's survey does little to challenge this perception of corporate sports museums as fuelling nostalgia. His work 'describes the hundreds of facilities around the world that honour the outstanding athletes and other sports personnel, trace the history of athletic events, and celebrate the great moments of sport worldwide' (Danilov 2005, 1). Many sports fans 'visit those temples of adulation – the sports museums and halls of fame – to celebrate the history, highlights and stars in various sports and perhaps to relive some precious sports moments they witnessed or remembered from the past' (Danilov 2005, 3). Redmond was the first to consider the 'quasi-religious quality' of 'halls of fame':

> Athletes become 'immortal heroes' as they are 'enshrined' in a sports hall of fame, when 'devoted admirers' gaze at their 'revered figures' or read plaques 'graven in marble', before departing 'often very moved' (or even 'teary-eyed') from the many 'hushed rooms, filled with nostalgia'. This is the jargon of the modern churches of sport in the twentieth century. The Basketball Hall of Fame at Springfield has seventy-six illuminated stained-glass windows, one for each of its immortals. Sunday prayer meetings have been held at the International Swimming Hall of Fame in Florida. (Redmond 1971, 46)

Snyder has explored collective and private nostalgia in the context of sports halls of fame and museums in the USA, concluding that

> the halls of fame and museums selectively preserve and thus create the past that is appropriate for nostalgic feelings … My use of nostalgia is related to, and supplements, the religious model. Indeed collective sport nostalgia extends the concepts of the 'sacred' and 'collective representations' explicated by Durkheim and of 'civil religion' developed by Bellah.
> (Snyder 1991, 237)

This links back to Danilov's (perhaps subconscious) use of the phrase 'temples of adulation'. Indeed, Snyder comments that 'most writers who consider sports hall of fame and museums emphasise the religious parallels of these "shrines"' (Snyder 1991, 228).

Vamplew comments that 'fans of the sport might be upset by the intervention of real history into the fantasy world of nostalgia' (Vamplew 1998, 275), yet this is an untested assumption. How do we know that fans are not prepared to see 'real' history rather than nostalgia? This argument also assumes that nostalgia is a bad thing. Who is to say that fans of a football club in visiting their club's museum want an objective history of their club, rather than a nostalgic wallow in the team's triumphs, or that this is necessarily problematic? As Snyder comments,

> Nostalgia is an important emotion in our society … for many people sport triggers feelings of longing for the past when they had pleasant experiences associated with sport. This reflection is most evident for the middle-aged and elderly, who have had more sport experiences, but perhaps most important, this is a period of their lives when concern about their own mortality is salient in their self-reflections. Consequently for those involved in sport, past or present, sport nostalgia may provide a source of consolation and a means of adjustment to the uncertainties of their lives. (Snyder 1991, 237)

Snyder concludes by quoting Davis as follows: 'Nostalgia re-enchants, if only for a while until the inexorable processes of historical change exhaust that past which offered momentary shelter from a worrisome but finally inexorable future' (Snyder 1991, 238). Nostalgia in the context of sports museums might therefore be performing an important social function, indeed an existential one, helping people to come to terms with their own mortality. Further, a commercial, corporate museum is a private institution and therefore has no responsibility to provide objective history for the public benefit. However, the adoption of the title 'museum' conveys such objectivity in the mind of the visitors and it would therefore be preferable if the term was not used in those contexts, although the lack of protection for the term in the UK means that this cannot be enforced. Yet all museums, and especially sports museums, should not entirely eschew nostalgia, but should find a way to harness its positive aspects.

Vamplew has commented that 'fortunately some museums have gone beyond the conventional boundaries of their sport' and, further, 'is there any reason why sports history exhibitions cannot be good history?' (Vamplew 1998, 272, 278). Popular exhibitions can be based on very thorough curatorial research, drawing on the work of academics. As Johnes and Mason noted in their review of the National Football Museum: 'We only noted one factual error in the text', and 'The NFM is thus taking forward the game's public history and helping it develop a more reflective and informed character that extends beyond nostalgia and an obsession with records and statistics' (Johnes and Mason 2003, 130). However, not all sports museums have the benefit of the independent governance status of, for example, the National Football Museum, which frees it from any direct or perceived pressure to positively reflect its sport.

The remaining three chapters in this section explore this issue in different contexts and from different perspectives. Walton and De Pablo consider how a serious and socially useful museum project at a football club can be devalued and distorted by commercial considerations relating to the issues of ownership of football clubs by transnational business figures. Vamplew considers the form of interpretation at the British Golf Museum and how this relates to wider issues in golf's heritage. Godfrey gives an insider's view of the development of the new Wimbledon Lawn Tennis Museum. These latter two chapters demonstrate the complexities of museum institutions that are run by governing bodies and sports clubs, and how the division between 'academic' and 'corporate' museums is too simplistic. The Wimbledon Lawn Tennis Museum was runner-up for European Museum of the Year in 2008. The chapters offer an interesting comparison, the first written by an academic, the second by a practitioner.

Sports museums are becoming a global phenomenon and sport is beginning to be reflected and interpreted much more widely in the museums sector as a whole. Academic analysis of sports museums, while of intrinsic value, will also greatly assist in the development of sport in museums. This introductory chapter has identified areas for future fruitful research. It has not considered how far there is a connection between the development of sport and the development of museums as aspects of modernism, or if there is any inter-relationship between the impact of postmodernism on both museums and sport, but both these questions are also worthy of further study.

BIBLIOGRAPHY AND REFERENCES

Adair, D, 2004 When the Games Never Cease: The Olympic Museum in Lausanne, Switzerland, in *Sport Tourism: Interrelationships, Impacts and Issues* (eds B W Ritchie and D Adair), Channel View Publications, Clevedon, 46–76

Alegi, P, 2006 The Football Heritage Complex: History, Tourism, and Development in South Africa, *Africa Spectrum* 41 (3), 415–26

Atherton, M, 2008 *The theft of the Jules Rimet Trophy: The Hidden History of the 1966 World Cup in England*, Meyer and Meyer, Germany

Brabazon, T, 2006a *Playing on the Periphery: Sport, Identity and Memory*, Routledge, London

— 2006b Museums and Popular Culture Revisited: Kevin Moore and the Politics of Pop, *Museum Management and Curatorship* 21, 283–301

Brabazon, T, and Mallinder, S, 2006 Popping the museum: the cases of Sheffield and Preston, *Museum and Society*, July 4 (2), 96–112

Danilov, V, 1997 *Hall of Fame Museums: A Reference Guide*, Greenwood Press, Westport, Connecticut

— 2005 *Sports Museums and Halls of Fame Worldwide*, Macfarland and Company, Jefferson, North Carolina, and London

Forslund, P, 2006 'Football is Forever'. The Establishment and Purposes of Football Museums, Masters Dissertation, International Museum Studies, Göteborg University

Frost, M, 2005 The sustainability of sports heritage attractions: lessons from the Australian Football League Hall of Fame, *Journal of Sport Tourism* 10 (4), 295–305

Greer, G, 2008 Football counts as culture just as much as opera does, *The Guardian*, 24 March

Hood, A, 2006 *Sports Heritage Network Mapping Survey: An Overview of Sports Heritage Collections*, Sports Heritage Network, Henley

Huntington-Whiteley, J, 1999 *The Book of British Sporting Heroes*, Richard Holt Books, London

Johnes, M, and Mason, R, 2003 Soccer, public history and the National Football Museum, *Sport in History* 23 (1), 115–31

Kellett, P, and Hede, A, 2008 Developing a sport museum: The case of Tennis Australia and the Tennis Heritage Collection, *Sport Management Review* 11, 92–8

Kohe, G Z, 2010 Civic representations of sport history: the New Zealand Sports Hall of Fame, *Sport in Society* 13, December, 498–515

Moore, K, 1997 *Museums and Popular Culture*, Leicester University Press, Leicester

— 2003a Marketing Sports Museums: Attracting New Audiences? *Revista de Museologia* 22 (2), 29–32

— 2003b The People's Museum of the Peoples Game? The National Football Museum England, *Revista de Museologia* 22 (2), 33–43

— 2004 Attracting new audiences: The National Football Museum, England, in *M: Museums of Mexico and the World*, Volume 2, Mexico City

— 2008 Sports Heritage and the re-imaged city: the National Football Museum, Preston, *International Journal of Cultural Policy* 14 (4), 445–61

— 2009 The National Football Museum, in *Sport in Manchester* (ed D Russell), *Manchester Region History Review* 20, 133–8

— 2012 Foreword, in *Representing the Sporting Past in Museums and Halls of Fame* (ed M G Phillips), Routledge, London, xi–xv

Osmond, G, and Phillips, M G, 2011 Enveloping the past: Sport stamps, visuality and museums, *The International Journal of the History of Sport* 28 (8–9), 1138–55

Phillips, M G, 2010 A historian in the museum: Story spaces and Australia's sporting past, *Australian Historical Studies* 41 (3), 396–408

— 2012a Introduction: Historians in Sport Museums, in *Representing the Sporting Past in Museums and Halls of Fame* (ed M G Phillips), Routledge, London, 1–21

— 2012b *Representing the Sporting Past in Museums and Halls of Fame*, Routledge, London, xi–xv

Phillips, M G, and Tinning, R, 2011 Not just 'a book on the wall': pedagogical work, museums and representing the sporting past, *Sport Education and Society* 16 (1), 51–65

Ramshaw, G, 2010 Living Heritage and the Sports Museum: Athletes, Legacy and the Olympic Hall of Fame and Museum, Canada Olympic Park, *Journal of Sport & Tourism* 15 (1), 45–70

Redmond, G, 1971 A Plethora of Shrines: Sport in the Museum and Hall of Fame, *Quest* 19, 41–8

Russell, D, 2004 *Looking North. Northern England and the National Imagination*, Manchester University Press, Manchester

Salazar, L, 2008 *Fashion V Sport*, V&A Publishing, London

Smith, C, 1999 This sporting nation, *Soundings: a journal of politics and culture* 13, Autumn, 18–34

Snyder, E E, 1991 Sociology of Nostalgia: Sports Halls of Fame and Museums in America, *Sociology of Sport Journal* 8, 228–38

Vamplew, W, 1998 Facts and Artefacts: Sports, Historians and Sports Museums, *Journal of Sport History* 25 (2), 268–79

— 2004 Taking a Gamble or a Racing Certainty: Sports, Museums and Public Sports History, *Journal of Sport History* 31 (2), 177–92

Victoria and Albert Museum, 1992 *Sporting Glory: the Courage exhibition of national trophies at the Victoria and Albert Museum*, Sporting Glory Exhibitions Ltd

Wood, J, 2005 Olympic opportunity: realising the value of sport heritage for tourism in the UK, *Journal of Sport Tourism* 10 (4), 307–21

8

The Everton Collection: Unlocking the Value of a National Football Archive

Max Dunbar

Britain, as the birthplace of many of the world's major sports, has a unique sporting heritage. However, the development of dedicated sports museums and archives in the UK has been comparatively late, in contrast with the situation in, for example, North America (Danilov 2005). Why, for example, was it that the National Soccer Hall of Fame and Museum opened in the USA in 1979 but that the National Football Museum for England, the birthplace of Association Football, opened in 2001? Moore has argued that this relates to the perceived lack of value and relevance placed on sport by the wider museums and archives sector in the UK, reflecting in turn issues of high and popular culture in museums, and ultimately issues of class (Moore 1997; 2008).

While the development of dedicated sports museums in the UK has been comparatively recent, there are now golf, tennis, cricket, horseracing, rugby, rowing and football museums. A number of Premiership football clubs have also opened museums and many other sports clubs have memorabilia displayed within their grounds. Yet our sporting heritage is not just preserved in museums or sporting venues. Sporting archives are held in record offices across the country. From sporting photographs and newspaper reports to match programmes, club publications and official papers, many of these sporting archives remain relatively unexplored. Furthermore, record offices themselves have yet to fully unlock the potential of their sporting archives. While there is a growing literature on sports museums, this is the first known study of a sports archive in a record office (Brabazon 2006a; 2006b; Brabazon and Mallinder 2006; Johnes and Mason 2003; Moore 2003a; 2003b; 2004; 2008; Vamplew 1998; 2004; Wood 2005). Sporting archives have huge potential to inform, inspire and educate a wide range of audiences. This study will assess the value of a football archive – The Everton Collection – not just to football fans but to sports fans, historians, academics, students and schoolchildren.

SPORTING ARCHIVES IN RECORD OFFICES

Record offices are the guardians of local history records and archives. There are around 300 publicly funded archive services across England and Wales that preserve records of both the past and present, making them publicly accessible. From archives of a wide variety of organisations to census records, business directories, old street maps and photographs, these archives have been described as 'the raw material of history' (HM Government 2009, 9).

In 2008 Liverpool Record Office accepted one of the most important long-term deposits in its history: The Everton Collection. National Museums Liverpool (NML) were originally considered as a home for the Collection, but it was felt that Liverpool Record Office would be more appropriate. This can largely be explained by the content of the Collection, as the vast majority of items were archival documents. While NML could have stored and displayed highlights from the Collection, the museum service did not have the staffing or resources to allow full public access to every item, as Liverpool Record Office did. By accepting this major sporting archive, Liverpool Record Office knew it had to deliver something special, beyond the scope of normal record office activities.

A football club archive containing match programmes, tickets, shirts, boots and balls was not a typical collection for a record office to house. Yet Liverpool Record Office recognised the significance of The Everton Collection to the people of Liverpool. Football has always played a major role in the social, political and even economic life of the city, and Liverpool Record Office knew the material in the Collection embodied this. The articles and adverts within the Everton match programmes, for example, offer a unique perspective on Liverpool's social and business history. The same could be said for many other items in the Collection. The Record Office fully understood the value of the Collection as a unique local history resource. The popularity of football in Liverpool also provided an opportunity for Liverpool Record Office to attract new users to its service. It was hoped that the Collection would interest working-class football fans and younger audiences who had never used an archive service before. As Tara Brabazon states, 'Sport has an intense and special commitment and zeal. Recognizing such commitment, football can be an apparatus to welcome non-traditional visitors' (Brabazon 2006b, 291). The case of the National Football Museum confirms this view, as 42 per cent of its visitors were from socio-economic groups C2, D and E, more than twice the average for national museums (Moore 2008, 455). The Everton Collection could therefore help Liverpool Record Office attract non-traditional users to its archive service.

However, there was no prior evidence to prove that a sporting archive would be used significantly by the public as a local history resource or that it would attract new users. This is not to say that other record offices do not hold sporting archives. A search for 'sport' on the National Archive's 'Access to Archives' database produced 120,000 sport-related archives in England and Wales,[1] including Doncaster Rovers publications in Doncaster Archives, Castleford Rugby League programmes at West Yorkshire Archive Service, the Whalley Range Amateur Football Club archive in Manchester Archives and the Ipswich Town Football archive at Suffolk Record Office.[2] In 2008 the National Football Museum negotiated the deposition of the archives of The Football League at Lancashire County Record Office in Preston, the city in which The Football League has had its headquarters for most of its history. In addition, a report commissioned by the Sports Heritage Network (the networking organisation formed by the UK's sports museums and archives) in 2005 found that there was a great deal of sports material in the UK's non-sports museums and archives (Hood 2006).

---

[1] Access to Archives (A2A) is part of the UK archives network and the A2A database contains catalogues describing archives held locally in England and Wales from the 8th century to the present day. See http://www.nationalarchives.gov.uk/a2a/ [13 January 2011].

[2] These were just some examples of catalogued sporting archives. According to the 'Archives for the 21st Century' report, there is currently online access to barely 50 per cent of the descriptions of archives across England and Wales. It seems likely that even more sporting archives exist in public record offices and have yet to be catalogued.

A wealth of sports heritage is clearly housed in record offices but has yet to be fully explored. It could be argued that sport is not considered a worthy subject within the archive community. This view is held in the museum sector, where 'sports heritage and sports museums are still the "other", viewed by the cultural elite as the least valuable part of the museums sector' (Moore 2008, 459). In record offices an emphasis is often placed on family history research and local history. Perhaps a more innovative approach in interpreting and using archives is now required. As stated in the 'Archives for the 21st Century' report, 'the value of archives has not been recognised in the same way as museums and libraries' (HM Government 2009, 11). The following study of The Everton Collection will demonstrate how valuable sporting archives can be for the archive sector. With pressures on record offices to unlock the rich potential of archives, it is hoped that the Collection will now set a precedent for work on other sporting archives.

THE EVERTON COLLECTION: A NATIONAL FOOTBALL ARCHIVE?

The Everton Collection Charitable Trust was established in 2005 to acquire The David France Collection. A lifelong Everton fan, David France spent years collecting Everton memorabilia through private sales and auctions. When he decided to sell his collection, the Trust was formed to prevent it from being broken up at auction. Working in partnership with Liverpool Record Office, the Trust secured funding from the Heritage Lottery Fund (HLF) in 2007 to purchase the David France Collection.[3] To secure the funding, Everton FC gifted the Club's own archive to the Trust. In 2008 The David France Collection was integrated with the Everton FC archive to form The Everton Collection. Independently from Everton FC, the Trust now aims to educate the public in the history and social impact of Everton FC through the acquisition, preservation, maintenance and display of Everton memorabilia.[4]

The Collection is now on long-term deposit at Liverpool Record Office. In June 2008 a Heritage Lottery-funded project, 'If You Know Your History', began.[5] The focus of the project was to catalogue, preserve and promote The Everton Collection to as many different audiences as possible. Within a year the Collection was fully catalogued to archival standards on the archive management system CALM and many fragile items, including early match programmes and photographs, were painstakingly preserved and repackaged in archival materials. The grant funding, totalling £954,000 from the HLF, enabled the appointment of three full-time professional staff to the project for a three-year period.

Despite its name, The Everton Collection is more a football archive than a football collection. The majority of the 18,000 items in the Collection, such as programmes, minute books, photographs and financial records, would be classed as archival material. To complement this archival material the Collection includes a range of objects, such as medals, trophies, shirts, boots and balls. With a run of programmes dating back to 1886 and minute books from 1887 there is no other football archive – or arguably sporting archive – as comprehensive. As a leading football academic wrote in a supportive letter to the Trust in 2007, 'It is an extremely exciting Collection

3   The Trust's other key partners include the National Football Museum, National Museums Liverpool and Everton Football Club.
4   The establishment of the Trust independent of Everton FC guaranteed that the Collection remained available to the public in the long term, whatever developments in the ownership of the club may occur in the future.
5   'If You Know Your History' is a line taken from a chant regularly sung by Everton fans at Goodison Park.

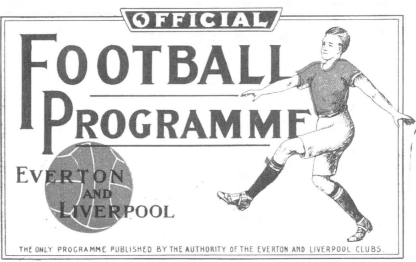

FIG 8.1. MATCH PROGRAMME: EVERTON V TOTTENHAM HOTSPUR AT GOODISON PARK AND LIVERPOOL RESERVES V BURY RESERVES AT ANFIELD, 21 OCTOBER 1933.

and potentially the most significant of its type in Britain. Its value as a resource to historians of sport is indisputable.'[6]

Arguably the most important items in the Collection are the club's official minute books. A complete run of 29 volumes from 1886 to 1964, the books contain the minutes from the meetings of the club's early management committees and later boards of directors. Every official decision taken by the club over a 78-year period is recorded in these volumes. As a primary source, these volumes provide a unique perspective on England's football history, with insightful detail on subjects such as the founding of the Football League (1888), the impact of war on football and the everyday struggles of running a top-flight football club. The volumes also provide valuable information for local historians, with first-hand accounts of the 'Anfield Split' which led to the creation of Liverpool FC and information on local players, officials, businesses and other local clubs.[7] The minute books offer a rare first-hand account of English footballing history, along with an insight into the social, political and economic history of Liverpool.

The 10,000 match programmes in the Collection are also an invaluable resource (Fig 8.1). With 4000 away match programmes, the Collection holds programmes from almost every English football league club. The earliest programme is from 1886 (Everton v Astley Bridge, 4 September 1886) and there are over 400 extremely rare and valuable pre-World War I programmes, including the oldest-known programmes for Manchester United (15 April 1889), Aston Villa (24 March 1888) and Celtic (5 April 1890). With a complete run of post-war programmes, it is estimated that the Collection contains 90 per cent of all Everton programmes issued, which equates to over 250,000 pages. This staggering week-by-week anthology has been described as 'the most complete compilation of archival material for any football club in the world' (France 2008, 55).

Along with the minute books and match programmes, other archival material includes original Goodison Park Gate Receipt books, showing precise match attendance figures from the 1900s, and the club's Cashbooks, revealing how the club was financially managed in the 1890s. Correspondence between directors, players and other clubs demonstrate how relationships within the game have changed throughout the 20th century and players' contracts from the 1890s to 1970s offer a valuable resource to examine trends in players' wages. Over 1500 photographs of teams, players, directors and supporters help bring the Collection to life, as do the many items collected by fans, including 1250 cigarette and trading cards, 300 postcards and hundreds of posters, autographs, dinner menus and prints.

Yet the Collection is more than just an archive. A collection of objects, including over 200 medals and trophies, complement the paper-based material. Highlights include FA Cup, League Championship and European trophies, along with medals from legendary players such as 'Dixie' Dean, Alan Ball and Brian Labone. The Collection also holds shirts, shorts, boots and balls, many worn and used by Everton players. Next to these iconic pieces of memorabilia are everyday

---

[6] Leading scholars, heritage specialists and politicians wrote letters to the Trust supporting the HLF bid, expressing enthusiasm for the Collection and an understanding of its historical significance.

[7] The Anfield Split happened in 1892. Between 1884 and 1892, Everton FC played at Anfield, now the famous home of Liverpool FC. The club rented the ground from a local politician and businessman, John Houlding. When Houlding requested an increase in rent the Everton Committee were split over a decision. Ultimately the Committee refused to pay a higher rent and so left Anfield for a new ground, their current home, Goodison Park. On the surface the Anfield Split was a rental dispute. However, under the surface there were deep political, moral and social disagreements between members of the club.

items such as toys, mugs, scarves and even beer mats, all Everton-related and all collected by fans. Presentation gifts from other clubs include models of Japanese geisha girls, Dutch windmills, a Bavarian bear and a Saudi Arabian aeroplane.[8] The memorabilia in the Collection complements the archival material, making The Everton Collection an outstanding and perhaps unparalleled collection on the history of a single English football club.

Despite the obvious links to Everton FC, the Collection should be considered a national football archive. The history and records of Everton FC and its players reflect the shared experiences of all top-flight English football clubs and players over the past 130 years. With 4000 away match programmes, as noted above, the Collection holds material from almost every league club in the country. Furthermore, the histories of other clubs and players can be explored in detail through the minute books, letters, contracts, photographs and other ephemera in the Collection. How, then, is such a valuable national football archive made publicly accessible?

Making the Collection Accessible

The Everton Collection is unique in the sense that it is a major football collection owned by an independent charitable trust and housed in a local authority record office. There was no specific target audience in mind when the Collection was first acquired. The Trust simply wanted to make the Collection available to as many people as possible. Had Everton FC owned the Collection it is likely that a commercial emphasis would have been placed upon it, with the main target audience being Everton fans. While the Trust is a fundraising charity and does generate income from the Collection, it recognises the historical and educational significance of the Collection for audiences other than Evertonians. The Trust had, therefore, always set the ambitious target of reaching as many audiences as possible.

An audience development plan was commissioned by the Trust in 2007 to explore the potential of the Collection. A series of focus groups was arranged to consult potential users of the Collection and to obtain ideas of how it may be used in the future. Five group meetings were held which included a selection of different audiences, ranging from Record Office users and family historians to Everton fans and young people. All groups showed considerable interest in the Collection and considered it to be of great historical importance to the city. A similar consultation process was undertaken with education sector professionals to consider the learning potential of the Collection. In addition, an online questionnaire was placed on Everton, Manchester United, Liverpool and Arsenal fans' websites. From all this research an action plan was drawn up identifying specific audience groups that were interested or potentially interested in the Collection. Groups included family historians, local historians, football historians and football finance academics. Art and design students were also included owing to the variety of adverts and graphics shown in the match programmes. Young people and the education sector were considered key target groups, as were Everton fans and football fans in general. This audience development plan made it clear that the Collection should be seen, used and experienced by a whole range of audiences, not just Everton fans.

When the Collection first arrived at Liverpool Record Office there was a genuine concern

---

8   Everton, like most top football clubs, are often presented with gifts on overseas tours or to commemorate important events or matches.

that staff would be overwhelmed with Everton fans desperate to see the Collection. However, the Record Office was not a museum and had no permanent exhibition area. How could all these fans access the Collection? And, aside from the Everton fans, how could other audiences access the Collection? Football historians were keen to gain access to the minute books and historians of other clubs were eager to search the programmes and other ephemera for information on their own club histories. The vast number of local people referred to or included in documents within the Collection was identified as a valuable source of reference for local historians and family researchers. How could all this information be easily accessed? The young people consulted in the focus groups were clearly interested in football history, especially the memorabilia, but admitted that it was unlikely that they would visit the Record Office or a museum. Where else, then, could they see the memorabilia? Teachers also recognised the huge potential in using the Collection to inspire and educate children, so how could this potential be realised? To unlock the historical, educational and inspirational value of the Collection and reach as many audiences as possible, three key areas were developed: an exhibition, a website and a learning programme for schools.

The 'Everlution' Exhibition

The exhibition 'Everlution: The Everton Collection' opened in September 2009 at Liverpool Central Library, where Liverpool Record Office is based. Significant anticipation had built up among Everton fans prior to the opening, as the Collection had always received a healthy amount of publicity from local press, the club and fans' websites. David France had also published a number of books about his collection, which meant that many Everton fans were already familiar with it. However, to maximise the full value of the Collection, the exhibition could not just be for these fans. The audience research suggested that the exhibition also needed to appeal to social historians, families, young people and all sports enthusiasts (Fig 8.2). Unlike many football club museums, this exhibition needed to be for more than just the fans.

The content and design of the exhibition was therefore carefully planned to appeal to a range of different audiences. The overall aim of the exhibition was to tell the story of Everton FC within the broader history of English football. The concept that Everton and English football had 'evolved' over the years prompted the aptly named exhibition title, 'Everlution'. Six exhibition themes were chosen: 'Origins', which focused on the club's early years; 'Anfield & Goodison', which explored Everton's early grounds; 'Players', which examined how the life of a footballer has changed; 'Club Management', which focused on the changes in running a top football club; 'Fans', which explored how supporters' experiences have evolved; and 'The Trophy Room', which highlighted Everton's honours. As the majority of visitors would be Everton fans the exhibition needed to include the club's successes (as well as failures) and great players, and so included images of memorabilia of star players in a 'changing room' setting. A 'trophy room' was also built, which contained trophies and players' medals and international caps. These celebratory 'hall of fame' features were considered necessary to satisfy the expectations of Everton fans. However, by creating these areas of 'fan worship', a 'hall of fame' atmosphere was contained. It was felt an exhibition that focused solely on Everton's achievements would have deterred most other audiences and would have been a pallid, partial and subjective interpretation of the club's history.

To appeal to sports historians and other fans, the exhibition drew on the shared histories and experiences of other football clubs and players. The exhibition explored many of the financial and managerial challenges faced by the club, in the knowledge that Everton's experiences mirrored

FIG 8.2. SCHOOLCHILDREN VISITING THE 'EVERLUTION' EXHIBITION.

those of many other football clubs. Likewise, players have always shared similar experiences regardless of the club for which they played. From the maximum wage law and retain-and-transfer system to contractual demands and changes in training, equipment and technology, the exhibition showed how life has changed for all footballers, not just Everton players.

While this approach would appeal to sports fans and historians it was also important to focus on the interests of non-sports enthusiasts. Within the exhibition there was an emphasis on wider social history. For example, in the 1880s new Liverpool laws gave workers a half-day holiday on Saturday afternoons. The impact of these laws was explored within the 'Origins' theme. Likewise, the 'Anfield & Goodison' theme provided detailed biographies on local politicians John Houlding and George Mahon and explored the influence of the local temperance movement on the Anfield Split. With 19th-century maps of Liverpool and articles from local newspapers on display, an emphasis on local history and local politics ran throughout the exhibition.

When writing exhibition text, young audiences and families were also considered. Short sentences, basic vocabulary and child-friendly 'Did You Know?' facts were used. Visitors entered the exhibition through a players' tunnel which complemented the players' changing room and trophy room. A 'football stand' set was also built where families could sit on original Goodison Park seats and watch an exhibition video. An interactive players' spinner was created, allowing children to spin images of players and compare styles in kits and haircuts. An All Time XI interactive game was also built so that fans could create their greatest ever Everton team line-up. With simple exhibition text, installations and interactives, the exhibition thus targeted family audiences.

The exhibition was staged in the impressive Picton Reading Room in Liverpool Central

FIG 8.3. 'EVERLUTION: THE EVERTON COLLECTION', EXHIBITION IN LIVERPOOL CENTRAL LIBRARY'S PICTON READING ROOM, SEPTEMBER 2009–APRIL 2010.

Library (Fig 8.3). Holding an exhibition in such a vast space proved challenging, particularly as the majority of displayed items were small paper-based documents. With bespoke exhibition structures installed in the room, the overall design of the exhibition ensured that the items were not lost in the space. However, with more than 18,000 items in the Collection and display cases to show just 1 per cent of this, there was an issue of what to display. In 1994 Nick Hornby wrote 'a couple of old medals, a few international caps and a pile of old programmes – the staple of football collections – hardly capture the essence of the game' (Hornby 1994, 44). The items selected for display were chosen to capture the essence, not of the game, but of Everton's and the city of Liverpool's heritage. With just under 200 items on show, such a relatively small amount of material embodied a wealth of footballing stories and emotions. Displayed items included early minute books with revelations about the Anfield Split, the oldest-known Everton team photograph from 1881, a player's contract from the 1890s and a training book from the 1930s. Contextualising these archival documents within broader social history displays brought them to life, particularly when displayed alongside iconic memorabilia such as 'Dixie' Dean's medals, Alan Ball's white boots and the first-ever League Championship medal from 1890.[9]

9   The first ever League Championship medals were presented to Everton players in 1890 by their own club. At that time the Football League did not present medals to Championship-winning sides. Of particular note for many Everton and Liverpool fans is the liver bird design in the centre of this medal. The liver bird, now a symbol strongly linked with Liverpool FC, was used in 1890 as it was (and still is) the symbol of Everton's home city, Liverpool. Liverpool FC was formed two years later.

The displayed items supported and complemented the exhibition themes, yet there was always a concern that something might have been missed. As Tara Brabazon states, 'In understanding popular culture, fans know more than the academics, journalists and museum curators ... the popular cultural past is owned by those who live it: it is not squeezed behind glass' (Brabazon 2006b, 285–6). However, most displayed items were extremely rare and as such were significant historical pieces in their own right. In this sense, the exhibition was as much about showcasing the treasures of the Collection as it was about interpreting the history of Everton and English football.

A number of events and activities were held alongside the exhibition. Former Everton players, including Graeme Sharp, Derek Temple and Duncan McKenzie, held question-and-answer sessions, while football historian Peter Lupson gave a series of talks on the shared histories of Everton and Liverpool FC (Lupson 2008). Football poetry sessions were held for schools in the exhibition's football stand and family exhibition tours were given during the school holidays. These events added further weight to the exhibition themes, encouraging debate and discussion among fans, historians and schoolchildren.

While a range of audiences experienced the exhibition in Liverpool Central Library, taking the exhibition to other venues ensured that even more audiences would see The Everton Collection. When the main exhibition closed in April 2010 a smaller travelling exhibition toured Liverpool venues. From the Metquarter shopping arcade in the city centre to Liverpool Anglican Cathedral, the travelling exhibition aimed to reach audiences that were not traditionally museum-goers. Subsequently the exhibition was installed in the 'Museum of Museums', a visitor attraction at the Trafford Centre shopping mall in Greater Manchester. Taking the exhibition out of Liverpool meant an even wider audience could be engaged.

The Online Collection

Audience research suggested that online access to The Everton Collection was essential, as it was not possible to display the entire Collection, with its hundreds of thousands of pages in programmes, minute books and other records, in an exhibition or museum. Liverpool Record Office does offer a research service for the public to access its archives, but with such a vast amount of information in the Collection researchers and fans required a more effective and immediate means of accessing material. As stated in the 'Archives for the 21st Century' report, 'individuals increasingly expect information to be accessible online as a right, not a privilege' (HM Government 2009, 4).

As with the exhibition, it was clear that most visitors to an Everton Collection website would be Everton fans. With so many fans' sites already online it was important that the Collection website stood out as something unique. But there had to be a balance between a website Everton fans would want to use and a professional heritage website for researchers. The site could not be treated like another fans' forum, nor could it appear as a specialist heritage site solely for academic researchers. In addition, the site needed to appeal to all football fans, and so it could not appear too Everton-centric. Researchers, academics and students would want to access the site so it had to distance itself from the look and feel of other football-themed websites. Furthermore, the site needed to attract younger users. In summary, the new Everton Collection website had to be a sports heritage website that appealed to sports fans, historians, academics and young audiences.

Given this remit, decisions regarding the material to be shown online were difficult. An

Everton fan might only be interested in viewing memorabilia of a popular recent player such as Duncan Ferguson, but a sports historian might want to access all the club's financial records. Audience research indicated that the minute books, programmes, medals and photographs were of particular interest to all targeted groups. As such, this material was classed as a priority for the website. Using an external digitisation company, every page of every minute book (over 10,000 pages) was digitised for the site, as was every pre-war programme, letter, medal and trophy. Other material, such as photographs, tickets, collectors' cards and postcards, was selected based on its significance in Everton's history. For example, photographs of prominent players were prioritised over less famous faces. In total, more than 30,000 images of material in the Collection were created for the website.

Through a heritage-based web design company a new Everton Collection website was developed: www.evertoncollection.org.uk. The main aim of the site was to encourage users to search and browse the 18,000 items in the Collection and discover the thousands of images noted above. Using the catalogued data from Liverpool Record Office, a fully searchable online catalogue was created which, in order not to appear complex and uninspiring, was accessible in various ways. A specific 'Collection' page was produced with eight distinct themes to explore: 'Players & Teams', 'Match Archive', 'Minute Books', 'Photographs', 'Publications', 'Kit', 'Fans' Memorabilia' and 'Club'. This page directs users to specific types of material and also encourages further exploration of the Collection. It was felt that this approach would be particularly favoured by Everton fans who perhaps needed some direction in browsing through their club's heritage. Simple and advanced search tools were placed in the header of every page. For users researching a specific player, team or subject, these were vital. For other football fans an 'Other Clubs' page was developed, listing over 400 British, European and international sides: clicking on a particular club would produce every item in the Collection that related to that specific club. Similarly, every Everton player on record and every Everton match played were listed in a 'Players' and 'Matches' page. These lists tempted users, especially fans, to click on a particular name or event to see what related material the Collection held. Sport statisticians could spend hours clicking on these pages.

Yet the greatest achievement of the online collection was the minute books. The digitised pages were fully transcribed to allow users to immediately access information in the minute books by keyword searches, instead of trawling through pages of minutes for a specific name, team or subject. Over 70 years of minutes documenting the development of Everton FC were thus instantly accessible to the world, forming a major new resource for historians, researchers and academics.

While the online collection formed a major part of the website, other features were developed to attract younger and diverse audiences. A series of online exhibitions were created, covering topics such as the life of 'Dixie' Dean and football fashions. Interactive features were produced, including 'Storyteller', which allowed users to submit their own illustrated Everton stories. For those conducting research or simply overwhelmed by the amount of material, a 'My Collection' feature was created, allowing users to build up and save their own collections. A group of volunteers working at Liverpool Record Office had also interviewed a range of Everton fans, from a 100-year-old supporter to the grandson of 'Dixie' Dean. These oral history recordings were added to the website for users to listen to. The overall feel of the site, with bright colours, clear text and easy-to-navigate pages, also aimed to attract younger, diverse audiences.

The Everton Collection website has set new standards for online sporting archives and online archives in general. The site now demonstrates how sports heritage can be presented online for a broad range of users, from serious academics and historians to sports fans and younger audiences.

The Collection in Schools

The potential to use The Everton Collection as a learning resource in schools was identified at an early stage. The Collection's content was not only relevant to the subjects taught in schools but also had the potential to inspire schoolchildren like no other resource could. Football is a topic that could stimulate challenging students, particularly young boys. Furthermore, football is a topic all children could relate to, particularly in a city with two major Premiership clubs. A dedicated Learning Officer was therefore appointed to use material in the Collection to develop school learning resources. A series of focus groups were held with teachers to determine how the Collection could be used by schools. From these three key areas of activity were developed: online learning resources, loan boxes and school outreach sessions.

Initially there were plans to create a teacher's pack showing images and information from the Collection. However, it was decided that these packs were outdated and rarely used by teachers. Instead a series of online learning resources was developed. Specifically designed for interactive whiteboards in school classrooms, these resources were available for teachers to download from The Everton Collection website. Using original source material from the Collection, 11 online learning resources were produced, each one making specific links to the National Curriculum. These resources included a 'football journalism' resource, where pupils compare football newspaper reports from the 19th century with those from today, and 'The World Cup 1966' resource, which uses photographs, programmes, tickets and oral history recordings to study British society in the 1960s. The English and Literacy resources included 'Football Advertising', where pupils explore persuasive texts through football kit adverts in match programmes, and 'Performance Poetry', which helps pupils write and perform their own football poem.

School loan boxes and outreach sessions also linked the Collection to the National Curriculum. A handling collection was sourced with replica objects including shirts, boots, balls, rosettes and programmes. Lesson plans were also produced, suggesting ways in which teachers could use these items in the classroom. The handling collection and lesson plans were sent out to schools in loan boxes for two weeks at a time, so that teachers could use material with different pupils in different lessons. The Collection's Learning Officer also delivered outreach sessions in schools. The handling collection was used in these sessions to prompt discussion and debate (Fig 8.4). Pupils were asked to compare old and new football equipment and would study maps and adverts in researching the history of their local area. For most pupils, the highlight of these sessions was dressing up as the legendary 1920s Everton striker 'Dixie' Dean. As with the online resources, all outreach sessions and loan box activities linked material from the Collection with the National Curriculum. By making these links with the National Curriculum, The Everton Collection was no longer just a football archive; it had become a valuable school learning resource.

Reaction to the Collection

The Everton Collection has the potential to reach a wide range of audiences. With no museum or permanent display area the challenge was to reach not just Everton fans but sports fans in general. The material within the Collection also potentially offered a unique resource for

FIG 8.4. LEARNING SESSION USING MATERIAL FROM THE EVERTON COLLECTION.

researchers, historians, students and schools. Through a major exhibition, website and schools learning programme it was hoped that Everton's sporting heritage would inform, educate and inspire all these audiences. To what extent was this achieved?

'Everlution: The Everton Collection' exhibition ran for seven months in Liverpool Central Library. The exhibition received over 30,000 visitors, making it the most popular exhibition ever staged in the Library.[10] As expected, twice as many exhibition visitors were men as women. Everton fans were clearly delighted with the exhibition, with many emotionally moved by the displays. 'Emotionally tear-jerking', wrote one fan, while another wrote 'Awe inspiring and emotional … brought a tear to my eye'. Other football fans who visited and responded positively to the exhibition included fans of top clubs (such as Manchester United, Arsenal and Chelsea), of smaller clubs (such as Wycombe Wanderers, Gillingham, Queen of the South and Charlton Athletic) and also many from Europe (including fans of FC Metz, Ajax, Napoli and Inter Milan). As one Chelsea fan wrote, 'A collection that is interesting even to non-Evertonians'. Yet the majority of these 'other' fans were Liverpool supporters. Despite the bitter rivalry between Liverpool and Everton fans, this was expected owing to the shared histories of the two clubs and

10 A visitor counter was used in the Players' Tunnel entrance of the exhibition. To collect valuable exhibition data visitors were encouraged to complete surveys and comment sheets throughout the duration of the exhibition.

the overall popularity of football in the city. Aside from the fact that the Anfield stadium has been the home ground of both Everton FC and Liverpool FC, both clubs also issued joint match programmes. Between 1904 and 1935 the two clubs shared more than 1100 programmes, with every front cover stating, 'Only Programme issued by Authority of the Everton and Liverpool Clubs' (an example from the 1933/34 season is illustrated in Fig 8.1). As one visitor wrote, 'I'm a Liverpool supporter but it is great to see as a lover of football history'. There was a general – though unproven – consensus that the exhibition educated visitors about Liverpool's past as much as it did Everton's, and linked this to the wider social history of the city. As one exhibition visitor wrote, 'An excellent cross-section of exhibits with an interesting historical perspective – offering the opportunity to broaden people's horizons on the history of the region and contrast between the past and present day conditions for society'.

To analyse the impact of the website, various data have been captured providing information on who is accessing the site and what they are looking at. In just over one year the website received 5.3 million hits, with 67,000 individual visitors looking at 1.2 million pages. By comparing the number of visits to the website with the number of visitors it is clear that these users are regular ones. Users from all over the world have visited the site. The majority come from European countries, followed by Australasia and the Americas, but the site is also accessed in more remote countries, including Ghana, Bermuda, Vietnam and Yemen. Almost a quarter of all users spend more than five minutes looking at the site, with 12 per cent of users spending more than quarter of an hour. This is a significant length of time for website usage, which suggests that visitors to the site are exploring the Collection in detail. Users are accessing the site to search for specific players, tournaments and other clubs. For example, in the first three months some of the top searches were 'Dixie Dean', 'Liverpool County FA Cup' and 'West Bromwich Albion'. By far the most popular type of material viewed is the club minute books, followed by home match programmes, FA Cup programmes and photographs. Users are therefore accessing the site from all over the world for significant lengths of time. Many of the top searches are 'Everton-centric', suggesting that Everton fans are, as expected, the main users. However, searches for specific football terms and other teams suggest fans of other clubs are also using the site. The overwhelming interest in the minute books, the repeated visits and length of time spent on the site also suggests that historians and researchers are accessing the online material – and are doing so in great detail.

The Collection's school learning programme was launched in September 2009. In its first year more than 5000 school children accessed the Collection through online learning resources, loan boxes or outreach sessions. By the end of the 2009/10 school year the 11 online learning resources had been downloaded 6599 times. This exceeded expectations by some margin and suggested the Collection was being used by schools across the country, not just in Liverpool. The loan boxes were used by schools throughout the year and reached 1843 pupils. All schools found the boxes useful; as one headteacher wrote, 'Teachers commented that the loan box brought life to local history and gave energy to speaking and listening. It was refreshing to see the children so enthusiastic (even the Liverpool fans) and they remained focused and on task for the whole of the session.' Likewise, the outreach sessions helped bring the Collection to life in the classroom. Over 2100 pupils participated in an Everton Collection session in 2009/10, with the vast majority finding the experience both fun and educational. As a 10-year-old pupil wrote, 'I enjoyed learning about football in the Victorian times. I think getting to feel all the objects was really fun.' The Everton Collection is now more than just a national football archive – it has become a valuable national learning resource that genuinely interests and inspires young audiences.

In housing the Collection, Liverpool Record Office hoped to attract new users to its service. The Collection certainly raised the profile of the Record Office through articles in the local press, match programmes and fans' websites. However, any expectations the Record Office had of attracting new users were dashed when the online Collection went live. Before the website was launched fans and researchers regularly requested access to material in the Collection. For example, the programmes and minute books proved an essential source of information for Peter Lupson when writing his book on the linked history of Liverpool FC and Everton FC (Lupson 2008). However, as soon as material such as the early programmes and minute books were available to view online, the number of viewing requests significantly dropped. Since the website went live in September 2009 only a handful of requests have been made to view the Collection at Liverpool Record Office. While this proves that the website is being used for research purposes it reflects a growing concern in the archive sector – that numbers of record office users will inevitably fall as more archives become accessible online. The Everton Collection website allows free, instant access to archival material, thus fulfilling the needs of fans, historians, researchers and all the other groups Liverpool Record Office was so keen to attract. As a result, the Record Office is now exploring further ways to use the Collection to attract new users. There is an emphasis on delivering more community projects, involving taking the Collection out to deprived communities to inspire and educate disadvantaged groups. At the same time, The Everton Collection Charitable Trust and the Record Office are working with other partners, such as the National Museums Liverpool, the National Football Museum and Everton FC, in creating new Everton Collection displays.[11]

Unlike most major sporting collections, The Everton Collection is housed in a record office, not a dedicated sports museum. There are no permanent displays showcasing the Collection; instead, material is stored in conservation boxes alongside the Liverpool city archives. Yet, over the past two years to January 2011, the Collection has reached almost 200,000 people, many of whom would have never experienced the heritage of Everton football club.[12] Through an exhibition, website and learning programme the Collection has shown how a sporting archive can be used to reach a wide range of audiences. An exhibition that glorified Everton's history in some areas while exploring the evolution of British football in others appealed to all sports fans. A sports heritage website for football fans and historians alike ensured that Everton's heritage could be easily accessed anywhere in the world. In schools across the country teachers have been using The Everton Collection in their classrooms, with pupils dressing up as 'Dixie' Dean while also studying local history.

The exhibition, website and learning programme have been a major success because sport is so integral to our everyday lives. Our sporting past can inspire, educate and inform like no other topic can. Football – and sport in general – is not just a part of life, it *is* life, embedding itself into our daily conversations, clothing, meals and metaphors (Brabazon 2006b, 285). The popularity of football in this country, particularly in Liverpool, ensured that there would always be a captive audience for The Everton Collection. Yet through some creative and innovative thought the Collection reached other audiences, all of whom could relate to football in one way

---

[11] At the time of writing, Everton FC was planning to open a museum at Goodison Park. Whilst many highlights of the Collection would be displayed in the Museum, the Collection would still be housed at Liverpool Record Office.

[12] Figures taken from HLF project evaluation report (January 2011) by heritage consultant Janice Tullock.

or another. The value of The Everton Collection lies not just in its rare archives and memorabilia but in its popular appeal to a diverse range of audiences. As such, it is to be hoped that more record offices will use their sporting archives to attract new users, and that this study will inspire other sports clubs, not just football clubs, to explore their own archives. As The Everton Collection has demonstrated, clubs do not always need a dedicated museum to promote their heritage. In setting the standard for other sporting archives it is hoped that The Everton Collection will now prompt further debate on the development of sporting collections in record offices and clubs across the country.

BIBLIOGRAPHY AND REFERENCES

Brabazon, T, 2006a *Playing on the Periphery: Sport, Identity and Memory*, Routledge, London

— 2006b Museums and Popular Culture Revisited: Kevin Moore and the Politics of Pop, *Museum Management and Curatorship* 21, 283–301

Brabazon, T, and Mallinder, S, 2006 Popping the museum: the cases of Sheffield and Preston, *Museum and Society* 4 (2), 96–112

Danilov, V, 2005 *Sports Museums and Halls of Fame Worldwide*, Macfarland and Company, Jefferson, North Carolina, and London

France, D, 2008 *Dr Everton's Magnificent Obsession, The David France Collection*, Trinity Mirror Sport Media, Liverpool

France, D, and Prentice, D, 2006 *Everton Treasures, The David France Collection*, Skript, Essex

HM Government, 2009 *Archives for the 21st Century*, Office of Public Sector Information, Surrey

Hood, A, 2006 *Sports Heritage Network Mapping Survey: An Overview of Sports Heritage Collections*, Commissioned by Sports Heritage Network

Hornby, N, 1994 The Arsenal Story, in *Museums in Britain* (ed M Wade), McMillan, Macclesfield, 43–4

Johnes, M, and Mason, R, 2003 Soccer, public history and the National Football Museum, *Sport in History* 23 (1), 115–31

Lupson, P, 2008 *Across the Park, Everton FC & Liverpool FC, Common Ground*, Trinity Mirror Sport Media, Liverpool

Moore, K, 1997 *Museums and Popular Culture*, Leicester University Press, Leicester

— 2003a Marketing Sports Museums: Attracting New Audiences?, *Revista de Museologia* 22 (2), 29–32

— 2003b The People's Museum of the Peoples Game? The National Football Museum England, *Revista de Museologia* 22 (2), 33–43

— 2004 Attracting new audiences: The National Football Museum, England, in *M: Museums of Mexico and the World*, Volume 2, Mexico City

— 2008 Sports Heritage and the re-imaged city: the National Football Museum, Preston, *International Journal of Cultural Policy* 14 (4), 445–61

Vamplew, W, 1998 Facts and Artefacts: Sports, Historians and Sports Museums, *Journal of Sport History* 25 (2), 268–79

— 2004 Taking a Gamble or a Racing Certainty: Sports, Museums and Public Sports History, *Journal of Sport History* 31 (2), 177–92

Wood, J, 2005 Olympic opportunity: realising the value of sport heritage for tourism in the UK, *Journal of Sport Tourism* 10 (4), 307–21

9

Culture, Commerce, Capitalism and Commemoration: Dmitri Piterman and the Alavés Football Museum

SANTIAGO DE PABLO AND JOHN K WALTON

This chapter is a case study of the tensions between international business, a powerful entrepreneurial drive and a dominating personality, and an Association football club which represents civic pride and provincial and regional identity, together with the aspirations to on-field success and glory of an extensive popular membership. It connects with debates about globalisation and identities, the commercialisation of sport and the exploitation of the club as brand and marketing tool and the multiple roles of sport in the economies and polities of advanced capitalist societies (Guilianotti and Robertson 2009). It has two central themes: the shifting and contested relationships between external capital on the one hand and local loyalty and sense of identity on the other, in the intensively commercial environment of professional football; and the relationships between clubs, management, fans and local and regional economic and political actors in the articulation and expression of cultures of pride, commemoration and celebration through representations of identity by way of history and heritage. The first has yet to attract sustained attention from academics, although some excellent investigative journalism has illuminated its hidden workings and disreputable corners (Conn 2005). The second intersects with an established area of debate on the applicability of the concept of topophilia, defined here as emotional attachment to places and their associations, to sporting arenas. This has particular force when clubs are moving to new locations or transforming existing stadiums, processes which require careful emotional as well as economic management (Bale 1993; Vamplew *et al* 1998). But this chapter adopts a different angle of approach, examining the role of the football museum as an expression of loyalty to and identification with a club, a celebration of its past, and, inevitably, a marketing opportunity. This reflects the importance of the stadium as '"a tourist place", a heritage site or a museum, where visitors … connect with the club's history and traditions through touring the ground or looking at material artefacts of the past' (Taylor 2008, 352). The setting is Spanish, but the contextual literature deals largely with England, especially the English Premier League.

The case study focuses on the conflicts surrounding the development of a football museum at the Mendizorroza football stadium of Club Deportivo Alavés in Vitoria, the administrative capital of the Basque Country of northern Spain, when the club's new owner Dmitri Piterman tried to appropriate the museum's designated space to display his collection of Dalí reproductions. At the time, Alavés had just enjoyed its most successful period on the pitch, becoming internationally visible through an exciting 5–4 defeat against Liverpool in Dortmund in the

2001 UEFA Cup Final. The museum episode was a part of wider conflicts about the running of the club and the intentions of the owner which acquired political resonance through the involvement of municipal and provincial government and provincial financial institutions. Some details are specific to a particular culture and political system, but the story contributes to the understanding of widespread phenomena in football in the new millennium. It illuminates the tensions that arise when external, itinerant capital and entrepreneurs, increasingly international or transnational, buy into established football clubs for profit-seeking and reputation-enhancing motives, without necessarily being aware of, or even interested in, the history and nature of the organisation or its relationship with its support base.

This can be represented as a working-out of tensions between the local and the globalising, between a social enterprise whose goals are civic pride, success and indeed glory on the field, and the sporting representation of a collective identity, and a commercial enterprise whose aim is profit maximisation (and in some cases the creation or reinforcement of a global brand which may be intended to transcend the foundational local loyalties) (Giulianotti and Robertson 2004). For the former, commercial success is a means to sporting glory; for the latter, profit may be an end in itself, and civic pride and supporter loyalty are assets to be exploited for that purpose. This is a strong statement of the case: individual owners may be, or become, attached to 'their' clubs, and may also be more interested in reputation through glory than in direct commercial returns. But the basic dichotomy holds good.

Football Clubs and Globalisation

The involvement of international entrepreneurs and businesses in professional football clubs originates in the late 20th century. Hitherto, the relationships between clubs and businesses had generally been rooted in the localities in question. Bob Lord, 'the Khrushchev of Burnley … presiding over the club and his butchery business from his office at his Lowerhouse meat factory' (Bagchi 2009), is often regarded in England as the epitome of the local business magnate who also ran his town's football club. The era of the local business bestriding provincial urban politics was in sharp decline by the 1970s, as was that of the successful English club rooted in a small or medium-sized industrial town. Lord was one of the last representatives of this culture in the top flight (ibid).

Lord gave up the chairmanship of Burnley in 1979 and died in 1981, as his club fell into the lower divisions. In the following year the Football Association removed the historic limit of 7.5 per cent on the level of dividend football club shareholders could receive, and a year later Tottenham Hotspur became the first club to be floated on the London Stock Exchange. These were not merely symbolic juxtapositions: they marked an incipient transition to football as profit-maximising 'big business', with a new breed of directors who saw clubs primarily *as* businesses, with their older functions as focus of supporter loyalty and emblem of civic pride increasingly subject to commercial exploitation and relegated to a subordinate role (Taylor 2008, 342; King 1998). This in turn reinforced existing trends towards the monopolisation of playing success into a few big city clubs, opening the way to the secession of the Premier League in 1992 and the disproportionate concentration of television revenues into the coffers of a prosperous elite. This attracted internationally mobile capital in search of opportunities for profit and display, although the biggest multinational conglomerates tended to content themselves with shirt sponsorship and other product placement and public relations interventions. Even in the 21st century most direct investors in individual clubs were individuals and syndicates, outside the 'big league' of global capitalism.[1]

An early exception was the attempted purchase of Manchester United in 1998 by the genuinely global media magnate Rupert Murdoch; but up to that point external entrepreneurial ventures in football club ownership had involved purchasers and investors lower down the food chain. Specific threats to the identity of historic clubs through the pursuit of profit maximisation had emerged in 1983, when the publishing and media tycoon Robert Maxwell attempted to merge Oxford United and Reading as the Thames Valley Royals, on a new site between the cities. Maxwell showed no insight into the fierce rivalry between the clubs and the strong identification of supporters with their grounds and traditions. The proposal collapsed after (but not because of) angry campaigns by both sets of fans. One commentator labelled the scheme 'a move that has only since been outdone for sheer brazenness and disregard for history by those who relocated Wimbledon to Milton Keynes' (Andrews 2008).

The case of Wimbledon is indeed revealing. This small club in south-west London rose rapidly from obscurity to become established in the Premier League, but lost its original ground to a speculative development transaction by the then owner in 1991, whereupon the club itinerated through a series of ground-shares. At the turn of the millennium it was sold on to two Norwegian businessmen who intended it to become the Dublin 'franchise' of the Premier League; and when this failed the Football Association approved a move to the new city of Milton Keynes, more than 60 miles away. This was strenuously opposed by Wimbledon's fans, who founded a new club, AFC Wimbledon, and started (successfully) all over again. The Milton Keynes 'franchise', as it was derisively labelled, changed its name to reflect the new location. Significantly, during 2005–6 pressure from the national Football Supporters' Federation helped to ensure that Milton Keynes Dons renounced all claim to the original Wimbledon's history, returning the 'patrimony' of replica trophies and memorabilia to its 'spiritual home' in the London Borough of Merton, to borrow the language used by the borough's Deputy Leader at the official repatriation ceremony on 2 August 2007 (Conn 2009a; Merton Council 2007; The Football Supporters' Federation 2007).

Wimbledon's sporting history had followed a similar trajectory to that of Alavés, and the episode demonstrates the determination and creative resistance that fans could muster against the power of international finance. A similar fans' rebellion occurred when Manchester United was taken over by the Glazer family from the United States using borrowed finance, and then loaded with debt and 'sweated' to generate profit over and above the interest payments. For some fans, protests at matches were not enough: they formed their own breakaway club, FC United of Manchester, which was organised as a members' club and registered with Co-operatives UK as a co-operative mutual, and won the Co-operative Excellence Award of 2009 for its work with local communities in the deprived Newton Heath area (Bose 2007; Coman 2010). This is an excellent example of the powerful dialectic between the global and the local that both calls upon and recreates imagined relationships between club, history, heritage and 'community' in response to external threat (Blackshaw 2008). But, as a study of the recent geographical expansion of the West Ham United fan base shows, the nature of the 'communities' at issue is itself

---

[1] Taylor (2008), 426–7, has surprisingly little to say about this.

changing, becoming more virtual, 'liquid' and volatile, and containing more detached and physically distant elements (Fawbert 2005).

Such attacks on clubs' traditions and links with their communities need not emanate from international capital, although there have been several recent cases in England, at clubs ranging from Liverpool to Notts County. They often originate closer to home. Some of the worst English examples have involved interventions at lower league clubs by corrupt or fraudulent local or regional business interests, as at Chesterfield, Doncaster Rovers and Chester City. But the role of international capital is especially seductive, and has been increasing, especially when clubs need access to additional resources to maintain or enhance their status, to finance ground improvements or to move to a new site. This is where globalisation imparts its own additional momentum. All of this has direct relevance to the case of Alavés (Conn 2009b).

Cultures of Commemoration and Celebration: The Rise of the Football Museum

The football museum fits into this picture as an aspect of the articulation of cultures of commemoration, pride in history and topophilia, and as part of the commercialisation and exploitation of heritage. Again, Britain set the pace in most respects. Potential tensions were expressed in England through controversies over the National Football Museum, originally located at the Deepdale stadium of Preston North End, pioneers of professionalism in English football and unbeaten winners of the FA Cup and League double in the first English League season in 1888–9. It opened in 2001 (seven years after the pioneer national football museum, that of the Scottish Football Association at Hampden Park, Glasgow), and won glowing reviews after initial teething troubles. But there was increasing pressure to move it to a higher-profile location. In 2010 it was controversially transferred to the Urbis museum site in Manchester, which had no links with football. Defenders of the Preston site emphasised its close relationship with the origins and grassroots of the game as well as the genuine accessibility of the setting; but Preston North End and the local sponsors, the city and county governments and the University of Central Lancashire lost out to more powerful external influences (see Culture24 2009).[2]

Meanwhile, the first purpose-built British football club museum, that of Manchester United, had opened as early as 1986, and Pelé opened an expanded and refurbished version in 1998. But it was easier for this, and subsequent club museums, to avoid controversy: there was no question about where they should be located or what they should display. The twin goals of commemoration and commerce were mutually compatible.[3] By 2010 Liverpool, Manchester City, Chelsea, Arsenal and West Ham United also had club museums (Martucci 2010). Museum initiatives lower down the pecking order were more likely to come from fans than club managements and to be run on a shoestring: interesting British examples are those of Bradford City (founded in 2005)[4] and Burnley, which remains a virtual online museum sustained by fans.[5]

2   See: http://www.scottishfootballmuseum.org.uk/the-museum/history.html [7 February 2012]
3   See: http://www.manchesterunitedmuseumguide.co.uk [25 December 2010]
4   See: http://www.bantamspast.co.uk [23 December 2010]
5   See: http://www.claretsmuseum.com [23 December 2010]

The Spanish Context

The first Spanish football club museum, that of Barcelona, was inaugurated in 1984, two years before that of Manchester United, and after amplifications in 1987, 1994 and 1998 it has become a staple element in the club's attractions, becoming the most visited museum in Catalonia in 2009, with more than 1.2 million visitors (Cvltvre.com n.d.). Martucci's global survey, published towards the end of 2010, identified further club museums at Real Madrid, Atlético de Madrid, Real Zaragoza and Athletic Bilbao, but it could not hope to achieve total coverage and (for example) it missed the museums at Sevilla[6] and Real Sociedad.[7] The new museum at Las Rozas, dedicated specifically to the history of the Spanish national side, which opened on 24 May 2010, appeared too late for inclusion (Martucci 2010).[8]

Barcelona apart, the development of football club museums in Spain lagged a little behind that in England. The Alavés project was developed in a national setting where football club museums were still unusual, although in a region where such expressions of heritage and identity were emerging at two of the major neighbouring clubs (and standard-bearers for the pride of their provinces), Athletic Bilbao and Real Sociedad. The limited extent and, above all, the nature of the football museum phenomenon in Spain is in keeping with more limited penetration of globalising influences in football finance in comparison with England. Even international player recruitment markets are dominated by Spanish-speaking parts of the world, away from the special cases of Barcelona and Real Madrid. Most clubs in the top divisions have been obliged to conform to a standard model of sporting limited company, the Sociedad Anónima Deportiva, although Real Madrid, Barcelona, Athletic Bilbao and Osasuna have kept to the older model of the club owned by its members and the influence of the membership remains a powerful force in other clubs, where the percentage size of shareholdings vested in particular individuals may be strictly limited. Grounds are often owned or part-owned by municipalities or other local public bodies and moves to new stadiums have also been unusual, certainly in comparison with England; since 1993 there have been only five cases. Clubs have usually met increasingly exacting expectations and requirements by redeveloping on the same site, without the challenges to heritage and identity that a move would entail (see, for example, Barba 2006).

Recent surveys have underlined that Spanish football clubs are not profit maximisers; that no club is publicly listed on the Stock Exchange; and that 'clubs are backed by the financial institutions and authorities of their regions', including elected local and provincial governing bodies as well as regional savings banks. Home-grown monsters such as Jesús Gil y Gil of Atlético Madrid appear occasionally, but their powers are usually limited by the ultimate veto of the members. Against this background, the Piterman affair at Alavés appeared even more lurid than it might have done in England, where both local malfeasance and controversial interventions on the part of global magnates were becoming commonplace in the early 21st century. Piterman fell squarely into neither category, which makes this case study even more interesting (Ascari and Gagnepain 2006; Barajas and Rodríguez 2010).

6   www.sevillafc.es [26 December 2010]
7   http://www.realsociedad.com/caste/home/real.asp?menu=020401 [26 December 2010]
8   http://www.rfef.es/index.jsp?nodo=8&ID=1538 [7 February 2012]

ALAVÉS: THE LOCAL AND REGIONAL BACKGROUND

To understand the Alavés case study we need some regional as well as local context. Alavés is the flagship club not just of Vitoria but also of Álava, the Basque province of which it is the capital, following a common Spanish pattern of clubs representing provinces as well as cities. Álava is the smallest of the three core Basque provinces which make up the Comunidad Autónoma del País Vasco, or Euskadi, with 320,000 inhabitants; and Vitoria, also known by its Basque name of Gasteiz, is the capital not only of the province but of the whole autonomous community, while with 240,000 inhabitants it is also unusually dominant demographically in its province, containing three-quarters of the population. Within the autonomous community the unique Basque language (Euskera) is a key emblem of identity, although less so in Álava than in the other two provinces, Guipúzcoa (whose capital is San Sebastián-Donostia) or Vizcaya (Bilbao); and questions of Basque identity are of central political and cultural importance, in ways that are also relevant to football (Mansvelt Beck 2004; Urla 1990).

Álava is distinctive. It is land-locked, with no Atlantic seaboard. It has a smaller population than Guipúzcoa (700,000) or Vizcaya (1,150,000). Throughout the first half of the 20th century it retained an agrarian economy, less developed than the other provinces, which had modernised very quickly owing to mining in Vizcaya, the industrialisation of the district around Bilbao and of much of Guipúzcoa, and coastal tourism in San Sebastián. Although Álava industrialised very rapidly from the 1960s, and has caught up with its Basque neighbours, people from Vizcaya and Guipúzcoa still refer jokingly (and disparagingly) to its inhabitants as 'patateros', a reference to the traditional cultivation of potatoes in the province (Rivera 2003).

Cultural differences between Álava and the other Basque provinces are also important. Castilian Spanish influences carry more weight in Álava than do traditional Basque culture and the Basque language. As a communications artery, the province has maintained intense relationships with Castilla, Navarra and La Rioja. Even now, although the Basque language is more widely spoken owing to recent Basque Government linguistic policies, only 25 per cent of Álava's population speaks Basque, compared with 53 per cent in Guipúzcoa (Gobierno Vasco 2009, 35). Vitoria itself retains a 'mixed' identity owing to the heterogeneous origins of its inhabitants. Rapid industrialisation between 1960 and 1975 attracted huge numbers of migrants, drawn as much from beyond the Basque Country in Castilla and León, Extremadura and Andalucía as from rural Guipúzcoa or Navarra. As the 'least Basque' among the Basque provinces, Álava sustains important affinities with such non-Basque territories. In 1975 only 40 per cent of Vitoria's residents had been born there, and in recent years it has attracted immigrants from outside Spain, with 10 per cent of its inhabitants being foreigners, mainly from the Maghreb, Latin America and Eastern Europe (Rivera 2009).

Álava's politics are also distinctive. Basque nationalism has played an important part in the construction of footballing loyalties in the other two provinces, but less so in Álava. From its origins in Bilbao in the 1890s, it sought the unification of Euskadi, Navarra and the French Basque Country in a single sovereign state. Within Basque nationalism a minority supports the violent revolutionary independence campaign of ETA, but most nationalists work peacefully towards enhancing sovereignty, especially through the dominant Christian democratic Partido Nacionalista Vasco (PNV). In most of the elections held after the death of Franco in 1975 and the subsequent 'transition to democracy', the nationalist parties have attracted the majority of votes cast in the Basque autonomous community, where the PNV was the ruling party, alone or in coalition, between 1980 and 2009 (Mees 2003; Woodworth 2007). But surveys of perceptions of identity indicate a broad spectrum of attitudes, from people who feel completely 'Basque' to those who are entirely 'Spanish', but with many gradations in between (De La Granja *et al* 2011, 153).

Within the Basque autonomous community (and in contrast with Catalonia) there are strongly felt provincial identities. The historical traditions of the Basques, linked to the 'Fueros' (traditional laws identified with each province, which were abolished at the end of the 19th century), ensured that Euskadi would be effectively a federation of three historic territories: Álava, Guipúzcoa and Vizcaya, each of which retained a strong internal autonomy, especially in fiscal matters. The Diputaciones Forales (provincial governments) retain important fiscal powers, and the Ayuntamientos (municipal governments) of the three provincial capitals are also important concentrations of political power, especially in Álava, given the macrocephalous nature of Vitoria.

These distinctive features have political consequences. For various reasons (historical traditions, limited use of the Basque language), Álava has always been the Basque province where nationalism has made least headway. The nationalist movement began later here than in the other provincial capitals, in 1907, and grew slowly. In Vizcaya Basque nationalism had a political majority for the first time in 1917, in Guipúzcoa in 1933 and in Álava not until 1979, after Franco's death. The nationalist share of the vote was always lower than in the other Basque provinces, but between 1979 and 1999 the PNV governed Vitoria and the province of Álava almost without interruption, during the most successful period for the nationalists throughout the Basque Country.

Although the dominant form of Basque nationalism in Álava was 'alavesista' (that is, it supported a Basque nation but sustained the distinctive identity of Álava), some local people accused nationalism of being a product of Bilbao, alien to Álava. In 1990 Unidad Alavesa, a conservative political party which defended the identity of Álava against the 'centralising' tendency of Bilbao and against the nationalist imposition of the 'alien' Basque language, emerged, and did well electorally during the 1990s. This anticipated the province's change of political direction in 1999, when the national conservative Partido Popular (PP), in power nationally under José María Aznar, defeated the PNV in Álava, running minority administrations at both city and provincial level. This was a hammer blow to Basque nationalism, which did not recover until 2007, when a change of strategy by the socialist PSOE, another party organised at Spanish national level, allowed it to regain control of the provincial government. For eight years (1999–2007) the fact that a conservative Spanish party ruled the two main institutions of Álava undermined nationalist claims of majority Basque support for independence and underlined that Álava, although Basque, was different from Vizcaya or Guipúzcoa (De Pablo 2008).

FOOTBALL, THE BASQUES AND ALAVÉS

These complex Basque and provincial identities were also expressed through football. The Basque Country was one of the earliest Spanish regions to embrace the sport, thanks to English influences on Vizcayan industrialisation. Athletic Bilbao, founded in 1898, is regarded as the second oldest Spanish club behind Recreativo Huelva. But, in contrast with Catalonia, where FC Barcelona draws support from the whole autonomous community and has become a symbol of Catalan identity, in the Basque case the strength and endurance of provincial attachments has prevented the identity of the whole of Euskadi from being focused on a single club.

The two historic clubs, Athletic Bilbao and Real Sociedad of San Sebastián, always expressed the idiosyncrasies of, respectively, Vizcaya and Guipúzcoa, the provinces they represent as the flagship clubs of the capitals, although each kept a clearly defined Basque character. At key moments they joined forces to affirm Basque identity (as when in 1976 both teams took the field at Real's Atotxa ground jointly carrying the ikurriña, the Basque national flag, whose display had been prohibited under Franco), but there is normally a fierce rivalry between the clubs and their fans, as displayed in local derby matches (Walton 1999; Walton 2001; Walton 2005; Unzueta 1999; and see also Burns 2009; Colomé 1997).

While Athletic and Real Sociedad are the standard-bearing clubs of Vizcaya and Guipúzcoa, in Álava Deportivo Alavés has this status. It was founded on 23 January 1921, replacing 'Sport Friend's Club', founded a year earlier. This replaced an 'exotic' English name by tapping into provincial identity. The name identified the club clearly with the province rather than the city or the Basque region.

The club's blue and white strip seems to have no significance for provincial identity, and nor does its heraldic shield, a triangular banner with the initials DA (Deportivo Alavés), although in some versions the shield of the province is added. But the club anthem or 'Himno al Deportivo Alavés', written by the local poet and composer Alfredo Donnay, expresses strong local and provincial sentiments.[9]

The limited extent of the club's ostentatious cultivation of Basque or even provincial identity may be symbolised by the problem of what its alternative nickname means. The official one is the grandiloquent (and Spanish) 'El Glorioso'; but fans also celebrate the club as the 'babazorros', which is widely used on websites. 'Babazorro' resembles a Spanish construction meaning 'slavering fox', and the club itself uses a fox as its mascot. But in Álava, and perhaps especially Vitoria, 'babazorro' in Euskera connotes the eating of broad beans as poverty food. The term is also used generically by Spaniards from outside Álava to imply backwardness and a lack of intelligence and urbanity (*Noticias de Álava* 2008; see also Sociedad Landázuri 2010). This suggests that fans were identifying with and celebrating the poverty of their province in a ritual of inversion, mocking external disparagement by embracing it. The British journalist Phil Ball noticed this, but preferred the idea that 'baba' is derived from the Spanish word for potato, while 'zorro' would connote 'some kind of tick or aphid that blighted the crop from time to time'. Alavés would then be the 'potato aphids'. This piece of creative etymology was pure invention, but Ball managed to include it in a *Guardian* report before the 2001 UEFA final. The *Daily Mirror* took it up as gospel, and Liverpool fans apparently paraded through Dortmund before the match bearing banners reading 'Scousers eat aphids'. Ironically, Liverpool has its own kind of poverty food, the stew called 'scouse', which gives its citizens their own (similar) label. The key point is that the source of the nickname remains unclear, not least at the club itself, which suggests at best a blurred sense of historical identity. This contrasts with the clear Basque communitarian identities of the Athletic and La Real, in spite of the latter's own Spanish and monarchist nomenclature (Basque nationalist fans prefer to refer to it as 'Erreala'). Ball has stuck to his invention, which could only gain traction in a setting where the club's Basque and provincial identities are blurred; and he reproduces it in the most recent edition of his book on Spanish football. Indeed,

9 Donnay began as an anarchist trade union activist, and was later a member of the Radical Socialist Republican Party, before abandoning politics to concentrate on apolitical songs of provincial nostalgia. See: http://www.alfredodonnay.com [12 January 2011]

this story is also a warning against putting too much trust in journalists when writing 'historia actual' (Ball 2003, 200–201).

The club's stadium, bearing the resoundingly Basque name of Mendizorroza, was opened on 27 April 1924. It has been remodelled on several occasions (it currently accommodates 19,900 spectators), but Alavés has remained on the same site since that date. It has never been able to use the development value of its ground as a bargaining counter to finance expansion: during the 1930s, owing to economic problems, it had to sell Mendizorroza to the Vitoria Savings Bank, which was linked to the municipality, which is still the owner of the stadium. This was to prove highly significant.

Deportivo Alavés began convincingly. In 1930 it was promoted to the First Division of the Spanish League, founded in 1928 and consisting of only ten teams. This was when Alavés acquired the title of 'El Glorioso', although most of its subsequent history has been anything but 'glorious'. Since its foundation the club has spent 11 seasons in the First Division, 33 in the Second Division 'A', nine in the Second Division 'B' and 22 in the Third. This is much inferior to the record of the other Basque provincial flagship clubs, especially Athletic Bilbao, one of only three Spanish clubs (along with Real Madrid and FC Barcelona) never to have been relegated from the top flight.

After a roller-coaster career spent mainly in the second, third and fourth tiers of Spanish football, the golden age of Alavés was precipitated by successive promotions to the Second Division B in 1990, to the second tier in 1995, and finally to the First Division in 1998. These were genuinely glorious years, in which the club qualified for the UEFA Cup in 2000, reaching the final against Liverpool on 16 May 2001. Although Alavés lost 5–4 in extra time, they had the distinction of being the first team to reach a UEFA final at the first attempt. This final is now considered the best in the history of the UEFA Cup (now Europa League), and in 2001 Alavés won UEFA's prize for having the best fans in Europe. These were years of sporting success, stadium improvements, prosperity and economic stability; but they proved short-lived.

In 2003 Alavés returned to the Second Division, and in the following year the then chairman Gonzalo Antón sold the club to the Ukranian–American tycoon Dmitri Piterman. After a brief return to the top division Alavés was again relegated, in the middle of a series of scandals and outrageous comments by Piterman which ended, as we shall see, in 2007. Piterman's incompetent management left the club severely wounded economically and it had to have recourse to a creditors' agreement through the 'Ley Concursal'. In 2009 the team was relegated to the Second Division B. As we write Alavés is battling to return to the Second Division A, to repair its financial situation and to secure survival with economic assistance from provincial and city governments (Gómez Gómez 1994; Fernández Monje 2001).

Until Piterman arrived Alavés had been a humble club, firmly grounded in its city and province. The local institutions had recognised not only the economic benefits to the province from having a professional football club (Periáñez 2002) but also its contribution to provincial pride, always with a jealous eye on Vizcaya and Guipúzcoa, on Athletic and Real Sociedad. The club's survival on several occasions when it seemed likely to go under reflects the interests of local institutions or business leaders in maintaining the team as an emblem of Álava's identity. Despite this, because of its modest history and the peculiarities of the province it has never aroused the overwhelming enthusiasm associated with Athletic or Real Sociedad; and it has never shared the nationalist pretensions of Athletic (especially) to recruit only Basque players.

Alavés is neither the only club in the province, nor in the city; but no rival has succeeded in displacing it as the club of Vitoria and Álava. The only serious challenger was CD Aurrera of Vitoria, which in 1996–7 almost joined Alavés in the Second Division A. However, in 2003 Aurrera was relegated administratively to the Third Division, where it remains, for failing to pay its players. It fell into a profound economic crisis, for which it blamed the municipal and provincial governments, which since the arrival of the PP in power in 1999 had withdrawn their economic support. While the PNV had assisted Aurrera when in power between 1979 and 1999, the PP abandoned this policy, claiming that the crisis arose from irregularities committed by Aurrera's management. The nationalists in turn accused the PP of assisting only professional sport (in other words, Alavés) while allowing Aurrera to be relegated. But Aurrera had become a feeder club for Athletic Bilbao, which some saw as a betrayal of provincial identity. Indeed, the PNV accused the conservatives of undermining Aurrera, which they saw as a better representative of Basque identity in the province, when it fell into crisis. After regaining power in the province in 2007, the PNV resumed economic assistance to Aurrera, in detriment to Alavés, provoking new disputes between the parties in Álava (see de Arri 2003; Martínez Viguri 2010).

Despite this confrontation, Deportivo Alavés has never been identified with a particular political ideology. From its inception the club has been run by people with diverse political affiliations, although conservatives have predominated. The first chairman was a journalist and newspaper proprietor from the political centre and centre-left. Others included a leader of traditional Catholic conservatism and a high-profile member of Acción Nacionalista Vasca, a left-wing nationalist party founded in 1930. During the Franco era the club was inevitably headed by 'suitable' monarchists, conservatives and Falangists. Many Alavés leaders were not defined by their politics, but were well-known provincial businessmen who saw the club not so much as an investment but as a way of identifying with local interests.[10]

Until Piterman's arrival the management of Alavés presented a serious image, closely tied in with local culture, drawing support from local and provincial institutions which saw it as representing provincial pride and values. The political and cultural differences between Álava and Euskadi as a whole sometimes produced confrontations. Some fans protested because the Basque Government, under PNV control between 1980 and 2009, gave more support to Athletic and Real Sociedad than Alavés, even when the latter was also in the First Division. They thought that Alavés was considered less 'Basque' than Athletic or Real, lacking as it did their links with nationalism. This was supported by the limited coverage Euskal Telebista (ETB), the public Basque television channel, gave to Alavés compared with Athletic and Real.[11]

ORIGINS OF THE ALAVÉS FOOTBALL MUSEUM

The UEFA Cup success of 2001 and the apparent consolidation of Alavés' position in the First Division seemed an appropriate moment for recovering the club's history and stimulating the pride of local supporters. The favourable economic state of club and local financial institutions opened out projects, including the museum, which would have been unthinkable with the return of economic crisis.

The museum project was entrusted to the Fundación Deportivo Alavés, a non-profit-making organisation which looked after aspects of the club's work that were not strictly economic nor

---

10   See: http://www.alaves.com/html/protagonistas.html [12 January 2010]
11   See: http://www.facebook.com/group.php?gid=120222988000755 [12 January 2010]

based on competitive sport, such as football in schools and the community or Third World solidarity campaigns. The Fundación had a social policy committee, with representatives from the main provincial institutions, including the provincial government, the city council of Vitoria, the savings bank of Vitoria and Álava and the University of the Basque Country.

Early in 2002 the director of the Fundación Deportivo Alavés, Alfonso Arriola, approached Antonio Rivera, a history professor who specialised in the province's history and was currently vice-rector of the Álava campus, to entrust the University with a preparatory study for the future museum. As the club itself had few trophies and historical materials to display, a research project was needed to catalogue suitable objects, photographs, documents and other items that were scattered in other locations or in private hands. The provincial government undertook to provide financial support, given the social, historical and cultural significance of the project for the province. The designated project director was Santiago de Pablo, professor of Contemporary History and author of several books on 20th-century Álava, and on 2 September 2002 the parties concerned signed a collaboration agreement by which he was to undertake 'the completion of a study which would identify the documentary sources and historical inheritance of Club Deportivo Alavés, which would then enable future consideration of a club museum' (Departamento de Juventud y Deporte de la Diputación Foral de Álava y el Departamento de Historia Contemporánea de la Universidad del País Vasco-Euskal Herriko Unibertsitatea 2002).[12]

In January 2003 a press conference announced that the future museum would be situated under the stand, next to the official club shop (Pernía 2003). This location reflected the dual role of the museum: conserving the historical memory of Alavés, but also stimulating trade at the shop. De Pablo's team brought together a variety of memorabilia which were donated by institutions and individual fans (*Deportivo Alavés Bizirik* 2003). On 30 December 2003 the club vice-chairman announced that the museum would open in 2005.

In March 2004 Deportivo Alavés selected specialist companies to present suitable projects, together with a budget. The club would choose its preferred option and hand the task over to the successful company. In July three projects were submitted, and the club announced that in the autumn one would be selected, and financial support finalised, for a 2005 opening. But at the same time (12 July 2004) Dmitri Piterman took charge of the company that ran the club, SAD Deportivo Alavés, after buying 51 per cent of the shares. His arrival stopped the museum project, with its focus on the history of the club and its relationship with the society of its province, in its tracks. On the same site, Piterman would propose a very different kind of exhibition.

PITERMAN AND DEPORTIVO ALAVÉS

When he took charge of Deportivo Alavés Dmitri Piterman was already well known in Spanish football. Born in the Ukraine in 1963, he was a United States citizen, having moved with his family to California when he was 12 years old. In 1990 he had moved to the Catalan city of Girona, where he continued the residential property speculations which had made his fortune, while becoming interested in football. In 1999 he took control of Palamós CF, a Third Division team from Girona province. His *modus operandi* in Palamós foreshadowed his activities in bigger

---

12   See also: 'A R', 2002 El museo del Alavés mostrará la relación del club con Vitoria, *El Correo* (Álava edition), 23 July, 43; 'J M / A G', 2002 El museo del Deportivo Alavés coloca su primera piedra, *El Periódico de Álava*, 23 July, 32

Fig 9.1. A demonstration of Alavés members passes through the centre of Vitoria, with a banner displaying the slogan 'Dimitry Kanpora' ('Dmitri [Piterman] out') in the Basque language.

clubs: he looked for clubs with economic problems, or whose owners needed ready money, took complete control of the organisation, ran it as if it were his own private property, brought in his own trusted manager (especially Chuchi Cos) and took personal charge of the team, despite having no official qualifications for the role.

After a frustrated attempt to acquire Badajoz, then in the Second Division A, in January 2003 Piterman bought 24 per cent of the shares of First Division Racing Santander. As the remaining shares were held in small parcels, Piterman took control of the team, presenting himself as a photographer or kitman to gain access to the bench, and managing in such a 'hands-on' way that the League took proceedings against him for acting as a manager without a licence. His unusual personality soon ensured the deterioration of his relationship with the other Racing shareholders, and he was driven out.

Piterman continued his search for control of a professional football club. Alavés became a preferred target because it played in the Second Division A and its chairman, the hotelier Gonzalo Antón, was desperately seeking a buyer to solve his liquidity crisis. In July 2004 the Ukranian–American bought the majority of the Deportivo Alavés shares. With 51 per cent of the company in his hands he could manage the club as he pleased, in contrast with the situation in Santander.

At first Piterman was accepted in Vitoria. Despite his eccentricities, which had yet to become disturbing, many people saw the possibility of heavy investment, the arrival of famous players and, above all, the return of Alavés to the First Division. But some already recognised the dangers he brought to Alavés, threatening a break with the tradition of an unglamorous club strongly attached to its province. But in 2004–5 the club was successful on the field. With Chuchi Cos as manager and some impressive signings, Alavés returned to the First Division (Goñi 2004).

Although the problems of Piterman's distinctive management style were now apparent, relega-

Fig 9.2. The Alavés players hold a press conference in opposition to Piterman, 30 November 2006.

tion to the Second Division A in 2005–6 brought complaints to a head. During this season, with Chuchi Cos as director of football, Piterman went through three different managers, one of whom was sacked, despite a series of good results, for resisting the chairman's attempts to influence team selection. The powerful local institutions broke off relations with Piterman, who threatened to take legal action against the Vitoria city government, which owned the stadium. Not content with barracking the chairman at matches, the fans organised demonstrations against him (Fig 9.1). Piterman reacted by referring to the campaigning group 'Sentimiento Albiazul' ('Blue-and-White Passion') as 'riffraff' ('gentuza'). This organisation had been established to recover the 'real' Alavés, freeing the club from Piterman's control; and his response merely made matters worse. Finally, Piterman also fell out with the squad when he threatened and illegally dismissed one of the players, for which he was legally punished (Fig 9.2). Further eccentricities also disgusted the fans, such as posing nude for the magazine *Interviú* in the city government's Mendizorroza stadium.

Economic problems were added to the list, including the non-payment of players' wages, and the situation became unsustainable. After further protests by the fans (Fig 9.3), pressure from the local institutions and complex negotiations, in March 2007 Piterman sold his majority share in Alavés to a group of investors led by the new chairman, Fernando Ortiz de Zárate. Apparently, during Piterman's four years in charge of Alavés the club's debt multiplied threefold, reaching 23 million euros. Piterman's financial record at the club is currently *sub judice*, but in 2008 the commercial court of Vitoria embargoed his assets in Spain to the value of 13 million euros. So far, the only judgement presented has required him to return 120,000 euros for having used club funds for personal expenditure (EFE/Vitoria 2009; Mallo 2010).

FIG 9.3. ALAVÉS SUPPORTERS PROTEST
AGAINST PITERMAN IN THE STANDS AT
MENDIZORROZA STADIUM, DISPLAYING A
COFFIN WITH A PHOTOGRAPH OF PITERMAN
AND THE SLOGAN 'RIP' (*REQUIESCAT IN
PACE*: REST IN PEACE).

THE PITERMAN EFFECT: DALÍ IN THE ALAVÉS MUSEUM

It was soon obvious that Piterman was not interested in the Alavés museum. In autumn 2004 all
that was needed was a decision on which of the three projects to choose. When Alfonso Arriola,
still general manager of the Fundación Deportivo Alavés, arranged an interview with Santiago de
Pablo in his role as project director for 14 October 2004, De Pablo assumed that they intended
to agree on the best project before proceeding. Great was his surprise when Arriola, who was
accompanied by José Carmona, a trusted lieutenant of Piterman, told him that the club museum
would not go ahead because the agreed site was to be used for the installation of a selection of
reproductions by Salvador Dalí owned by Piterman, who since his time in Catalonia had been
known for his passion for works of art, especially those of Dalí (Álvarez 2002).[13] In this meeting
De Pablo was invited to collaborate on the design of the Dalí museum, but when he declined
and expressed astonishment at such a radical change of objectives, Carmona told him that work
had already begun on the new project.

[13] For Piterman's angry dispute with the Artium, the city's museum of contemporary art, over his Dalí collection
      see Goñi, A, 2004 Bronca en el Artium, *Dato Económico* 45, November, 20.

A fortnight later Piterman dismissed Arriola as general manager of Deportivo Alavés. This was a further step in a clear-out of former employees, as the new management replaced them with trusted collaborators of Piterman. A little later the press learned of the Dalí museum project and the abandonment of the Alavés museum, sparking widespread opposition (de Esquide 2004). As the PNV was then in opposition both in the city and provincial government (which were run by the PP), this was an opportunity to put pressure on both institutions, which were involved as proprietor of the stadium and provider of financial support for the football museum research project. The nationalists had already accused the PP of having assisted the professional and 'globalised' Alavés in detriment to the voluntarist and 'Basque' Aurrera. A PNV councillor in Vitoria, Íñigo Antía, asked Encina Serrano, who held the municipal Culture and Sport portfolio, for explanations about the Deportivo Alavés museum project. He wanted to know specifically whether the city government had authorised the work on the Dalí museum, now being installed in a building that it owned, and what had happened to the Alavés museum. Responding to the pressure from the PNV, the city government opened an investigation to find out whether Piterman's project was actually legal ('J A M V' 2004). It then instructed Alavés to stop the building work until the nature of the museum had been clarified. Antía accused Piterman, and indirectly the PP, of 'throwing so many years of history out with the rubbish' by abandoning the Alavés museum (de Arrilucea 2004).

Now that the museum question had gone public the provincial and city governments tried to rectify the injustice, interviewing members of Piterman's management team (Rivera 2004; Loza 2004). Each institution had different objectives, although both were governed by the PP. The provincial government, led by Federico Verástegui, the portfolio holder for Culture and Sport, required Alavés to comply with the agreement signed two years previously and move ahead with the football museum. The city government, through its own Culture and Sport cabinet member, Encina Serrano, displayed its anger because the planning of both museums had taken place behind its back, in spite of its ownership of Mendizorroza. Serrano was right: the club, supported by the provincial government, had indeed prepared the original project without the city government's consent. Piterman had begun the work without proper permission, presenting it as 'minor alterations' when it actually entailed a fundamental reconstruction of the foundations of the stadium. As the PNV was threatening to use the museum issue as a weapon against the PP, the conservative politicians sought an agreement with Alavés to avoid opening a new front in the hidden struggle between the parties.

At last, on 2 December 2004 a meeting of all interested parties (Deportivo Alavés, the provincial and city governments, and De Pablo as director of the original project) was called to seek resolution of the conflict. Piterman's management team claimed that the previous management had told them nothing about the Alavés museum project. This was hard to believe, as although Piterman had been removing the trusted employees of Gonzalo Antón others who knew about the project had continued working for Piterman for some time and some remained in post, including his legal adviser. It seemed more likely that nobody within Alavés wanted to defy the new chairman by reminding him of the existing project and that the stadium was not the club's property. Piterman's representatives accused Antón of having removed the club's most precious trophy (the plaque for the UEFA runners-up, which was in the chairman's office and was said to have vanished at the moment of Piterman's arrival) and insisted that all documentation relating to the Alavés museum had disappeared from the club offices. Piterman's team, which consisted of people from Palamós or Santander with no connection with Álava, was only interested in opening the Dalí museum as soon as possible. The Alavés museum was irrelevant to them, as they had no interest in the club's history.

In the end a compromise was reached: Mendizorroza would house a museum which would reflect the history of Alavés but, in one or two rooms allocated to temporary exhibitions, Piterman's Dalí collection could be displayed first.[14] The problem was that, although completing the Dalí section of the museum would be easy, the Alavés section required more preparation time. The Piterman team proposed that the Dalí section should be opened first and that of Alavés some months later, confirming that the museum was really a pretext for displaying the chairman's art collection. But both the city and provincial government rejected the proposal, thinking about the political cost to the PP of appearing to support Piterman against a project linked to local history (Serrano said there had to be 'something' of Alavés, because otherwise 'the PNV people will kill me'). The institutions wanted above all to reach an agreement, avoiding political confrontations with either Piterman or the opposition (especially the PNV).

On 27 December the city government and Alavés announced that a final agreement had been reached, and that the museum – dedicated partly to Alavés and partly to Dalí – would open at the end of January 2005. In reality this proved impossible, above all because the Alavés section, held back by Piterman's intervention, needed extra time. Piterman's deputy tried to bring back De Pablo, the historian who had directed the Alavés project, but he refused. In the end a young journalist took charge of the Alavés part of the museum, while a trusted confederate of Piterman prepared the Dalí part.

The museum was inaugurated on 18 March 2005. As envisaged, it contained some rooms displaying works by Dalí – basically lithographs – and others dedicated to the history of Alavés, with trophies, shirts, photographs and memorabilia. Among those present were representatives of local institutions (provincial and city government, etc) and political parties, the local business and cultural worlds, sporting figures and former Alavés players. Piterman – accompanied by his family – emphasised the legacy of the Catalan artist, reminding those present that, like Dalí, they should keep an open mind and that 'in many cases the purest mind is that of the sports player'. One of the politicians remarked that this 'cocktail of sport and art' was an 'attractive proposition' (de Esquide 2005; Fiestras 2005). Both Piterman and the local institutions had finally achieved their objectives: that of Piterman, to display his collection and gain publicity; that of the city and provincial governments, to avoid a major dispute and silence the nationalist opposition. The best news was the reappearance of the UEFA runners-up plaque. Its whereabouts had remained unknown until, on the opening day, someone left it in a Vitoria church, informing the priest so he could return it to the club (Fig 9.4). This strange occurrence encapsulated the history of the project as a full-scale soap opera.

In practice, things did not run smoothly. The museum's design was less than elegant, put together by someone who lacked expertise, as illustrated by the lighting, low ceilings and round arches. In private, the politician who had described the combination of art and sport as an 'attractive proposition' commented that the museum's design 'was like a brothel' (anonymous *pers comm*). If Piterman thought that 'thousands of people' would come to see Dalí's works (and not

---

[14] The city government announced that each exhibition of art works could last for a maximum of three months; Piterman would not be able to keep his Dalí collection on show for ever ('L M', 2004 El Ayuntamiento limitará a tres meses las muestras artísticas en Mendizoroza, *El Correo* (Álava edition), 28 December, 45). This requirement was not enforced when the museum opened.

Fig 9.4. The plaque and one of the medals obtained by Alavés in the UEFA Cup Final of 2001, as displayed in the club museum.

the heritage of Alavés), it was soon apparent that he was being highly optimistic. In a city with relatively little tourism, where people were unaccustomed to pay for their culture (most local museums belonged to the provincial government and were free to enter), the price of a ticket, although cheap at three euros, seemed a lot after the journey from the city centre to Mendizorroza. The subsequent sporting trajectory of Alavés and the scandals of the Piterman era did not encourage many fans to identify with the football museum side of the project. Finally, the idea that the Dalí exhibition might only be temporary was soon forgotten. When in 2007 Piterman left Alavés, taking his Dalí pictures and lithographs with him, the new management closed the museum. Not until July 2010, as part of the preparations for the club's 90th anniversary, was it reinstated after renovations and improvements, including additional football memorabilia in part of the former Dalí zone. The new mayor of Vitoria, the socialist Patxi Lazcoz, attended the opening ceremony, but there was no representative from the provincial government, now under PNV control.

The new museum was closely linked to city and province, capturing the relationship between the club, its fans and Álava society. Reflecting the club's modest history, next to the UEFA runners-up plaque was a 'multitude of trophies – most of them from local competitions – souvenirs of clubs from every division …' (Barrio 2010). Alongside memorabilia donated by current First Division sides were those from more humble clubs, which had passed through Mendizorroza at low points in the history of 'El Glorioso': Valvanera, Club Sporting Rubí and Briviesca

FIG 9.5. A GROUP OF CHILDREN VISITS THE TROPHY SECTION OF THE DEPORTIVO ALAVÉS MUSEUM.

(Fig 9.5). Pictures by pupils of the School of Arts and Crafts replaced Dalí's works. This was symbolic of the values of the new museum, which the mayor described as 'cosy and attractive', unpretentious like the city and completely remote from the idea, linked with the forces of capitalism and globalisation, which had impelled Piterman to install Dalí in a local football museum (*El Correo* 2010).

The new management intended to open the museum to the public from September 2010, coinciding with the start of the new football season, but the club's difficult economic circumstances made it difficult to promote it. Apparently the income from tickets did not cover staff and maintenance costs, and as we write the museum has closed its doors again, although it reopens for specially arranged visits by schools, Third Age groups and other organised parties. This is, ultimately, a highly cautionary tale.

CONCLUSION

This has been an essay in the perils associated with globalisation for football clubs, especially modest ones, which seek to continue to punch above their weight and need injections of capital to do so. The case of Alavés does not fit readily into predetermined boxes. The club is not a bearer of strong cultural traditions, at least when compared with other provincial standard-bearers in Spain, and especially the Basque Country. Its nemesis, Dmitri Piterman, was neither an indigenous manipulator of needs and opportunities 'on the make' in unscrupulous pursuit of profit, as in so many English cases, nor, on a more elevated sporting plane, the representative of powerful global industrial and financial interests in search of sporting glory to promote themselves or their brand. He fell in between these categories, and his sporting and cultural aspirations outran his resources and abilities, although it was always clear that he had no particular attachment to Alavés as a club with a history and a local and provincial identity. But the strange affair of the Alavés football museum does shed an interesting, and sometimes lurid, light on the potential political and cultural repercussions of this kind of external intervention in local sporting cultures and on the problematic relationships between commemoration and commerce, heritage and hubris. It presents itself as both a landmark and a warning for those who seek to negotiate the perilous waters of globalisation from what might appear to be the most secure and, on their own terms, successful of starting points, especially if they value the history and heritage that constitutes the essence of their club's identity and meaning.

Bibliography and References

Álvarez, R, 2002 Del triple salto al palco y el banquillo, *El País*, 6 November, available from: http://www. elpais.com/articulo/deportes/triple/salto/palco/banquillo/elpepidep/20021106elpepidep_5/Tes [2 February 2012]

Andrews, G, 2008 The rise and fall of Oxford United, *Soccerlens* [online], 27 February, available from: http://soccerlens.com/the-rise-and-fall-of-oxford-united/6095/ [8 February 2012]

Ascari, G, and Gagnepain, P, 2006 Spanish Football, *Journal of Sports Economics* 7, 67–79

Bagchi, R, 2010 Burnley are back – thankfully without caricature chairman Bob Lord, *The Guardian*, 27 May, available from: http://www.guardian.co.uk/football/blog/2009/may/27/burnley [23 December 2010]

Bale, J, 1993 *Sport, Space and the City*, Routledge, London

Ball, P, 2003 *Morbo: The Story of Spanish Football*, When Saturday Comes Books, London

Barajas, A, and Rodríguez, P, 2010 Spanish football clubs' finances: crisis and players' salaries, *International Journal of Sport Finance* 5 (1), 52–66

Barba, B, 2006 Grandes estadios (III), *Diarios de Fútbol* [online], available from: http://www.diarios-defutbol.com/2006/12/01/grandes-estadios-iii-atotxa/ [17 January 2012]

Barrio, D, 2010 Historia albiazul en el nuevo Museo, *El Correo* (Álava edition), 29 July, available from: http://alaves.elcorreo.com/noticias/2010–07–29/historia-albiazul-nuevo-museo-20100729.html [2 February 2012]

Blackshaw, T, 2008 Contemporary Community Theory and Football, *Soccer and Society* 9, 325–45

Bose, M, 2007 *Manchester DisUnited*, Aurum Press, London

Burns, J, 2009 *Barça, A People's Passion*, Bloomsbury, London

Caspistegui, F J, 2001 Osasuna y Navarra entre primera y segunda división, in *Guerras danzadas. Fútbol e identidades locales y regionales en Europa* (eds F J Caspistegui and J K Walton), EUNSA, Pamplona, 193–214

Colomé, G, 1997 Futbol i identidad nacional a Catalunya: FC Barcelona i RCD Espanyol, *L'Avenç* 211, 32–4

Coman, J, 2010 FC United: a punk football fairytale, *The Observer*, 21 November, available from: http://www.uk.coop/node/6354 [24 December 2010]

Conn, D, 2005 *The Beautiful Game? Searching for the Soul of Football*, Yellow Jersey, London

— 2009a Tears of joy as AFC Wimbledon prove they are in the wider interests of football, *The Guardian*, 28 April, available from: http://www.guardian.co.uk/sport/blog/2009/apr/28/afc-wimbledon-blue-square-conference-south-champions [23 December 2010]

— 2009b The noughties: a decade when football's rulers ducked responsibility, *The Guardian*, 23 December, available from: http://www.guardian.co.uk/sport/david-conn-inside-sport-blog/2009/dec/23/noughties-decade-review-football-money [18 January 2012]

Culture24, 2009 *National Football Museum move to Manchester Urbis sparks uproar* [online], 19 November, available from: http://www.culture24.org.uk/history%20%26%20heritage/art73485 [17 January 2012]

Cvltvre.com, n.d. *Museo Futbol Club Barcelona*, available from: http://www.cvltvre.com/pg/museums/view/14748 [26 December 2010]

de Arri, E O, 2003 El club olvidado, *El País* (Basque Country edition), 6 October, available from: http://www.elpais.com/articulo/pais/vasco/club/olvidado/elpepiesppvs/20031006elpvas_12/Tes [30 January 2012]

de Arrilucea, C P, 2004 Encina Serrano anuncia la 'paralización' del museo sobre Dalí en Mendizorroza, *El Correo* (Álava edition) 25 November, 57

de Esquide, F Ruiz, 2004 Piterman expondrá su colección de Dalí en un museo que ya prepara en Mendizorroza, *El Correo*, 18 November, 58

— 2005 El Alavés inaugura hoy su museo sin la placa de subcampeón de la UEFA, *El Correo* (Álava edition), 18 March, 48

De la Granja, J L, De Pablo, S, and Rubio Pobes, C, 2011 *Breve historia de Euskadi. De los Fueros a la autonomía*, Debate, Madrid

De Pablo, S, 2008 *En tierra de nadie. Los nacionalistas vascos en Álava*, Ikusager, Vitoria

Departamento de Juventud y Deporte de la Diputación Foral de Álava y el Departamento de Historia Contemporánea de la Universidad del País Vasco-Euskal Herriko Unibertsitatea, 2002 Convenio de colaboración para la realización de un estudio de recopilación documental de los fondos históricos del Deportivo Alavés, 2 September, Archivo Departamento de Historia Contemporánea de la UPV/EHU

Deportivo Alavés Bizirik, 2003 El museo sólo es posible con el esfuerzo de todos, *Deportivo Alavés Bizirik* 44, November, 8–9

EFE/Vitoria, 2009 Piterman deberá pagar 120.000 euros al Alavés, *Marca*, 24 April, available from: http://www.marca.com/2009/04/24/futbol/equipos/alaves/1240568785.html [2 February 2012]

El Correo, 2010 Programa. Museo, *El Correo*, 27 July, 46

Fawbert, J, 2005 Football Fandom and the 'Traditional' Football Club, in *The Bountiful Game? Football Identities and Finances* (eds J Magee, A Bairner and A Tomlinson), Meyer & Meyer Sport, 121–41

Fernández Monje, P X, 2001 Deportivo Alavés, in *Historia del fútbol vasco*, Aralar, Andoain, vol I

Fiestras, J, 2005 Recuerdos y surrealismo, *El Correo* (Álava edition), 19 March, 81

The Football Supporters' Federation, 2007 *Press Release*, 29 June, available from: http://www.fsf.org.uk/uploaded/press-releases/press%20release%20-%20mkdons%20-%2029%2006%2007.pdf [15 February 2012]

Giulianotti, R, and Robertson, R, 2004 The Globalization of Football: a Study in the Glocalization of 'the Serious Life', *British Journal of Sociology* 55, 545–68

— 2009 *Globalization and Football*, Sage, London

Gobierno Vasco, 2009 *2006. IV Mapa Sociolingüístico*, Servicio Central de Publicaciones del Gobierno Vasco, Vitoria

Gómez Gómez, J, 1994 *Deportivo Alavés y su historia albiazul*, Diputación Foral de Álava, Vitoria

Goñi, A, 2004 Dimitri Piterman ya genera dudas, *Dato Económico* 45, November, 14–19

Hopcraft, A, 1968 *The Football Man*, Collins, London

'J A M V', 2004 El Ayuntamiento vigilará si las obras del museo sobre Dalí se ajustan a la licencia, *El Correo* (Álava edition), 20 November, 55

Loza, R, 2004 Alavés y surrealismo, *El Correo*, 30 November, 3

King, A, 1998 *The End of the Terraces*, Leicester University Press, Leicester

Mallo, B, 2010 La justicia tras sus pasos: Piterman vende los inmuebles que él mismo ofreció como garantía de pago, *Diario de Noticias de Álava*, 7 April, available from: http://www.noticiasdealava.com/2010/04/07/deportes/otros-deportes/piterman-vende-los-inmuebles-que-el-mismo-ofrecio-como-garantia-de-pago [2 February 2012]

Mansvelt Beck, J, 2004 *Territory and Terror. Conflicting Nationalisms in the Basque Country*, Routledge, London

Martínez Viguri, 2010 El PNV afirma que destina 700.000 euros al Aurrera para rebajar su deuda, *El Correo* (Álava edition), 5 November, available from: http://www.elcorreo.com/alava/v/20101105/deportes/mas-futbol/afirma-destina-euros-aurrera-20101105.html [30 January 2012]

Martucci, M, 2010 *Football Story: Musei e Mostre del Calcio nel Mondo*, Nerbini, Florence

Mees, L, 2003 *Nationalism, Violence and Democracy. The Basque Clash of Identities*, Palgrave Macmillan, Houndmills/New York

Merton Council, 2007 Wimbledon FC memorabilia returns home [online], 2 August, available from: http://www.merton.gov.uk/press-release-details.asp?id=1579 [24 December 2010]

Noticias de Álava, 2008 Historias de 'zuqueros', 'judíos' y 'babazorros', *Diario* [online], 20 August, available from: http://www2.noticiasdealava.com/ediciones/2008/08/20/sociedad/alava/d20ala10.1000926.php [18 January 2012]

Periáñez, I (ed), 2002 *Medición del impacto socioeconómico de los éxitos deportivos del Deportivo Alavés, SAD y del Saski-Baskonia, SAD sobre la ciudad de Vitoria-Gasteiz*, Diputación Foral de Álava, Vitoria

Pernía, N, 2003 La tribuna de Cervantes del campo de Mendizorroza acogerá el futuro museo del Alavés, *El Periódico de Álava*, 24 January, 45

Rivera, A (ed), 2003 *Historia de Álava*, Nerea, San Sebastián

Rivera, A, 2004 Piterpan y el efecto Guggenheim, *El Correo*, 26 November

— 2009 De poblachón a posmociudad: la Vitoria revolucionada, in *El edificio transparente: la cultura vasca en Sancho el Sabio*, Fundación Sancho el Sabio, Vitoria, 61–90

Smart, B, 2007 Not Playing Around: Global Capitalism, Modern Sport and Consumer Culture, in *Globalization and Sport* (eds R Giulianotti and R Robertson), Blackwell, Oxford, 6–27

Sociedad Landázuri, 2010 Alaveses: Babazorros, *El Correo* (Álava edition), 2 August, available from: http://www.elcorreo.com/alava/v/20100802/alava/alaveses-babazorros-20100802.html [30 Jaunary 2012]

Taylor, M, 2008 *The Association Game: A History of British Football*, Pearson Longman, Harlow

Unzueta, P, 1999 Fútbol y nacionalismo vasco, in *Fútbol y pasiones políticas* (ed S Segurola), Debate, Madrid, 147–67

Urla, J, 1990 *Being Basque, Speaking Basque: the Politics of Language and Identity in the Basque Country*, UMI, Michigan

Vamplew, W, Coyle, J, Heath, J, and Naysmith, B, 1998 Sweet FA: Fan Rights and Club Relocations, *Football Studies* 1, 55–68

Walton, J K, 1999 Football and Basque Identity: Real Sociedad of San Sebastián (1909–1932), *Memoria y Civilización* 2, 261–89

— 2001 Basque Football Rivalries in the Twentieth Century: Real Sociedad and Athletic Bilbao, in *Fear and Loathing in World Football* (eds G Armstrong and R Giulianotti), Berg, Oxford, 119–33

— 2005 Football and the Basques: the Local and the Global, in *The Bountiful Game? Football Identities and Finances* (eds A Bairner, J Magee and A Tomlinson), Meyer & Meyer Sport, Oxford, 135–54

Woodworth, P, 2007 *The Basque Country: A Cultural History*, Signal Books, Oxford

10

Replacing the Divots:
Guarding Britain's Golfing Heritage

Wray Vamplew

Material Culture, Collections and Museums

An essential aspect of golfing heritage is the legacy of material culture from the three centuries or so that the sport has been played in Britain. This is broad and covers most of the categories outlined in Hardy *et al*'s (2009) recent typology. To the fore is *playing equipment*, with golfers changing over time from using fully wooden clubs to those with metal heads and (later) shafts and now the oxymoronic 'metal wood'. The ball that they strike with these implements has developed from the 18th-century version, stuffed with feathers, through the 19th-century gutta-percha to the rubber core, invented in the early 20th century and the basis of the modern golf ball, each of them promising the user longer distance and greater control. Then we have *prizes*: the Claret Jug, denoting the connection of golf with alcohol, awarded to the winner of the Open Championship; the medals for club champions attached to the shaft of a club displayed in the clubhouse; and the plethora of engraved spoons given to those who overcame their handicap in the monthly club tournament. As for *sportswear*, club regulations have usually reinforced social convention in terms of golfing attire. Edwardian men played in suits and ties while women wore long skirts and bonnets. These are brought to us in photographs and film, the latter capturing bodily movement, an essence of sport. Golf magazines of the time, as well as being material culture in their own right, advertised the latest in *training equipment and sports medicine technology*, the latter being still primarily liniments and embrocations. *Venues* are often still in existence, though rarely in their original form as club and ball 'improvements' have rendered old distances and hazards redundant and as members have demanded better facilities in the clubhouses. Nevertheless, the sites show the shift from seaside links to inland courses and the move from courses almost as nature intended to ones that were artificial 'natural' environments created by golf architects. Finally there is the mass of *emphemera and detritus*, ranging from autographs to artworks, from broken tees to old scorecards.

Compilations of such heritage material are labelled *memorabilia* by Hardy and his colleagues. There are many collectors of golf memorabilia. Some pursue it for investment reasons, looking for rare books and equipment, but most are hobbyists, people simply passionate, occasionally obsessive, about an aspect of the game's history. Some collectors are intensely private, indulging in self-gratification; others, such as the 700 or so members of the British Golf Collectors' Society (BGCS; formed in 1987), are enthusiastically open about their hobby. This group's aim was 'to introduce golf collectors to one another, to encourage them to meet to correspond and to disseminate news and information about our hobby through a newsletter' (BGCS 2010). This

FIG 10.1. THE BRITISH GOLF MUSEUM, ST ANDREWS.

publication has developed into *Through the Green*, a quarterly magazine freely available on the Society's website, which is a useful source for research on all forms of collectibles, personalities, history and historical changes in the rules of golf. In 1994 the Society inaugurated the Murdoch medal to commemorate the contribution made to the collecting of golf memorabilia by Joe Murdoch, the Society's first honorary member. It is awarded to a member who has made a major contribution to the heritage of golf. As explained to me by some of the members responsible for drawing up the award criteria, history was seen as 'specific and factual' whereas heritage 'embraced wider cultural values' including personal collecting and museum work (J Pearson *pers comm*; D Hamilton *pers comm*). However, the Society does not have a formal definition of heritage to distinguish it from history. Indeed, 'whilst the Society caters for those interested in collecting what has become known as "Golfiania", its dominant aim was and is always to promote an interest in the history and traditions of golf' (BGCS 2010).

There are many books filled with pictures of golf memorabilia and golfing art but the real thing is available to view (McGimpsey and Leech 1999; McClelland 2006). Some golf clubs display collections of material culture, though they tend to be restricted primarily to prizes, playing equipment and photographs and are usually limited in their scope. The BGCS often exhibits material, but mainly to its fellow collectors. It is to the museums that the ordinary golf enthusiast must turn to see golf's heritage of material culture.

The major repository of golf memorabilia in Britain is the British Golf Museum (BGM), sited to the east of the Royal & Ancient (R&A) clubhouse on the Bruce Embankment in St Andrews (Fig 10.1). Although proposals for a golf museum in St Andrews had been discussed since the early 1970s, it was not until June 1990 that the British Golf Museum first opened its doors to the public. By 1985 the R&A's growing collection of memorabilia meant that, as Denis Hayes told the General Committee (of which he was Chair), 'the desirability of a suitable museum for the housing and preservation of these priceless assets had been noticeably advanced', especially given severe limitations on display space within the clubhouse. Indeed, the Museum was the financial child of the R&A, the acknowledged ruling body of golf since 1897, which paid all the £2.1 million needed except for £300,000 that came from the Scottish Tourist Board and sponsorship for the interactive displays from Philips Electronics. The R&A still provide annual payments towards operating costs and artefact purchase. It was not an easy birth. Only a month after Peter Lewis had been appointed Museum Director, the local council refused planning permission for the building; malcontents within the R&A then proposed that the project be abandoned but were brought into line by the astute intervention of ex-Conservative minister Willie Whitelaw. A redesign into a single-storeyed building won over the Council and the rest is history ... or even heritage (Steel and Lewis 2004). As the Director aptly put it, within a few years 'it ceased being known as the controversial British Golf Museum and rapidly became known as the award-winning British Golf Museum' (Steel and Lewis 2004, 225).

The mission of the curatorial staff of the museum and heritage department is to promote, interpret and care for the history of golf, reaching the widest possible audience through the means at its disposal. These include, but are not restricted to:

- Creating high-quality displays in the British Golf Museum and Club properties
- Creating high-quality exhibitions and displays for R&A events, golf-related organisations and museums around the world
- Acquiring artefacts to enhance the collections of the British Golf Museum and those relating to the history of The Royal and Ancient Golf Club
- Research and publication in printed, website, multimedia and new media formats
- High-quality care of the Museum and Club collections
- Advising other golfing bodies (clubs etc) on the care and display of their collections
- Encouraging and providing assistance to golf club historians, academics and the general public who are interested in researching the history of the game
- Running education programmes in the British Golf Museum (A Howe *pers comm*)

After passing through the inevitable shop, visitors are welcomed by a statue of Old Tom Morris, Keeper of the Greens at St Andrews from 1864 to 1903. The introductory gallery greets them with a variety of information. They learn (hopefully) that the putter, alone among clubs, has retained its nomenclature through the ages; and that golf has had its own terminology, with an explanation of bogie, par, and the emergence of birdie and those much rarer creatures, the eagle and the albatross. There is a significant collection of old clubs made by local craftsmen the Auchterlonie brothers, and video of highlights from the Open Championship. From then on, with the exception of an art gallery, the presentation is essentially chronological. Completing the tour is a mini artificial putting green on which visitors can try their skill using replica 19th-century clubs and balls. Much of the Museum's exhibition is artefacts in display cases and explanations on panels. However, there are some interactivity stations at which visitors can test their knowledge of the rules of golf, select highlights of particular Opens to watch and look at 18th-century documents on the history of golf.

Museums can simply display artefacts; good museums offer some analysis of what they are exhibiting. Hardy and his colleagues have argued that material culture could be analysed according to six long-term residuals which, though sometimes changing in character, generally exhibit long-term continuity of belief and practice. They are *agon* (the core contest between opposing individuals or teams); *craft* (the skills, practices and technology required to achieve in the competition); *community* (the ways in which both athletes and spectators create bonds and bridges that simultaneously link and separate groups through shared sporting passions; *gambling* (the wagering on the outcome of competition which drives much of the passion surrounding sport); *eros* (the sexual attraction of agonal bodies); and *framing* (the tendency to surround the *agon* with frames of spectacle and festival).

With the exception of *eros* – presumably left to the media and Tiger Woods! – the BGM has explored some of these avenues, though not using such academic terminology. *Agon* is clearly seen in the chronological lists of winners of the Open and Amateur Championships. However, little is shown on team competitions: even the Ryder Cup, the major international challenge match between the PGAs of Europe and the United States, scarcely gets a mention. The Museum's galleries are dominated by the concept of *craft*, as changing technology is a major theme pursued by the curators. *Community* brings in the idea of social capital, 'bridging', with an inclusive agenda that cuts across class, religious, gender and other boundaries, or 'bonding', which infers the use of exclusionary practices to enforce a homogeneous group identity. Here the BGM picks up two issues. First, it emphasises the social, playing and rule-making role of the early golf societies, which were clearly exclusive in nature, and, second, it deals with the early definition of amateur and professional, where the latter was a non-gentleman earning money from golf by making clubs, manufacturing balls, caddying or looking after the course. In neither case, though, were these issues brought into the present. Similarly, the role of *gambling* in modern golf is ignored, although one panel states that some of the early societies had betting books for their members. It is a pity that the physical layout of the Museum, with occasional roped-off gaps allowing the visitor a glimpse of the future displays to be seen, is not replicated in the displays themselves. Although the themes of equipment and its manufacture, major tournaments and their winners, and golf course architecture and maintenance run through the galleries, other issues are raised and then ignored as one moves into the more modern era. Where today did feature strongly was in the *framing* of the Open. To celebrate the 150th anniversary of the Open, being held in 2010 at St Andrews, the Museum created the 'Open Trail', in which particular artefacts were highlighted both in the displays and in a free commemorative booklet.

So what is missing from the BGM? From a heritage viewpoint what the Museum lacks is ambience. Although this view is subjective and perhaps influenced by too many personal visits, nothing in the Museum grabbed my attention. In contrast, the atmosphere felt when standing on the first tee on the Old Course at St Andrews – with the expanse of the links in front and the imposing R&A clubhouse behind, the wind picking up from the sea and the pot bunkers waiting to trap the unwary, unskilled or just unlucky – more easily prompts the query 'when did all this begin?' Ironically, once past the entrance, the architecture of the Museum does not even allow a glimpse of the course just across the road.

As with many museums, sport or otherwise, the BGM resorts to traditional heroic narratives in order to attract visitors and thus there is an (undue) concentration on the elite players, both amateur and professional, and a concomitant neglect of ordinary golfers, who really get a serious mention only in the panel dealing with the coming of the rubber-cored golf ball in the early 20th century, an innovation resisted by the elite but adopted almost immediately by club golfers as it enabled them to hit the ball further and thereby increased the pleasure that they got from the game (Vamplew 2004). Many club golfers were women. Unlike many games, golf was played by both sexes and offered the possibility of mixed participation, providing an opportunity for a family or married couple to share recreation. Nevertheless, while the sport was not one of courage and overt masculinity, like cricket, football and rugby, it was still framed as a male-dominated activity and the history of women's golf is one of separate and often unequal development (George *et al* 2007). This is not adequately dealt with in the Museum. Although there are two displays devoted to women in golf, the fact that one is captioned 'Playing With Style' suggests a particular view of female golfers. Nowhere is there any mention of the continuing struggle that women have had to secure equal playing and voting rights. There is little, too, on the operation of golf clubs as social institutions except for a panel dealing with club life in the 19th century, but this looked at the R&A, scarcely a typical representative. Nor, unless I missed it, was there anything on the development of the handicap system – incidentally, a venture pioneered by women – which has enabled players at all levels of the sport to play together competitively. It should not be forgotten that without the ordinary golfer there would be far fewer golf clubs and significantly fewer opportunities for elite players to emerge. Finally, while acknowledging the limitations of space and the fact that golf was not a big spectator sport until well into the 20th century, the Museum also neglects the watcher of the game, other than a small section dealing with the fans' experience of the Open via a display of tickets, programmes, mugs and badges.

One strength of the BGM – to this historian – is its cautious approach. Its *Royal Troon* collection is *reputed* to be the oldest surviving set of golf clubs in the world and a diagrammatic representation depicts the *approximate* number of clubs in Britain by geographical area. Another admirable quality is its willingness to go beyond the obvious material culture; so we find displays dealing with golf in art and literature and with artists and writers who played the game. This is real cultural production rather than the cultural reproduction too common in sports museums. It also nicely contextualises the cost of playing golf in the 18th century, not by using a modern Consumer Price Index (which would have necessitated constant updating) but by comparing the price of balls and clubs with the cost of contemporary clothing, something that can be put into modern perspective relatively easily by any visitor from any country.

Scotland has another, much smaller, museum devoted to golf. This is the Heritage of Golf Museum located next to the professional's shop at Gullane Golf Club (Gullane Golf Club 2010). Despite its site, the museum is privately owned by ex-Gullane captain Archie Baird, winner of the Murdoch medal in 2000, and is essentially his personal collection of artwork, equipment and memorabilia. It is open only by appointment and is free of charge, though donations are appreciated. However, Baird's interest is in the years before the rubber-cored ball, which restricts the Museum's coverage and sets a time limit to a definition of heritage. To his credit, Baird acknowledges that golf probably began in Holland and was imported to Scotland where it became popularised.

Even those museums and other institutions not dedicated to golf occasionally hold exhibitions dealing with the sport's history. A prime example is the recent *A Swing Through Time: Golf in Scotland*, held at the National Library of Scotland in Edinburgh from June 2010 to March 2011, which 'charts the social history of the game in Scotland and highlights the influences that make golf the game we know today' (NLS 2010). Among over 200 exhibits are the first minute book of the world's oldest golf club, diaries and letters of golfers from 1574 to the present day and the first printed book devoted entirely to golf. Although it had film footage of Open winners it also featured material from the Scottish Screen Archive showing amateur players from the 1920s to the 1960s enjoying their sport. And a cautious approach was taken in describing the 260-year-old Musselburgh Cup, which was '*believed* to be the world's oldest golfing trophy still being played for'. It is a pity that the curators could not correctly spell the name of Harry Vardon, the greatest player of the Edwardian era and a golfer whose grip is still coached today: heritage indeed!

Then we have virtual museums, the most recent example of which is that for miniature golf, or, as it is labelled in Britain, Crazy Golf. Organised by two of the premier miniature golfers

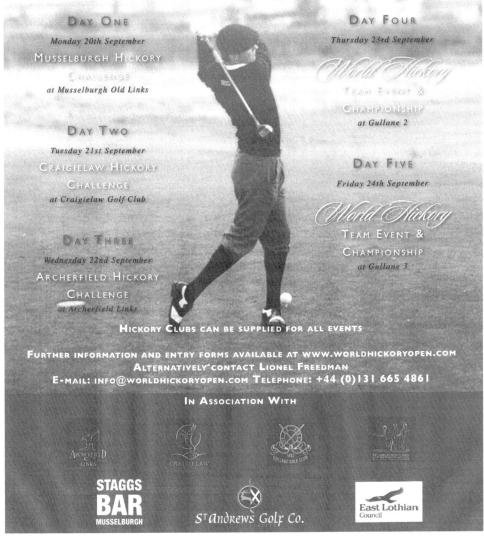

FIG 10.2. POSTER ADVERTISING WORLD HICKORY OPEN CHAMPIONSHIP.

in the UK, it offers 'a worldwide archive of miniature golf memories, histories and ephemera' (Davies and Gottfried 2010). The site is in its infancy and contains an appeal not only for sponsorship and advertising but also to course owners, suppliers, builders, clubs and associations for pictures and information. Internet golf ball supplier UK Lakeball host a virtual golf museum (Lake Balls Golf Museum 2010) which presents basic detail, including rough valuations of old balls, and an auction site. Its quality might be judged by some of its text, which describes the site as the place to be 'wether [sic] you are a serious collector looking to add to your collection or indeed if you are just begginning [sic] your collection'! In fact, this site is but one feature of a website mainly concerned with selling modern balls.

HERITAGE IN ACTION

The opportunity given to BGM visitors to try out 'old' equipment does tempt the user to admire the skills of the 18th-century players and realise how far club design has come. More regular demonstration of heritage in action comes from the BGCS, which organises golf tournaments in which the players employ hickory-shafted clubs and wear period dress. The American Society of Hickory Golfers has taken the lead by developing two main divisions of play. The pre-1900 group play with the old gutta-percha ball (or its equivalent) and clubs must have been produced before 1900 or be an authorised reproduction. The pre-1935 group play with modern balls, but clubs must have been manufactured before 1935 or be authorised reproductions. This is around about the time that steel-shafted clubs finally came to rule the golfing world (perhaps with the exception of putters) and matched sets of clubs were being introduced. However, there are no pre-game equipment inspections; as in most golf, the players are trusted not to infringe the rules.

It is in this area of golfing nostalgia that the private sector has found a market. The St Andrews Golf Company, which advertises itself as 'the last club maker in the world retaining the traditional skills to hand craft playable sets of hickory golf clubs' (St Andrews Golf Company 2010), has roots back to 1881 and offers not just handmade replica vintage clubs but also a repair service for old implements. There is a ready demand for its output as 'heritage' and 'hickory' tournaments have expanded in number, partly through the efforts of the BGCS but additionally via more commercial enterprises. Other companies in the golf heritage industry include Past Masters, now in its 15th year, and Timewarp Golf (Past Masters 2010; Bottrell 2010), who offer packages for club fundraisers and corporate golfing days in which holes or rounds are played with hickory-shafted clubs and sometimes also replica golf balls of the pre-rubber-core era. The inaugural World Hickory Open was held in 2005 at Musselburgh Old Links, appropriately claimed to be the longest continually played course in the world, and has continued under the aegis of a private promoter (Fig 10.2). The latest event, the sixth, was over five days at four different Scottish courses and, backed by the PGA and the Scottish Golf Union, included both professional and amateur players (Freedman 2010). Some of the proceeds were donated to the Keepers of the Green (a tribute to Old Tom Morris), an international St Andrews-based charity devoted to promoting 'the traditions of golf and to provide powered mobility for the needy' (Keepers of the Green 2010). But how do they help preserve such traditions? Essentially by playing with authentic sets of five hickory clubs (spoon, cleek, mid iron, niblick and putter) on the St Andrews links at their Spring and Autumn gatherings. They also recommend that members pursue another golfing tradition by organising challenge matches among themselves in two-ball foursomes. Yet their website has a section devoted to the history of golf which remains

Fig 10.3. David Joy in his role as Old Tom Morris, Keeper of the Greens at St Andrews from 1864 to 1903.

blank, suggesting that playing golf is more important to them than researching its past. Their patron is actor and golf historian David Joy, who makes some of his living by portraying Old Tom at golf and corporate functions. As an individual David, whose great grandfather was a caddie at St Andrews in the 1890s, has done much to conserve the heritage of golf in his paintings and drawings, his golf histories, his personal collection of old photographs and, above all, his dramatic representation of Old Tom Morris (Fig 10.3), whom he uses to illustrate the changes in golf during his lifetime, from 1821 to 1908 (Joy 2010).

Non-Material Heritage

Golf also has a less tangible cultural heritage associated with language and behaviour. Golf heritage has become part of our speech as the sport's terminology has entered the vernacular, with 'teeing off', 'bunkered', 'stymied' and 'rub of the green', although whether its users are aware that a stymie occurred when an opponent's ball blocked a direct putt at the hole (a rule removed in 1952) is debatable. Nor would most golfers appreciate that the green referred to was not the putting surface and the intricacies of its lawns, but the fairways, which in times gone by often included stones and other impediments from which even a well-directed drive from the tee could bounce into a bunker.

The sport prides itself on its player integrity and, at club level, its sociability. Although rules have recently been introduced to penalise players for intemperate language and equipment abuse, golf has a strong code of player self-regulation. It is rare among sports in that its rule book has a section on etiquette preceding the actual rules of the game. In the 2010 Verizon Heritage tournament in the United States, British professional Brian Davies called a two-shot penalty on himself, thus losing the playoff for the title. No-one else had seen the infringement but, when praised for his honesty, his replies evoked the response decades earlier of the great American amateur, Bobby Jones, who, when applauded for an act of sportsmanship in calling a penalty shot on himself in the 1925 US Open, responded 'You'd as well praise me for not breaking into banks' (Frost 2006, 179).

Central to the development of golf in Britain was the club. Golf was popularised from the 17th century primarily as a short game – little more than putting – played in churchyards and other small areas by a broad spectrum of the population using minimal equipment (Hamilton 1998). However, as golf developed into a longer game it required larger amounts of land and became a less democratic sport. The club, with its ability to raise funds collectively, became the instrument of golf expansion. Yet golf was more than a game. Out on the fairways and greens it was a participant sport but the organisation of golf as a club-based recreation meant that it offered, additionally, a social meeting place. A selection from prefaces to golf club histories shows that they make much of the (traditional) sociability of the clubhouse. At Bradford members 'over the past years' have created 'a happy golf club'; Langley Park 'has been fortunate over the years in having a membership resolved to maintain and foster friendliness and good fellowship'; at Hesketh 'tradition and good companionship are still considered to be of paramount importance'; golfers at Droitwich 'continue the genial atmosphere'; and Biggar still has 'a reputation for its hospitality, friendship and a warm welcome' (Richardson 1991, 7; MacDonald 1985, 10; Hick 1985, vi; Bromhead 1996, x; Ward and Ward 1995, 2).

Guardians of Golf's Heritage

No single institution, group of people or individual can claim to be *the* guardian of golf's heritage. Moreover, the term heritage can involve diverse narratives. Historians have a role to play as they document what has happened in the past to pass on to the future. The private sector has a role, often because it has the money. The new Dunes course at Machrihanish, as far west as you can go on the Scottish mainland, is being marketed as 'The Way Golf Began', but this is plainly hyperbole as, although only seven of the 250 acres could be cultivated by the designers and though it has the look of an old links course, the players venture forth with modern equipment (Ferrie 2010). In material culture terms the BGM is to the fore, supplemented (and in some areas outdriven and outbid) by the BGCS and other private collectors. Yet, except by the use of film, museums do not generally demonstrate how the equipment was used. It is almost taken as a given that the observer will know. But where is the evidence to show that the hickory club users actually play authentic shots with the balls and clubs of yesteryear?

But can museums tell us much about the non-material culture of golf? Should we look elsewhere for this? In the words of Professor Colin Tatz, author of histories of Royal Sydney and Monash clubs in Australia, 'a good golf club history' produces a 'sense of loyalty or tradition and, more important, [a] sense of soul' (Tatz 2007, 24). There is a caveat here. At the level of the club history the historians who painstakingly work their way through minutes, scrapbooks and other primary sources are generally golfers first and historians second. The club heritage which they depict is one based on a particular viewpoint. Club records are sites of privilege and contain material selected by the committees of the day. Moreover, few amateur historians, for all their detailed research, can match the analysis of an academic historian such as the late John Lowerson (Lowerson 1994 and 1995). Yet is his contextual examination of the role of class in the sport or his critique of the Scottish role in golf development what heritage is about, or should we stick to the narrative efforts of the amateurs? In many cases this would infer the acceptance that recycling conventional wisdom is heritage conservation.

Club historians do not always see the broad picture; their focus is usually on a micro aspect of golf's history. When they contextualise it is usually of the kind found in the history of Beaconsfield Golf Club, which notes:

> in April 1902 the Sino-Russian Treaty over Manchuria was concluded, a massive blaze destroyed a large area of the Barbican in the City of London, a state of emergency was declared in Ireland, twenty people died when a stand collapsed at the Ibrox Park football stadium in Glasgow and the Wilton Park Golf Club on the Du Pre Estate at Beaconsfield (population 1,524) was instituted. (Tuck 2002, vii)

However, they are thorough. Often derided by academic historians as antiquarians, amateur enthusiasts in all branches of history generally get the facts right. They have no time for the theory of Foucault and Bourdieu or theoretical concepts such as modernisation, materialism, hegemony, feminism, discourse and textualism. They would not necessarily accept that historical perspective is contested terrain with a plurality of meanings and that there are different versions of events depending on the perspective from which the narrative is being constructed. They may not appreciate Booth's argument that all 'facts are propositional statements about the nature of reality' and that all sources distort or filter the truth and all need interpretation (Booth 2005,

30). But certainly in golf they provide the raw material from which the sport's heritage can be constructed.

Golf clubs and their members can also contribute. Clubs themselves preserve courses and clubhouses, though rarely in their original form. But what about club archives? Too many have been lost over time, victims of fires, floods, removal men and, more distressingly, committee decision. Here a plea can be made for a set of photocopied records, especially of the early years, to be deposited in the local county record office. Then there are those who frequent the clubs. Golf is a game for all ages and the intergenerational aspect of club membership means that the standards of appropriate behaviour can be passed on by example more easily than, say, in a football club. Additionally, longevity within the club membership ensures a 'memory' of how things were (and should be) done.

Scotland and the town of St Andrews in particular have exploited the heritage of golf as a tourist attraction, but what have they done in return to preserve golf's heritage? St Andrews proclaims itself as 'The Home of Golf' and within the town there are commemorative plaques in older areas, and streets such as Tom Morris Drive in the newer ones. The St Andrews Links Trust, responsible for the maintenance of the Old Course, could not prevent the demolition of the 'Sheds' by the 17th tee but erected mesh fencing in the same dimensions as the removed buildings. Moreover, despite the unrelenting demand from visitors willing to pay a high price to play a round, they maintain significant and traditional access for local golfers. In terms of personnel, around 250 caddies are available in the summer season to carry the bags of those golfing tourists prepared to abandon their trolleys and play like an old-time golfer (Butler 2005). And the Cowie Photographic Collection, devoted to St Andrews and held at the University Library, has over 60,000 negatives with more than a quarter concerning golf.

The major golf-related institution in St Andrews is the R&A, which wears a guardianship mantle: indeed, one section of an information booklet about the Club is titled 'Keepers of Golf's Heritage' and one of the Club's four major objectives is 'to acquire and preserve records and artefacts relating to the history of the game of golf either directly or indirectly' (Lewis and Howe 2008). To this end they fund the BGM but have also published a three-volume history of the R&A as well as books on golf art and architecture and golf photography. The Club has also lent material to other institutions for special exhibitions and assisted bodies overseas in developing their own museums and collections. In recent years the R&A has built up an extensive film archive, particularly of the Open and Amateur Championships and the Walker Cup. Under the direction of Peter Lewis, the founding director of the BGM but now Director of Film Archive, a programme of early film restoration is being undertaken to preserve important footage. Details of this can be found in a series of articles in recent issues of *Through The Green*.

A DARK SIDE?

Not all of golf's heritage is to be applauded. There are negative and contentious aspects to golf's past, some of which continue today. Dress regulations imposed by clubs then and now are ancillary rules that have nothing to do with playing the game (Vamplew 2007; Cairns 2005). Similarly, although it has been shown that women were not as absolutely discriminated against as once thought in pre-World War I golfing society, they still faced difficulties of access and restrictions on both playing and voting rights, something that still persists in many clubs (Vamplew 2010).

Golf's handicapping system gave all players an equal chance on the course but social equality was less of a consideration. The social capital formation of the Edwardian golf club was of the bonding, not the bridging, variety. Golf clubs drew people together from a similar sociological niche and tended to reinforce exclusive identities and maintain homogeneity by such mechanisms as the level of fees, the wearing of uniforms and election procedures. Segmentation of clubs within the same area separated golfers from different social groups within the middle class without excluding them from playing: indeed, the social distance between neighbouring clubs could be far greater than the geographical (Vamplew 2010).

At the bottom end of the social scale, those few artisans who were allowed to share the course did so at times specified by the middle-class committee and often only in return for labouring on the greens and fairways. Even the elite working-class golfer in the guise of the club professional was barred from the clubhouse and its facilities. Surely such treatment is not part of a desired historical legacy? And what of the poor caddie, out in all weathers without the protective clothing worn by the club member, spending much of his time waiting for employment and learning few transferable skills along the way (Vamplew 2008)? Would the hickory club players of today want to have children as young as seven carry their bags? There are limits to the acceptable face of golfing heritage. Some aspects of golf's (un)sporting past are best remembered rather than reproduced.

BIBLIOGRAPHY AND REFERENCES

Booth, D, 2005 *The Field: Truth and Fiction in Sport History*, Routledge, Abingdon

Bottrell, G, 2010 *Timewarp Golf* [online], available from: http://www.timewarpgolf.com [16 September 2010]

British Golf Collectors' Society, 2010 *A Brief History of the B.G.C.S.*, available from: http://www.britgolfcollectors.wyenet.co.uk [15 January 2010]

British Golf Museum, 2010 *British Golf Museum* [online], available from: http://www.britishgolfmuseum.co.uk [20 September 2010]

Bromhead, J, 1996 *Droitwich Golf Club 1897–1997*, Grant Books, Worcestershire

Butler, R, 2005 The Influence of Sport on Destination Development: the Example of Golf at St Andrews, Scotland, in *Sports Tourism Destinations* (ed J Higham), Elsevier-Butterworth-Heinemann, Oxford, 274–82

Cairns, C, 2005 *No Tie Required: How The Rich Stole Golf*, Headline, London

Davies, T, and Gottfried, R, 2010 *The Crazy Golf Museum* [online], available from: http://www.crazygolf-museum.info [30 October 2010]

Ferrie, K, 2010 Machrihanish has a new top-class course to join Old Tom Morris one, Kevin Ferrie on Thursday in *The Herald* (Scotland), 29 July, 16, available from: http://www.heraldscotland.com/blogs/stramash/kevin-ferrie-on-thursday-machrihanish-has-a-new-top-class-course-to-join-old-tom-morris-one-1.1044408 [3 January 2012]

Freedman, L, 2010 *World Hickory Open Championship* [online], available from: http://www.worldhickoryopen.com [16 September 2010]

Frost, M, 2006 *The Grand Slam*, Time Warner Books, London

George, J, Kay, J, and Vamplew, W, 2007 Women to the fore: accommodation and resistance at the British golf club before 1914, *Sporting Traditions* 23 (2), 79–98

Gullane Golf Club, 2010 *Golf Scotland – Gullane Golf Club* [online], available from: http://www.gulla-negolfclub.com/visitor [9 November 2010]

Hamilton, D, 1998 *Golf: Scotland's Game*, Partick Press, Kilmacolm

Hardy, S, Loy, J, and Booth, D, 2009 The Material Culture of Sport: Towards a Typology, *Journal of Sport History* 36 (1), 129–52

Hick, K C, 1985 *The Hesketh Golf Club 1885–1985*, Hesketh GC, Southport

Joy, D, 2010 *David Joy* [online], available from: http://www.golfhistorian.co.uk [20 September 2010]

Keepers of the Green, 2010 *Keepers of the Green* [online], available from: http://www.keepersofthegreen.org [20 September 2010]

Lake Balls Golf Museum, 2010 *Golfball Museum* [online], available from: http://www.golfballmuseum.co.uk [30 October 2010]

Lewis, P N, and Howe, A, 2008 *The Royal and Ancient Golf Club of St Andrews*, R&A, St Andrews

Lowerson, J, 1994 Golf and the Making of Myths, in *Scottish Sport in the Making of the Nation* (eds G Jarvie and G Walker), Leicester University Press, London, 75–90

— 1995 *Sport and the English Middle Classes 1870–1914*, Manchester University Press, Manchester

MacDonald, A, 1985 *The History of Langley Park Golf Club 1910–1985*, Langley Park GC, Beckenham

McClelland, J, 2006 The History of Golf: Reading Pictures, Viewing Texts, *Journal of Sport History* 33 (3), 345–57

McGimpsey, K, and Leech, D, 1999 *Golf Implements and Memorabilia*, Philip Wilson, London

National Library of Scotland, 2010 *A swing through time: golf in Scotland* [online], available from: http://www.nls.uk/exhibitions/golf [8 October 2010]

Past Masters, 2010 *Old Links Golf Events* [online], available from: http://www.oldlinksgolf.com [16 September 2010]

Richardson, G A, 1991 *The Hawksworth Hundred: Bradford Golf Club 1891–1991*, Bradford CG, Bradford

St Andrews Golf Company, 2010 *St Andrews Golf Company* [online], available from: http://www.standrews-golfco.com [16 September 2010]

Steel, D, and Lewis, P N, 2004 *Traditions and Change: The Royal & Ancient Golf Club 1939–2004*, R&A, St Andrews

Tatz, C, 2007 Writing a Golf Club History, in *Writing a Golf Club History: Some Experiences* (eds J Pearson and B Leithhead), British and Australian Golf Collectors' Societies, York, 19–24

Tuck, G, 2002 *Beaconsfield Golf Club 1902–2002*, Grant Books, Worcestershire

Vamplew, W, 2004 Sporting innovation: the American invasion of the British turf and links 1895–1905, *Sport History Review* 35, 122–37

— 2007 Playing with the Rules: Influences on the Development of Regulation in Sport, *International Journal of the History of Sport* (24), 843–71

— 2008 Childwork or Child Labour? The Caddie Question in Edwardian Golf [online], available from: http//www.idrottsforum.org [10 June 2010]

— 2010 Sharing Space: Inclusion, Exclusion, and Accommodation at the British Golf Club Before 1914, *Journal of Sport and Social Issues* 34 (3), 359–75

Ward, H, and Ward, A, 1995 *Biggar Golf Club: A History 1895–1995*, Biggar GC, Biggar

11

Upping Our Game:
The New Wimbledon Lawn Tennis Museum

Honor Godfrey

The analysis of sports museums by interested academics is on the increase, although the number of academic reviews of new museums or exhibitions remains limited, beyond the 'Museum Reviews' section of the *Journal of Sport History* (see, for example, Adair 2004; Alegi 2006; Brabazon 2006a; Brabazon 2006b; Brabazon and Mallinder 2006; Johnes and Mason 2003; Kohe 2010; Moore 2008; Osmond and Phillips 2011; Phillips 2010; Phillips and Tinning 2011; Ramshaw 2010; Vamplew 1998; Vamplew 2004). The publication in 2012 of a major edited volume by historians on the representations of sporting history in museums (Phillips 2012) is therefore welcome. Lacking, too, is much published self-reflection by the museum professionals concerned with interpreting sporting history. Short reviews in professional forums such as *Museums Journal* have to suffice. Yet museum displays, in sports museums and elsewhere, have long moved on from simply objects in cases and the 'book on the wall' approach to images and text. Museum exhibitions are increasingly sophisticated, technologically complex and based on extensive audience research. They typically involve scores of specialist contractors with a wide range of skills. A close consideration of the development of new museums can be useful to both the practitioner and the critic. This chapter is offered as a detailed examination of the process of creating the new Wimbledon Lawn Tennis Museum from my perspective as Curator.

Wimbledon Lawn Tennis Museum was formally opened on 19 May 1977 as part of the celebrations surrounding the Centenary of the first Championships. The idea for a museum sprang from the success of a historical tennis display at Leamington Spa Art Gallery and Museum in 1972. This commemorated the Centenary of the playing of lawn tennis in Leamington, and the founding of the first lawn tennis club in the world. Subsequently, historical material was allowed to accumulate at the premises of The Lawn Tennis Association (LTA) in Barons Court, London, and donations to a homeless National Lawn Tennis Museum began. With the approaching Centenary at Wimbledon, it was agreed that The All England Lawn Tennis & Croquet Club, the most famous centre of the game in the world, should house a permanent lawn tennis museum and archive. The Museum is owned by The All England Lawn Tennis Ground Ltd, and is jointly managed by The All England Lawn Tennis Club (Championships) Ltd and The Lawn Tennis Association.

In its infancy, the Museum drew heavily on the extensive private collection of tennis historian Tom Todd, made available to Wimbledon on permanent loan. This was strongest in early rackets, tennis figurines, Victorian knickknacks illustrated with a tennis theme and artefacts relating to early players. Other mainstays were the objects collected by the LTA and those found at the All England Club and around the Wimbledon site, including historical documents, tennis equipment, seating, honours boards and so on. The exhibition space, slotted into the east side of Centre Court, occupied a long narrow gallery covering 4600 square feet. The overall colour was grass green and the tennis theme was reinforced by tennis nets, white lines and bench seating from Centre Court. The displays ran chronologically, proceeding down one side of the gallery and up the other. Set pieces, like the original Men's Dressing Room, a Victorian Parlour and a Racket Maker's Workshop, were incorporated. At various points the displays opened out to include sections of tennis equipment, full-size costumed figures of 'tennis greats' and a free-standing umpire's chair. In terms of technology, match commentaries played continuously at two listening posts, where visitors were invited to plug in their personal stethoscope headsets to hear recorded interviews. A variety of films were shown in the Film Theatre. The *Museums Journal* review at the time was mostly complimentary: in particular, the link between the Museum and the Centre Court provided by a viewing platform was 'a touch of genuine inspiration'. However, it noted over-emphasis on the very early history of the game and a lack of devotion to the more recent great personalities 'who, after all, draw in public support and sustain the unique flavour of the game' (Pearce 1978, 63–4).

By 1984 the collection had grown significantly through acquisitions, donations and the purchase of two important private collections. Every effort had been made to add to the collections – photographs, ephemera, books, advertising and posters – but early material remained easier and less problematic to collect than contemporary material. In that year, extensions to the Centre Court East Building provided the opportunity for a complete redesign of the Museum and the development of the collection was reflected in the enhanced displays and the increase in exhibition area by 20 per cent. The Museum closed for a year while work was in progress and opened in its second incarnation on the eve of the 1985 Championships.

Throughout the 1990s the Museum continued to update its displays and to capitalise on any additional space it was offered. In 1991 redesigned modern galleries, covering the period from the 1930s to the 1990s, were opened. These relied heavily on graphics and focused on film and interactive computer exhibits in the absence of a wealth, or any great variety, of objects post-1930. In the following year a new special exhibition area was created by the Museum at the north end. This housed several temporary exhibitions before becoming a costume gallery in 1999. The displays dealing with the years 1968 onwards were further updated in 1996 to provide better coverage of players from the 1980s and 1990s, to highlight the impact of technology on the game and to reflect the role of the Grand Slam tournaments.

Nevertheless, by the end of the decade the Museum was outdated and in need of change. Beautifully maintained, it had become a 'period piece' and the limitations of putting 'new wine into old bottles' when developing new exhibits were only too evident. Sporting records had been broken, new talents had emerged, changes to Wimbledon were not documented. Some displays were repetitive, others were 'tired' or too wordy. Initial visitor research highlighted the demand for interactive displays, the lack of multilingual interpretation, the popularity of videos and film footage and the underwhelming nature of the Centre Court experience.

Positioning and Branding

The arrival of a Commercial Manager at the Museum in 1997 prompted a series of changes which allowed the Museum to move forward. A mission statement was agreed in April 1998:

> To present the story of The Championships at Wimbledon to the public for their enjoyment and education. This encompasses the origins of lawn tennis and its development and importance in today's sporting world, and the role of the All England Lawn Tennis Club and The Lawn Tennis Association. This will be achieved through an active policy of collection, preservation, research and interpretation and information dissemination.

A position statement followed:

> The Museum, set in the unique context of Centre Court, reflects the history of lawn tennis and explains many of the quintessentially British traditions associated with the game. Its exhibits encapsulate the prestige, the glamour and the glory associated with The Championships, the last being most clearly defined by the Trophies, which are on display in the Museum, and by the view of Centre Court itself.

> The Museum seeks to inform its visitors in an interesting and exciting way and to honour the greatest tennis players that the world has known. The Museum does not, however, simply recount the history of the game of tennis and of Wimbledon and of the AELTC, but reflects the state of the current game and the champions of today, and aims to encourage the interest of the potential champions of tomorrow. (Wimbledon Lawn Tennis Museum 1998)

Subsequently Wimbledon Lawn Tennis Museum was developed as a brand extension of the main Wimbledon Championships brand, retaining the core values associated with The Championships: Englishness, formality, lawn tennis, an upmarket position, stylishness, enjoyment and prestige. A new corporate identity was developed and adopted for the Museum's promotional material, advertising and signage, with The Championships' crossed rackets logo being used in every application.

At the same time, the Museum sought to discover more about its visitors. The introduction of ongoing nationality surveys enabled the Museum to identify the countries of origin of visitors, to build a relationship with the travel trade and to target potential visitors at the times when they made their decisions about travel and planned their holidays or their days out. Multilingual leaflets were introduced in five languages as well as English. By 2011 leaflets included eight languages, the latest addition being Croatian.

Tours of the Grounds

In 1999 guided tours of the grounds began for pre-booked groups under the aegis of the Museum. Led by Blue Badge guides, the tours covered No 1 Court, 'Henman Hill', the Fred Perry statue and Centre Court. Public tours were introduced from Easter 2002; they were initially confined to the April–October period, but were gradually extended to every month of the year. In the same year the Museum won the London Tourist Board Small Attraction of the Year Award for the introduction of the behind-the-scenes tour. The combination of the tour and the Museum is greater than the sum of the parts. For 50 weeks of the year the Museum is the public face of Wimbledon and the tour seeks to conjure up the atmosphere of The Championships. During Wimbledon Fortnight, when there are no tours, the excitement of the live presence on site of the players and champions of the 21st century, combined with the Museum's insight into both these players and the ghosts of the past, create a potent visitor experience.

Museum Master Plan

During 2000, a working party was set up to consider a master planning exercise for the Museum. The initial task was to interview and appoint a firm of design consultants to work with the Museum on the project. Five companies were approached, four were interviewed, and Mather & Co were appointed. Before any work had started on the master plan the Museum was offered 110 square metres at the south end of the Museum in the former international press writing rooms. The space, developed as an Art Gallery and AV Theatre, was flexibly designed by Mather & Co in order to allow additional use of the whole area for corporate hospitality functions. The white walls, wooden floor and contemporary design finishes gave a good indication of how the whole Museum could look and helped to 'sell' the master plan.

In broad outline, the Museum master plan looked at the whole Museum from point of entry to point of exit as well as the wider context of the Museum's environment. It considered the following components:

- Approaches to the Museum
- Café Centre Court
- The Stairwell and Lift to the Museum
- The Museum Shop
- The Centre Court Experience
- The Museum's Exhibitions
- Integration of the Tour and Museum visit

A series of 'new vision' design team meetings, coupled with staff brainstorming sessions incorporating feedback, enabled the designers to produce a schematic plan for the existing Museum space. This consisted of a series of zones through which the visitor would travel in an anticlockwise direction:

- Quintessentially British: the approach stairwell, looking at fans, strawberries and cream, champagne, weather, records, etc
- Orientation Area: past, present and future
- Historic Gallery: beautiful showcases with artefact-based displays up to 1968 (advent of Open Tennis)
- Playing the Game: rules, tactics, scoring and officials, with a strong interactive component
- Tennis Equipment: rackets and balls with interactive space relating to the power of the serve
- Cinema: AV presentation, *Power*, focusing on the changing nature of tennis
- Art Gallery: special exhibitions, flexible space for corporate hospitality
- Costume and Player Memorabilia: changing fashions and memorabilia of modern players

- On the Circuit: lifestyle of contemporary players
- Tennis Today: live information on world tennis
- Trophies: artefact display linked to Winners and Losers AV presentation
- Viewing Platform: comedy, tragedy and victory on Centre Court

A New Museum for Wimbledon

Unfortunately, realisation of the master plan in the existing Museum was not to be. The announcement in 2002 of the Club's plans for a retractable roof on Centre Court and the redevelopment of the east side of the stadium necessitated – once again – the complete removal of the Museum and all its associated activities. These by now included the Library, the Library Extension, staff offices, three stores, the Education Department and the Playing for Success Centre. The Museum was given three options: (1) reinstate the existing Museum in another location; (2) close until a new space became available in Centre Court; or (3) create a new Museum for the 21st century.

The first option was not feasible as the structure of the Museum was custom-fitted and would be lost in deconstruction. The second was untenable – the Museum would lose the identity and audience it had worked so hard to establish and there was no immediate guarantee of a space in Centre Court. With the master plan already in place, the third option was viable provided an appropriate space could be found. The Club, meanwhile, had secured planning approval for a two-storey building with half basement to replace the Championship Entrance Building ('the Turnstiles') adjacent to Gate 3 on Church Road. Initially designed to provide Club offices, shop, bank and ticket office, the plans were amended to include a double basement to house the Museum and Library at Level Minus 1 and storage for all concerned, including the Museum, at Level Minus 2. The timetable was tight: the new building, soon known as the Museum Building, was scheduled for occupation by December 2005. The building programme was dictated by the three interim Championships (2003, 2004 and 2005) with their associated build-up and breakdown periods. For each one of them there still had to be turnstiles, bank, shop and ticket office.

The work was programmed as follows. During 2003 and 2004 the Championship Entrance Building was demolished and the double basement subsequently excavated. The Museum Building is at the lowest point on the Wimbledon site, on heavy clay, and the basement is constructed in waterproof concrete. During The Championships work ceased at ground level and temporary facilities on the concrete base were provided for a turnstile entrance, museum shop and bank. In 2004–5 temporary facilities were removed. Work on the above-ground structure of the Museum Building was commenced and nearly finished. The new turnstile facility, a Wimbledon Shop (shortly to become the Wimbledon Shop at the Museum) at ground level at the south end, and a bank at Level Minus 1 at the north end were available for The Championships. In 2005–6 the Museum began a staged decant from Centre Court, starting with the closure of Café Centre Court in July and the transfer of catering facilities for visitors to part of the Renshaw Restaurant in No 1 Court. Museum Education and the Playing for Success Centre were relocated to three hospitality suites in the same court. At the end of October the Museum and Library closed, the new Wimbledon Shop in the Museum Building opened and a temporary Visitor Centre welcomed the public in part of the Renshaw Restaurant. The Visitor Centre offered frequent short tours of the grounds, provided audiovisual presentations on the new Museum and the retractable roof, showcased the Wimbledon Singles trophies and hosted the inaugural exhibition of 'Winning Shots', images of tennis by the photographer Michael Cole.

VISITOR RESEARCH

The next step in the development of the new Museum was the investigation of the opinions of key markets via focus groups or in-depth interviews. The target markets identified were:

- Educational visit decision-makers/teachers
- Education consumers (primary school pupils – Year 5, aged 9–10 years)
- People with an active interest in tennis (LTA members)
- Local people (within postcode areas SW15 to SW20)
- Overseas visitors

General research issues included:

- Perceptions of the current Museum
- Facilities that visitors would expect to find within the new Museum
- Good and bad practice in museums/attractions
- Opposition to any of the exhibits shown in the current Museum and concepts for the new Museum
- Visitor expectations of a tennis museum
- The balance between contemporary exhibits and historic exhibits required in the new Museum
- The importance of the view of Centre Court
- Attitudes towards an underground Museum
- Visitor requirements for the audio guide system

Two mood boards, one reflecting the current Museum and one the new Museum, were used as prompts for the focus groups and interviews.

The key findings for each group were as follows. Educational decision-makers and teachers wanted touch screens, themed interactive areas, screens showing matches, costumes for dressing up, excellent facilities (lunchroom, coat/bag area, shop with child-price items). Primary school children were interested in recent history, particularly the trophies and current player memorabilia. The children suggested a virtual-reality tennis player to provide information and tips about the game. LTA members were concerned about the new Museum being underground – tennis was about outdoors, open air, English summer days. It was important to include the traditions of the game. Above all, the Museum must convey the 'uniqueness' of the Wimbledon experience. 'What stands out for me is the grass. It's almost where lawns were invented isn't it … it's a continuing fascination, that aspect of Wimbledon' (LTA member). Locals were positive about the roadside location, which would make the new Museum more obvious. Their main reason for visiting was to get the players' experience of The Championships. They were proud of Wimbledon and wanted the venue to befit the status and importance of The Championships and The All England Lawn Tennis Club.

Overseas visitors were engaged through on-the-spot interviews. Their reasons for visiting were sports-related attractions, keen tennis fans, pilgrimages to Wimbledon, shopping for relatives. They were especially keen to see Centre Court. 'I like the idea of seeing Centre Court – the view is really good. It's the first thing I'd want to see' (visitor from India). In the new Museum they expected to find the history of The Championships and the champions, player memorabilia, film clips, interactives, the science behind the game and its equipment, the evolution of the game and an insight into how staff cared for the grounds. Most particularly, they wanted to see players from their countries and matches from the eras they remembered.

A careful planning and balancing act was therefore required to ensure that the main needs of these key audience segments would be met. Drawing on the visitor research, a series of recommendations was made for the content of the new Museum, as follows:

- Ensure the Museum offers a view of Centre Court
- Give visitors a good insight into the players' experience of The Championships
- Balance historical content with modern themes
- Enable visitors to see all sides of the trophies
- Allow visitors to see players and matches from their own countries and eras
- Provide a range of interactive exhibits from simple mechanical to hi-tech
- Reduce the amount of text on graphic panels and use different fonts and textures
- Minimise the number of exhibits in showcases
- Retain player memorabilia and increase player endorsement
- Present information via touch screens
- Use floor space to introduce different court surfaces
- Use light and sound effects
- Retain the Club's colours of green and purple
- Save the best till last!

Key recommendations for the layout of the new Museum included:

- Develop a clear route around the Museum which minimises bottlenecks but allows visitors the freedom to return to all areas
- Use a bright colour scheme
- Ensure the pace is varied
- Balance light and dark areas
- Use fun images eg a tennis ball to guide people round

Recommendations for the location and exterior were as follows:

- Utilise the roadside location of the new Museum to create excitement and curiosity
- Locate the museum below ground but include an area which captures the 'summer feel' of the game and The Championships
- Ensure the new building is in keeping with the style of the All England Club

Design Brief

The Museum's brief to the designers encapsulated the findings and recommendations of the visitor research, provided for the adaptation of the existing Museum master plan for incorporation in the new location (see Fig 11.1 for the Floor Plan) and took into account branding considerations. It was also informed by the findings of Museum staff, who visited newly opened

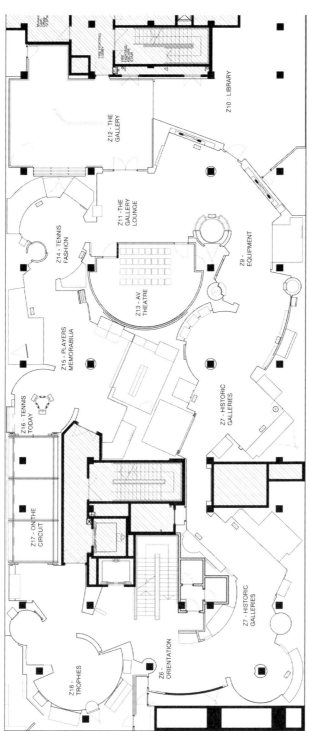

Fig 11.1. The general arrangement of the Museum, based on circles, provides imaginative use of the available area, given the constraints of 34 columns in the space. Columns which are not behind the scenes are, wherever possible, used for zone introductions or interactive stations.

museums, galleries and attractions seeking best practice. Of particular interest were interpretive methods, ranging from touch screens to audio guides, mechanical interactives and film presentations. Not to be overlooked from a practical standpoint were the years of experience of running the existing Museum. The durability and easy management of exhibits, the cost of maintenance and the mode of operation in terms of staffing and security were of paramount importance. The planned physical life of the new displays was 10 years, with the knowledge that certain technical components would have a 5-year lifespan. In essence, the brief called for the following:

- Creation of 'the best tennis museum in the world', reflecting the status of the collections and the standing of Wimbledon
- Provision of a Library doing justice to the finest collection of tennis books in the world
- Access for all, both physically and intellectually
- Combination of chronological and thematic displays with the opportunity to provide a different 'feel' in each element
- Contemporary overall 'look' with an impression of space and light
- Changes of pace and provision of 'highs' at varying points around the Museum
- Recognition of the fact that objects are static and tennis is about movement
- Inclusion of all those who contribute to Wimbledon – from players and spectators to groundsmen, umpires, queuers, fans, official suppliers etc.

DESIGN DEVELOPMENT

Mather & Co put together a creative team to work on the design development of the Museum. This included 3D designers, graphic designers, audio guide suppliers, film and touch screen programme-makers, interactive designers, cinema film-makers and Museum staff. Peripheral to, but also included in, this team were costume mannequin-makers, suppliers of special effects and lighting consultants. Though this group met infrequently every effort was made to keep in touch, particularly as many exhibits drew on several different groups, making programming critical. For example, the mechanically rotating racket 'wheels' involve real objects, in showcases, interpreted via interactive touch screens. From the outset the Museum recognised that visitors would dip in and out of the interpretation on offer. Some would rely on the audio guide, while others would read captions, play with mechanical interactives or just watch players in action. Whatever the visitor's preferred method of interpretation it was thought important that information was not repeated elsewhere, so different stories are told across the various interpretive media.

Museum staff worked to supply information to all the creative team members. Object lists, interactive treatments, storylines for the audio guide, research, images, fact checking, text writing – the requests came thick, fast and relentlessly. The Museum took on one additional member of staff, a researcher, to support the Curator. Ideas flowed, and most found their way into the final design. Throughout the process, Chris Mather, head of Mather & Co, cajoled the team and drove the programme.

MUSEUM FIT-OUT WORKING PARTY

In May 2003 the Club established a working party, chaired by a Director of the All England Ground Company, to take the new Museum project through to completion. Other members of

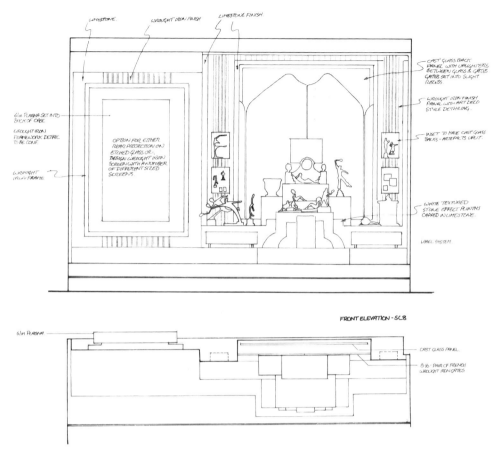

Fig 11.2. Elevation of Art Deco showcase, indicating the arrangement of objects, and detailing period case fittings, suggested screen frame structure and proposed finishes.

the working party were the Chairman of the Museum Committee, the Club's Finance Director, a Project Manager, Chris Mather, and the Museum's Commercial Manager and Curator. The Working Party met monthly to receive progress, design and research reports and to review the project timetable and the costs. The meetings provided excellent discipline for all parties and ensured that the interface with the Club's long-term plan objectives was met. A virtual walk-through of the new Museum, available by May 2004, gave a remarkably accurate impression of how the Museum would look and was of inestimable value in marketing terms.

Showcases

The wealth and variety of objects on display in the Museum demanded a wide range of showcase solutions. Needless to say, use of conservation-grade materials, conformity to British standards and attention to security, access and lighting design were of paramount importance. As the

Museum layout is based on a series of circles, the cases were all customised to suit the floor plan. The larger showcases contain a fixed section – often behind a touch screen – with either one or two access doors. Cases range from the floor-mounted to the wall-mounted, from free-standing frameless to custom-built interactive. Horizontal drawer units provide opportunities to focus on small objects in the collections, like marking pins and tape measures for laying out courts or fashion accessories such as Victorian tennis jewellery. Vertical drawers allow the display of objects such as outsize rackets and posters. All showcases have grey powder-coated steel finishes with case furniture in white for the first half of the Museum and grey from the 'Fashion' zone onwards.

Using object lists supplied by the Museum, a design manual for the showcase interiors was issued, containing meticulous front elevations and plan views for each case (Fig 11.2). This became the 'bible', providing all the necessary information for the design of case graphics and object labelling, as well as for the making of object mounts when the time came for installation.

Audio Guides

Underpinning the interpretive strategy is that foreign language provision is made by audio guide and that the cost of that audio guide is included in the Museum admission charge. Hand-held players with headsets were chosen rather than wand-style audio guides on the basis that visitors can, by using the integral lanyard, be hands-free to experience other interactive devices. Yellow tennis ball symbols are used to identify the objects or zones of the Museum under discussion. The length of the guide is 45 minutes, and the visitor is given the opportunity to discover more by listening to further 'layers'. These layers draw on different voices of Wimbledon to delve into subjects such as racket stringing, what it is like to be an umpire, how the Museum collects and what happens in the dressing rooms. Comedian Tony Hawks, a tennis devotee, is the presenter of the English version, moving the story along with a blend of information and humour. The audio guide is also available as a 'VIP' tour for visually impaired visitors. It follows the English version but gives additional directional advice as well as highlighting objects that can be touched – a column from Centre Court, the old tarpaulin court covers, racket grips and fabrics for tennis outfits. Designed to work alongside the audio guide is the handheld console for deaf visitors in British Sign Language. Here the content is augmented with interpreted video highlights from the Museum.

Interactive Touch Screens

Seventeen interactive touch screens throughout the Museum invite visitors to engage with specific ideas and focus in detail on individual objects, and via games and humour highlight topics from the history of lawn tennis and the present day. Variety in presentation styles is used to draw the visitor in and the tone of the presentations is always positive. If multiple-choice questions are used in a quiz, the selection presented is the right answer, a plausible – but wrong – answer, and a humorous, unlikely one. There is usually an amusing pay-off to be achieved. If the visitor makes the right choice, he is congratulated and if he does not, he is encouraged to try again.

In the 'Historic Galleries', film clips of real tennis, rackets and badminton being played answer questions on how these games relate to lawn tennis. Close-up footage of decorative items from a Victorian parlour can be called up to reveal an early tennis fan's obsession. Visitors can dress an on-screen figure in a mix and match game entitled 'The Rise and Fall of Men's Trousers', charting the history of men's tennis wear. 'Ask Eddie' gives the chance to glean push-button tips on caring for the grass from Wimbledon's Head Groundsman. Experts were consulted at every opportunity in the development of all these games.

The 'Tennis Today' zone has touch screens that deal with issues of the moment and houses three new games, installed in 2011. In response to a request from the Museum's Education department, the 'Eat to Win' touch screen has a perky cartoon tennis player choosing what to eat and drink to fuel his game, prompted by the visitor. 'Turning Points', a film-based guessing game, challenges the player to spot the momentum swing in famous matches, while 'Hot Topics' gives the visitor a chance to vote on issues that are being talked about by experts and fans in the tennis world right now.

Mechanical Interactives

It was the intention that not everything interactive in the Museum should be screen-based and computerised. Simple hands-on mechanical interactives have been used whenever appropriate, although in some cases the simplicity of the action required from the visitor belies the sophistication of the mechanics underneath. The various activities require the visitor to pull, rotate, feel, lift and wind. For 'On the Pull', visitors pull out old canvas court covers and new nylon ones, weighted on the roll to simulate the real thing, and compare the strength needed to do the job in different eras. 'Get a Grip' consists of racket handles of different materials to feel for preference. 'On the Ball', a multiple-choice game about ball boy and ball girl training, has the visitor rotating segments of a cylindrical drum to choose an answer. 'Reaction Station', a customised batak wall, is more hi-tech and electronic in its make-up, but simple to play and very popular with competitive visitors of all ages. Players test the speed of their reactions by extinguishing tennis ball lights with their hands as they flash up on the wall. More restful is a tiny Pepper's Ghost of Centre Court coming into being in 1922, which is accompanied by a conveyor belt of news photographs of the build and opening ceremony, operated by winding a handle. In the 'Fashion' zone, two sets of weights, housed in a table-top console, can be lifted to prove that a lady of 1881 wore a tennis costume twice as heavy as that of her gentleman partner. 'You cannot be serious!', a testingly difficult game about tennis rules devised in collaboration with the Referee, asks the visitor to revolve a wall-mounted disk to match the correct answers with the questions around the rim.

Special Presentations

A series of special presentations was designed for the Museum that, while fulfilling their interpretive role, would provide the 'wow' factor. These 'shows' are carefully placed around the Museum and, when encountered, serve to change the tempo of the visit. Visitors usually spend longer with these presentations than at other stopping points.

Early in the 'Historic Galleries', E F Brewtnall's 1891 tennis painting 'Wimbledon Tennis Party' is interpreted with film. The painting shows a garden party scene in which a group of new devotees to the game cluster around an outdoor tea table while tennis is played in the background. The purpose of the presentation is to bring the painting to life and introduce the viewer to the social environment in which the sport developed. On an adjacent screen, actors play the characters from the picture, dressed and performing as they are seen on canvas. As the camera pans across the scene, snippets of conversation reveal each character's view of the new pastime.

The reconstruction demanded scrupulous attention to detail. The actors were costumed exactly as their characters appear and, if their clothes could not be sewn, they were created. Props were hunted down that convincingly matched the originals: a silver tea urn, rackets of exactly the right shape and period, a generously proportioned slice of iced sponge cake. The trees in the chosen location – a Manchester park in May – provided the perfect canopy of leaves. And fortunately, on the shoot day, in this stand-in for a Victorian suburban garden, the sun shone.

In the 'Fashion' zone one large showcase displays a selection of the Museum's collection of ladies' tennis clothing from the 1920s to the present day. The large-screen film that is integral to the showcase has two elements: a documentary that charts three key periods and specially shot footage that shows important outfits from these periods being worn in action. The aim was to show how the clothes players wore and the developing game influenced each other. In the first segment, the balletic on-court movements of Suzanne Lenglen are echoed by ballerinas in 1920s tennis dresses. In the second part, a section devoted to the impact Ted Tinling's designs had on ladies' tennis wear in the 1950s and 1960s, three fashion models strut their stuff in dresses made by Tinling for players such as Ann Jones. The final part, shot in the blackness of a high-ceilinged film studio, has gymnasts in slow-motion flights, tumbling and twisting through the air off an unseen trampoline. The clothes that they wear, from the 1980s onwards, are made of modern stretch fabrics that enable an ease of movement not possible before.

Three-quarters of the way round the Museum, at the start of the 'Modern Galleries', a John McEnroe Pepper's Ghost has proved to be a highpoint and encourages a dwell time of the complete six-minute show for most visitors. This combination of an old illusionist trick and contemporary projection techniques enables a life-size 3D image of John McEnroe to inhabit a recreation of the Gentlemen's Dressing Room c. 1980 and seemingly interact with real objects. He flicks his headband into his locker, tests his racket strings, bounces a ball and picks up Bjorn Borg's shirt. From visitor research, McEnroe emerged as the most favoured player to inhabit the dressing room, to talk to the visitor about his Wimbledon career and to describe his epic battles with contemporaries Connors and Borg. In his current role as a commentator, McEnroe is ideally suited to bring the tennis story up to date and then look ahead to the game's future in a way that might have seemed inappropriately judgemental if done by the Museum. The presentation was researched by the Museum, scripted by McEnroe's biographer and filmed in New York for projection into the set. Adjacent to the dressing room is a showcase containing the actual shirt that is worn by Borg in the Wimbledon film clips McEnroe narrates for his audience and held in his hands by the 'ghost'.

It was always the intention of the Museum designers that the Museum experience should send the visitor out on an emotional high. Visitors enter the final 'Trophy' zone of the Museum under the inscribed wooden plaque that once hung at the entrance to Centre Court and under which, in its modern form, today's players still pass. The inscription is the Kipling quote: 'If you can meet with triumph and disaster and treat those two impostors just the same'. This message sets the scene for a high-impact two-screen film presentation of highs and lows in Finals matches at Wimbledon. Players are seen winning and losing with heart-breaking intensity of emotion and the background music, 'Requiem for a Tower', was chosen to stir up empathy in the viewer. As the final chords sound, light is brought up on three showcases of glittering trophies.

Fig 11.3. The completed Art Deco showcase. Tennis players were an inspiration for decorative artists who produced fine statuettes in chromed metal, bronze and ivory, capturing the balletic movements of Suzanne Lenglen and the dynamic style of the 'Bounding Basque' Jean Borotra. The players are shown in action on the adjacent screen.

'Science of Tennis' Film

Designed to be a highlight of the Museum experience, the 200-degree panoramic cinema is located halfway round the Museum. Its show immerses the viewer in the physiology, technology and infrastructure of the science of tennis, presented through an imaginary game featuring Maria Sharapova. The film shoot raised unique challenges: how to capture live action over 180 degrees at a suitable resolution, and how to get the required five-camera high-definition rig positioned on Centre Court during The Championships. Post-production included a year's worth of computer-generated 3D modelling, animating and rendering of everything from the ball to Centre Court. A surround-sound music and effects track was created to add emotive excitement. The cinema, with two designated wheelchair positions, seats 20 and there is standing room for a further 10 people. It is operated on demand by an attendant, rather than at fixed intervals, in order to conserve projector hours.

Museum Installation

The new Museum space was handed over during January 2006, with just three months to go until the Royal opening on 12 April. During this time showcase interiors were fitted out and all

objects put on display, set pieces were arranged, touch screen programmes and special presentations were tried and tested, mechanical interactives were installed and lighting and sound effects
were incorporated. A temporary workshop in the new Museum Gallery (special exhibitions
space) was established where display plinths were fashioned and object mounts made, showcase
by showcase. The Gallery's first exhibition, of framed tennis cartoons and caricatures, was deliberately planned in the knowledge that there would be only a three-day window of opportunity
for installation in April. Nervousness on the part of the Club as to 'what they were getting' was
understandable. It was deemed important to provide an example of the finished product as soon
as possible. With this in mind, the showcase devoted to the link between Art Deco and tennis
in the 1920s and 1930s was installed as soon as possible after handover (Fig 11.3). This case was
chosen as it contains decorative objects, largely of figures in action, with context provided by a
specially made film, designed into the showcase as a backdrop.

Some installations took much longer than anticipated. Days of discussion and adjustment
were involved in getting the ambitious John McEnroe exhibit up and working. It became clear
that the revolving racket wheels would require that all rackets had individually balanced mounts
to ensure their safe revolution and the smooth movement of the wheels. The installation of the
Museum's heaviest exhibit, part of a Centre Court column, turned out to be a job for the professionals. And, as always, the object labels were put in at the very last moment.

Reviews and Awards

Enthusiastic reviews followed the opening of the new Museum. Sarah Hodgson wrote in *South
West* magazine:

> You can still see the wonderful memorabilia – rackets, clothes, shoes, paintings – and many
> unseen exhibits which have been brought out of storage. But now, in the bold new space,
> there are state-of-the-art interactive exhibits, games, computer graphics, that blow your socks
> off, exhibits that dazzle and amaze – a 'real' John McEnroe reminiscing about his times at
> Wimbledon, whilst moving around the old Men's Dressing Room (I loved this) … You do not
> need to be a tennis fan to enjoy the breathtaking content. (Hodgson 2006, 10–11)

The *Museums Journal* praised the 'heady mixture of gorgeous objects, sumptuous audiovisual
displays and responsive interactives'. It commented on the tongue-in-cheek humour permeating
the Museum, 'not least in the costume interactive "The Rise and Fall of Men's Trousers"'. It drew
attention to the 'Modern' section where 'visitors walk through an (object-free) tunnel where
they are bombarded with sounds and images of aeroplanes taking off, fashion shoots, television
interviews, product launches, flashbulbs, and the endless circuit of tournaments. The pressured,
claustrophobic superstar lifestyle of the elite athlete is perfectly expressed.' Small quibbles aside,
the reviewer concluded: 'this accessible and wonderfully designed exhibition is essential viewing
for everyone with the slightest interest in museums. The rest of us need to raise our game' (Smith
2006, 40–41).

Awards followed. In 2006 the Museum achieved the Bronze Visit London Large Visitor
Attraction of the Year Award for its relocation, redesign and refurbishment. Following the award,
Andrew Shields, writing in *Time Out*, commented that the Museum 'acknowledges the past but
appreciates that, for most visitors, faded photos of the stars from years gone by have far less

impact than "Matrix"-style 3D effects capturing the explosive power and speed of modern sport'
(Shields 2007, 30). The following year brought two awards: the Gold Visit London Best Tourism
Award for the Museum and tour and the Bronze Visit London Accessible Tourism Award for the
Museum. In 2008 the Museum received a Special Commendation in the European Museum of
the Year Award. The citation read:

> Wimbledon Lawn Tennis Museum was relocated and modernised, and a multi-dimensional
> exhibition installed which communicates very successfully with its visitors. In the opinion of
> the judges, by using a well-balanced combination of traditional and state-of-the-art methods
> of interpretation, the museum has created a show that holds the attention of the visitor from
> beginning to end. Mention was also made of the way the museum tells the story of all the
> people involved in the game, and of the museum's impressive marketing strategy. (European
> Museum Forum 2008, 11–12)

Cost of Ownership

Bearing in mind the effort that had gone into the interpretation in the Museum and the reliance
on state-of-the-art technology, the aim has always been to ensure that all of the equipment is
kept working all of the time. Hardware was initially under warranty and comprehensive maintenance agreements were taken out with suppliers. The best investment was a new member
of staff, dedicated to Museum maintenance, who carries out preventative checks and provides
on-demand support. After three years of operation it became possible to reduce 24-hour support
agreements to a limited number of annual call-outs as the ability of staff to diagnose problems
grew. The Museum's rack room, situated on the floor below, contains computers, amplifiers, mp3
players, video servers – standard definition and high definition – AMX show controller, audio/
video processors, lighting controllers and network equipment. It is protected by gas suppression
systems and a water alert sensor cable. When electrical surges and power switching before The
Championships were found to be damaging and disruptive to restarting the Museum, UPS
battery back-up was added.

Every interactive provides its own maintenance challenge. Computers and touch screens will
not go on for ever, motors need maintaining, projectors require expensive new lamps and fibre
optic lamps need replacing. As equipment has reached the end of its normal life span it has
been replaced with the latest technology to handle modern software and the introduction of
high definition film and images. General wear and tear provides evidence of use and is to be
expected. The white walls of the Museum are painted annually before The Championships, with
touching up in between. The renewal of worn-off silk-screened instructions, washing of fabric
swatches and replacement of handling rackets happens regularly. Damage by visitors, brought
about by chewing gum, pencils and coins finding their way into mechanical interactives, has
been minimal.

CentreCourt360

It was not until three years after the Museum opened that the elusive view of Centre Court
was achieved for visitors. The programme of works to Centre Court had included replacement
terraces, the extension of the bowl, the removal of the existing fixed roof, a new fixed roof and

– finally – the installation of the retractable roof. On 19 May 2009 a 'Centre Court Celebration' trialled the new roof to a full house with tennis provided by Andre Agassi and Steffi Graf and Tim Henman and Kim Clijsters. That day, the Museum organised 360-degree filming of Centre Court, with and without visitors, for inclusion in its new experience CentreCourt360. Centre-Court360 was installed in the north-east corner of Centre Court after The Championships 2009. It consists of a multi-sided glass viewing platform perched a few metres back from the grass and above the seating, reached via a tunnel placed inside one of the stadium vomitories. Its construction necessitates the removal of 109 Centre Court seats and it is designed to be demountable. It is taken down at the end of May so that the seats can be put back in for The Championships, and is re-erected after the tournament for an August re-opening. Capable of holding 15–20 visitors, the viewing platform is heated in winter and air-conditioned in summer.

Interpretation is primarily by means of two multilingual interactive touch screens which enable the visitor to 'fly' round Centre Court – up into the roof, down to the grass and around the seating. The visitor can call up the view from a variety of points – the umpire's chair, the photographers' pit, the Royal Box, the TV stand-up position, the journalists' benches and the very centre of the court. Some of the time the court is empty, but other views show the photographers and journalists in action, spectators in their seats, and Agassi and Henman conversing in the front row of the Royal Box. Four tactile drawings for sighted and non-sighted visitors are applied to a horizontal leaning rail around the inside of the viewing platform. These provide a cross-section through the bowl of the stadium along the line of the tennis net, an annotated layout of Centre Court and of the court itself, an outline of one of the moving trusses, and the Club's logos. Explanations are in English and Braille.

On either side of the entrance tunnel to CentreCourt360 is a small interactive room fitted in under the terraces. The first is devoted to the grass and includes two multiple-choice interactives. One of these covers the groundsmen's year and looks at their tasks during the four seasons. The second tests the visitor's knowledge of who is allowed to go on the grass – hawks yes, foxes no, Sue Barker yes, streakers no, and so on. The interactives are supported by graphics outlining the Head Groundsman's day during The Championships and the way in which wear and tear on the grass is measured. The second interactive space looks at technology. Visitors can take the Hawk-Eye challenge, pitting their observational skills against real match footage. Or they can try their hand at closing the new roof; success results in a small model of the retractable roof closing over an on-screen Centre Court while failure brings on a deluge of rain which submerges Centre Court, bringing ducks, balls and panamas floating to the surface. Finally, a looping video charts the making of the retractable roof – trialling it on the ground, lifting the roof trusses into position, engineers working aloft and the roof in action.

Conclusion

In the five years since the Museum opened, annual visitor numbers have grown from 52,000 to 76,000, with 75 per cent of visitors now coming from overseas. The Museum has not rested on its laurels. More languages are offered on the Tours and on the audio guide. Updating of graphics, touch screen programmes, film content and player records is constantly taking place. Replacement of hardware and routine maintenance is ongoing. There have been five special exhibitions in the Museum Gallery. The most recent innovation 'What's in Store?', a new interactive touch screen experience, offers visitors the opportunity to interact with a selection of objects that are not currently on show. The Museum has also gone beyond its own walls with showcases of Museum objects in Centre Court and No 1 Court, and displays of Wimbledon images around the grounds. An ambitious new five-year plan is being drawn up, taking into account the requirements of escalating visitor numbers, the Museum's growing collections and – once again – the need for more space.

Sports museums have sometimes been criticised for offering a partial history, one which encourages nostalgia and celebration, rather than objectivity. They may be thought to be over-influenced by the sport's governing body if it manages the museum, or by sponsors (see, for example, Vamplew 1998 and 2004). When making such an assessment, however, allowance needs to be made for the highly complex process involved in deciding and shaping the content and form of exhibitions, the large number of specialists involved, the decisions to be made, the inevitable compromises and the over-riding practical constraints of time, budget and space. This is the case for most museums, but special consideration should be given to sports museums which record an ever-evolving game and where there is a constant need to keep up to date. Sport is about challenge, movement, emotion, winning and losing, not only for those that participate but also for those that watch. Nostalgia and celebration are essential parts of the experience, and if they stir the visitor by bringing inanimate museum objects to life, and by rousing emotion, so much the better.

Bibliography and References

Adair, D, 2004 When the Games Never Cease: The Olympic Museum in Lausanne, Switzerland, in *Sport Tourism: Interrelationships, Impacts and Issues* (eds B W Ritchie and D Adair), Channel View Publications, Clevedon, 46–76

Alegi, P, 2006 The Football Heritage Complex: History, Tourism, and Development in South Africa, *Africa Spectrum* 41 (3), 415–26

Brabazon, T, 2006a *Playing on the Periphery: Sport, Identity and Memory*, Routledge, London

— 2006b Museums and Popular Culture Revisited: Kevin Moore and the Politics of Pop, *Museum Management and Curatorship* 21, 283–301

Brabazon, T, and Mallinder, S, 2006 Popping the museum: the Cases of Sheffield and Preston, *Museum and Society* 4 (2), July, 96–112

European Museum Forum, 2008 *European Museum of the Year Award*, May 17, 11–12

Hodgson, S, 2006 High net worth, *South West*, June, 10–11

Johnes, M, and Mason, R, 2003 'Soccer, public history and the National Football Museum', *Sport in History* 23 (1), 115–31

Kohe, G Z, 2010 Civic representations of sport history: the New Zealand Sports Hall of Fame, *Sport in Society* 13, December, 1498–515

Moore, K, 2008 Sports Heritage and the re-imaged city: the National Football Museum, Preston, *International Journal of Cultural Policy* 14 (4), 445–61

Osmond, G, and Phillips, M G, 2011 Enveloping the past: Sport stamps, visuality and museums, *The International Journal of the History of Sport* 28 (8–9), 1138–55

Pearce, S M, 1978 The Wimbledon Lawn Tennis Museum – a review, *Museums Journal*, September, 63–4

Phillips, M G, 2010 A historian in the museum: Story spaces and Australia's sporting past, *Australian Historical Studies* 41 (3), 396–408

— 2012 *Representing the Sporting Past in Museums and Halls of Fame*, Routledge, London

Phillips, M G, and Tinning, R, 2011 Not just 'a book on the wall': Pedagogical work, museums and representing the sporting past, *Sport Education and Society* 16 (1), 51–65

Ramshaw, G, 2010 Living Heritage and the Sports Museum: Athletes, Legacy and the Olympic Hall of Fame and Museum, Canada Olympic Park, *Journal of Sport & Tourism* 15 (1), 45–70

Shields, A, 2007 Supreme Courts, *Time Out London*, 6–12 June, 30

Smith, J, 2006 Advantage Wimbledon, *Museums Journal*, July, 40–41

Vamplew, W, 1998 Facts and Artefacts: Sports, Historians and Sports Museums, *Journal of Sport History* 25 (2), 268–79

— 2004 Taking a Gamble or a Racing Certainty: Sports, Museums and Public Sports History, *Journal of Sport History* 31 (2), 177–92

Wimbledon Lawn Tennis Museum, 1998 Position Statement (internal document)

Survivals and Legacies: Sport, Heritage and Identity

12

Survivals and Legacies: Sport, Heritage and Identity

Jason Wood

In my first year at secondary school I won an essay competition. The title was intriguing and, as it turned out, prophetic. It read: 'Imagine you are an archaeologist in the year 3000. Describe and interpret your discoveries resulting from the excavation of Anfield Football Ground in Liverpool.'

It is at times like this when you wish your parents had kept all your school work. I do, however, dimly recall that the Anfield excavation revealed an enclosure of concrete terraces and turnstiles. The conclusion reached was that the building was an open-air prison (the turnstiles only permitting entry one way) and, to judge from the graffiti, the inmates had taken to worshipping a God named Shankly.

Fast forward 40 years to June 2010, and a meeting to explore the heritage implications of the decision to redevelop the site of Anfield when Liverpool's proposed new stadium across the road in Stanley Park is completed (Wood 2010). I am sitting in 5-star luxury in one of the executive boxes in the Centenary Stand, staring incredulously at a wall poster on which some corporate sponsor has contrived to misspell the name Shankly. A quote from another famous manager, Brian Clough, springs to mind:

> A lot of people are coming to games who wouldn't know Stanley Matthews from Bernard Matthews. The stands are full of people who can't tell you anything about the game unless it happened after 1990. They're either so conceited or so stupid that they believe football was invented just five minutes before they became interested in it. (Hamilton 2007, 197)

This opinion holds true for the majority of football clubs. They simply do not 'do history'; do not 'do old'. Their focus is on the here and now, with an unimpeded view to the future – the next game, the next win, the next balance sheet. Rarely do they engage with the past, and when they do it is a past foreshortened, with Year Zero being the creation of the Premier League: 'Way back in 1992 … in the depths of history', as one BBC Radio 5 Live commentator recently put it.

But Liverpool is different. As Andrea Titterington and Stephen Done's chapter explains, history and heritage infiltrate everywhere at Anfield and the club, established way back in 1892, takes its responsibilities very seriously. The club's decision to relocate its 'spiritual home', the way this decision was reached and the commitment shown in pursuing the project in full consultation with the local community are all explored here. It is a clear demonstration of how sport, history and heritage interests can be made to work together.

The existing stadium tour and intimate club museum already acknowledge the importance of history, even if the club website is a little effusive, welcoming visitors to 'one of the world's true sporting cathedrals' and inviting them to soak up 'the peerless heritage of England's most successful Football Club' (Liverpool Football Club 2011). Inevitably there are many objects and displays recalling Liverpool's European and domestic titles, especially the club's last great triumph in 2005, and a strong focus on charismatic personalities such as Bill Shankly. But there are also welcome features on less familiar names, such as John Houlding and John McKenna, who were instrumental in founding the club and securing its home ground.[1] Unfortunately, one piece of heritage no longer seen on the stadium tour is the legendary Boot Room – the 'think tank' and personal domain of the coaching staff from the 1960s, which became synonymous with 'The Liverpool way'. Insensitively, in the early 1990s, this historic and significant space gave way 'to the necessity of a media and press room' and, as serendipity would have it, Liverpool has not won a domestic title since. The Boot Room's name lives on in a sports café close to the museum and it was recently celebrated in a photographic exhibition in the city centre at the Reds Gallery at the Bluecoat (The Famous LFC Boot Room 2011).

One of the highlights of the tour is touching the famous 'This is Anfield' sign as you enter the players' tunnel. As Titterington and Done reveal, 'This is Anfield' is the current working title for the redeveloped site of the existing stadium that will form a grand entrance to the proposed larger stadium in Stanley Park, with hotels, restaurants and shops grouped around an open plaza. The key will be to ensure that the scheme is of high quality, reflects the club's history and heritage and allows the spirit of Anfield to live on. This will almost certainly include a memorial garden and space for fans to mark and celebrate their individual associations with the 'hallowed ground'. It might also involve artists and even a community archaeology project. Questions remain, however, over how best to accommodate the surviving landmarks they describe: Stanley House (John Houlding's former home and pivotal in the early history of the club – perhaps a possible future acquisition as an adjunct to the museum?); Houlding's original Sandon Hotel; the curious Flagpole Corner; the extraordinary fossilised remains of Archibald Leitch's pioneering reinforced concrete stand; and the numerous commemorative statues, gates and memorials.

Liverpool's fresh American owners, the Fenway Sports Group, are still considering options regarding the new stadium. Since acquiring the club in October 2010 the Group's principal owner, John Henry, has hinted he may choose to redevelop Anfield rather than build a new stadium in Stanley Park (BBC News 2011). The fervent atmosphere at the present stadium appears to have swayed his thinking, notwithstanding the difficulties of expanding Anfield owing to problems with planning, ownership and land assembly. The Fenway Sports Group takes its name from Fenway Park, the historic home of the Boston Red Sox baseball team, which Henry took over in 2002. There, the dilemma to relocate or redevelop was settled in favour of refurbishment. Fenway Park now looks forward to celebrating its 100th anniversary in 2012. Whatever final decisions are made, it is overwhelmingly clear that Liverpool will proceed only on the basis of partnership with the local community and the city council to achieve maximum benefits for the Anfield/Breckfield area and its regeneration. This is not just some box-ticking exercise to satisfy the planners; the club is really committed to it. As the chapter emphasises, this commitment is not just because permission for the new stadium was conditional on the full restoration of the historic core of Stanley Park. The club was already a catalyst for investment in the surrounding Victorian housing stock, initiating, with the expectation of little or no financial return, refurbishment of homes on Skerries Road, adjacent to the Centenary Stand, as a template for reha-

---

[1]   See http://www.sportcloseup.co.uk/liverpool-museum-and-stadium-tour.

bilitation of other terraced streets in the immediate vicinity. Happily, the objectives of the club and the aspirations of the communities of Anfield and Breckfield coincided. The club wished to stay in its historic home and expand its match-day capacity, while local people wanted to have their houses and park restored, as well as new homes, schools, sports fields, health facilities and match-day parking improvements.

Of course, an over-riding concern will be the destination of the various memorials at Anfield, especially the Hillsborough Memorial. This is an acutely sensitive issue that will have a profound impact on the Hillsborough families and supporters of the club in general. As well as being 'repositories of history', football stadiums such as Anfield, as Mike McGuinness' chapter demonstrates, have increasingly become 'repositories of public memory'. The recent 'memory boom' of statues and memorials at football grounds is revealed here, together with the importance of associated spontaneous shrines, stylised rituals, symbols and collective memory processes through which sporting loyalties, identities and pride are expressed. Saturated with cultural meaning, such 'memoryscapes' or 'lieux de mémoire' grow to be places of remembrance that shape knowledge of history as well as history-shaped identity.

Memorialisation and commemoration studies have seen something of a revival in cultural history and heritage studies in recent years and these contextual themes are explored in relation to the emerging literature relating to sacred places and sporting heroes. By way of example, McGuinness focuses on the Munich air disaster of 1958 and how this event became so deeply engrained into the collective memory of Manchester United and into the fabric of the club's Old Trafford stadium. But the key premise underlying his discussion is 'the canonisation of common people' – the commemoration of football fans themselves. Nowhere is this more potently demonstrated than at Anfield, home to two memorials to fans who died at the stadium disasters at Hillsborough in Sheffield (UK) and Heysel in Brussels (Belgium). These disasters and their aftermaths play significant but sharply different roles in the narrative of Liverpool as a football club. Relative to the 96 Liverpool fans who lost their lives at Hillsborough, the 39 Juventus fans who died at Heysel have been largely forgotten, save for a small display of artefacts in the club museum and a website presence. Indeed, it was not until the 25th anniversary of the Heysel disaster in May 2010 that a permanent commemorative plaque was unveiled at Anfield, and then only in a semi-public area facing the car park behind the Centenary Stand.

But this is nothing compared to the unhappy situation at Heysel itself, which I visited in September 2010. A quarter of a century ago the stadium was a shabby and dangerous venue, completely unsuited to stage a European Cup final. But stage it it did, with disastrous consequences. It would be ten years before the stadium hosted another football match, by which time it had been almost completely rebuilt and cosmetically renamed the King Baudouin Stadium. It is still an ugly hulk of a place; and unwelcoming too, as I was to discover. All I wanted was to photograph the memorial to the 39 Juventus fans, in this, the 25th anniversary year of their death. But the rather undistinguished plaque, on a wall close to the site of the tragedy, was inaccessible behind a steel fence and surrounded by the accoutrements of the ground staff's equipment. My attempts to photograph this scene through the fence were intercepted and my subsequent request to gain access shamefully denied. If I wanted to photograph the memorial, I was told I would have to pay to join the stadium tour. It seemed that I would have to pay to pay my respects. When I protested I was directed to another smaller plaque on an outside wall. This commemorated the names of the dead but was ignominiously flanked by two wheelie bins. I was eventually permitted entry by a security man – perhaps, because of my faltering

French, he thought I might be Italian. Whatever his reasoning, I was grateful. He rang upstairs and then directed me to a suite of offices. Here, the atmosphere became more cordial but not before I had been forced to divulge my nationality and place of work and confirmed to my female interrogator that I was not a journalist. I explained I was an archaeologist undertaking research on football grounds. This unlikely justification was met with the reconciled 'so we are antiquity already?' I thought better of an academic defence of the heritage of the recent past, superfluous anyway as the lady was warming to the quirkiness of the situation. My request to photograph the memorial was granted on the condition that I could not publish the results, an assertion I would have gladly controverted if the series editors and publisher of this volume had countenanced it.[2] Like the naive handling of events 25 years ago, and the subsequent avoidance of responsibilities, this little episode does no credit to the Belgian authorities. The Heysel disaster clearly remains a touchy subject and an embarrassment from which they would rather, like the memorials, hide away.

In this and other respects, Croke Park in Dublin is the antithesis of Heysel. When the Republic of Ireland's national sports stadium and spiritual home of Gaelic sports was rebuilt, the authorities, in the guise of the Gaelic Athletic Association (GAA), sought to reaffirm and amplify the stadium's symbolic position in Irish life through the re-commemoration of a past event. There is no hidden history here; rather a source of lasting political provocation and an officially sanctioned history of nationalism – themes explored in the chapter by David Storey.

The event in question was of course the first in Ireland to become known as Bloody Sunday, when Croke Park was the scene of an infamous massacre by British forces during a Dublin–Tipperary Gaelic football match on 21 November 1920. Retaliating for the assassination of 14 British Intelligence officers earlier that day, the Royal Irish Constabulary, supported by the British Auxiliary Division, entered the ground, shooting indiscriminately into the crowd, killing or fatally wounding 14. The dead included 13 spectators and Tipperary's right full back and captain, Michael Hogan. It was a seminal moment in the Irish War of Independence and became a major touchstone of the GAA and Croke Park. Four years later, the GAA took the political decision to name a new stand in Hogan's honour.

The GAA was founded to roll back the tide of British influence in Ireland, but its political stance hardened after Bloody Sunday. No longer just a stadium, Croke Park became a place infused with memory and meaning; an important focus of Irish nationalism; a salient expression of an Irish identity and cultural heritage. These points were reinforced by Tim Carey, the former curator of the GAA museum at Croke Park, in his book *Croke Park: A History* (Carey 2007) and in an interview he gave to BBC Radio 4's *Today* programme on the occasion of the Queen's emotionally charged visit to the stadium in May 2011 (BBC Radio 4 2011). The Queen was met by GAA officials under the new Hogan Stand – the name lives on – and shown out on to 'the hallowed nationalist turf' of what is now, following major redevelopment, the third largest stadium in Europe after Barcelona's Nou Camp and Wembley in London, boasting a capacity of over 82,000. As the Irish writer Fintan O'Toole put it: 'That amateur sports … can fill such a stadium is extraordinary. Much more extraordinary, though, is that the stadium can now play host to a British monarch' (O'Toole 2011).

---

2   Instead, see http://www.facebook.com/pages/You-Cant-Photograph-That/220710408014769.

The Queen's visit, in seeking to lay the past to rest, may be seen as the culmination of a process of modernisation within the GAA, aligning it 'more closely to the mainstream of Irish nationalism … which hankered for ideas of Irish identity that were positive and open rather than embittered and embattled' (O'Toole 2011). As Storey's chapter explains, some of the long-standing rules that protected the GAA's old exclusive attitudes have slowly undergone change. The organisation lifted the ban on its members playing 'foreign' games or the playing of 'foreign' sports at GAA grounds. It allowed *God Save the Queen* to be played at Croke Park in 2007 when the England rugby team came to play Ireland. Most importantly, members of the Northern Ireland police and British armed forces are no longer barred from joining.

As the Queen toured the GAA museum she doubtless found many of the notions that characterised the old Corinthian spirit – character, community, playing for the sake of it – alive and well and living in Croke Park. And here is the irony, as O'Toole neatly expresses it:

> The GAA is a quintessentially Victorian institution. It is a classic creation of the late 19th-century English drive to codify sports with written rules and centralised organisations. The men who established the GAA in 1884 saw themselves as traditionalists and cultural nationalists, preserving the ancient games of the Gael from the new vigour of rugby, soccer and cricket. But their reaction took the form of emulation – they did for Gaelic football and hurling what the English were doing for other sports. … The GAA … has been much more faithful to its origins in late-19th-century sporting culture than the English sports that influenced it. If you want to get some sense of the ethos of English sport before the rise of professionalism, without the snobbery that went with it, the best place to look is probably the GAA. (O'Toole 2011)

The symbolism and exploitation of the stadium to suit certain political and ideological purposes are investigated further in Daphné Bolz's chapter on the heritage of the modern Olympics. As Bolz stresses, from 1896 Olympic stadiums always expressed the position of the host city and country in terms of innovation, prestige and identity. The social identity of the International Olympic Committee (IOC) and its quest for an idealistic, democratic Modern Olympia are revealed in the early Games and venues. But all changed after World War I, and especially in 1930s Germany and Italy, when the Games became increasingly hijacked as a vehicle to showcase nationalistic, militaristic fascist regimes, heavily influencing the architecture and environment of the Olympic spectacle, with the stadium employed as a metaphor for political success.

Bolz also touches on the use of the term 'legacy' in Olympic discourses, signifying the IOC's desire to go beyond the foundational triangle of performance–media–money and give a stronger or renewed moral sense to the Games. Within minutes of London being awarded the Games of 2012, the UK government's then culture secretary and Olympics minister, Tessa Jowell, was claiming that, through regeneration, the Olympic legacy 'will transform communities of east London and lives of countless people across the country' (quoted in Wood 2005a, 10). Even before building work had begun, 'legacy' was repeatedly seized upon by the New Labour administration in its attempts to justify the inflated costs of staging the 2012 Games and to counter accusations of 'white elephantitis'. Moreover, an Olympic Park Legacy Company (OPLC) was in existence well before the building work was completed in order to manage the expectations these legacy assurances had raised. However, as I write (in October 2011), negotiations to sell the Olympic stadium to the football club West Ham United, in partnership with Newham Council, have been abandoned by the OPLC (BBC Sport 2011). This is an embarrassing set-back, with

unknown consequences for the long-term legacy for the stadium. For months the only information on the London 2012 website regarding what is called 'legacy after the Games' (as distinct
from the oxymoronic 'pre-Games legacy' of earlier announcements) refers in general terms to
the transformation of the Olympic Park 'into one of the largest urban parks created in Europe
for more than 150 years' and the adaptation of sports facilities for community use. Transport
improvements and more training and job opportunities are promised, as are 'national benefits
in culture, sport, volunteering, business and tourism' (London 2012 n.d.). The OPLC website
is equally unforthcoming and littered with unsubstaniated pledges of vibrancy and optimistic
claims to global attractiveness (OPLC n.d. a). Blow away the froth and what is left amounts
to a considerable blurring and paring of the original legacy proposals which may yet be further
eroded amid fears of spending cuts.

    But it is not all disheartening news. At least some of the new Olympic venues for 2012 will
be retained 'in legacy'. Unfortunately, this was not the case for the two previous London Games
and consequently very little Olympic heritage survives in the UK. The White City Stadium,
venue for the 1908 Games and the world's first purpose-built Olympic stadium of the modern
era, was demolished in 1985, while the original Wembley Stadium, used for the 1948 Games,
suffered the same fate in 2002. Coincidentally, the Wembley running track used in 1948 was
later re-laid at the Eton Manor Boys' Club sports ground, but cleared away during construction of the present Olympic Park. Other venues used for the 1948 Games, such as the Palace of
Engineering at Wembley, Empress Hall at Earl's Court and Harringay Arena, have all been lost.
Notable survivors, however, are the Empire Pool at Wembley (now the Wembley Arena) and
the delightful Herne Hill Velodrome in south London, one of the oldest cycling tracks in the
world, having been built in 1891 and refurbished for the track cycling events in 1948. It is still
in active use today but under threat, although the track itself was resurfaced in 2011 (Herne Hill
Velodrome 2010; DCMS 2011).

    I visited Herne Hill in November 2010, shortly after the 'Save the Velodrome' campaign was
launched, accompanied by my friend Neville Gabie, the Olympic Delivery Authority's Artist
in Residence at the Olympic Park (ODA 2011, 10). Neville was keen to learn more about what
physically remains of the 1908 and 1948 venues, to see how he might use some of the historical
places and events to make a connection to the present Olympic Park and the people building it.
A pleasant time was had talking to enthusiastic and helpful staff. Later that day we went to the
BBC Media Village built on the site of the White City Stadium, where we were met by a less
than welcoming reception. We wanted to photograph the 1908 Olympic medal table and list of
athletes commemorated beside the entrance to the BBC Broadcast Centre, and what pertains
to be the finish line marked in the paving outside the building. A repeat of my Heysel experience ensued when a security man intervened. Apparently it is not allowed to photograph a BBC
building without a permit. But we were not photographing the building, we explained, we were
photographing things in front of or attached to the building, things we presumed were in the
public realm. In which case, we were told, we would also need a permit from Hammersmith and
Fulham Council – an even more unlikely excuse. We retired to a coffee shop next door. It was
too dark now for photography anyway. The irony was not lost on us. The BBC is not unknown
for poking a camera in front of the faces of complete strangers when it suits it and its thirst for
a news story, and the security man knew we were there only because we had been observed on
CCTV. 'I don't recall giving the BBC permission to film me', complained Neville, as he leant

over the table to show me the photographs he had taken surreptitiously, and which I gratefully reproduce here (Fig 12.1).

In 2013, London's Olympic Park will be renamed the Queen Elizabeth Olympic Park. According to the OPLC's website:

> The combined Olympic and Royal heritage emphasises quality, history and innovation all at the same time. It will enhance the offer for the Park by appealing to international visitors and UK nationals of a variety of ages and backgrounds. This name reflects a real tangible legacy from the 2012 Games, and reflects our plans for making the Park one of Europe's premier visitor destinations. (OPLC n.d. b)

The OPLC probably overstates its case. Time will tell whether the two main London 2012 venues – the Stadium and the Aquatics Centre – will be 'at the heart of an exciting new visitor experience' (OPLC n.d. c), but the OPLC is right to anticipate a spike in tourism statistics in the years following the Games, since visits to sports venues increasingly make up many tourists' itineraries. As the work of Sean Gammon and others demonstrates, levels of public interest and visitation are also motivated by the popularity of sports museums (see Section II of this volume), halls of fame and stadium tours, and events such as seniors' tours, heritage classics and even fantasy camps (themed vacations with sporting professionals) (see Gammon 2002; 2004; Gammon and Ramshaw 2007). However, to date, such developments have largely been *ad hoc* and the benefits of so-called 'nostalgia sport tourism' have been overlooked and undervalued. It is perhaps for this reason that unfortunately there appear to be no plans for an Olympic Museum in the Park to capture the 'tangible legacy from the 2012 Games' and also celebrate London's unique position of being the only city to have hosted the Olympics on three occasions. This is a significant oversight.

The growing realisation of the value of sports history and heritage to tourism and the increase in 'secular pilgrimages' to famous sporting landmarks and locations are themes explored in Jean Williams' personal perspective on the enduring appeal of the Indianapolis 500. The Speedway at Indianapolis may not be the oldest operational motor sport venue in the world – that distinction belongs unexpectedly to Shelsley Walsh in Worcestershire (UK), the international home of hill racing since 1905[3] – but it does claim to be the world's largest spectator sporting venue and home to the largest one-day sporting event in terms of live audience. Indianapolis is described as the epicentre of motor racing in America and 25 years ago its Speedway and Hall of Fame Museum were recognised as a National Historical Landmark.

A visit to the museum is integral to the day's activities. These are cleverly portrayed in Williams' individual memoir, told from the point of view of the non-enthusiast and patient accompanying spouse. The chapter is all the more immediate and relevant for it, and an important testament to the pilgrimage. In it she ranges over a cultural geography of emotion and imagination, a cultural landscape of consciously constructed ceremonies, 'kinetic' rituals and invented traditions, and sustained historical atmospheres providing her with an extraordinary and sensory experience of 'being there'.

---

[3]   See http://www.shelsley-walsh.co.uk.

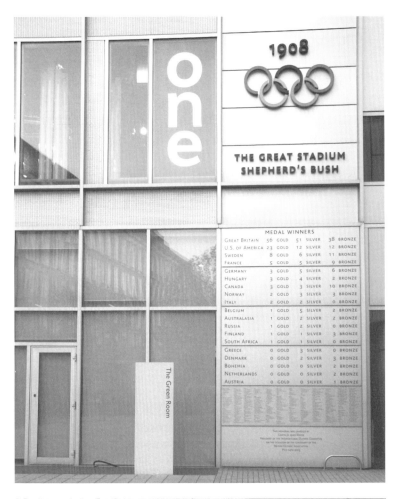

Fig 12.1. The 1908 Olympic medal table and list of athletes commemorated beside the entrance to the BBC Broadcast Centre, and the 'finish line' of the White City Stadium.

Williams visited Indianapolis in 1996, since when there have been two centennial celebrations to mark the 100th anniversaries of the racetrack (in 2009) and first Indy 500 (in 2011). The latter centennial was also marked at the Goodwood Festival of Speed, the UK's own nostalgia trip and 'invented tradition' of motor sport history (inaugurated in 1993), at what is billed 'the world's biggest motor culture event' (March and Sutton 2004, 8). The Indianapolis Motor Speedway Hall of Fame has supported the Goodwood Festival since 1998, and in 2011 over 40 significant and rarely seen Indy 500 race cars were displayed to create Goodwood's very own 'Gasoline Alley', accompanied by a host of successful Indy 500 drivers. Moreover, in a symbolic gesture, a number of authentic red 'Culver Block' bricks from the original track surface were appropriated and relaid at the hill climb start line, as a permanent 'reliquary' to the Indy 500 race among the flint walls of the Goodwood Estate (Goodwood Estate 2011).

My first venture in writing on sports heritage was published as a think piece at the end of a round-up of work in *British Archaeology* in 1992 (Wood 1993). It concerned the fate of some of Britain's historic football grounds in the wake of recommendations for all-seater stadiums and argued that they were as relevant to the study of early modern society and culture as hotels, theatres, cinemas and railway stations which seemed better served by statutory designation. Nobody in the heritage sector was listening, and some famous and popular football landmarks continued to disappear without a nod of recognition below housing estates, retail parks and supermarkets, presumably to await discovery by archaeologists in the year 3000. It was not until a meeting in 2001 that I was finally able to persuade English Heritage, the UK government's heritage agency for England, to commission a pilot study on various aspects of the history and heritage of sport. The pilot area was to be Manchester, the driver being the Commonwealth Games due to be held in the city in 2002. The date of the meeting was 11 September. After it, I left English Heritage's offices and made my way across London to Sportspages bookshop, where I watched the live coverage from New York and Washington. Getting 'official' approval for a sports heritage project was not, of course, such a defining moment in history as the other events of 9/11, but since that date, and much to the bewilderment of some of my former archaeological colleagues, I have rarely looked back.

As an archaeologist, I first approached the heritage of sport from a conservation management perspective, the results of the Manchester study being a case in point (Heritage Consultancy Services 2002). But I was also developing research interests in the rapidly developing fields of public history and the changing perceptions of and conflicts around the heritage of the recent past, with a view to promoting programmes that offered a more inclusive reach in terms of community participation. The Manchester study had shown that achieving a balanced approach to the wide range of values and benefits that flow from sports heritage required more than understanding and respecting special historical, architectural and landscape significance. It must also include celebration of local customs, traditions, routines and practices that people associate with such places, recognising their importance as repositories for and conduits of public memory, and actively promoting forward-looking strategies that are sensitive to the richness of sports history and its personalities, including investment in 'live' schemes and events (Wood 2005b).

At this time I began to initiate discussions with the UK government's Department for Culture, Media and Sport. The DCMS was, after all, responsible for sport and for heritage, and therefore joined-up government, I naively thought, ought to pose no problem. I firmly believed that sports heritage offered a new and dynamic focus for public engagement that chimed well with the delivery of a number of key government strategies and priorities across the social and cultural spectrum (regeneration, education, healthy living, tourism), especially in the build up to the London Olympics in 2012. Sport doubtless had the potential to attract new audiences to heritage, I said, particularly young people and others who may feel excluded from traditional ideas about heritage. The discussions were all one way. Unperturbed, I called for the creation of a British Trust for Sports Heritage and for the sport and heritage sectors to join forces to deliver imaginative projects for the Cultural Olympiad (Wood 2005c). Frustratingly, all of these efforts came to nothing.

Likewise, the Manchester pilot was grounded before it could take off and the report found a convenient bottom drawer in an English Heritage office. The project did spawn the excellent *Played in Britain* series,[4] but the original concept was never rolled out across the country as had been hoped. English Heritage failed to deliver the necessary planning and design guidance for owners and developers of historic sports venues or to engage with relevant communities. There was, therefore, a lack of coherent policy, organisation and documentation. Consequently, sport continues to linger below the heritage radar and the sector's responses to redevelopment have been inadequate, belated or inconsistent – sometimes all three. Today, the scale of loss and change is unprecedented. Controversial closure and disposal of sports facilities by public and private bodies continues unabashed and with too little regard for their historic and heritage values. This has led to increased planning casework, political interest or interference and media representation (often misrepresentation), but also to a growing number of public protests and demonstrations (Walton and Wood 2007).

In subsequent articles I have tried to focus attention on the positive, mutually reinforcing role of sport, history and heritage in the place-making agenda, regeneration and identity, and especially the potent roles of place, memory and meaning in the historic sports landscape. These themes are particularly acute in football (see Wood 2011) and my current work explores marking and celebrating the tangible and intangible heritage of former football grounds such as Ayresome Park in Middlesbrough (Wood and Gabie 2011). Of especial interest here is revealing how sports venues such as football grounds are valued as emblematic of aspiration and achievement, and understanding the intense sense of identity and of place which they convey in popular culture. Exploring people's emotional and subjective attachment to these cherished locations, and the different ways in which this attachment is expressed, constitute the most pertinent and most challenging components of this research.

There have been a number of false starts in mobilising the sports heritage agenda. Opportunities have been missed for improving integration of management and conservation action in the historic sports environment; missed too in terms of innovative community participation through the Cultural Olympiad. However, the chapters that follow are a timely reminder that academic curiosity and challenge in the fields of sport, heritage and identity are now firmly up and running.

---

[4]   See http://www.playedinbritain.co.uk.

BIBLIOGRAPHY AND REFERENCES

BBC News, 2011 *John Henry hints Liverpool may stay at Anfield* [online], 4 February, available from: http://news.bbc.co.uk/sport1/hi/football/teams/l/liverpool/9387492.stm [25 October 2011]

BBC Radio 4, 2011 Queen 'reconciles' with Irish history, *Today* [online], 18 May, available from: http://news.bbc.co.uk/today/hi/today/newsid_9489000/9489498.stm [25 October 2011]

BBC Sport, 2011 *West Ham to continue Olympic Stadium bid – Karren Brady* [online], 11 October, available from: http://news.bbc.co.uk/sport1/hi/olympics/15253276.stm [25 October 2011]

Carey, T, 2007 *Croke Park: A History*, 2 edn, The Collins Press, Cork

DCMS, 2011 *1948 Olympic track brought up to date* [online], available from: http://www.culture.gov.uk/news/news_stories/8415.aspx [25 October 2011]

Gammon, S, 2002 Fantasy, Nostalgia and the Pursuit of What Never Was, in *Sport Tourism: Principles and Practice* (eds S Gammon and J Kurtzman), Leisure Studies Association, Eastbourne, 61–71

— 2004 Secular Pilgrimage and Sport Tourism, in *Sport Tourism. Interrelationships, Impacts and Issues* (eds B W Ritchie and D Adair), Channel View Publications, Clevedon, Buffalo and Toronto, 30–45

Gammon, S, and Ramshaw, G (eds), 2007 *Heritage, Sport and Tourism: Sporting Pasts – Tourist Futures*, Routledge, London

Goodwood Estate, 2011 *Indy 500 Centenary: Goodwood Confirms Indy 500 Centenary Celebrations at the 2011 Festival of Speed* [online], available from: http://www.goodwood.co.uk/festival-of-speed/news-and-coverage/articles/indy-500-centenary.aspx [25 October 2011]

Hamilton, D, 2007 *Provided You Don't Kiss Me: 20 Years with Brian Clough*, Fourth Estate, London

Heritage Consultancy Services, 2002 A Sporting Chance: Extra Time for England's Historic Sports Venues – Manchester Pilot Study, Internal Report for English Heritage

Herne Hill Velodrome, 2010 *Save the Velodrome!* [online], 17 September, available from: http://www.hernehillvelodrome.com/save-the-velodrome [25 October 2011]

Liverpool Football Club, 2011 LiverpoolFC.TV [club website], available from: http://www.liverpoolfc.tv/history/tour-and-museum [25 October 2011]

London 2012, n.d. *Legacy after the Games* [online], available from: http://www.london2012.com/legacy-after-the-games [25 October 2011]

March, C, and Sutton, R (eds), 2004 *Goodwood Festival of Speed: A Celebration of Motorsport*, CollinsWillow, London

ODA, 2011 *Art in the Park*, Olympic Delivery Authority, London

Olympic Park Legacy Company, n.d. a *Resources* [online], available from: http://www.legacycompany.co.uk/news-events/resources [25 October 2011]

— n.d. b *The future of the Park* [online], available from: http://www.legacycompany.co.uk/legacy-plans/ [25 October 2011]

— n.d. c *Sport: Everyone's an athlete* [online], available from: http://www.legacycompany.co.uk/future-plans/sport [25 October 2011]

O'Toole, F, 2011 Can the Queen win over Croke Park? *The Observer*, 8 May

The Famous LFC Boot Room, 2011 The Reds Gallery at the Bluecoat, 14 May–11 August

Walton, J K, and Wood, J, 2007 History, Heritage and Regeneration of the Recent Past: The British Context, in *Interpreting The Past V, Part 1. The Future of Heritage: Changing Visions, Attitudes and Contexts in the 21st Century* (eds N Silberman and C Liuzza), Province of East-Flanders, Flemish Heritage Institute and Ename Center for Public Archaeology and Heritage Presentation, Brussels, 99–110

Wood, J, 1993 Demolishing the Idea that Football Grounds Don't Count, in *Archaeology in Britain 1992* (ed M Heyworth), Council for British Archaeology, York, 176–8

— 2005a Team Effort, *British Archaeology* 85, 10–13

— 2005b Talking Sport or Talking Balls? Realising the Value of Sports Heritage, *Industrial Archaeology Review* 27 (1), 137–44

— 2005c Olympic Opportunity: Realizing the Value of Sports Heritage for Tourism in the UK, *Journal of Sport Tourism* 10 (4), 307–21

— 2010 A Day in the Life … Sporting Archaeologist: Best Career Ever? *Current Archaeology* 248, 52

— 2011 Topophilia, Reliquary and Pilgrimage: Recapturing Place, Memory and Meaning at Britain's Historic Football Grounds, in *Local Heritage, Global Context: Cultural Perspectives on Sense of Place* (eds J Schofield and R Szymanski), Ashgate, Farnham, 187–204

Wood, J, and Gabie, N, 2011 The Football Ground and Visual Culture: Recapturing Place, Memory and Meaning at Ayresome Park, *International Journal of the History of Sport*, 28 (8–9), 1186–202

13

Anfield: Relocating Liverpool's Spiritual Home

Andrea Titterington and Stephen Done

Anfield, home to Liverpool Football Club since 1892, is no ordinary sports venue. The stadium is synonymous with Liverpool and a powerful repository of the history and heritage of 'England's most successful football club'. This chapter explores that legacy in light of the club's wish to create a new home, either by rebuilding Anfield or relocating to a completely new stadium. Such are the passion and pride of the fans and the local community, and such are the profundity and resonance of the implications throughout the district, the city and across the football world, that this move is something the club is committed to getting right.

Stanley Park and the Genesis of Anfield

The remarkable history of Liverpool FC and its Anfield stadium are woven into the fabric of the surrounding area, in particular that of Stanley Park. Opened in 1870, and explicitly dedicated to the recreation of working people, the park's grounds were landscaped by Edward Kemp (1817–1891) and the buildings designed by Borough Surveyor E R Robson (1835–1917) (Layton-Jones and Lee 2008). One year later, only a short walk from Stanley Park, the first services were held at the newly constructed St Domingo Methodist Chapel (now demolished), located at the junction between Breckfield Road North and St Domingo Vale in Everton. Here, the Revd Benjamin Swift Chambers preached the doctrine of 'Muscular Christianity' and soon formed a 'special affinity with the members of the Young Men's Bible Class in the Sunday School, most of whom were in their late teens … Within only a month of his arrival he had persuaded them to form a chapel cricket club' (Lupson 2008). By the winter of 1878, the members of the Bible Class were inspired to take up the fledgling new sport of Association Football and formed the St Domingo Football Club in order to extend their enthusiastic physical endeavours outside the cricket season. Being closest to where most of them lived, the team chose to play their matches at the south-east corner of Stanley Park.

Within a year, St Domingo's had adopted the name Everton Football Club to better reflect the wider catchment area of their team. It was in this guise that they attracted the attentions of John Houlding (1833–1902), a wealthy and ambitious brewer who lived in a villa overlooking the area of the park where the club played. Houlding took over the club and became its president. When Everton FC were asked to vacate Stanley Park it was Houlding who found them an alternative ground in 1884, leasing an adjacent area of land between Anfield Road and Walton Breck Road from two fellow brewers, on what is now the site of the present Anfield stadium. The Sandon Hotel, owned by Houlding, provided the club's first offices and changing rooms. In 1888, Everton FC became a founder member of the English Football League, winning their first title in 1891, but within a year the club had severed all connections with Houlding and built a new

FIG 13.1. THE PROXIMITY OF LIVERPOOL'S ANFIELD AND EVERTON'S GOODISON PARK HAS ITS ORIGINS IN THE DISPUTE OF 1892. STANLEY PARK ACTS AS A 'BUFFER ZONE' BETWEEN THE TWO CLUBS. NOTE PARTICULARLY HOW ANFIELD IS BOXED IN BY ROWS OF CLOSELY TERRACED HOUSING.

ground at Goodison Park, about half a mile away on the other side of Stanley Park. Houlding's immediate response in 1892 was to form a new club to take over the tenancy of Anfield. Thus was born Liverpool FC, soon after admitted to the League and winning their first title in 1901, a year before Houlding died (see Lupson 2008; Menuge 2008, 61–73; Williams 2010, 24–86).

Anfield's spartan facilities of the 1880s were upgraded in 1894 and 1903 and subsequently substantially rebuilt to the designs of Archibald Leitch in 1906. Leitch's work included a new Main Stand (more correctly known as the Lake Street Stand after an adjacent, and now demolished, row of terraced houses), the re-erection of its predecessor on the opposite Kemlyn Road side of the ground and the creation of the famous south terrace or Spion Kop. Anfield's Main Stand was Leitch's first in reinforced concrete, and probably the first in Britain (Inglis 2005, 86–9).

The stadium emerged simultaneously with surrounding streets of predominantly two- and three-storey terraced houses, rows of small shops and many corner pubs that provided homes and services for the people who would become the first supporters of Houlding's football club. The area is a 'microcosm of the townscape of working-class Victorian suburbia' (Pollard and Pevsner 2006, 393) (Fig 13.1).

FIG 13.2. STANLEY HOUSE, HOME OF JOHN HOULDING FROM 1876.

ANFIELD'S SURVIVING HISTORICAL LANDMARKS

Today Anfield retains several buildings and features in and around the stadium that reflect the celebrated, and sometimes tragic, history of Liverpool FC. Perhaps the most significant is Stanley House, 73 Anfield Road, built as the private home for the brewer and football promoter John Houlding in 1876 (Fig 13.2). This large villa is one of the best preserved, externally, of what was once an elegant row of such houses overlooking Stanley Park to the rear. It was one of the latest to be built and 'as brash as any in the area' (Menuge 2008, 23–4) – an observation perhaps reflecting the self-confident nature of its owner. The outlook to the park is 'emphasised in the form of a tall, well-lit stair turret rising on the garden elevation, while towards the street a stable and coach-house block is set to one side of a large forecourt' (Menuge 2008, 24). The location of Stanley House was pivotal in the history of Liverpool FC. It lay equidistant between the Anfield ground and the area in Stanley Park where the St Domingo's team had first played. And it was here, in April 1892, that Houlding and his supremely gifted football administrator, John McKenna, created Liverpool Association FC[1] from the fall-out of the terminal dispute with the board of Everton FC.

A short distance from Stanley House lies Houlding Street, retaining one original cast-iron street sign on the side of a barber's shop and commemorating the influence of Houlding on the developing townscape of the late 19th century. On the corner of Houlding Street and Oakfield

---

[1] The word 'Association' lingered for many years, the club dropping and re-introducing it in a whimsical and thoroughly inconsistent manner until at least the immediate post-World War II period.

FIG 13.3. HOULDING'S SANDON HOTEL, THE BIRTHPLACE OF LIVERPOOL FC.

Road is Houlding's Sandon Hotel. As well as providing changing room space for Everton FC, the hotel was also the base for Houlding's cycling club (the 'Black Anfielders') and a crown green bowls club, complete with pavilion. It was this pavilion that in 1892 provided the backdrop for one of the first photographs of Liverpool FC. Although The Sandon (now a public house) was refaced in a rather gaudy art deco style in the 1930s and is much altered inside, the outline of the pavilion is echoed by the modern covered area to the rear and the walled car park retains the size and outline of the former bowling green. The Sandon has also been used in recent times as an official corporate hospitality area on match days, in a fascinating return to something like its original relationship with the football club and ground (Fig 13.3).

Leaving the Sandon and walking along Oakfield Road towards the stadium, the visitor's attention is often drawn to a tall, white-painted wooden flagpole placed slightly back from Walton Breck Road. This unusual artefact is a top-mast from Isambard Kingdom Brunel's *SS Great Eastern*, purchased by the club from Henry Bath and Sons, the company responsible for breaking up the ship at Rock Ferry on the river Mersey. Launched in 1858, it was the world's largest ship, but it served its final years as a showboat, music hall and advertising hoarding for Lewis's department store, until Lewis's sold it for scrap. The flagpole was probably installed in the early 1890s, during ground improvements, perhaps to mark Everton's first title. Ever since, it has remained an unchanging fixture at this corner of the ground.

Redevelopments to the stadium took place throughout the 20th century. This was especially true during the 1990s, following recommendations for all-seater stadiums after the Hillsborough disaster. This period saw the Kemlyn Road Stand (and indeed Kemlyn Road itself) replaced by the Centenary Stand (1992), the construction of a new Kop Stand (1994) and new Anfield Road Stand (1997). There is little of any great age immediately obvious to the untrained eye. Nothing remains of the 1894 or 1903 buildings but one significant part of Leitch's reinforced concrete Main Stand of 1906 does survive entombed in the present enlarged structure. The brick rear wall of the paddock remains unchanged, and is clearly visible, while the upper tier's original 18 rows of wooden tip-up seats, on a four-inch thick slab of concrete, remain in use (Inglis 2005, 89). In such a modern stadium, they are quite extraordinary survivors from over 100 years ago (Figs 13.4 and 13.5).

Anfield is also home to a remarkable number of commemorative landmarks and memorials. The first to be erected – but probably the least recognised today – is a plaque dedicated to the memory of John McKenna, unveiled in February 1937 by William Cuff, the well-known Everton FC chairman who helped form the 'School of Science' team of the interwar period, and a close friend of McKenna.

> In the course of the ceremony Cuff handed Liverpool's chairman, W J Harrop, a silver casket containing an address presented to McKenna by all 88 clubs in the Football League in recognition of his long and distinguished service. Cuff told the audience they were 'perpetuating the memory of a great British sportsman … he was a football genius and meritoriously earned all the honours the game had to give'. (Lupson 2008)

The bronze plaque is now on the wall at the top of the stairs leading to the former Trophy Room inside the Main Stand; the silver casket is displayed in the club museum.

Bill Shankly, the legendary manager of Liverpool FC (1959–74), has no fewer than two memorials. The first of these to be erected was the Shankly Gates, bearing the words of what has become the club anthem, *You'll Never Walk Alone* (Fig 13.6). The gates, unveiled by Shankly's widow Nessie in 1982, formally tie the song into the very fabric of the club. The gates also became part of the redesigned club crest in the centenary year of 1992. The statue of Bill Shankly standing outside the club museum entrance in the Kop Stand was commissioned by Carlsberg (then the club's main sponsors) in 1997 (Fig 13.7). Created by Liverpool's most prolific and notable living sculptor, Tom Murphy, who numbers a statue of John Lennon among his public works, it depicts the manager with arms defiantly outstretched in a pose he famously adopted while addressing the vast crowd assembled outside St George's Hall in May 1971, having narrowly lost the FA Cup final to Arsenal. 'He made the people happy' reads the inscription, and his memory and legacy continue to do so to this day.

Bob Paisley was Shankly's famously reluctant successor to the managerial position (1974–83), but he became the 20th century's most successful football manager, taking Liverpool to new heights. In particular, Paisley's European Cup triumphs were instrumental in laying the foundations for the truly global support the club now enjoys. The gateway erected in his honour in 1998 stands before the Kop Stand and, appropriately, displays images of his three European Cup successes.

On Anfield Road, beside the Shankly Gates, is the Hillsborough Memorial, dedicated in 1990 (Fig 13.8). This red marble edifice records the names of 96 fans who died as a result of the darkest

FIG 13.4. THE MAIN STAND UNDER RECONSTRUCTION IN 1970, RETAINING ELEMENTS OF LEITCH'S 1906 STAND.

FIG 13.5. ANFIELD STADIUM TODAY, VIEWED FROM THE KOP STAND WITH THE MAIN STAND TO THE LEFT, THE CENTENARY STAND TO THE RIGHT AND THE ANFIELD ROAD STAND IN THE DISTANCE.

FIG 13.6. A YOUNG FAN LOOKS UP AT THE SHANKLY GATES.

FIG 13.7. TOM MURPHY'S STATUE OF BILL SHANKLY OUTSIDE THE CLUB MUSEUM.

day in the club's history, when on 15 April 1989, at the start of an FA Cup semi-final match at Sheffield Wednesday's Hillsborough Stadium, an avoidable crush on the terraces led to the deaths of so many, and caused countless thousands more to live with the pain and suffering that followed. The memorial includes a living flame and remains a poignant focal point for visitors to the ground, with floral and other tributes laid before it on a daily basis, a great many from 'rival' football clubs from across the globe. Everton fans were the first to show their respect in the days immediately following the Hillsborough tragedy, when they linked scarves with Liverpool supporters in a powerful show of unity and shared mourning. 'The first scarf was tied to the gates of Goodison Park by Everton star Ian Snodin and from there, the chain continued out of Bullens Road, over Walton Road, across Stanley Park and through the Bill Shankly Memorial Gates at Anfield to the Kop' (Lupson 2008). A second memorial to the 96, in the form of a huge ceramic wall plaque bearing shirts with the names of the fallen, was installed in 1998 on a wall close to the entrance to the club museum.

On the outside wall of the Centenary Stand a commemorative plaque affords a permanent tribute to the 39 Juventus fans who lost their lives in the Heysel Stadium disaster on 29 May 1985, when Liverpool played Juventus in the European Cup final in Brussels. Senior club officials and dignitaries from both clubs came together at a ceremony in which the plaque was unveiled on the 25th anniversary of the tragedy in 2010. The plaque augments a smaller one that was

FIG 13.8. THE HILLSBOROUGH MEMORIAL.

unveiled in 1986 and is now displayed in the club museum alongside appropriate artefacts. The Hillsborough Memorial and Heysel plaque are discussed in greater detail by Mike McGuinness in the chapter below.

BACKGROUND TO THE RELOCATION AND PLANNING PROCESS

Following the redevelopments in the 1990s, Anfield's capacity stood at 45,000 (44,375 with restrictions), but with a waiting list for season tickets of around 60,000 the need for increased capacity (plus extra revenue and modernisation for fans' comfort) led to a decision by the club in 1999 to replace and expand the existing Main Stand. Unlike some professional football clubs at this time, Liverpool was committed to staying in its historic home and not relocating to a motorway junction out of town. A plan called 'Anfield Plus' was offered to local residents for discussion. It was not well received, principally because the expansion of the Main Stand and its associated infrastructure would have led to the demolition of 300 homes in the Rockfield area. As a result, the chief executives of the club and the city council pledged to work with local residents to ensure that the club's investment would reconnect the threads of Anfield's historic fabric and be a catalyst for the area's regeneration.

Residents formed the Anfield Breckfield Community Steering Group (now the Anfield Breck-field Partnership Forum) from two neighbourhood councils with representation from every resi-dents' association. GVA Grimley was appointed to work with all parties to address the question: 'Is it better for the regeneration of Anfield/Breckfield for LFC to expand in situ or to build a new stadium on Stanley Park?' (GVA Grimley 2002). Sub-committees considered the needs for housing, open spaces, environment, community facilities, transport, education, health, youth and community safety and retail and local economy. A complementary report on tourism was prepared by Locum Destination (GVA Grimley 2002). Exhibitions were held on the options. The conclusion was that a new stadium at the eastern end of Stanley Park (now mostly given over to car parking) was the best solution. Thereafter a survey of 19,500 households was conducted using PPS (probability proportional to size) sampling, which supported the proposition by 82%. Only then did the club begin to work on its planning application which, as well as the stadium design, also included restoration of substantial parts of the grade II-listed Stanley Park.[2]

The initial scheme, designed by AFL Architects, was for a stadium with a 60,000-seat capacity with community facilities to the west. Because it was necessary to demolish the Vernon Sang-ster Sports Centre (VSSC, a 30-year-old community-run business in poor premises) in order to build the stadium, the club was required to provide replacement community facilities and to ensure that the activities were maintained throughout the stadium build. To meet the latter requirement the city council worked with the club, VSSC and the Anfield Youth Club (AYC) to form Anfield Sport and Community Centre Ltd (ASCC), with the intention of restoring and expanding the former AYC premises at Lower Breck Recreation Ground, less than a mile from

---

[2] AFL's stadium design was submitted on 8 October 2003 with consent issued on 11 April 2006 (valid for 5 years): LPA reference: 03F/3214. There were 73 conditions as part of this consent and 16 primary obligations on the club as part of a Section 106 agreement; 30 of these were pre-commencement requiring the submission of details prior to starting on site. All of these conditions have now been discharged.

Stanley Park. Between 2003 and 2009 the council and club raised £4.2 million to improve ASCC and its surrounding football pitches.[3] The club carries out many of its community programmes at ASCC, which also houses facilities for a nursery, education, crafts, dance, music and drama, a fitness suite, outdoor multi-use games areas and offices for the Hillsborough Families Support Group.

Delays in the programme initially arose while the council awaited the approval of grant funding from the North West Development Agency (which had expressed interest in being a partner in the overall regeneration plans). During the delay, the cost of the new stadium tripled. Notwithstanding this, the VSSC was vacated on 19 March 2007 in readiness for construction of the AFL-designed stadium to begin on 7 April. However, the club's then-new American owners, Tom Hicks and George Gillett, called a halt. They wanted the stadium redesigned, so accordingly appointed Dallas-based HKS Architects to start anew. The revised brief was for a distinctive stadium with an initial 73,500 capacity. The HKS design was based upon the primacy of the Kop and kept the pitch orientation the same as the existing stadium while respecting the contours of the sloping site. The requisite community facilities were duly incorporated and all other planning requirements complied with. The close involvement of English Heritage and the Commission for Architecture and the Built Environment was maintained. Planning approval for this design was achieved in June 2008. The cost estimates for the first HKS scheme were such that the building was recast on a smaller footprint during the planning process.[4]

Unusually, despite the scale of the new stadium and its location in a listed park, the planning application was never called in for a public inquiry. The government deemed that so much work had been done to knit the new stadium plans into the overall regeneration programme that a public inquiry process was not necessary and the local planning authority's decision could stand. Objectors to the scheme were vociferous, if not as numerous as supporters: on the club website, more than 2500 fans from over 80 countries expressed their approval for the new stadium.

However, while matters now looked set fair for the new stadium to proceed, the credit crunch in world markets affected the plans and, owing to a number of factors, the owners were increasingly losing support from players and fans. A protracted legal battle followed that saw Hicks and Gillett lose the club to the present owners, the Fenway Sports Group, and the deliberations about whether to build new or redevelop have started afresh.

The highly complex nature of the debate and the lack of an obvious solution were perfectly summed up in a public statement on the stadium issue:

> Liverpool FC today made clear its frustration at the obstacles facing the potential re-development of Anfield. The Club has been comprehensively exploring all options open to it in terms of new stadium development or expansion, which has included a study into the refurbishment of both its Main and Anfield Road Stands to increase capacity beyond 60,000 seats.

---

3   Phase 1 of the improvements to the former AYC was funded through the Neighbourhood Renewal Fund and Barclays Spaces for Sport. Phase 2 of the restoration and extension of the facilities was funded using European Social Fund monies (Objective 1).

4   HKS's stadium design was submitted on 25 July 2007 with consent issued on 19 June 2008 (valid for 3 years): LPA reference: 07F/2191. There were 69 conditions on this consent and 15 primary obligations as part of the Section 106 agreement (as some had been completed as part of the work on the AFL scheme). All of the pre-commencement conditions for the HKS scheme have been discharged.

Managing Director, Ian Ayre, said: 'In the nine months since the new ownership, an enormous amount of work has been undertaken in conjunction with leading architects, consultants, other industry experts and with Liverpool City Council to explore the building of a new stadium as well as exploring a refurbishment solution that could deliver the necessary growth in capacity, whilst maintaining the heritage and atmosphere that make Anfield uniquely Liverpool FC. However, with land/property acquisition, environmental and statutory issues creating barriers to our ambition, it looks increasingly unlikely there is any way we can move forward on a refurbishment of Anfield unless there are significant changes in those areas'.

Commenting further on the options open to the Club, Ayre explained: 'In terms of a Stanley Park stadium versus redevelopment, there is absolutely no question that a refurbishment of Anfield would come at a significantly lower cost than a new build. A new stadium of course also has its merits, being modern, more functional, and easier to construct. However, a new 60,000 capacity ground also comes at a significantly higher price, while at the same time only delivering roughly the same amount of revenue as a refurbishment of Anfield – with both options offering an uplift of approximately 16,000 seats each'.

Ayre added: 'It's disappointing that based on where we are at the moment, we seem to be unable to press on with the more viable economic option of a refurbishment, but we remain committed to finding the best possible long term solution. We already have a very healthy dialogue in place with several leading brands regarding naming rights for a new stadium, but like every major deal we have ever done, that just takes time to explore in full. Our challenge now is to try to find a way to bring all of those elements together in a solution that is in the best interests of Liverpool Football Club and its fans. We are mindful that supporters have been promised a solution in the past and have been disappointed, and also that local residents would like to know what direction we are headed in, however just like any other business, we can only proceed as and when we are clear on all elements and we will not be forced to make a decision that is not in the best long term interests of our club and we will not make any promises to our fans that we can not keep. We will continue to work diligently on this project and keep our fans informed of any progress.' (Liverpool FC 2011)

Regeneration and Community Involvement

As a pre-requisite of the Centenary Stand building process Liverpool FC acquired 20 terraced houses on the west side of Skerries Road. As it was not necessary to demolish the houses, long-standing Anfield residents remained as tenants. In 2001 the club invested in a major refurbishment, managed by the Maritime Housing Association, of ten of these properties for its remaining tenants. The homes were attractively restored to a very high standard to meet modern needs and aspirations, including conservatories and extended gardens. The architect, Ken Martin, even overcame the problem of wheelie bin storage by designing brick stores at the front of the houses that blend perfectly with the style of the Victorian terrace. On completion, the club held 'open days' for Anfield residents, in whose eyes the project was a great success. However, the biggest issue for the club was the cost–value relationship. At the time it cost £65,000 to restore each of the houses, but once refurbished they were worth only £35,000 each: on the face of it, not an attractive investment proposition. Subsequently the city council funded external works to the houses on the east side of Skerries Road, and as wider regeneration plans for the area were

FIG 13.9. THE END OF THE ROW OF THE REFURBISHED HOUSES IN SKERRIES ROAD, WITH THE CENTENARY STAND BEHIND.

approved as part of the Housing Market Renewal Pathfinder, New Heartlands, property prices gradually began to increase.[5] The club eventually sold the remaining ten houses in Skerries Road to the Affordable Housing Development Company (AHDC) at below market value. After refurbishment and with confidence boosted by the overall regeneration plans associated with Housing Market Renewal Pathfinder investment, these houses sold at prices ranging from £85,000 to £115,000 in 2005–6 (Fig 13.9).

In recent years regeneration has focused on homes in the Rockfield area, to the west of the stadium. Here, the residents of Anfield and Breckfield have devised a housing strategy and, working with AHDC, have begun the restoration of more than 300 properties, some of which had been derelict for some time. Keepmoat was selected as the new-build developer for the areas where houses had to be replaced. However, the economic slowdown in finance caused by the

5   In 2003 a large proportion of Anfield and the neighbouring suburban district of Breckfield were designated as a target area under the government's Housing Market Renewal Initiative, which envisaged a combination of clearance, refurbishment and new housing and infrastructure as a vehicle for economic and social regeneration. English Heritage undertook an architectural and historical assessment of the affected areas as a necessary preliminary to this process (Menuge 2008).

credit crunch and public sector spending cuts from 2010 have combined to slow the realisation of the overall housing master plan.[6]

When the club first began working with the city council and local residents on regeneration plans related to its new stadium, Stanley Park's historic architectural and landscape features lay dilapidated and vandalised and its public football pitches neglected and underused. As mentioned above, restoration of the park and its continued maintenance was written into the club's successful planning applications and endorsed by English Heritage. More importantly, an innovative solution to guaranteeing revenue for future management of the park was found through the creation of the Stanley Park Company Ltd, a 50/50 partnership between the club and the council. This joint venture ensures that the club's rental payments for the lease of the new stadium site are ring-fenced for maintenance and further regeneration works in the park as required.

By 2009, thanks to a £9 million investment from the club, matched by a similar amount from European Objective 1, plus a contribution of £1 million from the Housing Market Renewal Pathfinder, New Heartlands, the restoration of Stanley Park is complete and vandalism has all but disappeared. It is important to note that Planit EDC, the landscape architects for the stadium site, held the same role for the park's restoration, thus ensuring that the changes to the landscape were conceived as a whole. Improvements to the football pitches now enable upwards of 1000 young people to play at weekend matches organised by the Anfield Junior Soccer League, while at the western end of the park the original historic features (pavilions, bridges, lakes, Rose Walk, etc) have been renovated and made accessible. The derelict Gladstone Conservatory, a glasshouse gifted to the park in 1900, has been reborn as the Isla Gladstone Conservatory,[7] named after the textile designer. Here, the objective of the architects Lloyd Evans Prichard was to create a high-quality venue that would restore pride in the park as well as respecting its architectural excellence. The Conservatory operates as a bistro and events venue, including corporate entertaining on match days (see Layton-Jones and Lee 2008; Pearson 2010).

The club has been and continues to be engaged in all of the community networks involved in the wider regeneration of Anfield and Breckfield: the restoration of housing in Rockfield, the master planning of new housing in Breckfield, community safety, Stanley Park events, new schools, new health facilities and new arts programmes. From 1999 onwards the club expanded its community programmes from football coaching after school and during the holidays to a wider range of activities in education, health, physical activities, social inclusion and support for community organisations and charities. The club works with numerous public and third sector partners and contributes hundreds of thousands of pounds per annum for these community programmes. It is one of the few Premier League clubs which offers its coaching programmes free of charge and with open access.

'THIS IS ANFIELD': REDEVELOPING THE SITE OF THE EXISTING STADIUM

'This is Anfield' was the working title for what was called 'Anfield Plaza' in the outline planning consent for the redevelopment of the site of the existing stadium (Fig 13.10). The consent allows

---

[6]   In 2010 the coalition government abolished the Housing Market Renewal Pathfinders 7 years into a 15-year programme. Uncertainty surrounds the realisation of the agreed master plan for the area.

[7]   See http://www.theislagladstone.co.uk.

FIG 13.10. 'THIS IS ANFIELD' TAKES ITS NAME FROM THE FAMOUS SIGN ABOVE THE PLAYERS' TUNNEL.

for the complete demolition of the stadium, but discussions are still ongoing regarding the best way to reflect the significance of the site and all that it encapsulates for the club since 1892. As 'no net loss of open space' is a condition of the planning approval for the new stadium being sited in Stanley Park, over 1 hectare of open space is an integral requirement of any proposals for the Anfield site. Moreover, a benchmark has now been set by the high-quality design of the stadium and the restoration of Stanley Park. Any new buildings or public realm works will have to replicate that quality. However, with the debate on renewal or new-build still ongoing there is no certainty that this aspect of the regeneration will take place and, if it does, it may well be subject to revision.

Proposals have been worked up with a sub-committee of the Anfield Breckfield Community Steering Group. Fundamental to their aspirations was the provision of job opportunities for local people provided by businesses offering sufficient 'dwell time' for the anticipated 1.7 million visitors per annum. Tourism inspired by the club is seen as the unique selling point of any regeneration. Should the new stadium proposals be realised, plans anticipate a development of mixed uses reflecting the desire of local people to have premium restaurants, hotels and shops in a distinctive public realm that serves not only as the grand entrance to the new stadium but as a place where people will choose to stay. At the appropriate time, the sub-committee would become involved in the detailed design process. Indeed, the club has already held workshops with pupils at the North Liverpool Academy about proposed designs and looks forward to engaging local people of all ages and possibly inspiring architects or developers of the future.

However, this is not just another new public space: 'This is Anfield'. Great efforts will have to be made to capture the long history and heritage of Liverpool FC and especially to mark and celebrate the site of the stadium and people's individual attachment to the place. In this respect the destination of the various memorials will be an over-riding concern to many, and the club has already signalled that any decision on relocating the Hillsborough Memorial will be left to the Hillsborough Families Support Group. Discussions are also in progress on where the club museum might eventually reside.

Yet so much of what is being achieved by the club's decision to remain in Anfield preserves an intangible heritage – the memories of fans, players, managers, residents and visitors. Each day visitors come from all corners of the globe to visit this 'hallowed ground'. For many it is a sacred place; a place of pilgrimage; a place with spirit. It is an awesome responsibility to respect that aura and engender hope and optimism about the future: *You'll Never Walk Alone*.

BIBLIOGRAPHY AND REFERENCES

GVA Grimley, 2002 *A Regeneration Strategy for Anfield/Breckfield*, GVA Grimley, Manchester

Inglis, S, 2005 *Engineering Archie: Archibald Leitch – Football Ground Designer*, English Heritage, London

Layton-Jones, K, and Lee, R, 2008 *Places of Health and Amusement: Liverpool's Historic Parks and Gardens*, English Heritage, Swindon

Liverpool FC, 2011 *Public Statement*, 10 July, Liverpool FC Press Office

Lupson, P, 2008 *Across the Park*, Sport Media, Liverpool

Menuge, A, 2008 *Ordinary Landscapes, Special Places: Anfield, Breckfield and the Growth of Liverpool's Suburbs*, English Heritage, Swindon

Pearson, A, 2010 Stanley Park and the Gladstone Conservatory, Liverpool, in *Historic Gardens 2010*, Building Conservation Directory Special Report, Cathedral Communications, Tisbury

Pollard, R, and Pevsner, N, 2006 *Lancashire: Liverpool and the South-West*, The Buildings of England, Yale University Press, New Haven and London

Williams, J, 2010 *Red Men. Liverpool Football Club: The Biography*, Mainstream Publishing, Edinburgh and London

14

The Canonisation of Common People:
Memorialisation and Commemoration in Football

Mike McGuinness

[The] desire to commemorate is … the prime historical phenomenon of our time.

(Runia 2007, 314)

Public statues that commemorate the lives and achievements of athletes are pervasive and influential forms of social memory within the cultural landscape of Western society.

(Osmand *et al* 2006, 83)

On 29 May 2008 Sir Alex Ferguson, manager of Manchester United Football Club, unveiled a statue outside the club's Old Trafford stadium to who are commonly considered to be three of United's greatest players: George Best, Denis Law and Bobby Charlton. This continued a process which began with statues of the former manager Sir Matt Busby (standing over the main entrance to the stadium) and Denis Law (on the concourse of the upper tier of the West Stand, formerly the famous Stretford End). Manchester United, of course, also has significant memorials to the dead of the Munich air disaster of 1958, which killed eight of Busby's young team.

Sporting heroes are increasingly being celebrated, commemorated and memorialised across the full spectrum of sport, and a significant feature of the sporting landscape in recent years has been a growth, especially in the world of football, of the memorialisation and commemoration of people and events associated with various clubs and fan groups. This chapter will explore the role and function of memorials and remembrance in football, taking examples primarily from the UK.

According to Russell (2006, 3), commemoration in football has altered both quantitatively and qualitatively, particularly since 1985. This includes the erection of statues and memorials, the naming of roads, stands, retail outlets and hospitality suites and the retiring of shirt numbers. These practices have become a feature of the modern development of football; they are symbols of the growth in its importance in society and part of the reconstruction of its sporting space. The relatively recent character of this phenomenon can be chronicled through the work of Simon Inglis. In Inglis' earliest work on football grounds (1983) there are very few representations of the above: only a few stands bore the names of individuals associated with their clubs – for example, Eric Miller at Fulham, Bob Lord at Burnley and John Ireland at Wolverhampton Wanderers (noticeably none of these are ex-players, but directors); there are some named roads, such as Bartram Close at Charlton Athletic and Iremonger Road at Notts County; and there is also the Jeff Hall Memorial Scoreboard at Birmingham City (demolished 1993, now replaced). Ten years later John Bale (1993; 1994), in discussing the place of the sports stadium in the community, found that examples of memorialisation and commemoration, at least in the UK, were still very limited. Inglis produced a third and expanded edition of his book in 1996, just as new and upgraded stadiums were being developed in line with recommendations by Lord Justice Taylor (1990) following the Hillsborough disaster of 1989 (Inglis 1996). In this work Inglis recorded more instances, particularly in the naming of stands, such as the Revie Stand at Leeds United and the Billy Wright Stand at Wolverhampton Wanderers. The practice has grown ever since and today it is nearly impossible to find a football club without some form of memorialisation or commemoration.

The limited amount of research focused on the processes of memorialisation and commemoration in sport tends to be very specific in its orientation, focusing for instance on the Munich air disaster in 1958 and Manchester United, about which more later. In order to attempt to place sport in this context, some of the work associated with the development of memorialisation after World War I (for example, Winter 1995; King 1998) and the processes of remembering or commemorating the past (Lowenthal 1985) will be utilised. These studies have been related to public commemoration, with remembrance and honour being heaped upon political leaders, military figures and so on, but more recent commemorations have developed in a different direction and have ceased to be a source of lasting political provocation (Michalski 1998, 201). One exception to this, in respect of sporting commemoration, is the naming of grounds used by the Gaelic Athletic Association for its sports. Mike Cronin (1998, 92) has stated that, in comparison with the rest of Europe, Ireland seems unique in 'its continued celebration of the political in the naming of grounds'. Much of this is in the nature of a rejection of the 'foreign' (British) games of colonialism and is a celebration of a 'shared and officially sanctioned history of political nationalism' (Cronin 1998, 93; see also Storey, this volume). In the USA a statue was erected at San Jose State University to honour the contribution to the civil rights movement of Tommie Smith and John Carlos by their actions at the 1968 Mexico Olympics (Mackay 2005). However, commemoration has increasingly been more associated with the canonisation of the fans' heroes and in some cases the fans themselves. King's study of World War I memorials (1998) emphasised the point that they were about remembering the ordinary soldier – the canonisation of common people. This is the theme underlying this discussion, as is the place of the stadium as a 'site of memory' or 'place of memory' (see Mitchell 2003; Taylor 2000, 36).

For many the stadium has become a place to which people develop ties and quasi-religious attachments (Bale 1993, 64). Bale (1993; 1994) uses the concept of topophilia, as first expounded by Yi-Fu Tuan (1974), to explore the extent to which human beings are tied to the material environment, coupling sentiment with place or an expression of love and affection for place. The affection for stadiums comes close to the affection shown to more traditional places of worship and by those with devout religious adherences. This may be irrational, but these secularised 'icons' of the 'sportscape' carry a very heavy conceptual and emotional weight and have some aspect of the sacred (Bale 1994, 134–5). Armstrong (2003/2004) suggests that memorialisation in sport is organised into acts of ritual commemoration, giving social substance to collective memory. This is aided by the proposition that sport can transcend speech in creating these discourses. The monuments or memorials associated with this become selective aids to memory and nowadays can be seen as natural and inevitable (see Mitchell 2003, 445–6, although she was not talking about sport in this instance). Survivors of loss integrate themselves into visions of the world and use rituals and narrative to create new meanings (Niemeyer *et al* 2002, cited in Dennis and Kunkel 2004, 706). They can be manifested in a very physical sense or through the practice of 'retiring' shirt numbers for the living and the dead (in relation to the dead see Armstrong 2003/2004).

The nature of sporting heroes (less so heroines) is built around the concept that different ages and different cultures have their representative heroes who are products of their period (see Holt and Mangan 1996, 5). They possess a number of perceived qualities which include being models of athletic competence, being admired for outstanding and skilful athletic performance and having courage, expertise, perseverance, dependability, honesty and character (Vande Berg 2000, 138). Not all will live up to every one of these standards but they are representative of a community or era. In this they are seen as people of action, often moulders of history, demonstrating qualities of universal excellence with grit and determination (Holt and Mangan 1996, 6). North *et al* (2005, 40) suggest that they are famous people 'whose achievements persist through time'.

Memorials and commemorative artefacts, and the ceremonial acts that often go with them, act as focal points to 'conjure up the memory of the dead' (King 1998, 173). However, in sport commemoration is not always associated with the dead. Indeed, many sporting heroes have been commemorated while they were still alive, the aforementioned Denis Law and Bobby Charlton being good examples, while others include Tom Finney at Preston North End and Bobby Robson at Ipswich Town. Taylor (2000, 36) sees this as a reinvention as 'places of memory' and it is often a reconstruction that suits the needs of the present because the 'story of remembrance needs a place where it can continue to be told and retold' (Marshall 2004, 38). Mellor (2004a, 267) suggests that these kinds of memorial have a place in the construction of 'communities' and serve as an important cultural resource in bonding people together. Phillips *et al* (2007, 284) state that rarely are monuments to sports stars 'simple paeans to sporting achievement', but they celebrate moments and events which have cultural significance. Sometimes, as at Munich, these processes are associated with disasters. Indeed, football in the UK has been particularly beset by these, with crowd disasters at Burnden Park (Bolton Wanderers) in 1946, Ibrox Park (Glasgow Rangers) in 1971, Valley Parade (Bradford City) in 1985 and Hillsborough (Sheffield Wednesday) in 1989 (see Darby *et al* 2005).

These occurrences, and their commemorations, can be seen as part of the process, albeit adapted, of site sacralisation as described by Dean MacCannell (1999, 43) in his study of the tourist and their relationship with tourist sites. The first stage in this process is the distinguishing in some way of a sports site, person or event as worthy of preservation or commemoration. The second stage is elevation, in that an object is put on 'display', as in the case of statues, gates, the naming of stands and so on. This can lead to a third stage, that of enshrinement, as the object becomes the focus of attention and veneration (MacCannell 1999, 44–5). Adapting some of the headings that Bale (1993; 1994) uses to show the importance and relevance of the sports stadium within the community and beyond provides further illustrations of memorialisation and commemoration. Bale identifies a number of factors: the stadium as a sacred place, as a home, as a scenic place, as heritage and as providing economic benefit. His reference to the role as a sacred place is based on the way in which the stadium can stimulate emotional bonds and an almost quasi-religious devotion from fans. As a home the stadium and its environs is a place where fans can develop bonds that can be likened to the sentiments associated with home. As a scenic place the stadium provides and develops a character to which people and a community can identify. As heritage the stadium can engender local pride, retain architectural significance and act as a tourist attraction. Linked to these factors is the extent to which economic benefits can be provided for the community (Bale 1993, 65–86).

Using a range of examples to illustrate particular forms of use, the remainder of this chapter now examines sites commemorating sporting heroes and their sacred connotations, and the concept of the canonisation of common people in relation to the commemorating of fans.

SACRED PLACE AND SPORTING HERO

A significant example from outside the world of football is the memorial to the British cyclist Tom Simpson near the summit of Mont Ventoux in France. Simpson, an Olympic medallist and World Champion, died during the 1967 Tour de France while racing on Mont Ventoux. His demise near the summit had a profound effect on many cycling fans and professional cyclists (Fotheringham 2003, 11). The memorial was unveiled a year after his death and has become a site of pilgrimage. Cyclists stop on their way up the mountain and visitors leave items of cycle paraphernalia and memorabilia as offerings. Fotheringham (2005) identifies this as one of the 'small number of holy places' associated with the Tour de France. What makes the devotion to Simpson surprising is the fact that his death was caused, at least in part, by his use of performance enhancing drugs, in which sense he could be described as a 'cheat'.

In football, the Munich memorials at Manchester United's Old Trafford stadium are very important examples of the development of sacred places associated with a sports venue. The Munich air disaster of 6 February 1958 was a profound occurrence in the history of Manchester United and of football in England (Taylor 2000; Mellor 2004a; Woolridge 2009). An airliner carrying Manchester United players and officials and some newspaper reporters home from a European Cup quarter-final match against Red Star Belgrade of Yugoslavia (now Serbia) crashed after refuelling in the German city of Munich. It resulted in the deaths of 23 passengers, including 8 of the so-called 'Busby Babes'.[1] Gavin Mellor (2004a, 265) has stated that it was a disaster of national, and even international, importance and a 'black day for football'. Taylor (2000, 27–8) believes Manchester United, as it is understood today, to be the 'child of the Munich air crash' and that the club acquired its foundation myth at Munich, effectively defining it and precipitating its full transformation into the first 'national' club side in England. It has been mischievously suggested by David Winner (2005, 102) that the disaster, among other things, has helped turn the club into a semi-religious cult. Mellor argues that the disaster and its place in the history of the club are 'central to how rival fans perceive United', suggesting also that the club has 'wallowed in the misery of Munich' and possibly utilised the disaster as part of an overall 'branding' exercise (Mellor 2004b, 28–9). The 'othering' of United has been a result of this, and in many respects the club has become, at least at the 'rhetorical level', everybody's local rivals (Brick 2001, 15, 19).

The disaster is commemorated on a memorial plaque and illuminated clock, both unveiled in February 1960. According to Joyce Woolridge (2009, 120), these memorials reveal the influence of mourning practices from World War I. The plaque takes the form of a plan of Old Trafford

---

[1]   The 'Busby Babes' refers to the group of football players developed through Manchester United's youth policy by Matt Busby and his coaching team. They were young and gifted and formed the backbone of the successful First Division Championship sides of 1955–6 and 1956–7 and the unsuccessful FA Cup Final side of 1957. The players killed in the Munich air disaster were aged between 21 and 28.

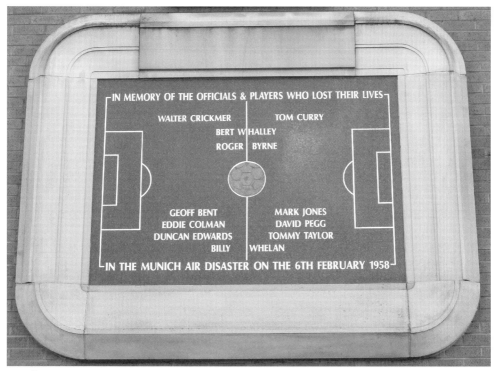

FIG 14.1. THE MUNICH MEMORIAL PLAQUE AT OLD TRAFFORD.

with the names of the dead officials and players within the confines of the football pitch (Fig 14.1). It was chosen and paid for by Manchester United themselves after the launch of a Disaster Fund in 1958. The rectangular clock was paid for by the Supporters' Club Grand Committee and Woolridge sees this as both a utilitarian monument as well as a traditional reminder of one's mortality (*momento mori*) (2009, 125). These public expressions of grief were seen as exceptional and broke the mould, and might be considered an 'early indicator of new trends within English culture' (Russell 2006, 10).

For a number of years fans have been paying their respects at the match closest to the anniversary of the disaster. Such is the interest that numbers have been increasing and it is planned to make it a more formal annual event. Regularly on 6 February at 3.04pm (the time of the crash), fans would gather at the memorial to pay their respects, songs were sung (notably *The Flowers of Manchester*) and flowers and tributes were placed at the site throughout the day. In September 2004 the process of remembrance was further developed when a memorial was unveiled at Munich airport on the site where the crash had happened, replacing a temporary and unofficial memorial which had nonetheless become a place of pilgrimage. The 50th anniversary of the disaster in 2008 saw a number of commemorations which reinforced the image and memory. Coincidentally, the closest home fixture to the anniversary was on Sunday 10 February 2008 against local rivals Manchester City. Despite the forming of close relationships between the Manchester clubs after the disaster, in what David Conn (2008) has described as 'a city united in sorrow', a strong antipathy had developed between the fans. Manchester City fans see themselves as the 'real' Manchester club, the people's club, rather than the national and international brand of Manchester United. Against this background it is unsurprising that concerns were expressed over whether the 3000 City fans attending the match at Old Trafford would behave and observe the minute's silence and the rest of the ceremonials arranged for the day. Despite the fact that one of the reporters killed at Munich was the former Manchester City and England goalkeeper Frank Swift, a number of tasteless songs referring to the disaster had been a feature of matches between the teams and it was hoped that this would not recur on this occasion. Thankfully, the day appeared to pass off quietly, respectfully and without any major incidents.

COMMEMORATING THE FANS

The Hillsborough Memorial at Liverpool Football Club's Anfield stadium, discussed in the previous chapter by Andrea Titterington and Stephen Done, commemorates the 96 Liverpool fans who died in a crush on the terraces during an FA Cup semi-final match between Liverpool and Nottingham Forest at the Hillsborough stadium in Sheffield on 15 April 1989 (Fig 14.2). Ian Taylor (1989, 90) felt that Hillsborough had joined the list of 'post-war graveyards on European or, more particularly, on English soccer grounds'. Phil Scraton, in his studies of the Hillsborough disaster (1999a; 1999b), shows how this has had a profound impact on the supporters of Liverpool, made worse by the gross injustice meted out to them in the media and subsequent official enquiries. According to Tony Walter (1991, 620), it was as though the very soul of the city had been attacked, which only added to the bad press the city of Liverpool had received prior to Hillsborough. The memorial, therefore, has had the particular function of representing the feelings of the fans, and especially the families of the dead, by allowing them to acknowledge the truth as they see it. The disaster and its aftermath have significant roles to play not only in the narrative of the club but also in that of the city. Economic problems caused by structural unemployment, a declining dock industry and manufacturing base and demographic changes (Jemphrey and Berrington 2000, 472), coupled with Liverpool's unique blend of Celtic expressiveness and 'celebratory culture' (Walter 1991, 607; Brennan 2008a, 11; 2008b, 340), provides the city with a strong sense of identity and 'otherness' from the rest of the UK, producing a local 'structure of feeling' (Brennan 2008b, 341) and a projection of 'topographic cultural heritage' (John Belchem 2000, cited in Power 2011, 100).

The feelings and ceremonials connected with Hillsborough are in sharp contrast to the memorialisation associated with the earlier disaster at the Heysel stadium in Brussels during the European Cup final match between Liverpool and Juventus on 29 May 1985. Here, 39 Juventus fans died in a crush against a stadium wall which subsequently collapsed. Relative to the Liverpool fans who died at Hillsborough, these 39 Italians have been largely forgotten. Paul Kelso (2005, 4), writing in a *Guardian Sport* special, suggested that this was because, at Hillsborough, Liverpool were the victims and that it was easier to come to terms with this than acknowledging even the smallest culpability for the earlier disaster at Heysel. Indeed, Heysel is often seen as an afterthought in some discussions on Hillsborough (see, for example, Moneypenny 2001, 230–31). On the 25th anniversary of the Heysel disaster a plaque was unveiled on the Centenary Stand at Anfield in honour of the 39 fans killed.

The fire at Bradford City's Valley Parade ground on 11 May 1985, in which 56 people died, does not seem to have had the same impact, despite the high cost in lives and consequent changes

FIG 14.2. THE HILLSBOROUGH MEMORIAL AT ANFIELD IS MADE OF RED MARBLE WITH THE NAMES OF THE 96 DEAD IN GOLD LETTERING, AN ETERNAL FLAME AND WITH LEDGES 'ON WHICH VISITORS AND MOURNERS REGULARLY PLACE WREATHS, MEMENTOES, SCARVES AND PENNANTS' (INGLIS 1996, 223).

to health and safety regulations at football stadiums. In the immediate aftermath there was a wave of sympathy which resulted in over £1m in donations being raised, exhibition football games being played and a short remembrance ceremony being held at the start of the 1985 FA Cup Final (Taylor 1987, 172–3). Permanent memorialisation and commemoration includes a memorial in Centenary Square outside Bradford Town Hall donated by the City of Hamm in Germany, Bradford's twin town, a memorial next to the entrance to a stand and a sculpture above the entrance to the Executive Suites. This is much more of a local process.

HERITAGE AND TOURISM

Bale (1993, 75) suggests that stadiums can become places to be enjoyed through the perspective of the tourist and visitor, and, as such, the development of the infrastructure to provide things for them to see becomes important. As stadiums expand into these markets, providing tours, museums, halls of fame, hospitality and so on, the idea of selling images of locality and history (Crawford 2004, 80) and of the heritage and identity of the club becomes quite central to this. Canter *et al* (1989, 82) have stated that a large part of the spirit of a football club lies in its past, including the 'roll call of star players and managers, the history of glorious victories and igno-minious defeats'. Associated monuments and memorials provide embellishment of the past by

FIG 14.3. 'THE SPLASH'. THE STATUE OF THE FOOTBALLER TOM FINNEY IS SITED OVER A FOUNTAIN AND IS BASED ON A FAMOUS PHOTOGRAPH OF FINNEY SLIDING THROUGH A WATERLOGGED PITCH DURING A MATCH BETWEEN CHELSEA AND PRESTON NORTH END AT STAMFORD BRIDGE IN 1956.

evoking a particular epoch's splendour, a person's power or genius or a unique event (Lowenthal 1985, 321), although they do not simply bear the imprint of the past. By offering a means for its articulation they are also implicated in the reproduction of the past and designed and planned with narrative choices and biases (Dwyer 2004, 425). As Crawford (2004, 67–8) suggests, linked to this is the view that sport is extremely powerful in stimulating local, regional and national pride, and will hold great sentiment for supporters. Moreover, Taylor (2000, 36) states that in football, as elsewhere in life, 'the past helps to order and give meaning to the present' and that, with the refurbishment and relocation of stadiums, clubs are 'naturally anxious to retain a link with the past'.

The role of heritage can be divided into a number of aspects in the context of the memorialisation and commemoration of sport and sporting personalities. Heritage is inevitably entwined with the ambivalences of nostalgia, or what has been described by Chase and Shaw (1989, 9) as an imagined past, where the generation of objects, images and texts are powerful talismans of how things used to be. Chase and Shaw suggest (1989, 4) that for this to be possible there ideally needs to be a secular and linear sense of time, apprehension about the failings of the future and availability of evidence of the past. Sport embraces all of these and is able to generate the conditions under which heritage and nostalgia can come together with representations of, *inter alia*, a 'Golden Age', sometimes with a glorification and bowdlerisation of the past and the creation of mythologies, icons, heroes and stars (see Snyder 1991). One of the impacts of this is to provide an economic windfall, especially with regeneration of the sporting environment or where sport is used as a focus for regeneration. According to Giulianotti (2000, 83), there is a post-modern development which involves the 'museumification' of football grounds, with nostalgia becoming a key marketing tool in selling sport to its fans (Crawford 2004, 75).

For example, the redevelopment of Preston North End's football ground at Deepdale incorporates a number of 'heritage' features. There is a statue of one of its greatest players, Tom Finney, called 'The Splash' (Fig 14.3). Within the stadium the faces of former heroes are 'picked out' in the seating. And, in a bold move, Deepdale was chosen as the location of the National Football Museum, as both the club and the city have played key roles in the development of the modern game (see Moore 2009). The museum opened in 2001 but will be relocating and reopening in Manchester in 2012.

Conclusion

It is impossible to chronicle all of the developments taking place in the processes of memorialisation and commemoration in football, let alone sport as a whole. Sporting heroes have a significant place in history and celebrations have taken a number of forms, from music and song in the 19th century (see Huggins and Gregson 2007) to the more modern and recognisable manifestations discussed above. It is also fair to say that some manifestations are not always favourably received; a recent statue to honour Ted Bates, former manager at Southampton Football Club, had to be changed because it was said to make him look like one of the Krankies, a popular comedy duo. Despite this, these processes will continue to try to reflect the needs and desires of the supporters and the wider community. It may also be that the practices will spread further, to include those who represent sport at all levels; as Projit B Mukharji (2008, 1612) suggests, sports stars are not just those who make a living or name out of sporting exploits – every village has its stars. Across the sporting scene, in different localities and at different times, there is a wide variety of memorialisation and commemoration, as Hill and Williams (1996, 10) have observed. In recent years the development of these processes has had a profound effect on the way in which sport, and significantly football, is seen in the wider community. Along with the modernisation of the facilities has come the establishment of the stadium as an important part of the social and cultural infrastructure. At a more extreme level the stadium can be seen to take on the status of a religious icon or symbol, or a phenomenon generating a 'quasi-religious experience' (Gammon 2004, 35). The main element of the role as a sacred place is strongly linked to the stadium's role as a heritage site chronicling the football club and furthering the growth of tourism.

Bibliography and References

Armstrong, E, 2003/2004 Memorializing in Sport: a Comparison of the Responses to the Deaths of Dale Earnhardt and Darryl Kile, *Sociology of Sport* 6 (2) [online], available from: http://physed.otago.ac.nz/sosol/v6i2/v6i2_1.html [12 October 2010]

Bale, J, 1993 *Sport, Space and the City*, Routledge, London

—— 1994 *Landscapes of Modern Sport*, Leicester University Press, Leicester

Brennan, M, 2008a Mourning and Loss: Finding Meanings in the Mourning of Hillsborough, *Mortality* 13 (1), 1–23

—— 2008b Condolence Books: Language and Meaning in the Mourning for Hillsborough and Diana, *Death Studies* 32 (4), 326–51

Brick, C, 2001 Can't Live With Them. Can't Live Without Them. Reflections on Manchester United, in *Fear and Loathing in World Football* (eds G Armstrong and R Giulianotti), Berg, Oxford

Canter, D, Comber, M, and Uzzell, D L, 1989 *Football in its Place. An Environmental Psychology of Football Grounds*, Routledge, London

Chase, M, and Shaw, C, 1989 The Dimensions of Nostalgia, in *The Imagined Past. History and Nostalgia* (eds C Shaw and M Chase), Manchester University Press, Manchester

Conn, D, 2008 Manchester's Shared Tragedy has been Redefined by Senseless Hatred, *The Guardian*, 9 February, 2

Crawford, G, 2004 *Consuming Sport. Fans, Sport and Culture*, Routledge, London

Cronin, M, 1998 Enshrined in Blood. The Naming of Gaelic Athletic Association Grounds and Clubs, *The Sports Historian* 18 (1), 90–104

Darby, P, Johnes, M, and Mellor, G (eds), 2005 *Soccer and Disaster: International Perspectives*, Routledge, London

Dennis, M R, and Kunkel, A D, 2004 Fallen Heroes, Lifted Hearts: Consolation in Contemporary Presidential Eulogia, *Death Studies* 28 (8), 703–31

Dwyer, O, 2004 Symbolic Accretion and Commemoration, *Social and Cultural Geography* 5 (3), 419–35

Fotheringham, W, 2003 *Put Me Back on My Bike. In Search of Tom Simpson*, Yellow Jersey Press, London

—— 2005 Tour's Tragedy Still Resonates 10 years on, *The Guardian*, 16 July, 4

Gammon, S, 2004 Secular Pilgrimage and Sport Tourism, in *Sports Tourism. Interrelationships, Impacts and Issues* (eds B Ritchie and D Adair), Channel View Publications, Clevedon

Giulianotti, R, 2000 *Football. A Sociology of the Global Game*, Polity Press, Cambridge

Hill, J, and Williams, J, 1996 Introduction, in *Sport and Identity in the North of England* (eds J Hill and J Williams), Keele University Press, Keele

Holt, R, and Mangan, J A, 1996 Prologue: Heroes of a European Past, in *European Heroes. Myth, Identity, Sport* (eds R Holt, J A Mangan and P Lanfranchi), Frank Cass, London

Huggins, M, and Gregson, K, 2007 Northern Songs, Sporting Heroes and Regional Consciousness, c. 1800–c. 1880: 'Wor Stars That Shine', *Northern History* 44 (2), 141–58

Inglis, S, 1983 *The Football Grounds of England and Wales*, Willow Books, London

—— 1996 *Football Grounds of Britain*, CollinsWillow, London

Jemphrey, A, and Berrington, E, 2000 Surviving the Media: Hillsborough, Dunblane and the Press, *Journalism Studies* 1 (3), 469–83

Kelso, P, 2005 Liverpool Still Torn Over Night That Shamed Their Name, *Guardian Sport*, 2 April, 3

King, A, 1998 *Memorials of the Great War in Britain. The Symbolism and Politics of Remembrance*, Berg, Oxford

Lowenthal, D, 1985 *The Past is a Foreign Country*, Cambridge University Press, Cambridge

MacCannell, D, 1999 *The Tourist. A New Theory of the Leisure Class*, University of California Press, Berkeley

Mackay, D, 2005 Power Runners Handed Honour, *Guardian Sport*, 28 May, 3

Marshall, D, 2004 Making Sense of Remembrance, *Social and Cultural Geography* 5 (1), 37–54

Mellor, G, 2004a 'The Flowers of Manchester': The Munich Disaster and the Discursive Creation of Manchester United Football Club, *Soccer and Society* 5 (2), 265–84

— 2004b 'We Hate the Manchester Club like Poison'. The Munich Disaster and the Socio-historical Development of Manchester United as a Loathed Football Club, in *Manchester United. A Thematic Study* (ed D L Andrews), Routledge, London

Michalski, S, 1998 *Public Monuments. Art in Political Bondage 1870–1997*, Reaktion Books, London

Mitchell, K, 2003 Monuments, Memorials and the Politics of Memory, *Urban Geography* 24 (5), 442–59

Moneypenny, C, 2001 Afterword: Hillsborough – Flowers and Wasted Words, in *Passing Rhythms. Liverpool FC and the Transformation of Football* (ed J Williams, S Hopkins and C Long), Berg, Oxford

Moore, K, 2009 The National Football Museum, in *Sport in Manchester* (ed D Russell), special issue of *Manchester Region History Review* 20, 133–8

Mukharji, P B, 2008 The Culture and Politics of Local Sporting Heroes in Late Colonial Bengal and Princely Orissa: the Case of Santimoy Pati, *International Journal of the History of Sport* 25 (12), 1612–27

Niemeyer, R A, Prigerson, H G, and Davies, B, 2002 Mourning and Meaning, *American Behavioral Scientist* 46 (2), 235–51

North, A C, Bland, V, and Ellis, N, 2005 Distinguishing Heroes from Celebrities, *British Journal of Psychology* 96 (1), 39–52

Osmand, G, Phillips, M, and O'Neill, M, 2006 'Putting Up Your Dukes': Statues, Social Memory and Duke Paoa Kahonamoku, *International Journal of the History of Sport* 23 (1), 82–103

Phillips, M, O'Neill, M, and Osmond, G, 2007 Broadening Horizons in Sport History: Films, Photographs, and Monuments, *Journal of Sport History* 34 (2), 271–93

Power, B, 2011 *Justice for the Ninety-six*: Liverpool FC Fans and the Uncommon Use of Football Song, *Soccer and Society* 12 (1), 96–112

Runia, E, 2007 Burying the Dead, Creating the Past, *History and Theory* 46 (3), 313–25

Russell, D, 2006 'We All Agree, Name the Stand after Shankly': Cultures of Commemoration in late Twentieth-century English Football Culture, *Sport in History* 26 (1), 1–25

Scraton, P, 1999a Policing with Contempt: The Degrading of Truth and Denial of Justice in the Aftermath of the Hillsborough Disaster, *Journal of Law and Society* 26 (3), 273–97

— 1999b *Hillsborough: The Truth*, Mainstream, Edinburgh

Snyder, E, 1991 Sociology of Nostalgia: Sports Halls of Fame and Museums in America, *Sociology of Sport Journal* 8 (3), 228–38

Taylor, I, 1987 Putting the Boot into a Working-Class Sport: British Soccer after Bradford and Brussels, *Sociology of Sport Journal* 4 (2), 171–91

— 1989 Hillsborough, 15th April 1989: Some Personal Contemplations, *New Left Review* 1/177, 89–110

Taylor, M, 2000 Football History and Memory: The Heroes of Manchester United, *Football Studies* 3 (2), 24–41

Taylor, The Rt Hon Lord Justice P, 1990 *The Hillsborough Stadium Disaster 15 April 1989. Final Report*, HMSO, London

Tuan, Y F, 1974 *Topophilia: A Study of Environmental Perception, Attitudes, and Values*, Prentice Hall, Englewood Cliffs, NJ

Vande Berg, L, 2000 The Sports Hero Meets Mediated Celebrityhood, in *Mediasport* (ed L Wenner), Routledge, London

Walter, T, 1991 The Mourning after Hillsborough, *Sociological Review* 39 (3), 599–625

Winner, D, 2005 *Those Feet. A Sensual History of Football*, Bloomsbury, London

Winter, J, 1995 *Sites of Memory. Sites of Mourning. The Great War in European Cultural History*, Cambridge University Press, Cambridge

Woolridge, J, 2009 'They Shall Not Grow Old': Mourning, Memory and the Munich Air Disaster of 1958, in *Sport in Manchester* (ed D Russell), special issue of *Manchester Region History Review* 20, 111–32

15

Heritage, Culture and Identity:
The Case of Gaelic Games

DAVID STOREY

THE RISE OF HERITAGE

The growing importance of heritage would seem to be due to a complex array of inter-locking factors: educational, cultural, political and commercial. There seems a desire by many people to know more about the history of a place, person or event, to disseminate this knowledge and often to celebrate it. Heritage is intimately bound up with culture, whether on a local, regional or national scale, and the preservation or remembrance of lifestyles, work practices, musical or folk traditions and so on. Such emphases, in turn, are often linked to political considerations concerned with the promotion (or obscuring) of particular versions of the past which lend support to contemporary agendas (Lowenthal 1998). For example, arguments over national identity and the inculcation of loyalty to the state are often bolstered through reference to a shared heritage (Hobsbawm 1992; Gellner 1997; Smith 2001).

Whatever the underlying causes of the increased demand for heritage, it is clear that there is an expanding supply, so that heritage has become a recognised industry. The perceived economic potential of heritage means that it has become ever more utilised as a mechanism in regeneration strategies, mainly through the promotion of heritage sites and elements of local heritage as tourist attractions (Timothy and Boyd 2003). Moreover, the cachet attaching to ideas such as 'heritage' and 'tradition' has seen such terms applied (often in a very tenuous manner) to various products as a marketing mechanism. Heritage branding has developed into an additional device through which marketing techniques are applied to the heritage 'subject', whether it is a person, place or event (Misiura 2006). Although heritage is a means of representation through which particular meanings are conveyed, it is also an economic and cultural product which is both bought and sold, and the intertwining of educational, cultural and political objectives combined with this increased commodification of the past leads to inevitable tensions (Lowenthal 1985; Hewison 1987; Rojek 1993; Samuel 1994; Graham *et al* 2000; Storey 2010).

The production, performance and consumption of heritage have a range of social, cultural and political implications and one key debate has centred on the differences between heritage and history. For Lowenthal (1998), heritage is concerned with the utilisation of the past for the attainment of contemporary objectives. This necessarily involves selecting elements of the past, a process which raises 'political' questions centring on what is selected and by whom (Wright 1985; Walsh 1992; Storey 2004). One key issue is that of authenticity, with debates surrounding the accuracy (or otherwise) of depictions of the past. Political, commercial and practical considerations will influence the ways in which heritage is presented. Historic representations often convey a certain set of messages that suits contemporary agendas and the selection and presentation of material can be designed to support a particular narrative (with the obscuring or exclusion of others).

What contributes to a 'national' heritage often proves highly contentious and, as this chapter suggests, sport's role within this may be far from unproblematic. National heritage provokes considerable debate with dissonance over what might be seen as key elements of that heritage, and how and whether those elements should be preserved. While it might be argued that in an increasingly globalised world the nation is becoming less significant, nationalism remains a potent social and political force and, although it has many obvious manifestations, there is a myriad of mundane everyday ways in which people accept, reproduce and reinforce ideas of the nation (Billig 1995). People read *national* newspapers and support *national* sports teams, and in a wide variety of ways the nation is constantly reaffirmed and reproduced. Sport can serve as a useful arena in which a sense of identity and collectivity is nurtured, sustained and transmitted, contributing to the promotion of ideas of national identity and 'national character' and thereby reinforcing the bonds of the imagined community (Anderson 1991). Through this and many other subtle mechanisms the nation becomes naturalised (Paasi 1999; MacLaughlin 2001).

While acknowledging the pressures (political, cultural and practical) to sanitise (and sometimes romanticise) elements of the past, it is simplistic to assume that a truly authentic representation can actually be devised. Even were such authenticity agreed upon, the pragmatic issue of its depiction would remain because 'the sheer pastness of the past precludes its total reconstruction' (Lowenthal 1985, 214). More fundamentally, the complex and multifaceted nature of heritage means it may be interpreted quite differently by different people at different times, making it highly unlikely that there will be universal agreement over what constitutes an authentic representation of the past. Although this is generally acknowledged and recognised, concerns arise when the nature and form of representation become particularly controversial. That which is presented as historically accurate and authentic will be seen by some as distorted and misleading. The idea of an essentialised heritage built on the bedrock of an ancient and immutable cultural core is an unattainable (and probably undesirable) goal.

A useful insight into broader connections between cultural heritage and sport is provided by the example of the Gaelic Athletic Association (GAA or Cumann Lúthchleas Gael) in Ireland. This chapter highlights how this sporting organisation projects itself not only as an upholder of a specific form of sporting heritage but also as a conduit for the wider (re)production of Irish cultural and national identity. Against this backdrop, it explores how some of the tensions associated with heritage play out in relation to Gaelic sports, with particular attention focused on the GAA's balancing of tradition with modernising influences and commercial pressures.

The GAA and Irish Sporting Heritage

Although a British colonial presence in Ireland can be traced back many hundreds of years, the Act of Union in 1800 abolished an autonomous Irish parliament and imposed direct rule from London. Consequently, the 19th century witnessed a demonstrable growth in Irish nationalism. While this was most obviously manifested through increasing political agitation, it was also accompanied by a growing assertion of cultural identity. In this it was not dissimilar to nationalist movements elsewhere in Europe at the time. The revival and strengthening of the Irish language was one aspect of 'national' identity, alongside the promotion of a 'national' literature and the establishment of a 'national' theatre and other cultural institutions. Within this realm, sport played a key role as an arena in which demands for a separate Irish identity could be played out. The nature of Irish history and the island's complex political relationship with its British neighbour has, perhaps unsurprisingly, created 'a sporting culture … closely bound up with such potentially potent themes as the meaning of being Irish and the relationship of Irish people with each other and with the world beyond' (Bairner 2005, 1).

The GAA was founded in 1884 at a meeting in Thurles, County Tipperary, by individuals concerned with what was seen as the erosion of 'native' pastimes in favour of ones imported from England. It led to a number of codes being drawn up for what were deemed to be distinctive and historical Irish games. In pursuit of its objectives the GAA successfully organised its own games: Gaelic football, hurling, camógie, ladies football, handball and rounders. There is a certain irony in that the last of these is an Irish variant of a game considered to have originated in England. Hurling, as developed by the GAA, was based on pre-existing forms of the sport but Gaelic football in large part was invented at this time as a particular Irish version of football. From its very inception the GAA was envisaged as more than just a sporting organisation. Then, as now, it explicitly acknowledged its role in relation to the broader arenas of Irish national identity and culture. It continues to describe itself as a sporting and cultural organisation, one which permeates many aspects of Irish life both at home and among Irish emigrant communities abroad, asserting that it:

> has as its basic aim the strengthening of the National Identity in a 32 County Ireland through the preservation and promotion of Gaelic Games and pastimes [and it will] actively support the Irish language, traditional Irish dancing, music, song, and other aspects of Irish culture [and] foster an awareness and love of the national ideals in the people of Ireland. (http://www.gaa.ie)

A clear cultural element is displayed, but so too is an overtly political one. The GAA's premier competitions are the All-Ireland championships in an organisation that both explicitly and implicitly refuses to acknowledge Irish partition and allies itself to the irredentist territorial claim.

The GAA's organisational structure has a strong geographical base using Ireland's provinces, counties and parishes as its key units. This has helped to inculcate or reinforce a strong sense of place and an attachment to locality among its members where inter-parochial and inter-county rivalries are an important backdrop to fixtures. The major competitions are the annual inter-county All-Ireland football and hurling championships. Furthermore, this structure and the amateur status of the games means the organisation is firmly embedded at a local level and teams remain strongly connected to local communities. The GAA boasts over 2,300 clubs in Ireland, with many others abroad. Through its sporting activities, the GAA has successfully transmitted its heritage into the various everyday cultural practices of many Irish people in ways which especially link into religion and language. For many people GAA matches are a focal point of the week, whether as participants or observers, while associated activities run by local GAA clubs become major social events at the parish level. GAA pitches and facilities are therefore part of the cultural landscape of Ireland, and its activities form a key element in the life of many people throughout the country.

These connections with broader dimensions of Irish culture and politics are reflected in the names of clubs and Gaelic grounds, many of which commemorate religious leaders or Irish nationalist political figures. Markievicz Park in Sligo is named after Constance Markievicz, a participant in the unsuccessful 1916 rebellion against British rule and subsequently a politician; Tralee's GAA club and its ground are named after Austin Stack, a local-born revolutionary of the early 20th century. The GAA's principal stadium, Croke Park in Dublin, is named after a Catholic Archbishop and a section of the ground is named Hill 16 as it was reputedly built with some of the rubble from Dublin's General Post Office, damaged during the 1916 uprising. The Croke Park Bloody Sunday massacre of 1920 witnessed the deaths of 14 people at a Dublin–Tipperary football match at the hands of British forces. Among the dead was the Tipperary captain Michael Hogan, after whom a stand was subsequently named. In these sorts of ways, historical, political and religious reference points are embedded into commonplace discourse.

Beyond the playing of the actual sports themselves, the GAA's broader cultural activities have always been important and this was reinforced through the introduction of Scór in 1969. This is the explicitly cultural wing of the GAA, aimed at actively promoting aspects of Irish culture and which the GAA asserts 'has played a significant part in the revival of our culture and heritage in creating an understanding and interest in its importance' (http://www.gaa.ie). Through Scór, and through linkages with Irish language organisations and various other channels, the GAA has also maintained a close identification with the language. While Irish is spoken as a first language by only a small minority of people, the GAA continues to play a proactive role in its promotion and usage. On receiving the trophy at the end of an All-Ireland hurling or football final, it is now a well-established tradition that the captain's acceptance speech made to the crowd (and those watching or listening on television and radio) commences with a few sentences in Irish, even though the player may be far from fluent in the language. This use of *na cúpla focal* (the few words), while having become a ritualised phenomenon, serves as a clear reminder of the broader cultural role the GAA sees itself as playing. A recent agreement granting television coverage of the All-Ireland football and hurling minor finals from 2011 to the independent channel TV3 (instead of the state broadcaster RTE) led to concerns that the traditional use of an Irish language commentary for those matches (which precede the senior games) might be dropped (O'Riordan 2010).[1]

While Gaelic games are strongly associated with Ireland, the island's long history of out-migration has resulted in deep-rooted Irish communities abroad, especially in many urban areas in the UK, North America and Australia (MacLaughlin 1997; Bielenberg 2000). Out of these have emerged GAA clubs in places such as London, Paris and San Francisco, where local football and hurling leagues have been formed (Darby 2009; 2010). These have served to provide Irish migrants with familiar recreational activities and, moreover, have ensured that many migrants stay closely connected with aspects of Irish culture and heritage. In a study of Gaelic Park in New York, Sara Brady (2005) has cast light on the ways in which a particular cultural space works in this respect, providing not solely a venue for sport but also a social meeting space in which a sense of Irish cultural heritage is indulged, shared and reproduced. The existence of clubs outside Ireland reflects both the GAA's international influence and the desire by many Irish emigrants to stay in touch with a key element of their heritage and culture, and in so doing to retain a strong sense of national identity.

Even in its relative infancy GAA clubs travelled abroad to play against teams among Irish emigrant communities in the USA and elsewhere. The importance of this link to the Irish dias-

---

[1]   See also the online discussion on fora such as http://www.gaaboard.com.

pora was highlighted by the playing of the 1947 All-Ireland football final at the Polo Grounds in New York (in which Cavan beat Kerry), and these efforts can be seen as an attempt at connecting the Irish at home with those abroad and the inclusion of both within the compass of the GAA. Today, the importance of the GAA to emigrant communities, and vice versa, is manifested through the participation of teams from London and New York in inter-county All-Ireland competitions; for these purposes London and New York are treated as Irish 'counties'.

Conflict and Controversy

Gaelic games have been held up as a national cultural symbol of Irishness as pastimes to be preferred over imported 'foreign' games, especially those which were seen to be colonial imports from Britain. Soccer (as football tends to be known in Ireland, to distinguish it from Gaelic football) was often referred to as the 'garrison game' and seen as a sport played by British soldiers (Hannigan 1998). As might be expected, the aims and ethos of the GAA have created a number of controversies. In promoting its national sports the GAA maintained a long-standing rule banning its members from playing 'foreign' sports (principally soccer or rugby) or even attending them as a spectator, abolishing this only in 1971 (Rouse 1993). Alongside this was a ban on Gaelic sports grounds being used for such 'foreign' games. This resulted in some curious anomalies, as the likes of Tina Turner and American football teams could play at Croke Park but the Republic of Ireland football team could not. However, the ban on the playing of foreign sports at GAA grounds was temporarily suspended in 2007 to allow rugby and soccer to be played at Croke Park during the refurbishment of those sports' regular venue at Lansdowne Road. While this prompted some debate both within and outside the GAA, it is significant that opposition remained limited and relatively muted. Nevertheless, the rule continues to be a source of controversy and in 2010 the Cork club Nemo Rangers were censured for allowing the Irish rugby team to briefly use their training facilities (Keys 2010).

It is hardly surprising, given the nature of the organisation, that the GAA's position in the Northern Irish conflict has generated various strains. In a divided society relationships between sport and identity take on an added significance and the GAA has been heavily embroiled in the politics of the disputed territory (Sugden and Bairner 1993; Cronin 1999a; 2001; Bairner 2003; Hassan 2005). Although the organisation strove to cast itself in a non-overtly political light, this stance has always created tensions (Cronin, Duncan and Rouse 2009). For many northern nationalists, involvement with the GAA provided an obvious platform for assertions of an Irish identity within British-controlled territory. The GAA's emphasis on an Irish identity and its promotion of the Irish language and other aspects of Irish culture has led many unionists to view it as a hostile organisation, with loyalist paramilitaries characterising it as part of the broader Irish republican threat. Further controversy surrounded a GAA rule prohibiting members of British security forces and police in the north from membership. While many people within the organisation (and outside it) felt this was anachronistic, it was largely supported by those in northern counties, who tended to view themselves as living in an occupied territory. The rule was abolished in 2001 despite intense opposition from GAA members in the north. From the other side there were many reports of harassment of the organisation and its members. GAA pitches were occasionally commandeered by the British army, including in the early 1970s its main northern venue, Casement Park in Belfast. The long-standing British military occupation of the club ground of Crossmaglen Rangers in south Armagh was highly contentious. Incidents such as the killing of Aidan McAnespie, a 22-year-old Gaelic footballer, shot dead in disputed circumstances at a British army border checkpoint in County Tyrone as he was going to a match in 1988, served to increase such tensions. The significance of the Northern Ireland question for sections of the Irish diaspora is manifested in the naming of the leading Gaelic football team in Boston in the USA after McAnespie.

Balancing Tradition and Modernity

The strong cultural ethos espoused in various ways by the GAA since its foundation and the perceived intransigence of northern officials in relation to security force personnel have led to accusations that the organisation is living in the past, appearing to promote and hold onto an outdated and essentialised version of Irish identity underpinned by forms of sport considered to be indigenous (Arrowsmith 2004). From this standpoint the GAA can be seen as attempting to reproduce a version of Irish sports linked back to an 'authentic' pre-colonial set of pastimes unsullied by outside influences. In recent years the GAA has endeavoured to (re)emphasise aspects of its heritage. In what might be seen as a conventional practice, a GAA Museum was opened in 1998 within Croke Park and underwent a substantial refurbishment in 2010. The museum was established 'to commemorate, recognise and celebrate the GAA's enormous contribution to Irish sporting, cultural and social life since its foundation in 1884' (Croke Park 2011). In the museum a display describes the GAA as 'the pulse of a nation'. Its collection includes trophies, medals and other memorabilia. The museum also houses an archive of documentary material relating to the GAA. The organisation made much of its 125th anniversary in 2009 with a number of projects, one outcome of which was the publication of a volume dealing with various facets of the GAA throughout its history (Cronin, Murphy and Rouse 2009). Another was the creation of a GAA Oral History project aimed at unearthing 'ordinary' people's memories of specific sporting or other cultural events associated with the GAA, which provides ample evidence of the role of Gaelic games as a living heritage firmly rooted in people's everyday experiences (Cronin, Duncan and Rouse 2009).

However, while the GAA articulates a strong sense of tradition, its origins and founding vision reflect an engagement in a process of modernisation through the codification and regulation of sport within Ireland, thereby paralleling the increased regulation of sport and the creation of sporting administrative bodies in Britain and the rest of Europe in the late 19th century (Holt 2009). Moreover, while the GAA has been cast in some circles as a conservative and backward-looking organisation, it has shown itself very adept at modernising and accommodating changes for a variety of reasons, be they safety (wearing of helmets in hurling), playing regulations (introduction of ideas from other sports, such as yellow and red cards for player misdemeanours), broadcasting, or commercial matters (sponsorship and merchandising). Recent developments have seen the introduction of floodlights and all-weather training facilities at many clubs. Even some of the GAA's long-standing rules have undergone change. As already indicated, bans on its members playing 'foreign' games or the playing of 'foreign' sports at GAA grounds, and the prohibition on members of British security forces, have been either dropped or temporarily suspended. The emergence and marketing of GAA computer games and the success of a television programme in which celebrities managed GAA clubs seems to reflect a readiness to embrace and adapt aspects of contemporary forms of global entertainment.

In short, for all its emphasis on Irish sporting heritage, the GAA, particularly in recent decades, has shown a high degree of adaptability and pragmatism and the traditional–modern dichotomy serves to oversimplify a more complex reality where the local and parochial intertwine with the global and modern (Doak 1998; Cronin 1999b; Ó Tuathaigh 2009). Gaelic games, no more than any other sport (or for that matter broader elements of cultural heritage), are subject to a range of influences so that they constantly (though often imperceptibly) evolve, and debates over the authenticity of sporting heritage tend to miss this important point.

COMMERCIAL PRESSURES AND THE GAA BRAND

An obvious area of tension for the GAA (as for many sporting bodies) has been the marrying of its traditions with commercial imperatives. The major refurbishment of the Croke Park stadium completed in 2005 has resulted in the creation of one of the largest sporting venues in Europe (Fig 15.1). Unsurprisingly, such investment reflected more than merely sporting interests. The stadium boasts a conference centre and hospitality suites and can be booked for weddings and other functions. (A 2010 deal between the Irish government and trade unions on public sector reform was negotiated in the stadium's conference facilities and has become known as the Croke Park Agreement.)

As indicated earlier, the use of heritage branding as part of broader promotional strategies has become a prevalent feature in recent years (Misiura 2006), and the GAA is far from immune. The rise of sponsorship nationally and locally was a marked feature of the 1990s onwards as clubs endeavoured to raise money to improve training and playing facilities. The branding of Gaelic sport was elevated in 1995 when Guinness became official sponsors of the All-Ireland hurling championship. This was portrayed as a coming together of two uniquely Irish brands trading on the long heritage of both the drink and the sport and is in keeping with the broader symbolism attaching to ideas of Ireland and Irishness which operates in other place-promotional ventures (Gaffey 2004). Somewhat ironically, however, Guinness, although traditionally associated with Ireland, is part of a multinational drinks company headquartered in London. In recent years the GAA has actively engaged with marketing agencies in a conscious attempt at brand promotion mainly associated with the commercial sponsorship of selected events.[2]

The GAA has endeavoured to link their commercial involvement to broader national concerns through the promotion of a policy to buy Irish products wherever possible. Footballs and sports clothing are produced by the Irish company O'Neills, with whom the GAA has had a long-standing relationship. Many counties endeavour to maintain local links through sponsorship; for example, Donegal Creameries sponsors the county teams and has their logo emblazoned on the shirts. Merchandising has been a dominant feature of the last two decades, with sales of replica club and county shirts (Fig 15.2), flags, banners, hats and rosettes (both contemporary and historic) mirroring trends in other sports. This commercialisation results in younger fans having an eclectic array of sportswear with tops in the colours of, for instance, Barcelona, Newcastle United and Wexford. The major insurance company Allianz (with its headquarters in Germany) is the current sponsor of the GAA's national hurling and football leagues. Etihad Airlines and Toyota are sponsors of the All-Ireland hurling championship. Similarly, Vodafone, a sponsor of the All-Ireland football championship, has recently become shirt sponsor for the Dublin team,

---

2   See, for example, http://www.rebrand.com/2009-distinction-gaa-gaelic-athletic-association.

Fig 15.1. Croke Park, Dublin: home of the GAA and now one of the largest sporting venues in Europe.

Fig 15.2. Replica GAA county shirts showing sponsors, on display at Croke Park.

replacing a local department store (see Hancock 2009). This suggests that commercial pressures sometimes sit uneasily with both the amateur nature of the games and the nationalist political orientation. It might be argued that preserving a heritage seen as national, and with connotations of cultural purity attaching to it, risks being somewhat sullied by commercial deals. Nevertheless, and despite additional concerns such as ongoing tensions over payments to players, the GAA remains built on the efforts of community-based groups and enormous voluntary commitment (Cronin, Duncan and Rouse 2009).

CONTINUITY AND CHANGE

When placing the GAA and Gaelic games within the context of broader debates over heritage the issue of authenticity is (as elsewhere) something of a meaningless argument. As Cronin, Murphy and Rouse's (2009) overview amply demonstrates, the GAA has constantly evolved, controversially at times, but has shown an enormous capacity for adaptation. The games under the auspices of the GAA certainly may have deep historical roots but their initial codification and subsequent gradual rule adjustments mean that they periodically change. However, with the GAA's increased commercialisation, especially during the economic boom of the late 1990s and early 2000s, there have always been tensions and accommodations surrounding amateurism and broader commercial concerns (McAnallan 2009).

The GAA has also had to adapt to changing social circumstances. In the past, substantial emigration left some clubs finding it difficult to field teams owing to the loss of young talent, a concern that has re-emerged following the recent economic collapse (see, for example, Duggan 2011). Ireland's experience of substantial immigration from the mid-1990s through to about 2008 – a reversal of previous established trends – has resulted in immigrants and the children of immigrants becoming involved in Gaelic games. This, along with reported incidents of racial abuse at some games (see, for example, Foley 2008) contributed to the introduction of policies on racism and guidelines to clubs on dealing with the more multicultural backgrounds of some of its members. The GAA now has statements prohibiting discrimination on the basis of ethnicity and cultural background and has enshrined anti-racism principles within its regulations. Ireland's Celtic Tiger economic boom also witnessed Irish migrants finding themselves in some non-traditional destinations and as a result the GAA has established clubs and events in various parts of Europe and south-east Asia. An Asian County Board was established in 2006, governing more than 600 players from 18 nationalities at 16 clubs (such as the Arabian Celts, Dalian Wolfhounds and Singapore Gaelic Lions) taking part in a regional Gaelic games tournament (see GAA Overseas Work Group, n.d.). So a seemingly insular and nationally defined organisation, concerned with the preservation of a sporting and cultural heritage, benefited enormously from Ireland's global interconnections.

CONCLUSION

The GAA endeavours to present itself in a favourable light, emphasising its positive role in the broader preservation and strengthening of Irish identity and culture and its political role in promoting a sense of independence. To some extent there is an almost inevitable tendency towards simplifying the past and an association with romanticised versions of its history. However, the GAA has also dealt with a range of controversial issues, particularly in relation to events in

Northern Ireland. Moreover, even in its relationship to, and celebration of, Irish identity and cultural heritage, it has accommodated itself to shifting versions of identity and to changing political contexts on both sides of the border. The 2011 tour of Croke Park by Queen Elizabeth II as part of the itinerary of her historic Irish visit amply demonstrates a flexibility on the part of the GAA to changing circumstances, notwithstanding some dissenting voices (de Bréadún and Ó Caollaí 2011). More broadly, as Mike Cronin (1999b) has argued, the GAA is both local and global at the same time, simultaneously preserving and harnessing parochial identities while outwardly embracing modern global and local commercial opportunities. While the GAA has undoubtedly provided a focal point for local communities and fostered a strong sense of place, it has also responded in various ways to a series of outside influences. Although its core principles hark back to pre-modern sports, the GAA could, to a considerable extent, be said to have invented them in their contemporary forms. Its very existence has served to modernise those same sports of which it is the official custodian.

ACKNOWLEDGMENTS

This chapter has benefited greatly from the advice and insights provided by Michael Holmes and Anne Sinnott.

BIBLIOGRAPHY AND REFERENCES

Anderson, B, 1991 *Imagined Communities: Reflections on the Origin and Spread of Nationalism*, 2 edn, Verso, London

Arrowsmith, A, 2004 Plastic Paddies vs Master Racers: 'Soccer' and Irish Identity, *International Journal of Cultural Studies* 7 (4), 460–79

Bairner, A, 2003 Political Unionism and Sporting Nationalism: An Examination of the Relationship between Sport and National Identity within the Ulster Unionist Tradition, *Identities: Global Studies in Culture and Power* 10 (4), 517–35

— 2005 Sport and the Irish, in *Sport and the Irish: Histories, Identities, Issues* (ed A Bairner), University College Dublin Press, Dublin, 1–4

Bielenberg, A (ed), 2000 *The Irish Diaspora*, Longman, Harlow

Billig, M, 1995 *Banal Nationalism*, Sage, London

Brady, S, 2005 Performances of Irishness at New York's Gaelic Park, *New York Irish History* 19, 17–34

Croke Park, 2011 *About the GAA Museum: GAA Museum at Croke Park* [online], available from: http://www.crokepark.ie/gaa-museum/about [31 October 2011]

Cronin, M, 1999a *Sport and Nationalism in Ireland: Gaelic Games, Soccer and Irish Identity since 1884*, Four Courts Press, Dublin

— 1999b Global, Parochial, Still Anti-imperialist and Irish, *Peace Review* 11 (4), 517–22

— 2001 Catholics and Sport in Northern Ireland: Exclusiveness or Inclusiveness? *International Sports Studies* 21 (1), 25–41

Cronin, M, Duncan, M, and Rouse, P, 2009 *The GAA: A People's History*, The Collins Press, Cork

Cronin, M, Murphy, W, and Rouse, P (eds), 2009 *The Gaelic Athletic Association 1884–2009*, Irish Academic Press, Dublin

Darby, P, 2009 Gaelic Games and the Irish Immigrant Experience in Boston, in *Sport and the Irish. Histories, Identities, Issues* (ed A Bairner), University College Dublin Press, Dublin, 85–101

— 2010 The Gaelic Athletic Association, Transnational Identities and Irish America, *Sociology of Sport Journal* 27 (4), 351–70

de Bréadún, D, and Ó Caollaí, É, 2011 GAA says Croke Park visit honours association, *Irish Times*, 19 May

Doak, R, 1998 (De)constructing Irishness in the 1990s – The Gaelic Athletic Association and Cultural Nationalist Discourse Reconsidered, *Irish Journal of Sociology* 8 (1), 25–48

Duggan, K, 2011 Reality of emigration is starting to hit home, *Irish Times*, 5 February

Foley, C, 2008 GAA Issues Racism Apology, *Irish Independent*, 25 July

GAA Overseas Work Group, n.d. *GAA Overseas Units. Contact Information Booklet*, GAA, Dublin

Gaffey, S, 2004 *Signifying Place: The Semiotic Realisation of Place in Irish Product Marketing*, Ashgate, Aldershot

Gellner, E, 1997 *Nationalism*, Weidenfeld and Nicolson, London

Graham, B, Ashworth, G, and Tunbridge, J E, 2000 *A Geography of Heritage. Power, Culture and Economy*, Arnold, London

Hancock, C, 2009 Dublin GAA Scores with €6m Vodafone Sponsorship Deal, *Irish Times*, 12 December

Hannigan, D, 1998 *The Garrison Game. The State of Irish Football*, Mainstream, Edinburgh

Hassan, D, 2005 Sport, Identity and Irish Nationalism in Northern Ireland, in *Sport and the Irish. Histories, Identities, Issues* (ed A Bairner), University College Dublin Press, Dublin, 123–39

Hewison, R, 1987 *The Heritage Industry: Britain in a Climate of Decline*, Methuen, London

Hobsbawm, E, 1992 *Nations and Nationalism since 1780. Programme, Myth, Reality*, 2 edn, Cambridge University Press, Cambridge

Holt, R, 2009 Ireland and the Birth of Modern Sport, in *The Gaelic Athletic Association 1884–2009* (eds M Cronin, W Murphy and P Rouse), Irish Academic Press, Dublin, 33–46

Keys, C, 2010 Croker Issue Warning to Nemo, *Irish Independent*, 5 May

Lowenthal, D, 1985 *The Past is a Foreign Country*, Cambridge University Press, Cambridge

— 1998 *The Heritage Crusade and the Spoils of History*, Cambridge University Press, Cambridge

McAnallen, D, 2009 'The Greatest Amateur Association in the World'? The GAA and Amateurism, in *The Gaelic Athletic Association 1884–2009* (eds M Cronin, W Murphy and P Rouse), Irish Academic Press, Dublin, 157–82

MacLaughlin, J (ed), 1997 *Location and Dislocation in Contemporary Irish Society: Emigration and Irish Identities*, Cork University Press, Cork

— 2001 *Reimagining the Nation-State. The Contested Terrains of Nation-Building*, Pluto, London

Misiura, S, 2006 *Heritage Marketing*, Butterworth-Heinemann, London

O'Riordan, I, 2010 TV3 and Newstalk make gains, *Irish Times*, 10 November

Ó Tuathaigh, G, 2009 The GAA as a Force in Irish Society: an Overview, in *The Gaelic Athletic Association 1884–2009* (eds M Cronin, W Murphy and P Rouse), Irish Academic Press, Dublin, 237–56

Paasi, A, 1999 Boundaries as Social Practice and Discourse: the Finnish–Russian Border, *Regional Studies* 33 (7), 669–80

Rojek, C, 1993 *Ways of Escape: Modern Transformations in Leisure and Travel*, Macmillan, London

Rouse, P, 1993 A History of the G.A.A. Ban on Foreign Games, 1884–1971, *International Journal of the History of Sport* 10 (3), 333–60

Samuel, R, 1994 *Past and Present in Contemporary Culture*, Routledge, London

Smith, A D, 2001 *Nationalism: Theory, Ideology, History*, Polity Press, Cambridge

Storey, D, 2004 A Sense of Place: Rural Development, Tourism and Place Promotion in the Republic of Ireland, in *Geographies of Rural Cultures and Societies* (eds L Holloway and M Kneafsey), Ashgate, Aldershot, 197–213

— 2010 Using the Past: Heritage and Re-imagining Rural Places, in *Geographical Perspectives on Sustainable Rural Change* (eds D G Winchell, D Ramsey, R Koster and G M Robinson), Rural Development Institute, Brandon University, 374–83

Sugden, J, and Bairner, A, 1993 *Sport, Sectarianism and Society in a Divided Ireland*, Leicester University Press, London

Timothy, D J, and Boyd, S J, 2003 *Heritage Tourism*, Prentice Hall, Harlow

Walsh, K T, 1992 *The Representation of the Past: Museums and Heritage in the Post-modern World*, Routledge, London

Wright, P, 1985 *On Living in an Old Country: The National Past in Contemporary Britain*, Verso, London

16

Olympic Heritage – An International Legacy: The Invention of the Modern Olympic Stadium from Coubertin to 1948

Daphné Bolz

From their revival at the end of the 19th century at the instigation of Pierre de Coubertin, the modern Olympics have progressively developed to meet the needs of various sports and the expectations of spectators. However, what has changed little is the central position of the Olympic stadium. Throughout the 20th century, stadiums have become landmarks in Olympic history and a focus for national pride and representation. Their design and development reflects improvements in sporting achievements and in technical competence. And they set a clear legacy which has a double dimension: on the one hand, stadiums supply a material legacy in terms of infrastructure; on the other hand, they create an image for both the Olympic movement and the hosting city.

The aim of this chapter is to examine the concept of the Olympic stadium in the first half of the 20th century (see Wimmer 1976; Schmidt 1986a; 1986b; 1988) and in particular to see how successive Games built on previous experiences of stadium design as part of a perpetual and always evolving legacy. The use of the word 'legacy' has become fashionable in the Olympic movement's discourses: adoption of the term 'Olympic legacy' makes clear the shift from being a 'peace movement' to a 'brand' (MacAloon 2008, 2061). For academic purposes, 'legacy' embraces the effects of *all* previous Olympic Games in terms of facilities, memory, philosophy and image. Since 'the modern Olympics are a heritage of the complex currents of modernity' (Dyreson 2008b, 2118), it is the ongoing definition and renewal of the Olympic movement's identity that we will explore through the lens of the Olympic stadiums.

The Stadium in the History of Olympics

Theoretical considerations of what an Olympic stadium should look like have existed since the end of the 19th century. The 1896 Games were staged in the reconstructed remains of an ancient Greek stadium in Athens, but after the disappointing experiences of Paris in 1900 and Saint Louis in 1904 Coubertin underlined the importance of having a proper stadium to host future Olympic celebrations. Central to the Olympic Charter 'was the notion of "Olympism", the humanistic philosophy that mediated the cultural construction of the revived Games and guided the development of the supporting ceremonial content that steadily accumulated in the subsequent years' (Gold and Gold 2007, 21). For this reason Coubertin would very much have liked the Games to be held partly in the ruins of ancient Rome (Coubertin 1931, 70; Wimmer 1976,

21) and he strongly supported the successful bid of the eternal city for the 1908 Olympics; Rome, however, eventually had to withdraw and the Games went to London.

In 1910 the International Olympic Committee (IOC) launched an architecture competition for a Modern Olympia ('*cité olympique moderne*') – an ideal 'Olympic place'. The *Revue Olympique* considered it a good idea to help interested parties by publishing a series of articles on the expectations for such a new concept (Anon 1909a; 1909b; 1910). Here the inconsistencies between the ancient Games and the modern Olympic movement immediately become apparent. The articles mention only vaguely the necessity to take into account 'antique customs' but then go on to say that what is wanted is 'innovation and useful innovation' (Anon 1909a, 147) and the will to create a particular, almost quasi-religious, atmosphere (Anon 1909b, 153). The winning design by Monod and Laverrière, also published in the *Revue Olympique*, is a 'huge stadium' at the heart of a complex dedicated to sport and the arts. The results of the architecture competition are presented as examples of projects which successfully offer responses to 'social evolutions'. Most important of all is the claim that democracy is a central value in the idea of a Modern Olympia (Trelat 1911). Indeed, the stadium was understood as a hub of democratic gathering to celebrate human performance and to share the knowledge and the experience of these.

In the first years of the 20th century, when sport increasingly became a spectacle, Coubertin was more and more preoccupied with the characteristics of newly built stadiums. For him these were too many and too big; they were the expression of a kind of deviance of sport. In the *Revue Olympique* he claimed that big stadiums should be reserved for the Olympics, festivals which celebrate more the achievements of humanity than the records of individuals (Coubertin 1911, 158–60). So angry was he about the proliferation of stadiums for spectacle that he even argued that Olympic stadiums should be temporary (Coubertin 1911, 159). After all, the aim of the IOC was to promote the practising of sport and not the passive watching of it. Writing 20 years later, he ended his *Mémoires Olympiques* with a charter for sport reform, asking that city councils renounce the building of huge stadiums in favour of modern Hellenistic gymnasia (Coubertin 1931, 216–17).

A Sporting Legacy: Stadiums to Practise Sport

The idealistic approach of Coubertin was at odds with the evolution of (spectator) sport at this time. By the interwar period, for example, most of Britain's major stadiums hosted professional football matches. The charge of people such as engineer Archibald Leitch (Inglis 2004) – the central figure in the domain of British stadium-building in the first part of the 20th century – was not to create an ideal democratic venue to host sportsmen; instead 'designing a football ground in Leitch's time was basically a question of filling the space left available once the pitch had been marked out. With the money available one had to try and fit in as many spectators as possible' (Inglis 1983, 20). Indeed, as the Olympic movement grew, idealistic visions of sport and the development of stadiums had to be accommodated with real life social and economic expectations.

The technical history of Olympic stadiums is one of constant evolution, building legacy upon legacy. The bringing together of sport and the arts and the associated technical aspects of design were central to Coubertin's project and an essential part of the identity of an Olympic stadium. However, this was not the case at the outset. The refurbished Panathenian Stadium in Athens, used for the 1896 Games and having no modern 'Olympic' stadium to take as its model, presented an elongated shape which was far from ideal for competitors. Yet it was specifically because of the stadium's shape, and the chosen building material (white marble), that the event and the venue acquired some distinction and dignity. At the beginning of the 20th century the Olympic movement hit hard times and Coubertin's project had trouble surviving. The 1900 Paris and 1904 Saint Louis Games were disappointing experiences. It was bad enough that Coubertin's project was not understood; worse were the venues and conditions for staging the events. Not much can be said about the Paris stadium, as there was none; sport was basically practised in nature (Gold and Gold 2007, 23). In Saint Louis things were comparatively better with at least a stadium being provided for competitors, even though the Saint Louis Exhibition completely overshadowed the Games.

Modern Olympic sport came to be celebrated properly from 1908, when a purpose-built stadium, the Great Stadium, was erected for the London Games at White City. Although the White City Stadium, as it became known, was not without its disadvantages, it was large and impressive enough to make it a fitting venue for Olympic competitions and celebrations, with a running track, a cycle track and even a 100m swimming pool, as well as room for 93,000 spectators. The architectural style and building materials reflected the typical 'industrial' construction techniques of the time, with steel and wood predominating and concrete used only for the cycling track. The White City Stadium was an experiment that suited the Coubertin idea of having a central place for as many disciplines as possible. While it may have left a 'considerable legacy' for the Olympic movement (Gold and Gold 2007, 23), in later years it failed to keep pace with the development of modern spectator sport and was demolished in 1985.

The White City Stadium had a strong influence on the design of major stadiums built in the years that followed. The *Revue Olympique* drew attention to direct influences on the stadium built at the Grunewald racecourse in Berlin, especially the provision of a 100m swimming pool (Anon 1910, 58). This 'Deutsches Stadion' was inaugurated in 1913 for the 1916 Games (cancelled owing to the outbreak of World War I) and is a perfect embodiment of the Olympic ideal, accommodating both a large number of spectators and a huge variety of sports. It was the most important stadium in Germany and its legacy was long-lasting, influencing not only stadium design but associated urban planning, especially in the 1920s (Schmidt 1990, 67). Other German cities, such as Cologne, Frankfurt or Nuremberg, also consciously developed stadiums along the same lines. Together with Berlin, all three of them applied to host the 1936 Games.

During the interwar period the design of stadiums, including Olympic ones, moved away from the antiquity of Athens and the huge London-style stadiums. The elliptical shape of the stadium survived at the Olympic stadiums at Antwerp (1920), Paris (1924) and Amsterdam (1928) (Agostinelli 1989, 58), but developments in the 1920s and 1930s saw, for example, swimming pools leaving the stadium arena to become separate venues.[1] Some non-Olympic venues, such as the Vienna Stadium by O E Schweizer (Schweizer 1938), had a huge influence on future design, big and small. Moreover, at this time physical education was becoming a 'new' political cause across continental Europe. When the fascists came to power in Italy new sporting facilities were built nearly everywhere (Bolz 2008). Italian architects were invited to design stadiums that

---

[1] The only exception was the *Stadio del PNF* in Rome, where a pool was built during refurbishment of the U-shaped stadium in 1928.

would be convenient for spectators and allow the practice of a variety of sports – mini Olympic stadiums in a way.

STADIUMS TO ATTRACT PEOPLE: CREATING SPORT TOURISM AND THE SPREAD OF SPECTACLE

Spectacles such as Olympic Games require spectators and the income generated from them. From the very beginning of the 20th century stadiums were increasingly considered in economic terms as mass entertainment venues. The IOC encouraged this, recognising that local (ie regional or national) economic ambitions also played an essential part in promoting the Games. In the interwar period, for example, American sports promoters began to believe 'that an Olympic spectacle in the US could challenge major-league baseball and college football for paying customers' (Dyreson 2008a, 1477).

The lure of gain had implications for the stadiums themselves. From the beginning of the 20th century, and especially from the interwar period onwards, Olympic stadiums were more than technically proficient venues for sport. From 'industrial'-style engineering, they came to be viewed as architectural statements, sometimes following an ideological line that combined nationalism with a fascination for antiquity. The Olympic stadium of Colombes, built for the Paris Games of 1924, may be seen as the last of its kind (Fig 16.1). Its functional, 'industrial' style was in part due to a restricted budget following huge financial problems between the organisers and the local authorities in Paris and Colombes (Schmidt 1986a, 401; Pizzori Itié 1992; Schut and Terret 2008). A new functionalist style, inspired by Frank Lloyd Wright, is evident at the Amsterdam stadium built for the 1928 Games (Schmidt 1986b, 466).

The Los Angeles Games of 1932 set a new milestone not only for the Olympic movement but also for the city itself: Olympic expansion and economic successes went hand in hand and have marched together ever since. The 1932 Games were the first successful 'city marketing' experience, an expression now routinely used when considering Olympic city applications (Ward 2008, 120). For Los Angeles, organising the Games was clearly a way to advertise the city, to put it on the world map and to attract tourists and investors. The money for the palm trees of Los Angeles came from the Olympic budget, a decision that has proved itself invaluable in terms of the city's image worldwide (Riess 1981, 51).

As far as the stadium itself is concerned, the Los Angeles Coliseum is a good example of local ambition meeting the Olympic movement's opportunism. Its construction had been imagined after World War I to raise the profile of Los Angeles – at that time far from being a leading city in America – and to boost tourism, which was in decline. When a member from the Community Development Association (CDA), a body formed to smarten up the city and especially to attract money, proposed in 1920 that Los Angeles should host the Games, the city was far from ready or aware of the duties this implied (Riess 1981, 51–3). Success was finally achieved through political determination. The CDA's chairman, William May Garland, lobbied hard and was even elected an IOC member in 1921. Although Los Angeles was not selected to stage the Games this did not stop construction proceeding nor the Coliseum being called 'Olympic stadium'. It opened in 1923, nine years before it staged an Olympic Games. Built of concrete and designed in the classical style by architect John Parkinson, it was the biggest and most expensive public stadium in the USA (Riess 1981, 56). It was (and still is) one of the distinctive landmarks that makes Los Angeles a world city (Fig 16.2). The 1932 Games were the first where the ambitions of a city in terms of urban development met the globalising ambitions of the IOC. This was not only true

Fig 16.1. The Colombes stadium, venue for the 1924 Games in Paris.

for the stadium, which became 'the central architectural legacy of the games': the Olympic aspiration of Los Angeles 'ensured that their Olympics left several legacies' of infrastructure across California (Dyreson and Llewellyn 2008, 1995–8).

The development of the media intensified the importance of the Olympic stadium as a displayed element for the promotion of the Games. Improvements in photography and film techniques had a strong impact on the growing importance of the *visual* identity of the Games and in 'selling' the event. Spectators' interest in the Olympics rose with the ability to 'see' the dramatic actions of the athletes and the impressive venues where the Games were being celebrated. First to exploit this were the Berlin organisers in 1936,[2] though with limited success (Haynes 2010, 1031–3). Generally speaking, the stadium has to answer the intertwined interests of both the Olympic movement and the local organisers in terms of performance, image and money. While the aesthetic shape of the stadium itself is perfect to link the Games to a romantic vision of 'Olympic' brotherhood, it is inevitable that 'one of the legacies of the modern games is consumption' (Maguire *et al* 2008, 2042). On most occasions, the expenses for the Olympic venues were justified against the general 'legacy' of the event and especially against the economic profit the venues themselves would generate. Olympic tourism, for example, was one key element to maintain the London Games in 1948 and help offset the cost for Olympic facilities – though not for the stadium (Bolz 2010) – in a post-war, devastated London.

---

[2] Leni Riefenstahl's film exemplarily presented not only the individual actions of the athletes but also the collective feelings of the crowd in an aesthetically 'perfect' stadium. But what was transmitted here was more than commercial.

FIG 16.2. A SYMBOL OF LOCAL AND OLYMPIC SUCCESS: THE LOS ANGELES MEMORIAL STADIUM HOSTING THE 1932 GAMES.

A POLITICAL LEGACY: THE OLYMPIC STADIUM AS A SYMBOL

For Coubertin, sport was a tool to promote international peace and friendship and in this sense 'politics' was a core dimension of the Olympic movement from the very beginning (Guttmann 2002). In architectural terms, Olympic stadiums clearly were and still are a way of expressing the position of the host city and country in terms of innovation, prestige and identity. Inspired by the Greek experiences, Olympic stadiums had a particular relationship to building materials and design. From the prestigious marble stadium of 1896, all Olympic stadiums stood for both ancient Olympic heritage and the contemporaneity of the Olympic cause. Not all organisers could count on the generosity of a rich benefactor, as in Athens, but all used the stadium as a hub for celebrations and festivities that would spread outside the venues.

The first Games and venues revealed little about the *political* identity of the Games themselves; they were much more about the *social* identity of the IOC. The classical inspiration for Olympic stadiums was due to the fact that the members of the IOC were a group of men from elite society whose education had been grounded in a knowledge of ancient history (Dyreson and Llewellyn 2008, 1993). The reach of Olympic ideology, however, was much broader than references to antiquity. It had to embrace the era of the masses under the umbrella of 'modernity'. Indeed, the Olympic movement was born at the same time as the international fair movement that aimed to exhibit the scientific progress of the Western World (Dyreson 2008b, 2118; Roche

2000). It is unsurprising that the Olympics of 1900 and 1904 were organised in the context of these world exhibitions. As Mark Dyreson has noted, 'the practice of circulating the Olympics through the world's greatest metropolises evolves from the traditions of the expositions and not the model of antiquity with its singular stage at Olympia' (Dyreson 2008b, 2119); by doing so, the Olympic movement aimed at globalising an occidental way of practising physical activities. The disappointment for Coubertin was that these early Games were largely invisible and left little in the way of any substantial legacy, owing mainly to the relative lack of power and money of the Olympic movement compared with the international fairs. Certainly, after these episodes, he was more determined than ever to make the Olympics autonomous and visible in the cultural and urban landscape.

The architecture of Olympic stadiums therefore expresses the uneasy position of the Olympic movement in embracing both progress and conservatism. This is exemplified by the Stockholm Olympic stadium of 1912, which contains both modern (concrete) and traditional (lime granite and brick) elements which give the stadium an impression of solidity (Schmidt 1986a, 399). The same technique, but on a larger scale, was to be used for the 1936 stadium in Berlin – an overtly political symbol, as we shall see.

By the interwar period the quality of sporting infrastructure became a barometer for national prestige, especially in Europe, where the trend to build 'national stadiums', often in conjunction with applications to hold an Olympics, was established. In the US the situation was different. From the early 20th century many American sporting authorities thought that 'the United States risked falling far behind in future competitions if a sparkling Olympic movement was not quickly erected on American soil' (Dyreson 2008a, 1476). In 1916, the American Olympic Committee official Bartow Weeks 'asserted that the US could stage the games as part of a grand Fourth of July festival to honour the American republic's emerging role as the world's leading power' (Dyreson 2008a, 1479). The construction of an American national stadium was a means to this end, although the plans were eventually dropped. Twenty years later it was for the Nazis to use the Berlin Olympics as a clear political and ideological tool. The stadium was one key element in their demonstration of power.

The Berlin Games of 1936 have been extensively studied (see, for example, Mandell 1971; Alkemeyer 1996; Krüger and Murray 2003). The organisers' plans had been limited until Hitler came to power. While the Nazis were not ideologically attuned to hosting a global sports event designed to celebrate international friendship, high party members, including Hitler himself, quickly understood that it was in the Nazi movement's best interest to put on a great show and use the Olympics as a vehicle for the regime. First and foremost, the Olympic facilities were to be the most gigantic and perfect ever built, setting a landmark in Olympic and stadium building history (Kluge 1999; Schäche and Szymanski 2001; Bolz 2008). The stadium was the centre of the Games' success – and a metaphor for the success of the regime. Festivities were prepared and organised in respect of the new policies developed by the regime, and so was the stadium. After visiting the future Olympic park in November 1933, Hitler ordered the complete reorganisation of the venues. Buildings across the area were to be distributed around two main symmetrical axes, which enhanced the monumental aspect of the whole complex. Funding was to no longer be a problem. Unemployed locals were hired, thus combining the preparation of the Olympics with an effective economic policy. The stadium that resulted subtly, and therefore perversely, merged the reference to antiquity (to satisfy the IOC and the media), the use of modern techniques (without which it would not have been possible to achieve the construction) and the Nazi

FIG 16.3. SETTING A TECHNICAL AND POLITICAL LANDMARK IN STADIUM HISTORY: THE 'REICHSSPORTFELD' IN BERLIN, VENUE FOR THE 1936 GAMES.

doctrine (not mentioned except to stress how devoted Nazis were to the Olympic movement). The various buildings and functionalities of the Olympic park were said to be inspired by the Greek model. The main stadium and other central venues were constructed in concrete but clad in monumental masonry: while concrete stood for modernity and innovation for the Italian fascists, the Nazis rejected it in architecture, for it was in ideological conflict with their praise for 'soil' and nature (Fig 16.3).

Leaving aside the moral legacy of the Berlin Games, the Olympic park illustrates the perfect adaptation of architecture and environment to the Olympic spectacle. In this respect it is unsurprising that the IOC was very enthusiastic in the end. Later, of course, Germany had the opportunity to organise the Games again in Munich in 1972, which was also an opportunity to overcome and replace the memories of the 'Berlin Games' (Schiller and Young 2010, 56–86), particularly through the extraordinary Olympic stadium's airy style (in total contrast to Berlin) as a representation of (West) Germany's open democracy (Schiller and Young 2010, 87–126; Modrey 2008).

In the immediate aftermath of the 1936 Games it was difficult to imagine how future Olympics could surpass the Berlin experience. But in Italy and also Japan (for which see Collins 2006; 2007) competition to stage an even better event was stirring. Indeed, Italy offers an interesting example, with its first proper Olympic stadium inaugurated in 1932 and extended in 1937: the Stadio dei Cipressi in Rome (later substantially refurbished for the 1960 Games). The fascist regime had pursued the idea of organising the Olympics in Rome for some time but, on the

FIG 16.4. A NEW START IN A LEGENDARY VENUE: WEMBLEY STADIUM, VENUE FOR THE 1948 GAMES IN LONDON.

orders of Mussolini, the eternal city withdrew her application to host the 1940 Games at the last minute in favour of Tokyo (Collins 2006, 1132–4). The Stadio dei Cipressi is at the crossroads of several influences. On the one hand, it exemplified the ideal Olympic stadium – large enough to accommodate 90,000 spectators and embedded in the natural landscape (Caporilli and Simeoni 1990, 118). Built in a physical education complex, it was also aligned with Coubertin's idea of the Modern Olympia. On the other hand, the stadium itself was part of the Mussolini Forum, a huge and impressive complex of sports venues originally intended to educate Italians physically but gradually extended to encompass the idea of cultivating the fascist sporting hero (Greco and Santuccio 1991; Masia *et al* 2007; Bolz 2008). Rome could have considered organising the Olympics in its Stadio del Partito Nazionale Fascista (stadium of the Fascist National Party), where the final of the 1934 football World Cup had been won by the Italian team. However, by the end of the 1930s Italy had become an Empire and the regime's ambition was such that this stadium was now too small and too dull to showcase the 'new Italy'. The booklet *Roma Olimpica*, prepared for the bid competition to host the 1940 Olympics, shows a monumental U-shaped stadium with a capacity of 50,000 by architects Moretti, Frisa and Pintonello that reflected the self-perception of the fascist government (CONI 1935; see also Toschi 1990). By 1939, when Rome was seeking to host the 1944 Games, another promotional brochure (CONI-ENIT 1939) anticipated enlargement of what is now the Stadio Olimpionico to a capacity of 100,000 and the development of other major facilities (Toschi 1995, 291).

World War II put the Olympics on hold. There were no Games in 1940 or 1944 and no new

Olympic stadium for 12 years. In awarding the 1948 Games to a war-torn London, the IOC made a wise choice. A key element in this choice was the existence of Wembley Stadium, which had been built for the British Empire Exhibition of 1924 (Hill and Varrasi 1997) (Fig 16.4). Also important were Britain's sporting traditions and heritage, and her role in the spread of a world-wide sports culture, which chimed well with the Olympic movement's global ambition. So, after having stood for the British Empire's achievements, Wembley stadium now stood for Olympic global friendship of nations. The design of the stadium suited both roles.

Conclusion

The aim of this chapter has been to present and discuss the legacy question related to Olympic stadiums. The elements presented here illustrate how complex and wide-ranging the topic is. No Olympic stadium is similar to another but all have something in common. Moreover, every newly built Olympic stadium takes its pedigree from a long and evolving heritage while at the same time it is the implicit duty of the host organisers to display a new stadium that embodies the progress of the Olympic movement. Within less than two decades the stadium moved away from a theoretical and impracticable 19th-century idea of a Modern Olympia to take into account the technical realities of sport development and performance and the heightening of spectator and media interests. From the first Games, financial issues and local prestige were interwoven when considering building an Olympic stadium. After World War I, politics clearly entered the Olympic scene, turning stadiums into ideological showcases. In more recent times Olympic stadiums have echoed to the mantra of modern sport: performance–media–money. Nowadays, as we look forward to a third London Olympics in 2012, the emphasis has shifted to new forms of legacy promise – 'lasting community benefits at each stage of an Olympic project, not just when the games are concluded' (MacAloon 2008, 2065) – to give a stronger or renewed moral sense to the Games.

Bibliography and References

Agostinelli, F, 1989 Stadi. Dalle Prime Olimpiadi Moderni ai Campionati del Mondo di Calcio del 1934, *Parametro* XX (172), 56–65

Alkemeyer, T, 1996 *Körper, Kult und Politik. Von der 'Muskelreligion' Pierre de Coubertins zur Inszenierung von Macht in den Olympischen Spielen von 1936*, Campus Verlag, Frankfurt and New York

Anon, 1909a En Vue du Concours International d'Architecture, *Revue Olympique*, October, 147–8

— 1909b Une Olympie Moderne. I. Le Cadre, *Revue Olympique*, October, 153–6

— 1910 Stades Anciens et Modernes, *Revue Olympique*, April, 56–60

Bolz, D, 2008 *Les Arènes Totalitaires. Fascisme, Nazisme et Propagande Sportive*, CNRS Editions, Paris

— 2010 Welcoming the World's Best Athletes: an Olympic Challenge for Post-war Britain, *International Journal of the History of Sport* 27 (6), 1006–28

Caporilli, M, and Simeoni, F (eds), 1990 *Il Foro Italico e lo Stadio Olimpico. Immagini dalla Storia*, Tomo Edizioni, Rome

Collins, S, 2006 Conflicts of the 1930s Japanese Olympic Diplomacy in Universalizing the Olympic Movement, *International Journal of the History of Sport* 23 (7), 1128–51

— 2007 The Spectacle of Olympic Tokyo and Imperial Japan, *International Journal of the History of Sport* 24 (8), 1064–96

CONI, 1935 *Roma Olimpiaca*, Rome

CONI-ENIT, 1939 *Roma Olimpiaca*, Rome

de Coubertin, P, 1911 Partie Officielle. Bulletin du Comité International Olympique, *Revue Olympique*, October, 158–60

— 1931 *Mémoires Olympiques*, Bureau International de Pédagogie Sportive, Lausanne [reprinted 1996, Editions Revue EPS, Paris]

Dyreson, M, 2008a If We Build It Will They Come? The Plans for a National Stadium and American Desires, *International Journal of the History of Sport* 25 (11), 1475–92

— 2008b Epilogue: Athletic Clashes of Civilizations or Bridges Over Cultural Divisions? The Olympic Games as Legacies and the Legacies of the Olympic Games, *International Journal of the History of Sport* 25 (14), 2117–29

Dyreson, M, and Llewellyn, M, 2008 Los Angeles is the Olympic City: Legacies of the 1932 and 1984 Olympic Games, *International Journal of the History of Sport* 25 (14), 1991–2018

Gold, J R, and Gold, M M, 2007 Athens to Athens: the Summer Olympics, 1896–2004, in *Olympic Cities. City Agendas, Planning, and the World's Games, 1896–2012* (eds J R Gold and M M Gold), Routledge, London and New York, 15–47

Greco, A, and Santuccio, S, 1991 *Foro Italico*, Multigrafica, Rome

Guttmann, A, 2002 *The Olympics. A History of the Modern Games*, 2 edn, University of Illinois Press, Urbana-Chicago

Haynes, R, 2010 The BBC, Austerity and Broadcasting the 1938 Olympic Games, *International Journal of the History of Sport* 27 (6), 1029–46

Hill, J, and Varrasi, F, 1997 Creating Wembley. The Construction of a National Monument, *The Sports Historian* 17 (2), 28–43

Inglis, S, 1983 *The Football Grounds of England and Wales*, Willow Books, London

— 2004 *Engineering Archie. Archibald Leitch – Football Ground Designer*, English Heritage, London

Kluge, V, 1999 *Olympiastadion Berlin. Steine Beginnen zu Reden*, Parthas-Verlag, Berlin

Krüger, A, and Murray, W (eds), 2003 *The Nazi Olympics. Sport, Politics and Appeasement in the 30s*, University of Illinois Press, Urbana and Chicago

Liao, H, and Pitts, A, 2006 A Brief Historical Review of Olympic Urbanization, *International Journal of the History of Sport* 23 (7), 1232–52

MacAloon, J J, 2008 'Legacy' as Managerial/Magical Discourse in Contemporary Olympic Affairs, *International Journal of the History of Sport* 25 (14), 2060–71

Maguire, J, Barnard, S, Butler, K, and Golding, P, 2008 Olympic Legacies in the IOC's 'Celebrate Humanity' Campaign: Ancient or Modern? *International Journal of the History of Sport* 25 (14), 2041–59

Mandell, R D, 1971 *The Nazi Olympics*, Macmillan, New York

Modrey, E M, 2008 Architecture as a Mode of Self-representation at the Olympic Games in Rome (1960) and Munich (1972), *European Review of History – Revue Européenne d'Histoire* 15 (6), 691–706

Masia, L, Matteoni, D, and Mei, P, 2007 *Il Parco del Foro Italiaco. La Storia, lo Sport, i Progetti*, Silvana Editoriale/CONI, Milan

Pizzori Itié, F (ed), 1992 *Les Yeux du Stade. Colombes, Temple du sport Français*, L'Albaron-Musée d'Art et d'Histoire de Colombes, Thonon-les-Bains

Riess, S A, 1981 Power without Authority: Los Angeles' Elites and the Construction of the Coliseum, *Journal of Sport History* 8 (1), 50–65

Roche, M, 2000 *Mega-events and Modernity. Olympics and Expos in the Growth of Global Culture*, Routledge, London

Schäche, W, and Szymanski, N, 2001 *Das Reichssportfeld: Architektur im Spannungsfeld von Sport und Macht*, be.bra Verlag, Berlin

Schiller, K, and Young, C, 2010 *The 1972 Munich Olympics and the Making of Modern Germany*, University of California Press, Berkeley, Los Angeles, London

Schmidt, T, 1986a Architecture at the Service of Sport (Part I). The Olympic Stadiums from 1896 to 1936, *Olympic Review* 225, 397–402

— 1986b Architecture at the Service of Sport (Part II). The Olympic Stadiums in Los Angeles and Berlin, *Olympic Review* 226, 466–70

— 1988 Olympic Stadiums from 1896 to the Present Day: the Architects (Final Part), *Olympic Review* 249, 376–80

— 1990 Stadionbauten in Berlin. Zur Planungsgeschichte und zu den Gestaltungsmerkmalen des ersten Deutschen Stadions und zum nachfolgenden Stadionbau in den Sportparkanlagen, *Sozial- und Zeitgeschichte des Sports* 4 (2), 67–77

Schut, P-O, and Terret, T, 2008 Quitte ou Double: les Paris des Infrastructures et du Budget, in *Les Paris des Jeux Olympiques* (ed T Terret), vol I, Atlantica, Biarritz, 125–52

Schweizer, O E, 1938 *Das Wiener Stadion*, Berlin

Toschi, L, 1990 Uno Stadio per Roma. Dallo Stadio Nazionale al Flaminio (1911–1959), *Studi Romani* XXXVIII (1–2), 83–97

— 1995 Sport e Urbanistica a Roma Durante il Fascismo, *Studi Romani* XLIII (3–4), 277–96

Trelat, G, 1911 Rapport sur le Concours d'Architecture, *Revue Olympique*, August, 116–20

Ward, S V, 2008 Promoting the Olympic City, in *Olympic Cities. City Agendas, Planning, and the World's Games, 1896–2012* (eds J R Gold and M M Gold), Routledge, London and New York, 120–37

Wimmer, M, 1976 *Olympic Buildings*, Edition Leipzig, Leipzig

17

The Indianapolis 500:
Making the Pilgrimage to the 'Yard of Bricks'

Jean Williams

Back Home again in Indiana
And it seems that I can see
The gleaming candleight
Still shining bright
Thru Sycamores for me   (MacDonald and Hanley 1917)

I married an engineer. As someone who read books like Germaine Greer's *The Female Eunuch* (1970) while waiting for the school bus, it is perhaps a miracle that I married at all; but who could resist the charm of a first date to the Sutton Cheney Steam and Country Fair in rural Leicestershire? The honeymoon was four days in York. This included a full day in the National Railway Museum. On the way back we stopped off, mercifully only for the afternoon, at the Crich National Tramway Museum. Calling at a supermarket before getting home, I asked my husband to get whatever he fancied, meaning quite clearly for the evening meal. He returned with a £40 trolley-jack for the car and asked what was for supper. We survived a decade together thus, occasionally attending slightly more glamorous European events, such as the British Grand Prix and the Le Mans 24 Hours. I had by now discovered that part of Simon's agenda for our combined 'bucket-list' (of things to be accomplished before we die) was a visit to the Indianapolis circuit for the 500-mile event. So we went to the self-styled 'motor-racing capital of the world' for our tenth wedding anniversary in May 1996.

These domestic snippets are by way of introduction to a serious point made by Honor Godfrey in her chapter earlier in this volume. Unlike art galleries and other museums, which are generally supposed to be educative, morally improving or emotionally stimulating in some way for all concerned, the sports museum is often thought to be an indulgence for the anorak fan. How, then, can the sports museum be perceived as relevant, intellectually attractive and worth a day out for the non-fan and, in particular, for the accompanying partner or family? This chapter therefore approaches tourism to sports museums partly from the point of view of my day-job but more so from the point of view of the accompanying spouse. It attempts to build on the work of the editors of this book and others to give an individual memoir of an international event (see, for example, Hill 1996; Moore 1996 and 2008; Wood 2005; Brabazon 2006). I could not call myself a motor-racing enthusiast, even if I am perplexed that academic sports history has largely overlooked the range of activities that this implies, along with a vast literature, fashion, art and collectibles market. Most people who go to sports museums and sites of sporting interest are, after all, fans on some level, though it has become something of a cliché to say that a particular stadium is our 'spiritual home' even while we take 'going to the match' for granted. This micro-history is offered as a reminder that sometimes people do particular things for quite specific reasons: being a patient companion is among them. Paradoxically, movement, and the meaning we place on it, is an under-explored aspect of our understanding of how sport is 'done'.

The first section gives a brief historical overview of the Indy 500 and argues that 'the most famous automobile race in the world' dominates the IndyCar and United States racing mythology compared with the other meetings in the annual calendar (Hulman George 1996, 1). With the Le Mans 24 Hours (since 1923) and Monaco Grand Prix (since 1929), it forms the classic trio of must-see races in world motorsport (O'Kane 2011). This discussion is the longer portion of the two, not least because motor-racing is often overlooked in sports history more generally. Addressing Eurocentric views of the importance of Formula One racing is part of that revision. The Indy 500 is the culmination of three weeks of qualifying activity and sees itself as the largest one-day sporting event in the world in terms of live audience (Hulman George 1996, 1; Powell 2010). On a 559-acre site six miles north-west of Indianapolis, the Motor Speedway is the world's largest spectator sporting facility, with more than 250,000 permanent seats (Indianapolis Motor Speedway 2011). The crowds inside the circuit in 1996 numbered approximately 350,000 spectators. Joined by millions of viewers on television, they watched 33 drivers compete over the 500-mile race for a total prize purse which exceeded US $7.5 million. The spectacle and its value has increased since then: for example, the 2010 race, won for the second time by Scottish-born Dario Franchitti, earned him almost $3 million from an overall prize fund approaching $14 million (Powell 2010). In effect, the whole of May is dedicated to the schedule of events in and around the town of Speedway. If the size and scale of Indy makes it an important example, another reason for the in-depth treatment is that motor museums span the sports-transport divide and so have some links with what might be perceived as mainstream national collections (Indianapolis Motor Speedway Hall of Fame Museum 2010; Brooklands Museum 2010). And a third reason for looking at the history is the permanence of the oval, as opposed to the temporary nature of events held on street circuits, such as the Monaco Grand Prix. The Indy 500 as an event has consciously constructed historical rituals since at least 1946 and the museum is part of that self-definition. In this chapter I want to draw attention to the idea of 'kinetic rituals' in relation to sport and tourism – of actively moving bodies toward a site to participate in a system of 'rites' (hence our physical trip to the circuit) – and to some of our experiences at the site before, during and after the race.

The 2.5-mile Indianapolis oval was inaugurated in 1909, shortly after the slightly longer Brooklands motor-racing circuit was opened for racing in Britain in 1907 (Clymer 1946, 7). Both were determinedly nationalistic initiatives intended to stimulate public interest in, and to advance the technology and achievements of, their respective automobile industries (Boddy 1957, 10). The last race at Brooklands took place in 1939, before the circuit was lost to World War II. The Indy 500 is therefore somewhat, but not entirely, justified in calling itself 'the most historic motor race in the United States of America': first held in 1911, there will have been 95 editions by 2011. Indianapolis cannot claim to be the oldest race in America. The Chicago Herald organised the first road race in the United States in November 1895, won by Frank Duryea in his petrol-powered Valvoline Oil-lubricated car at speeds of up to 7 miles per hour (Perkins 1993, 16). Nor can it claim to be the oldest circuit: Narragansett Park at Cranston Rhode Island enclosed a dirt track of one mile and charged the huge crowds attending to see five laps in 1896. An electric car reaching 24 miles per hour proved the commercial success of this enterprise. Championship races from 1902 were decided by the media rather than race wins, and European marques, such

The city of Indianapolis was a leader in the fledgling automobile industry when the Speedway was built as a combination race track and testing facility in 1909. The 500-Mile Race was first held in 1911 as it has been ever since with the exception of the war years, 1917-18 and 1942-45.

The original track owners, headed by Carl Fisher and James Allison, turned it over in 1927 to a group led by WWI ace Capt. Eddie Rickenbacker, who later sold it to Anton Hulman, Jr. of Terre Haute, Indiana, in 1945. The Hulman family continues to perpetuate the traditions established by Tony well into the 90's.

FIG 17.1. HALL OF FAME IMAGE TAKEN FROM THE RACE-DAY BROCHURE OF 1996 AND OUTLINING THE PLACE OF INDIANAPOLIS AS THE 'RACING CAPITAL OF THE WORLD'.

as Renault, Fiat and Mercedes, dominated events. Formal races and record-breaking attempts had also been held on Daytona Beach since 1904 (Clymer 1946, 9; Perkins 1993, 18). So the Indy 500 joined the Atlanta oval (opened in 1908) and the other 22 American Automobile Association Championship circuits somewhat belatedly as a permanent year-round site.

What makes Indianapolis special to a race fan? In seeking to answer why a motor-racing fan from the British midlands wanted to visit the Indy 500, my second, shorter, section looks at my experience of the Indy day in 1996. Each element was independently organised, as there were no package holidays of this kind. Soon afterwards, the internet made the organisation of travel the matter of credit card ownership and a few clicks of a computer mouse, and lifestyle travel for all kinds of speciality interest has been a beneficiary of that change. The discussion of pilgrimage literature in this section looks at some of the experience of attending the Indy, an integral part of which is going to the site. This includes visiting the fan-fest and the Indianapolis Motor Speedway Hall of Fame Museum, which Tony Hulman and Karl Kizer, the museum's first director, established in 1956 before it moved to its current site in 1976. Our visit happened to coincide with the combined 40th/20th anniversary celebrations of these occurrences. The museum, located inside the grounds of the circuit, is open every day of the year except Christmas and Thanksgiving. In 1996 its brochure claimed that it had hosted some 400,000 visitors by the time of the race itself (Fig 17.1). Had we gone for the full Indianapolis Motor Speedway experience we could have stayed at the Speedway Motel and played at the Pete Dye-designed Brickyard Crossing 18-hole golf course just outside turn two of the circuit. What attractions, then, did 'The Greatest Spectacle in Racing' hold for someone who was, and still is, not *that* interested in the sport?

The Indianapolis Motor Speedway and its Museum and History

If William Boddy's *The History of Brooklands Motor Course* (1957) is the 'bible' among Brookland's many enthusiasts, for fans of the 'Brickyard' circuit it is Floyd Clymer's *Indianapolis 500 Mile Race History* (1946), which predated the former by 11 years. Clymer began the process of issuing yearbooks from 1946 and, like cricket, motor-racing is obsessively statistical in its narrative. The 'Brickyard' nickname is the result of the decision in late 1909 to pave the track's racing circuit with 3.2 million bricks. (An earlier crushed rock and tar course was deemed inadequate and contributed to the loss of the lives over three days in August 1909 of one driver, two riding mechanics and two spectators, plus other serious injuries.) The vast majority of the 'Culver Blocks' used for the paving (named after patent holder Ruben Culver) came from the Wabash Clay Company in Indiana. These were considered the finest material available at the time. Each brick weighed ten pounds and the paving was completed, so it is generally said, in 63 days, with the State governor, Thomas R Marshall, dedicating the new surface by placing a 'gold' brick (of gold-plated brass) in the track to inaugurate its first time trials on 17 December 1909. This local engineering feat became part of the 'invented tradition' of the course's design. The term 'invented tradition', coined by Eric Hobsbawm and Terence Ranger, has been widely applied and defined as a set of practices 'which seek to inculcate certain values and norms of behaviour by repetition which automatically implies continuity with the past' (Hobsbawm and Ranger 1992, 10). Sentimental branding, a sense of place and conscious reinvention of the past are very apparent at Indianapolis today (Fig 17.2). For example, when the asphalting of parts of the track began in 1936 to allow faster racing, the process was so gradual that it was not completed until the main

Fig 17.2. The cover of a 1996 race-day brochure, dominated by a rather placeless image of motor-racing. This 'open-wheel' race could be anywhere, were it not for the distinctive winged wheel logo of the Indianapolis Motor Speedway.

straight was covered in time for the golden anniversary of the first race in 1961. A symbolic 'Yard of Bricks' was left at the start and finish line. The seats aligned with these three feet of the circuit have since become the most coveted, and hence the most expensive, for the Indy 500 event.

This narrative of motor-racing circuit construction as exemplifying nationalistic civil engineering 'can-do' spirit is not confined to Indianapolis. For example, Dame Ethel and Captain Hugh Locke-King founded Brooklands in Surrey, UK, in 1906 on 330 acres of farmland. It opened as the world's first purpose-built motor-racing circuit on 6 July 1907 and is said, mainly by the British, to have been the inspiration behind Indianapolis. The Locke-Kings spent more than £150,000 of their own money and employed over 2000 men in the construction of the concrete track, and its distinctive green-domed clubhouse for officials and stewards, to help promote the British motor-racing industry. The Brooklands Automobile Racing Club had their HQ at Carlton House, in Regent Street, London. Their attitude can perhaps best be illustrated by the fact that in 1931, the Racing, Aviation, Election and House and Wine Sub-Committees were all busy throughout the season but the Safety Sub-Committee's work was deemed to be complete and it was accordingly dissolved. There were 'only' two fatalities that year (Brooklands Automobile Racing Club Minutes 1931, 10). Although it nominally held 30,000 spectators,

Brooklands was much more about the enjoyment of the classes, rather than being a spectacle for the masses. While it was open to all who could afford the fees, its club slogan was 'The Right Crowd and No Over-Crowding'. (In 1907, entry fees ranged from 15 to 50 sovereigns, while prize money in the first six races ranged between 250 and 1400 sovereigns.) Brooklands chose 1000-mile races as its most prestigious events but these gradually declined in spectator popularity even though increasing numbers of racers (including women) were breaking the 120 mph and 130 mph barriers in the 1920s and 1930s. The circuit was bought in 1936 by the Weybridge Company, who were more interested in aviation than the track, which fell into disrepair during World War II. The museum at Brooklands is therefore much more of a nostalgic experience than is that at Indianapolis (Brooklands Museum 2010).

Importantly, the Indianapolis Motor Speedway Company was officially formed as a business, rather than a member's club, on 9 February 1909 and capitalised at $250,000 (Clymer 1946, 24; Fox 1984, 10). There seems to have been a delay in either registering or signing the papers but both Clymer and Fox agree this date for incorporation. Having already attracted crowds of 50,000 in 1910, the management considered a single major racing event for 1911 featuring a huge purse, in the range of $25,000, as a way of attracting more publicity. After initially discussing a 1000-mile or 24-hour race, a 500-mile event was scheduled to take place on Memorial Day in 1911. The then-titled 'International Sweepstakes' was won on 30 May in front of more than 80,000 spectators by Ray Harroun, competitor number 32 of 40, in his Marmon 'Wasp', helped by the innovation of a rear-view mirror (and without the weight of a riding mechanic). For 1912 the number of competitors was reduced to the now standard 33 and riding mechanics made mandatory. By 1913 several European factories began to enter cars and Jules Goux won in his Peugeot by over 13 minutes; he was reportedly refreshed in so doing by six bottles of champagne, one for each of his pit stops (Fox 1984, 11). Victory for René Thomas in a Delage in 1914 again brought a European success. The following year saw the inauguration of the numbering of cars according to their qualifying speeds, with number one starting on pole. In recognition of the war in Europe, the 1916 event was only 300 miles, with Dario Resta leading in his Peugeot from the 18th lap to win. After a suspension of two years the Indianapolis 500 resumed in 1919 and was subtitled 'The Victory Stakes'. American 'Howdy' Wilcox won in a Peugeot. The quest for international motor-racing success in the later 1920s became so keen that some manufacturers overspent. Racing went through a bleak period which coincided with the Wall Street Crash of 1929 and subsequent world slump. Bentley, for example, became synonymous with Le Mans by winning five times and more American cars began to enter European races. However, the liquidation of Bentley in 1931 led many to ask whether racing was too expensive. Some race organisers chose to promote less expensive car events instead of Grand Prix, and it is here that the Indy 500 mythology really developed.

Niels Kayser Nielsen, drawing on Yi Fu Tuan's and John Bale's work in relation to topophilia or an affection for place (Tuan 1974; Bale 1982; 1993), has theorised the symbolic importance of the stadium in the collective imagination of a city and region in this way:

> The stadium is also the place where the city and its inhabitants inherit themselves. Here, the city's sense of history is expressed, not only through museum-like antiquity and the aura of the stadium buildings, but also through the lived history prolonged by the sustained traditions and myths which are an integral part of stadium culture. (Kayser Nielsen 1995, 25)

To build on this idea of a geography of emotion and imagination, there seem to have been three main elements to a process whereby the 500 and the Motor Speedway gradually developed in the interwar years as a synecdoche, not just for the city of Indianapolis but for the Midwest more generally, as the epicentre of car racing as a particularly American pursuit. First was the likes of Steve Hannagan, taking over as publicity director in 1921, followed in August 1927 by Eddie Rickenbacker, a World War I 'air ace' and former driver, buying the Indianapolis Motor Speedway. He was to own it until 1945. A sense of masculine glamour and modernity in the way that Indianapolis was promoted by these men combined with the second factor – an improvement in racing spectacle. By 1927 minimum qualifying and lap record times for the Indy 500 went up to 90 miles an hour and 120 miles an hour respectively. Technological developments were in part responsible for this, such as the new Firestone low-pressure tyres and increased speed as a result of centrifugal superchargers. However, rule changes made by the circuit were also designed to promote faster racing, such as that forcing cars to carry riding mechanics being rescinded in 1923 and the raising of the prize money to over $60,000 the following year. More importantly, responding to the economic conditions, Rickenbacker lowered the piston displacement from the 91.5 cubic standard to the 366 cubic inches of cheaper semi-stock engines in 1930. It appeared to make the race more democratic, so that factory brands including Chrysler, Reo, Hudson, Buick and Hupmobile were able to compete against specialised race cars (Hulman George 1996, 6; Clymer 1946, 52). The third element was a form of Americanisation. While the United States circuit was regularly populated by the finest drivers of the day, such as Jimmy Murphy (who won a Grand Prix at Le Mans in 1921 before becoming the first Indy 500 competitor to start on pole and win the race in 1922), it seemed to tell a story of European manufacturers' decline, as Maserati was the next foreign-made car to win in 1939.

During the 20 years that a foreign-made car did not win at Indy, international car racing had became increasingly political: from the 1934 Grand Prix season onwards Mussolini had supported, threatened and cajoled Alfa Romeo and Maserati to win races as an example of Italian superiority. Hitler subsidised both Auto Unions and Mercedes-Benz to the extent that, from May 1934, the silver arrows German cars were unbeatable for the next six years, dominating European Grand Prix. The lack of an overseas victory at Indy also highlighted several domestic developments during this time in the United States. They highlighted the car as an identifiably American form of travel, appropriate to a wide range of people. Individual brands with particular rivalries became increasingly important. Individual racers became famous through Indy promotional material, and the idea of a warm 'Hoosier' welcome that stood apart from either East Coast, West Coast or European style became increasingly important. While space precludes the detailed treatment of each of these fairly large issues, Hoosier has been a self-mocking nickname for over 150 years for someone who comes from Indiana, often used in relation to various sports teams. It has both 'white trash' and 'blue collar' connotations as well as rural or 'hick' variants. Running the first Indy 500 on Memorial Day was designed in part to attract farm workers who would have identifiable free-time that day, for example. This 'homeliness' is epitomised by drinking a bottle of milk in victory, as Louis Meyer, the winner in 1936, was photographed doing supposedly at the instigation of his mother, who claimed it would refresh him more than alcohol. Unsurprisingly, the national milk council was happy to support repetition of this innovation, which is only unobserved when lactose intolerance forbids. There is consequently perhaps as much self-mockery as pride in claiming a Hoosier culture for an event that, in Anton Hulman George's words, 'has always been a part of Indiana as the Derby is part of Kentucky' (1996, 4). By the time we visited

The Indianapolis Motor Speedway Hall of Fame Museum was built in 1976 and is located within the famed 2.5-mile race track. The museum contains more than 30 Indianapolis 500 winning cars and a world-class variety of antique, classic racing cars and passenger cars. Also on hand is a superb collection of racing technology, art, trophies and memorabilia.

Adjacent to the track is the Brickyard Crossing, a newly re-designed 18-hole golf course by renowned architect Pete Dye. The Speedway Motel (top), offering year-round lodging, dining and conference facilities, also contains the Golf Shop.

Exit 16A, I-465 West

Indianapolis Motor Speedway
Hall of Fame Museum
Hours: — 9 a.m. to 5p.m., EST 364 days a year (closed Christmas Day)
4790 West 16th Street • Indianapolis, IN 46222

FIG 17.3. THE BACK COVER OF A 1996 RACE-DAY BROCHURE CITES THE HALL OF FAME MUSEUM AS INTEGRAL TO THE DAY'S ACTIVITIES INCLUDING MORE THAN 30 RACE-WINNING CARS, COLLECTIONS OF ART, TECHNOLOGY AND OTHER ARTEFACTS.

Indianapolis was Indiana's largest city (population c. 750,000), the 14th biggest in the United States and the third (behind Chicago and Detroit) in the Midwest. Given Detroit's development of its image as 'the motor city' through car manufacturing and the music industry, and Chicago's metropolitan dominance of the area, Indianapolis' claim to international motor-racing fame is an ongoing project to define itself, in part, against larger neighbours (Fig 17.3).

After World War II it looked as though a dilapidated Indianapolis might go the way of Brooklands, before it was purchased in 1945 by Tony Hulman, an industrialist from Terre Haute, Indiana. He either renewed or reinvented the routines of the Indy 500 as part of his overall strategy to reinvest money earned by the circuit into its own development as a venue. The Speedway became a National Historic Landmark in 1987, overseen by his surviving family ten years after his death. Family, ceremonial remembering and legacy are therefore integral to the meaning of the Indy 500. This is in part expressed by the patterned repetition of the determinedly nostalgic and pastoral song *Indiana*, which Hulman inaugurated in 1946, lines from which appear at the opening and closing of this chapter (see Davidson 1996). First sung by the famed opera tenor James Melton, and conveyed to the large crowd (many of whom could not see him) by the public-address system, it has become one of the moments of communion designed to link all those who are present (and past). Putting Indianapolis at what Anton Hulman George (1996, 2) called the epicentre of racing in the United States has been a slow and gradual process. For example, the American Automobile Association (AAA) and other official bodies sanctioned the museum as of national importance after the AAA had previously withdrawn from racing activities and participation in the Hall of Fame from 1955 until 1961. It then sanctioned records and correspondence from the Ford museum to go to the Indianapolis Motor Speedway museum. The elevation to 'national' status has seen, amongst other developments, the 500 Oldtimers Club become a more formal dinner of honour from 1991 while the museum collection now stands at over 300 cars. Building a museum is then part of a process of taking the race, circuit and history of Indianapolis more seriously.

If anyone was under any illusions about the strength of feeling that Indianapolis was an All-American circuit under Hulman and his family's patronage, then Floyd Clymer's foreword to the 1966 Yearbook should remove doubt:

> The Indianapolis 500 is no longer the isolated event it once was, as foreigners not only fly over in a matter of hours now but do exceptionally well at the brickyard. Since the first 500 in 1911, few foreigners have had success. In the early years such famous drivers as Jules Goux of France and Dario Resta of Italy were winners, and added interest. Then came a long dry spell when the foreigners did nothing. Best of the bunch was the late Alberto Ascari, who was doing real well in 1958 until a wheel collapsed. In the fifties few foreigners seemed interested. I saw Stirling Moss and Mike Hawthorn drive at Monza in 1958. They compared favourably with our best. I told them both that they should do well at Indy, and urged them to come over. Both 'poo-pooed' the idea … like most European drivers they felt that Indy drivers, turning to the left always, were not really great drivers – that road racing was a tougher test.… But times have changed. Clark and Brabham have shown that the road-circuit men have the ability, stamina and courage to do a real job in the 500. (Clymer 1966)

Even with the British influence since Brabham's time, the four-time winners are A J Foyt, Al Unser and Rick Mears. Mario Andretti is one of the best-known Indy 500 personalities and his son Michael has made this a dynastic link.

Because my husband Simon grew up in the 1960s and 1970s, increased British interest in the Indy 500 influenced his wish to go and see the race. In the 1990s Nigel Mansell was a particularly important figure for British, European and worldwide motor-racing fans, though he was by no means a charming champion in his relentless will to win. Mansell drew attention to the Indianapolis 500 because after he won the 1992 Federation Internationale de l'Automobile (FIA) World Championship title in a Honda McLaren, against the seemingly dominant Ayrton Senna, he dramatically decided not to defend his FIA title and instead signed with the Paul Newman and Carl Haas team (Newman-Haas) to drive a Lola/Ford/Goodyear design for a reported $4.5 million for the 1993 IndyCar series (Perkins 1993, 10). Mansell went on to win the season's first race in Australia from pole and became the first driver to win the series in his first year of racing in it, narrowly beating fellow Formula One and IndyCar winner Emerson Fittipaldi. The British interest in IndyCar racing, and in particular the Indy 500 itself, had been of longer standing, however. Colin Chapman had brought over two rear-engined Ford-powered Lotuses in 1963 and Jim Clark had come a narrow second that year. The 1966 winner, Graham Hill, became the first rookie to win the Indy 500 since 1927, with Clark second and Jackie Stewart sixth.

MAKING THE PILGRIMAGE

The word pilgrimage usually connotes a spiritual journey to a place of religious significance as an act of piety on the part of an individual. The Christian, Hindu, Jewish, Islamic and Buddhist faiths all incorporate this element of worship in their observance and it would be crass to try to make some connection between this primary meaning of the word and sport as some kind of 'modern-day' religion. The attendant idea of the pilgrim undertaking a long and difficult ascetic journey has been lost in the search for more material pleasures as secular travelling became part of 'event' tourism from the Great Exhibitions of the Works of Industry of all Nations in 1851 in London's Hyde Park at least. These and other exhibition events combined a sense of place, potential for the future and transition in relatively banal expressions of faith. Since the advent of the cult of personality amongst Communist leaders, a visit to Lenin's tomb became something of a cliché for those whose inspiration was political rather than spiritual, though the connection between the two remains a point of academic contention (Coleman and Eade 2005, 5–15).

In setting out from midlands England to the American Midwest as non-believers in any of the world religions in order to see a motor race, we did not expect the experience to be morally improving. However, even though the IndyCar series has a reputation of being anti-intellectual in its rituals, this does not mean that participants do not place spiritual value on their activities. More importantly for this discussion, it represents a specific and public articulation of American-ness in sport and the way that it is memorialised. What our going there can be argued to share with the idea of pilgrimage is the concept of voluntary mobility for liminal purposes. The Indy 500 has become part of the national sports-scape in America just as American football's Superbowl (in January), baseball's World Series (in October) and golf's US Masters at Augusta (in April) are part of it. While sedentarism enables the armchair fan to experience the mediated aspects of their sport, only 'being there' can tell us what 'it feels like'. This sensory experience is one that sporting museums have begun to try to replicate in terms of including sights, sounds and so on. Treating each sense in turn would require an article in its own right, perhaps, but we are all familiar with a particular smell as part of our kinetic ritual of going to sporting events. Scent is one of the most evocative of senses and changes all the time as part of our changing consciousness. On a rainy day in May, the Indy 500 has a characteristic and distinctive aroma.

While pilgrimage may mainly have been explored by academics in its religious sense, an attendant aspect is making a journey intending to join with a wider collective, present and past. Having paid £300 for a pair of race tickets that had a face value of $75 each (Fig 17.4), everything else except the accommodation was relatively cheap. Like many other sports fans we set out to experience an event in the company of a cross section of people who have a common (and in my case not very intense) interest, for a brief amount of time. On our first visit to the United States we flew into Chicago's O'Hare airport and drove to what we imagined, before we travelled, to represent the highlights of the Midwest. In two weeks we went to Graceland and Beale Street in Memphis, Nashville, St Louis (including a baseball game at the Cardinal's), and as far south as Lynchburg, Tennessee, before returning to Chicago. This can be related to the emergent field of pilgrimage studies, which has an agenda incorporating non-religious roots tourism and 'such travel as one of the twenty-first century's many forms of cultural mobility … locality and belonging' (Coleman and Eade 1995, 1). While a wish to go to a Chicago Blues club or to see Elvis' grave would not in themselves have been enough to motivate us to travel, the road trip (itself a stylised form of travel celebrated in movies, literature and song) was part of our shared

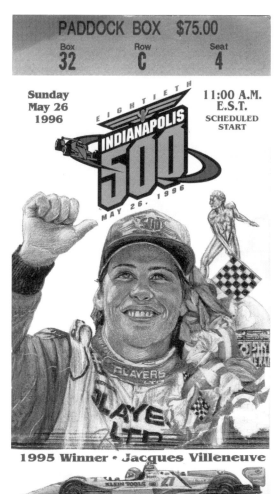

Fig 17.4. Race-day ticket of 1996. This piece of ephemera makes the point that the Indy consciously represents the races' past, present and future as a continuum. Just as fans are reminded that Jacques Villeneuve won last year, the victor of the event for that afternoon will feature on next year's race ticket. In these simple ways, fans are constantly reminded that they are watching history be made and re-made on race-day.

Midwest of the imagination. Neither of us had the creativity or resourcefulness to foresee that Dollywood, Dolly Parton's eponymous theme park, would be part of the reality.

Though there is no indexed reference to sport and only one mention of speed in Coleman and Eade's collection, many of the issues resonated in the research for this chapter. The citation of Victor and Edith Turner's *Image and Pilgrimage in Christian Culture* as the most influential text for consideration, for example, perhaps opens up the debate for sports historians, containing as it does reference to 'kinetic ritual' and populist spontaneously articulated 'antistructure' (Turner and Turner 1978, xiii). In this way, journeying to a site of individual and collective meaning brings a possibility of social or psychological transformation, even if only a temporary one. In discussing our secular but awareness-raising journey, the tensions between freedom and constraint implied by the 'kinetic rituals' of sport could perhaps be more fully explored. I want to build upon the work of the Turners and Coleman and Eade to suggest that for race fans Indianapolis Motor Speedway is an example of a secular shrine to a particular articulation of American motor-racing in a country which, arguably more than any other, is defined by the car. My experience, even as a non-fan, was comprised of 'various forms of motion – embodied, imagined, metaphorical – as constitutive elements of many pilgrimages' (Coleman and Eade 2005, 9). Having mentioned briefly movement *to* Indy, what of the movement at the track on race day? What did the day at the Indy 500 feel like and what was the experience of being there?

The first thing to say is that it is a long day, even if you are a race fan. At five in the morning a military bomb signals that the gates are opening and people can begin to drive into the centre of the circuit. As a logistical exercise the vast scale of the event involves a permanent staff of 200 full-time employees which grows by several thousand with security, parking and usher assignments, in addition to 1100 working in concessions and 250 doctors, nurses and medical technicians. Getting in, parking and getting a much-needed coffee was easy compared with European race-days. The time from 5am to 8am is a period of free-range across the course. The build up starts at 8am, with the spectacle of the cars positioned in front of the pits. At 9.45am the Purdue University Band played *On the Banks of the Wabash*, adapted from the song *Indiana*, written by James Hanley (music) and Ballard MacDonald (lyrics) in 1917. It may first have been played by the trackside band to accompany the 1919 victory laps, though I have been unable to verify this. It was sung for several years by the opera tenor James Melton, who was also president of the Antique Automobile Club of America. It is now as much of an anthem to the race as official songs are at other sporting events.

Communal singing is followed by featured events, presentations and introductions. The hour before the race starts at 11am becomes increasingly ceremonial and focused, though before it we have plenty of time to visit the relatively small museum and fan-fest for $2 and $15 respectively. We are encouraged to take a $2 narrated tour of the track in a minibus before the final track inspection is made at 10.35am, that year by a 1996 Dodge Viper. At 10.42am the National Anthem, again courtesy of the Purdue University Band, is followed by a military flyover and the Invocation. At 10.48am Taps is played by the US Armed Forces Color Guard to mark Memorial Day. At 10.51am the announcement 'Gentlemen, and lady, start your engines' is followed one minute later by the parade and pace laps and then, as they say, they are off. The race lasts for the next six or seven hours, depending on the various combination of crashes, rain, breakdowns, driver error and so forth. The winner, masking the fact that he is now a dollar-millionaire (even if he was not when he began the race), celebrates with a ceremonial bottle of buttermilk.

The smell obviously changes but is a combination of rain, sun-dried asphalt, food and drinks, other people in various states of relaxation and excitement, race fumes, grass and leather. What had been a thunderstorm with hailstones at 5am gave way to intense heat and by 3pm we were both badly sunburnt. Nor is this just an olfactory experience; as with many American experiences of sport it is as much about socialising in the crowd as slavishly following the action (Fig 17.5). A television crew had heard our accents in the fan-fest on the day before (yes, of course we had to go twice) and had featured an interview on a local cable channel the previous night. Quite a few people shouted 'Happy Anniversary' and remembered our names, which felt odd. While there was that kind of spontaneous friendliness, it is also an overwhelmingly male spectacle and one of the most chauvinistic crowds I have ever been a part of (even including the days of standing

Fig 17.5. Simon at the fan-fest. With imperfect technology and spur of the moment composition, this snapshot is testament to the pilgrimage. It records that 'we were there' but it also withholds as much information as it divulges. What did the experience feel like? Can sensory experience ever be satisfactorily mediated in language or image? How, then, can historians know what the fan's experience on race-day was even in recent times?

on terraces at football matches). Local residents who have put wire fences around their gardens to stop them being intruded upon are going to return to find them six feet high in empty beer cans. The crowd responded cheerily if attending celebrities appeared on the big screens around the circuit. Individual spectators were even more vigorous if they appeared for a brief time and choreographed little 'turns' to try to make this happen. I willed Lyn St James, the only woman in the race, to do better than her 32nd place of last year. It was 8pm by the time we began to drive out of the track and we exited easily before having to stop in a hailstorm with stones the size of golf balls. It was both like and unlike other motor races I have been to, mainly because of the intimacy with the cars, the track, the museum and the fan-fest, in spite of the scale of the undertaking, but I have never been to a racing circuit, before or since, where you can be so close to the cars and take a trip around the track up to an hour before the race starts. The pricing policy encouraged consumers to go everywhere at Indy, in contrast to the way that rather sniffy attitudes towards those not benefiting from hospitality packages, and exploitative charging at Silverstone for the British Grand Prix, for example, keep the public at arm's length.

In conclusion, then, one of the contributions of the Indianapolis Hall of Fame Museum to cultures of heritage and history is that, in the United States, classic automobiles were often preserved as part of transport history while pure race cars, prior to the 1950s, were less valued because of their 'inbuilt obsolescence'. However, the problem of tracing the provenance of motor cars that may have had parts cannibalised and recycled or allowed to rot because of redundant technology is an international issue in motor-racing history. There are contradictory processes at work here, as design and manufacturing of effective materials that have become increasingly specialised for use in sport are also part of the story since the 1950s. For this reason the use of materials, technologies and sciences such as bio-dynamics make motorsport an important 21st-century topic for further research. Some of the more ephemeral aspects of cultural heritage, and its relationship with history, remain to be analysed here. Racing at unprecedented speeds in Indy cars for the entertainment of others is a new trend in a long history. It may seem a long way back from a man-made infield to folk and 'nature' games but many sports have had transport history as a big part of their rationale. Whether it is moving through forests on skis, using natural forces to glide on a surfboard or a pole to vault across dykes, proponents were essentially combining scientific curiosity with technology to move through nature. How we contextualise and remember the history of motorsport in museums to house specific collections therefore links time and space with a distinct sense of place (De Bondt 2011).

The Indianapolis Motor Speedway museum is part of the 'info-tainment' of the Indy 500 weekend and clearly brands the race in large part as being about its own history. As an attendee you are asked to take part in ritualistic aspects of the day that are kinetic, metaphorical and embodied. We therefore not only went to the Yard of Bricks but became a very small part of that history by being immersed in the patterned behaviour in the last hour of focusing attention into the oval as the race starts. During the action there was the movement of the race but also a sense of mobility created by the changing crowd-scape and individual consciousness, such as I have briefly tried to capture here by recording some sights, sounds and smells of the day. The educational aspects of travelling to be entertained by sport bring in aspects of mild adventure, spectacle and fashion which have perhaps been under-written, even while a standard complaint of historians is that it is difficult to know precisely how participants experienced an event. If part of this work is about the building and protecting of monuments in the form of sporting museums and places, the more intangible aspects of experiencing them are no less significant.

Of course, since 1996 this process of building the profile of the Indy has accelerated both in terms of a more aggressive form of American nationalism after September 11 2001 and with the centennial edition of the Indy 500 in 2011. The atmosphere in museums, too, has become rather more commercially focused and, perhaps uniquely, this has been interpreted at Indy as being a centennial era, spanning three years of celebrations, rather than a single event. So festivities began at the 100th anniversary of the opening of the racetrack (2009) and have continued to the 100th anniversary of the inaugural Indianapolis 500 (2011). This has enabled the development of various vintage sub-brands of the main Indy 500 product. The use of social media such as Twitter and Facebook has enabled Indy to showcase its celebrity fans in endorsements and this use of new communication platforms as a vehicle for nostalgia is perhaps worth more investigation. The 100th anniversary Indianapolis 500 took place on Sunday 29 May 2011 and Englishman Dan Wheldon earned his second victory in 'The Greatest Spectacle in Racing' by overtaking the leader, rookie J R Hildebrand, who crashed in the final turn of the final lap. Wheldon was later killed in the last race of the Indy season in Las Vegas in October 2011: a reminder of the dangers of motorsport even for the most experienced and talented of drivers. Little wonder, perhaps, that the Goodwood Festival of Speed in the UK, itself a byword for all things nostalgic in motorsport, memorialised the centennial edition of Indy at its own celebrations in July 2011. In many ways, the history of Indianapolis Motor Speedway has developed the Indy 500, and its particular brand of middle-America, as its own theme.

> The new mown hay
> Sends all its fragrance
> From the fields I used to roam
> When I dream about the moonlight on the Wabash
> Then I long for my Indiana home.
>
> (MacDonald and Hanley 1917)

Bibliography and References

Bale, J, 1982 *Sport and Place: A Geography of Sport in England, Scotland and Wales*, Hurst, London

— 1993 *Sport, Space and the City*, Routledge, London

Boddy, W, 1957 *The History of Brooklands Motor Course: Complied from the Official Records of the Brooklands Automobile Racing Club*, Grenville Publishing, London

Brabazon, T, 2006 Museums and Popular Culture Revisited: Kevin Moore and the Politics of Pop, *Museum Management and Curatorship* 21 (4), 283–301

Brooklands Automobile Racing Club, 1931 BARC Club Minutes, sourced from the Brooklands Museum archives, Weybridge, Surrey

Brooklands Museum, 2010 *Welcome to Brooklands: Birthplace of British Motorsport and Aviation* [online], available from: http://www.brooklandsmuseum.com [1 June 2010]

Clymer, F, 1946 *Indianapolis 500 Mile Race History*, Floyd Clymer Publishing, Los Angeles

— 1966 *1966 Indianapolis 500 Mile Yearbook*, Floyd Clymer Publishing, Los Angeles

Coleman, S, and Eade, J (eds), 2005 *Reframing Pilgrimage: Cultures in Motion*, Routledge, London

Davidson, D, 1996 Back Home Again in Indiana, *Eightieth Indianapolis 500 May 26 1996 Official Programme*, Indy Publications, Indianapolis, 13–17

De Bondt, W, 2011 *Sportimonium: More than a Museum About Sports*, Openbaar Kunstbezit in Vlaanderen, Antwerp

Fox, J C, 1984 *The Illustrated History of The Indianapolis 500 1911–1984*, Carl Hungness & Associates, Indianapolis

Greer, G, 1970 *The Female Eunuch*, Paladin, London

Hill, J, 1996 Rite of Spring: Cup Finals and Community in the North of England, in *Sport and Identity in the North of England* (eds J Hill and J Williams), Keele University Press, Keele, 85–113

Hobsbawm, E, and Ranger, T, 1992 *The Invention of Tradition*, Cambridge University Press, Cambridge

Hulman George, A, 1996 President's Welcome, in *Indianapolis Motor Speedway Program 1996*, Indianapolis Motor Speedway, Indianapolis

Indianapolis Motor Speedway Hall of Fame Museum, 2011 History, available from: http://www.indian-apolismotorspeedway.com/facility/35204-Museum/ [16 November 2011]

Indianapolis Motor Speedway Website, n.d. available from: http://www.indianapolismotorspeedway.com [26 July 2011]

Kayser Nielsen, N, 1995 The Stadium in the City – a Modern Story, in *The Stadium and the City* (eds J Bale and O Moen), Keele University Press, Keele, 15–34

MacDonald, B, and Hanley, J F, 1917 *(Back Home Again in) Indiana*, Columbia Records, A2297, ODJB

Moore, K, 1996 *Museums and Popular Culture (Contemporary Issues in Museum Culture)*, Leicester University Press, Leicester

— 2008 Sports Heritage and the Re-imagined City, *International Journal of Cultural Policy* 14 (4), November, 445–61

O'Kane, P, 2011 A History of the 'Triple Crown' of Motor Racing: The Indianapolis 500, the Le Mans 24 Hours and the Monaco Grand Prix, *International Journal of the History of Sport* 28 (2), 281–99

Perkins, K, 1993 *IndyCar*, Osprey, London

Powell, E, 2010 Franchitti Earns $2.75 Million For Win; De Silvestro Chase Rookie of the Year, *Indianapolis Motor Speedway News/Blogs* [online], available from: http://blog.indianapolismotorspeedway.com/ [1 June 2010]

Tuan, Y F, 1974 *Topophilia: A study of Environmental Perception, Attitudes, and Values*, Prentice Hall, Englewood Cliffs, NJ

Turner, V, and Turner, E, 1978 *Image and Pilgrimage in Christian Culture*, Columbia University Press, New York

Wood, J, 2005 Talking Sport or Talking Balls? Realising the Value of Sports Heritage, in *Understanding the Workplace: a Research Framework for Industrial Archaeology in Britain* (eds D Gwyn and M Palmer), special issue of *Industrial Archaeology Review* 27, 137–44

Afterword: History and Heritage in Sport

Richard Holt

I will begin my short reflection on this timely, varied and innovative collection with a simple generalisation: history is how we explain the past; heritage is how we preserve it. Preserving the past comes in many forms, from acts of personal recollection to collective rites of public commemoration. In terms of sport this can range from memories of great matches or players to putting up statues outside stadia which themselves have become a focus of sporting heritage.

A simple distinction between history and heritage, however, is complicated by the fact that much popular 'history' is probably better characterised as 'heritage' in the sense that it evokes or records the past rather than analyses it. History as an academic discipline restricted to a relatively small readership is very different from heritage as a way of bringing the past to life through memory and material culture. Hence the heritage approach tends to reach a wider audience and have more influence on popular understandings of the past than conventional history. Few works of sporting heritage – the term itself was rarely used – appeared before the 1950s, when publishers such as Stanley Paul realised there was a lucrative market in the formulaic sports biography or the adulatory club history. The sheer volume of such work is striking, even if the literary or historical standards are low. The heritage of sport has frequently been conveyed in a simple biographical form that focuses narrowly on the experience of the player rather than the response of the fan.

I have started with a literary approach to sports heritage partly because it is often overlooked and partly because it prioritises the individual over the group. As individuals we live both in personal time and in historical time. The public both frames the private and is experienced through it. We inherit the past in all kinds of ways, from the micro world of family memoir to the macro processes of national and global history. Beyond private experience and beneath the public affairs of state, there was the everyday world of places and people, of neighbourhood, city and nation, of territory and identity which was evoked perhaps more powerfully by sport, especially in team ball games, than through any other form of culture.

Serious historical writing, including sports history, tries to link these cultural forms to the forces that have shaped the modern world – industrialisation, urbanisation, nationalism, imperialism and so forth – while heritage deals more directly with the hard and soft legacies of such change – the buildings, the places and the feelings they evoke. This has been a profoundly gendered world where male memory and commemoration have dominated – an implicit feature that comes across strongly in the collection.

How sporting memories and affiliations become collective myth and culture is the subject of the first part of the collection, introduced by Jeff Hill. It ranges from the commercialisation of rugby union's myth of origin, as described by Jed Smith, to Tony Bateman's distillation of the way cricket writing created its own English myths of the pastoral and a 'Golden Age'. In an innovative piece of doctoral research, Ray Physick rediscovers the engagement of the visual arts with 'The People's Game' in an early attempt to reveal its sporting heritage – a striking gap in the conceptually driven world of contemporary art. How a group of enthusiasts sustain the collective memory of a sport in its place and time is the subject of Neil Skinner and Matthew Taylor's study of the London Ex-Boxers' Association (LEBA), which has genuinely important implications for other associations of ex-players in other sports. Finally, Tim O'Sullivan reveals the beginnings of what has become arguably the most important channel of shared sporting experience. The voices of the commentators over the years are an intrinsic part of the story and deserve special attention as part of an auditory heritage of sport, along with the songs, chants and sounds of the crowd.

Museums are among the most important conduits of sporting heritage. The scale and nature of this phenomenon is the subject of the second and part of the third section of this collection. Kevin Moore sets out the facts and the agenda with the seasoned eye of the expert practitioner. Sport has been represented in museum collections long before the recent appearance of dedicated sports museums. This inviting topic, as he observes, deserves more attention. So too do those less tangible parts of sports heritage examined in part three of the volume. Jason Wood's essay calls attention to the relationship between place and memory, a difficult but important subject that historians of sport have found elusive and have often avoided. What Wood calls the 'cultural geography of emotion and imagination' is a recurring theme in the contributions here, each of which in different ways acknowledges the notion of 'lieu de mémoire'.

Some of the problems inherent in this project are revealed in the magnificently refurbished Scottish National Portrait Gallery in Edinburgh, which devotes a room to Scottish sporting heritage. However, this really amounts to a disparate collection of paintings, images and objects with archery, deer-stalking and curling alongside early photographs of Scottish rugby and football teams. The problem here is that, while 'fitba' is Scotland's most popular sport, earlier curators do not appear to have considered it worthy of their attention. A specially commissioned short film includes the curator of the Scottish Football Museum talking sensibly about the origins of the game, but the 'Wembley Wizards' and 'the Tartan Army' are strangely absent, although Kenny Dalglish gets a prominent spot in the café. This highlights a wider problem. Museums have collections on diverse topics, including sport, which they have sometimes built up over a long period. Displaying the 'heritage' takes priority over explaining the history.

The new Museum of Liverpool, opened in 2011, has a different remit and does a useful job of mapping the distribution of different sports across the city and its region. A short film of two boys playing together, one a 'Red' and the other a 'Blue', fictionally dramatises the distinctive culture of Liverpool, with families and friends split between Everton and Liverpool. However, the absolute requirement to give equal treatment to both clubs (despite Liverpool's greater achievements and global fan base) distorts the picture. So, too, does the heightened sensitivity of the city to the Hillsborough tragedy in comparison with the divisive impact of the Heysel disaster. How can a museum of the city, full of bright images of the Beatles, come to terms with the darker side of popular culture? The representation of sport within a mainstream museum is particularly subject to pressures which make presenting its own past problematic to the 'neutral'.

A different kind of problem arose when The National Portrait Gallery mounted an exhibition of 'British Sporting Heroes' in 1999 at the suggestion of Tony Banks, the newly appointed Minister of Sport. The problem here was where to start and what to choose. The period from the 18th to the mid-19th century was easier in the sense that there were a limited number of images and sports to choose from. But with the development of photography and the creation of new sports, especially association football and rugby, selection became more difficult. Renown and achievement – not always synonymous – were the guiding principles. The overall purpose was to show how sport had become central to British culture and identity. Gender and class had to be balanced with regional and national affiliation to present a nuanced account of how the sporting hero represented the nations of the United Kingdom. Reviews were favourable but its popular impact was limited. The conclusion of the curators was that the exhibition had been a good show and up to the high standards of that institution but that an exhibition devoted to a single sport, probably to football, might have brought in greater numbers and attracted more publicity. The collection, which could have formed the basis for the first national museum of the sporting image, was returned and the momentum was lost.

Given the importance of sport in our national culture, this omission is especially disappointing. The holding of the 2012 Olympic Games in London could have provided the perfect opportunity to set up a national sports museum – even a modest one such as the French have created. This seems to have been overlooked as part of the 'Cultural Olympiad', with the exception of the small-scale travelling exhibition of 'Our Sporting Life' – a laudable and innovative gesture rather than a permanent national initiative. Nor, to my knowledge, has permanent 'museum heritage' featured in the much vaunted multiple forms of 'legacy' of the London Games.

As Moore stresses, the bulk of effort that has gone into creating a sporting heritage has come from enthusiasts for a single sport rather than for 'sports' in general. Sports historically associated with the hegemony of a particular club or institution have been notably successful: the cricket museum at Lord's, the British Golf Museum at St Andrews, The River and Rowing Museum at Henley, and the tennis museum at Wimbledon, which is the one I know best.

The wealth generated by the Wimbledon Championships enabled the All England Club to lavish considerable expense on the museum. The fact that the French were building a tennis museum at Roland Garros in Paris was no doubt another factor. If Wimbledon was to sustain its reputation as the best tennis tournament in the world, it ought also to have the best museum. It certainly is an impressive museum, especially in terms of new technology, including a remarkable hologram of the former scourge of Wimbledon now turned licensed jester, John McEnroe. The museum dwells on the great players of the past. This is what the public wants to see. They are very keen to acquire the personal memorabilia of the champions. This understandable biographical and great match focus of the museum, however, inevitably overshadows the unique structure of 'the championships' and the role of the All England Club itself, as well as avoiding the awkward issue of how and why the tournament finally was opened to professionals. Here heritage seems to get in the way of history.

It would be wrong to end these short reflections on this major collection without a mention in dispatches for Simon Inglis and the 'Played in Britain' series. In conjunction with English Heritage, Inglis and his authors record and celebrate 'the pavilions and clubhouses, the greens, the grounds and grandstands, the parks, pools and pigeon lofts, the boathouses and billiard halls that form such an integral part of our urban landscape'.[1] Inglis is the Pevsner of our sporting architecture, under whose leadership a whole series of books has been produced to the highest standards

---

[1] The 'Played in Britain' series of books on sporting heritage, launched in 2004 in conjunction with English Heritage, is edited by Simon Inglis. By the end of 2011 the series contained some 17 extensively illustrated titles. They range from thematic studies (eg *The British Olympics*) to records of sport in particular cities (eg *Played in Liverpool*) and collections from the numerous Charles Buchan sport books and magazines of the 1950s and 1960s. See www.playedinbritain.co.uk.

of illustration and scholarship, culminating in Martin Polley's recent (2011) *The British Olympics: Britain's Olympic heritage, 1612–2012*, which offers an excellent example of how serious history and popular heritage can be combined. Inglis' forthcoming books on London will complete a magnificent series which has set new standards of scholarship and publishing in the field, from the shed to the stadium.

From writing to collecting to curating, the interest in our sporting heritage has never been greater. Over the past 30 years the entire area has flourished as never before and it shows no sign of abating. When it comes to private collections we have hardly begun to unearth the treasures that have been accumulated over a lifetime of love for a particular sport. David Rayvern Allen is well known as a cricket writer and biographer of John Arlott and E W Swanton, but he is also a private curator of cricket heritage with an extraordinary store of cricket books, prints, drawings, pamphlets, scrapbooks and songs. Few can amass such a collection but most of us are touched by the same impulse, whether it be to hoard match programmes, tickets or photographs or, in my own case, Chix No 2 Series 'Famous Footballers', collected at primary school on Tyneside in the late 1950s. As I write this I instinctively reach to the desk drawer and pull out my thumbed set held together by an elastic band – the greats, John Charles and Duncan Edwards, alongside the journeymen, Leyton Orient's Stan Willemse or Bill Dickson of Mansfield. Flicking through them, I reflect on my own attachment to playing and watching football and the innumerable lives which have been touched by its local and national heroes. I just enjoy the memories rather than trying to explain them. Heritage and history may go hand in hand for some but for most people it is the heritage of sport which is more important and which amply justifies the time and effort devoted by the editors and the authors to this collection.

BIBLIOGRAPHY AND REFERENCES

Polley, M, 2011 *The British Olympics: Britain's Olympic Heritage, 1612–2012*, 'Played in Britain' series, English Heritage

Contributors

Anthony Bateman is a freelance writer and editor and an Honorary Visiting Research Fellow at the International Centre for Sports History and Culture at De Montfort University, UK. He studied at the Royal Academy of Music, The Open University and The University of Salford, where he undertook a PhD on the literature of cricket and the construction of national identities. He is the author of *Cricket, Literature and Culture: Symbolising the Nation, Destabilising Empire* (Ashgate, 2009), a book that was shortlisted for the 2010 Lord Aberdare Literary Prize for Sports History. He has also contributed articles and chapters on cricket and its literature to a number of journals and books, as well as to the popular press. He is co-editor (with John Bale) of *Sporting Sounds: Relationships Between Sport and Music* (Routledge, 2008) and the *Cambridge Companion to Cricket* (with Jeffrey Hill) (CUP, 2011). He is currently editing a second volume of essays on interactions between sport and music for Routledge. A former professional musician, he writes on music for *The Guardian* and other publications.

Daphné Bolz is Assistant Professor at the University of Rouen, France, a member of the research centre CETAPS (EA 3832), and a former Marie Curie Fellow at the International Centre for Sports History and Culture at De Montfort University in Leicester, UK. Her research interests lie in sports architecture and the political dimension of sport at international level, especially in the interwar and post-war period in Germany, Italy and Britain. She is the author of *Les Arènes Totalitaires: Fascisme, Nazisme et Propagande Sportive* (CNRS Ed, 2008), based on her doctorate on sports architecture in fascist Italy and Nazi Germany. Her recent publications include an article on the 1948 London Olympic Games: 'Welcoming the world's best athletes. An Olympic challenge for post-war Britain', *International Journal of the History of Sport*, 27 (6), April 2010, 1002–24, and an article on sports facilities provision in Europe: 'Creating places for sport in interwar Europe. A comparison of the provision of sports venues in Italy, Germany and England', *The International Journal of the History of Sport*, iFirst article May 2012, 1–15.

Stephen Done has been Curator and Image Archivist at Liverpool Football Club since 1998. Prior to this he was Curator of the Cyfarthfa Castle Museum, Merthyr Tydfil. At Liverpool he established the club museum from scratch, developing the collections into one of the richest of any football club and enhancing the stadium tour operation into one of the top visitor attractions on Merseyside. Stephen also runs the club's photographic service and has created an image bank currently holding 28,000 pictures. In his spare time he is an author of historical crime fiction. The fifth of his Inspector Vignoles Mysteries, *The Last Train (to Brackley Central)* (Hastings Press, 2012), is set in Leicester along the former Great Central Railway line.

Max Dunbar is Chief Executive Officer of Manchester Jewish Museum. Prior to this, he worked in various roles within the sports heritage sector. After writing his MA thesis on sporting memorabilia in museums, he went on to become the Sporting Memorabilia Specialist at Christie's Auctioneers. From the commercial world of sporting memorabilia, he returned to the museum sector as Collection Manager at the World Rugby Museum, Twickenham. In 2008 he moved from rugby to football collections, spending three years managing The Everton Collection project at Liverpool Record Office. He now lives in Manchester with wife Zoe and daughters Poppy and Kitty.

Honor Godfrey is Curator of Wimbledon Lawn Tennis Museum, a post she has held for the past 12 years. During this time, she has overseen the development of a new Museum and the emergence of the Museum's Education Department, and has contributed to presentation displays of the heritage and traditions of Wimbledon around the grounds. She is responsible for Museum acquisitions and the programme of special exhibitions. Current work includes a major cataloguing project and research for an exhibition 'Tennis and the Olympic Games'. Previously she has worked as a company historian, putting together collections for Colman's, Sainsbury's and Zanussi, and she has taught Museum Studies and Heritage Interpretation at postgraduate level in Australia and England. She founded The Ephemera Society of Australia and was Deputy Editor and subsequently Editor of *The Ephemerist* for many years.

Jeffrey Hill is Emeritus Professor of Historical and Cultural Studies at De Montfort University, where from 2001 to 2007 he was Director of the International Centre for Sport History and Culture. He has worked at Nottingham Trent University and held visiting positions at the University of British Columbia and Columbus State University, Georgia, USA. His research interests are in sport, politics and popular culture, and among his recent publications are *Sport in History: An Introduction* (Palgrave Macmillan, 2010) and, with Anthony Bateman, the *Cambridge Companion to Cricket* (CUP, 2011). He is currently working on the place of leisure and voluntary associations in Conservative Party politics during the interwar years.

Richard Holt is Professor in the International Centre for Sports History and Culture at De Montfort University. He is the author of general histories of sport in France and in Britain and has worked as an advisory editor for sport for the Oxford Dictionary of National Biography. In 1999 he was the academic adviser to the 'British Sporting Heroes' exhibition at the National Portrait Gallery and he is currently a member of the advisory board of the French national sports museum. He co-directed the AHRC 'Sport in Europe' project from 2008–2010 and at present is co-editing the 'Routledge Handbook of Sport and Legacy' with Professor Dino Ruta, Bocconi Business School, Milan.

Mike McGuinness is a lecturer in Sports Studies in the School of Social Sciences and Law at the University of Teesside, Middlesbrough, UK. Originally a political scientist, he has published and presented on the impact of European integration on identity, citizenship, racism and submerged nations working with European Union networks. His main research interests are in sport and national identity, especially the development of an English identity via sport and cultural representations of sport (ephemera, art, literature, popular music, etc). Present projects are looking at sport and the obituary in newspapers, and football in Middlesbrough linking Lady Bell's *At the Works* (1907) and Arnold Bennett's *The Card* (1911). Forced to give up football and cricket, he is kept busy considering the ups and downs of Birmingham City.

Kevin Moore has been Director of the National Football Museum, England, since the beginning of the project in 1997. The Museum opened in Preston in 2001, and is the permanent home of the world's greatest football (soccer) collections, including the FIFA Museum Collection. The new National Football Museum will open in Manchester in 2012. Kevin has published widely in museum studies and cultural studies, including the books *Museums and Popular Culture*; *Museum Management*; and *Management in Museums*. From 2004 to 2007 Kevin was the first Director of the International Football Institute (IFI), a partnership between the University of Central Lancashire (UCLAN), England, and the National Football Museum, to advance football research and to make the findings of this research available to a global audience. He is a Visiting Fellow at UCLAN and a Fellow of the RSA. He is Chair of the Sports Heritage Network, the professional organisation of the UK's sports museums.

Tim O'Sullivan is Professor of Media & Cultural History in the Faculty of Art, Design and Humanities at De Montfort University, Leicester, UK. His recent work has included (with Dr Alan Burton) *The Cinema of Basil Dearden and Michael Relph* (Edinburgh University Press, 2009) and a number of chapter-length studies concerning aspects of the entry of television into the British home in the immediate post-war period. See, for instance, 'Researching the Viewing Culture' in H Wheatley (ed), 2007 *Re-Viewing Television: Critical Issues in Television Historiography*, IB Taurus. He is currently working on a monograph on television in Britain, 1946–1960.

Santiago de Pablo is Professor of Contemporary History at the University of the Basque Country (Spain), and was Visiting Scholar at the Centre for Basque Studies (University of Nevada Reno, USA) in 2009–10. He specialises in political history and film history and he also works on the social history of sport in the Basque Country. His books include *En tierra de nadie: Los nacionalistas vascos en Álava* (2008); *Tierra sin paz: Guerra Civil, cine y propaganda en el País Vasco* (2006); *El Péndulo Patriótico: Historia del Partido Nacionalista Vasco* (1999–2005); and *The Basque Nation on Screen: Cinema, Nationalism and Political Violence in the Basque Country* (forthcoming). He is editor of the Basque academic journal *Sancho el Sabio* and member of the *Academia de las Artes y Ciencias Cinematográficas de España*.

Ray Physick is a full-time PhD student and a part-time lecturer at the University of Central Lancashire, Preston. His field of study for the PhD (due for completion in June 2012) is British 'Football Art' – how football has been represented in the fine arts c. 1850–2000. In February 2011 Ray curated *Football in the Frame*, an exhibition of contemporary work by artists who use football as a major focus for their work. His publications include *Played in Liverpool* (2007), which was the seventh book in the ground-breaking *Played in Britain* series, published by English Heritage and edited by Simon Inglis. Ray also wrote *Liverpool Boxing Venues* (2008), which was published by Trinity Mirror. Both books explore the rich cultural heritage of sport on Merseyside. In January 2011 Ray also curated a Heritage Lottery-funded exhibition for Hackney Museum about boxing in the East End of London.

Neil Skinner is a research student at the International Centre for Sports History and Culture at De Montfort University in Leicester. His thesis examines British boxing in the post-war period.

Jed Smith is the Collections & Exhibitions Manager at the National Sports Museum in Melbourne, Australia. He assisted with the building and development of the museum and curated a number of the permanent galleries including the *Champions* thoroughbred racing gallery, the *Australian Football Hall of Fame*, a film theatre, an interactives gallery and two 'Pepper's Ghost' multimedia displays. The number of sports included in the National Sports Museum allows Jed's team the opportunity to examine extremely broad themes. Future temporary exhibitions will include an analysis of the use of colours and symbols by Australian national teams and a show that will focus on Indigenous involvement in Australian sport. For 11 years Jed was curator at the World Rugby Museum (formally Museum of Rugby, Twickenham) in London, England. It was while in this previous position that Jed researched and wrote *The Little Book of English Rugby* and *The Original Rules of Rugby*.

David Storey is Senior Lecturer in Geography at the University of Worcester, UK. He has extensive research expertise in the interconnections between place, identity and territory, and in rural change and development. David has written extensively on the use of local heritage in rural place promotion in the UK and Ireland and on various dimensions of sport and national identity. He is the author of *Territories: The Claiming of Space* (2 edn, Routledge, 2012).

Matthew Taylor is Professor of History at the International Centre for Sports History and Culture at De Montfort University in Leicester. He has written widely on the history of sport and recreation, including *Moving With the Ball: The Migration of Professional Footballers*, co-authored with Pierre Lanfranchi (Berg, 2001); *The Leaguers: The Making of Professional Football in England, 1900–1939* (Liverpool University Press, 2005); and *The Association Game: A History of British Football* (Longman, 2008). His most recent book is *Football: A Short History* (Shire, 2011). Current research projects include a study of sport and civilian morale in World War II and a 20th-century social history of British boxing. He is also completing a number of articles and an edited collection on sport and global history. He is currently editor-in-chief of the journal *Sport in History* and an academic adviser to the National Football Museum.

Andrea Titterington has been Regeneration Director at Liverpool Football Club since 2003. She has worked in housing since 1969 in the US, UK, Germany and Tanzania. Before Liverpool her career in England was primarily with housing associations (including the Housing Corporation), most recently as Chief Executive of Maritime Housing Association (Group CEO of Regenda). While at Liverpool she has been a North West Representative for the Commission for Architecture and the Built Environment, a member of the North West Historic Environment Forum, a founding Board Member of Liverpool Vision and a former Board Member of The Mersey Partnership. She is Deputy Chair of Blackburn Cathedral Development Company, a former member of the North West Regional Design Review Panel of PlacesMatter! and an Academician of the Academy of Urbanism.

Wray Vamplew is Visiting Professor at the International Football Institute, University of Central Lancashire, and Emeritus Professor of Sports History at the University of Stirling. Author or editor of 27 books, he has also published over 150 articles and book chapters. His research has been awarded prizes by the North American Society for Sport History and the Australian Institute of Sport. Currently he is working on a study of the golf club as a social institution and looking at the relationship between sport and charity. He is immediate past Editor of the *Journal of Sport History* and the Managing Editor of the *International Journal of the History of Sport*. Recent keynote lectures were given at the NASSH Conference, Asheville (2009), and the Taiwan International Sports Sociology Conference (2010). In 2011 he was given the ISHPES Scholar Award to commemorate his career in sports history.

John K Walton has worked since January 2010 as a research professor for IKERBASQUE, the Basque Foundation for Science, in the Department of Contemporary History at the University of the Basque Country UPV/EHU, Leioa, Bilbao, Spain. A graduate of Merton College, Oxford, and Lancaster University, he has published extensively on histories of tourism, sport and identities, especially in Britain and Spain, and edits the *Journal of Tourism History* for Routledge/Taylor and Francis. He was the founding president of the International Commission for the History of Travel and Tourism. With F J Caspistegui he edited *Guerras Danzadas* (Barañain, 2001), one of the first academic histories of sport in Spain, and his most recent publications include (with Keith Hanley), *Constructing Cultural Tourism* (Bristol, Channel View, 2010), and (edited, with Peter Borsay) *Resorts and Ports: European Seaside Towns Since 1700* (Bristol, Channel View, 2011).

Jean Williams has been a Senior Research Fellow at the International Centre for Sports History and Culture at De Montfort University in Leicester, UK, since 2006. She is the author of *A Game For Rough Girls: A History of Women's Football in England* (Routledge, 2003) and *A Beautiful Game: International Perspectives on Women's Football* (Berg, 2007). Jean's recent projects include a research monograph entitled *A Contemporary History of Women's Sport* (Routledge Research, 2012), a £6000 network examining swimwear and dancewear history 1890–1940, and a 17,000 Euro UEFA-funded project *Women's Football, Europe and Professionalization 1971–2011*. As well as researching a collective biography of the Brooklands' women racers 1906–1939, she is working on *Send Her Victorious: A History of British Women Olympians 1900–2012*, for Manchester University Press in 2013. She has been awarded a John H Daniels Fellowship to the National Sporting Library, Middleburg, Virginia, in 2013.

Jason Wood has been Director of Heritage Consultancy Services since 1998. His other posts have included Professor of Cultural Heritage at Leeds Metropolitan University, Head of Heritage at WS Atkins Consultants Limited and Assistant Director of Lancaster University Archaeological Unit. He has been Chair of the National Trust's Archaeology Panel since 2005, and played an influential role in the affairs of other heritage organisations, such as the Institute for Archaeologists, the Royal Institution of Chartered Surveyors, the International Council on Monuments and Sites UK and UNESCO. Jason's research interests lie in public history and heritage of sport and leisure. He was the lead consultant for an English Heritage pilot study in Manchester on the heritage of sport in 2002. His current projects include investigating the sporting connections of historic properties and collections belonging to the National Trust.

Index

HERITAGE MATTERS